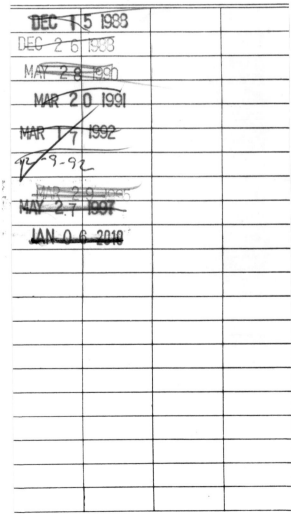

DATE DUE

DEC 15 1988		
DEC 2 6 1988		
MAY 2 8 1990		
MAR 2 0 1991		
MAR 17 1992		
12-9-92		
MAR 2 0 1995		
MAY 2 7 1997		
JAN 0 6 2010		

DEMCO NO. 38-298

Mexican Politics in Transition

About the Book and Editor

Initiated in the mid-1970s, Mexico's program of political reform was designed to provide a new opportunity for political competition. In this book, contributors examine the significance political mobilization has had and the extent to which the reform has served as a vehicle for defusing discontent in the wake of Mexico's failed oil-based development program and the related financial collapse. Specifically, they analyze the Institutional Revolutionary Party's (PRI) performance within the more fluid political context, the development of expanded organized political opposition, the renewal of activity by the National Action Party (PAN), and the response of the Mexican citizenry. The book provides the only detailed empirical analysis of the outcomes of reform initiatives currently available and makes a valuable contribution to the theoretical literature on the process of political "democratization" within authoritarian systems. The case of Mexico is particularly interesting from a theoretical perspective, given the earlier absence of a fully functioning multiparty system in the postrevolutionary period, the development of wholly new instruments for the representation of opposing interests, and the transformation of the roles of established organizations.

Judith Gentleman is assistant professor of political science at the State University of New York, Geneseo, New York.

Mexican Politics in Transition

edited by
Judith Gentleman

Westview Press / Boulder and London

Westview Special Studies on Latin America and the Caribbean

Copyright © 1987 by Westview Press, Inc.

Published in 1987 in the United States of America by Westview Press, Inc.; Frederick A. Praeger, Publisher; 5500 Central Avenue, Boulder, Colorado 80301

Library of Congress Cataloging-in-Publication Data
Mexican politics in transition.
  (Westview special studies on Latin America and the Caribbean)
  Includes index.
  1. Mexico—Politics and government—1970-
2. Partido Revolucionario Institucional. 3. Political
parties—Mexico—History—20th century. 4. Opposition
(Political science)—Mexico—History—20th century.
I. Gentleman, Judith, 1950- . II. Series.
F1236.M49 1987   320.972   86-4036
ISBN 0-8133-7210-0

This book was produced without formal editing by the publisher.

Printed and bound in the United States of America

The paper used in this publication meets the requirements of the American National Standard for Permanence of Paper for Printed Library Materials Z39.48-1984.

10   9   8   7   6   5   4   3   2   1

Contents

Part One
Introduction

Part Two
Political Reform and Economic Crisis in Mexico

Part Three
Recent Performance in the Political System

Part Four
Perspectives on the Political Opposition

Tables and Figures

Preface

This volume is the outgrowth of a panel on "Politics and Political Parties in Contemporary Mexico" convened at the XII International Congress of the Latin America Studies Association held in Albuquerque, New Mexico, in 1985. Subsequent to the panel's convening, invitations were extended to several additional scholars to contribute works to a book that would provide a comprehensive analysis of recent political development in Mexico. The volume that has emerged thus brings together the revised works of the original panelists along with the invited contributions of other scholars.

Many thanks are owed to Barbara Ellington at Westview for her encouragement and assistance in the development and completion of the volume. To Miriam Gilbert, Bruce Kellison, Alice Levine, and Lauri Fults, also at Westview, thanks are due for assistance with the project. At SUNY-Geneseo, support for the project has been provided by grants from the Geneseo Foundation and the College Senate Faculty Research Program. I am grateful to Pamela Thomas, who helped in numerous ways with manuscript preparation. Thanks are also due to Catherine Lewis for her work on the project, along with Mark Arlaukas.

Without the continuing help, cooperation, and commitment of the contributors, however, the project would have remained only a concept. It is to these scholars that I owe the greatest thanks.

Judith Gentleman

PART ONE

Introduction

1

Political Change in Authoritarian Systems

Judith Gentleman

Mexico's political system has successfully weathered crises in the past, and indeed as Martin Needler observes in his contribution to this volume, crisis is hardly a new experience for Mexico. Despite this fact, some have suggested that the current crisis plaguing the nation is of a degree of severity that may well set it apart from previous experiences and may be creating a context in which there could emerge important departures from past political practices. As such, the current period may be viewed as a period of transition for Mexico's authoritarian political system potentially leading to an intensification of the authoritarian framework in response to crisis, or perhaps shifting to a more liberal competitive mode, or perhaps simply leading to an erosion of state power and a growing political vacuum in which oppositional interests might organize on an independent basis.

Contributors to this volume have examined this transitional phase from differing points of view and with a variety of emphases. All, however, share in a recognition of the enduring strength of the political system even in the face of overwhelming crisis. Nonetheless, the interest that has drawn the contributors together is the consideration of the potential sources of change in the political system, recent experiences with political reform, the sources of elite resilience in managing the current crisis, and the impact of the crisis experience upon the structure of political authoritarianism in Mexico.

Authoritarian systems have traditionally been distinguished from other political systems on the basis of several distinctive traits. In his recent study of the process of industrialization in Mexico, Dale Story specifies three key features of such systems including "limited political pluralism, low subject-mobilization and hierarchical ordering of relationships."[1] Others, including Juan Linz, Wayne Cornelius and Ann Craig, have further noted the tendency for such systems to be subject to weak ideological constraints.[2] In Mexico, political life is conducted not only within an authoritarian political system but also within an authoritarian tradition that transcends the nation's

3

experience of revolutionary transformation, as both Lorenzo Meyer and José Luis Reyna have argued.[3]

What was elaborated by the Mexican Revolution politically, it may be argued, was not a system derived from the reformulation of class relations, the destruction of the class system or the development of a new belief system, but ultimately a reorganization of intra-elite interests with the acceptance of state sector management of the process of capital accumulation, and the development of an effective structure for the corporatist-authoritarian management of the broader society. The ruling elites sought to legitimize the new political approach to the management of the society on the basis of a "loosely connected set of goals or symbols,"[4] none of which were fundamentally destructive of the essential interests of elites, in particular, the hegemony of the dominant class.

While a "political revolution," in Theda Skocpol's conceptualization of the phenomenon, did occur, the transformation of political structures was not accompanied by the degree of social transformation that one might argue has taken place even in some non-revolutionary situations. In Argentina, for example, the convergence of labor mobilization with Perón's populist authoritarian leadership induced changes in society that in the long run created a basis for the pluralist, post-authoritarian situation present in Argentina today. In the Mexican case, the political transformation was accomplished at a point prior to the successful independent formal organization of non-elite interests in society, leaving to the state the opportunity for such organization.

Mexico's political revolution was always much more convincing in terms of its corporatist-structural accomplishments than in terms of the development of a legitimizing corporatist ideology. As Roger Hansen has pointed out, the chief innovation of the post-revolutionary period was in the structural dimension of politics with the creation of the official party designed for the purpose of organizing and managing the expression of potentially conflictive interests in society while providing for the reconciliation of elite interests on an independent basis. Story observes that authoritarianism in Mexico has meant the effective incorporation of non-elite interests into a closely controlled framework for political involvement while elites have remained comparatively free to pursue their interests.[5] This approach of course is a direct function of the fact that the revolution led to the further entrenchment of a state capitalist model of development. In short, the post-revolutionary political system that developed in Mexico was clearly characterized by limited political pluralism and low subject-mobilization.

The dominant party system which emerged actually espoused an official ideology of political democracy and even lent some symbolic legitimacy to the concept of political competition in the system by permitting auxiliary political parties to exist although within strictly defined parameters. Nevertheless, as John Booth and Mitchell Seligson have pointed out,[6] the agents of "liberalism" and liberal reforms in the Mexican system have always been the effective managers of the authoritarian political system, thus conveying decidedly mixed signals, a situation which in and of itself, has provided substantial political advantage and minimal constraint. The regime has tended to characterize competitive political systems as fundamentally suspect owing to their tendency to be dominated by elites and to display frequent deficiencies in terms of mass participation and the defense of mass interests.

By contrast, a system that emphasizes substantive democratic outcomes rather than emphasizing rules governing the procedural aspects of political competition is a more probable guarantor of democratic ideals according to the regime's advocates. Ultimately, however, the traditional argument over the relative merits of so-called "substantive" versus "procedural" democracies has been decided in the Mexican case, one might argue, in favor of neither as measured by the regime's record of political and economic performance.

That Mexico's inclusionary corporatist authoritarian regime has endured with relative ease especially in contrast to the experience of many of the bureaucratic-authoritarian regimes that populated the region in the 1960s and 1970s has remained a question of substantial theoretical interest. The political "liberalization" or "reform" initiated in Mexico in the late 1970s along with rapid and dramatic political changes elsewhere in the region have pressed social scientists to renew consideration of the process of political change, a process that is, even now, poorly understood.

In a recently published compendium of works on theories of change in Latin America, one of the volume's editors, Thomas J. Bossert, notes the rather limited accomplishments of social scientists to date in formulating "systematic explanations for regime changes." In particular, Bossert argues that scholarship has yet to specify the relationship that exists between "the character of the state" and the "particular demands of economic structures and class conflict."[7] Further, the nature of the relationship that exists between the dependent capitalist state and different forms of political regime remains unclear.

Many studies completed during the 1970s of the new bureaucratic authoritarian regimes of the Latin American region suggested that the rise of such exclusionary regimes was fully consistent with the cultural proclivities and socio-political history of the region. Efforts were further undertaken to demonstrate why such bureaucratic-authoritarian regimes were fully consistent with the character of the economic policy implemented in response to crisis. As work progressed in this vein, Mexico was always regarded as the exceptional case, having seen the establishment of an inclusionary authoritarian regime decades prior to the onset of the range of economic crises argued to have stimulated the imposition of brutal demobilizing regimes elsewhere in the region. Notably, however, the very same crisis of development in Mexico produced a state sector strategy purporting, at least, to introduce liberalization as a politico-economic strategy.

Throughout the period, Latin America's authoritarian regimes were depicted in fairly static terms, a tendency that was understandable in light of the widespread view that corporatist-authoritarian forms of political organization were essentially "natural" to the region. Pluralist options were commonly characterized as alien grafts upon the body politic and as such, consideration of change within authoritarian systems was virtually precluded. While some observers cautioned against viewing "corporatism or authoritarianism as the constant normative pattern,"[8] little attention was paid to the question of change in authoritarian systems. More recently as several states in the region have experienced substantial political change, efforts have been undertaken to examine more closely the dynamics of change in authoritarian systems.[9]

The Mexican political system's seeming immunity to massive dislocations stemming from economic stress has been attributed to a variety of factors. Fernando Cardoso has identified several key characteristics of the system that have served to stabilize Mexico's political life over time: massive cooptation, the incorporation of "broad sectors of society in national life," the openness of the system to "pressures and suggestions from the bottom," the "bureaucratic capacity for control," the "extensive system of bargaining with regard to economic interests, the system's "efficient financial and economic performance," and the governing class's "success in reorganizing society to cope with more complex forms of capitalist growth," including the state's ability to control labor, the "state bureaucracy" and "public enterprises."[10] Traditionally, the strength of the system was evidenced by its ability to overwhelm interests in society, including those seeking to challenge the system's insistence upon a limited, essentially coopted form of pluralism that was never based upon the acceptance of the principle of political competition. As Cornelius and others[11] have argued, while the state's autonomy has been limited, at the same time, the system has not permitted the emergence of "large, national level opposition parties and movements that are truly beyond governmental control." At best, as Cornelius and Craig note, such interests have managed to establish a bargaining relationship with the government but not upon an independent basis.[12]

Essential for the stability of the political system has been a low level of political participation.[13] As Susan Kaufman Purcell argues, the system rests upon and even counts upon the "passivity and apathy of large sectors of the population." The chief benefit of such a condition of political torpor is that political elites need only cope with intermittent demands from most sectors of society, permitting more energy to be devoted to the critical activity of harmonizing elite interests. Pablo González Casanova has argued, for example, that between 50 and 70% "of today's Mexicans are effectively barred from making any type of demand upon the political system."[14] Kaufman Purcell maintains that the real key to the maintenance of the Mexican system has been the political system's "wherewithal to institute the kinds of basic reforms required to defuse the potential for mass mobilization."[15] It may further be added that the maintenance of tranquility among competing elites also serves to forestall the potential mobilization of the mass of the population who might otherwise be recruited via an elite inspired populist vehicle during intensified elite competition.

As has been widely discussed, the current political-economic climate in Mexico has raised questions concerning the system's ability to sustain itself, its record in attempting to preserve the hegemony of its political elite and about the character of potential political change in the nation. Certainly the political reform of the late 1970s served to stimulate widespread speculation regarding Mexico's political future.[16] To what extent, if any, have the system's critical political capabilities been undermined by the strengthening of opposition under the aegis of political liberalization or has political reform enhanced the system's capabilities?

At issue it seems is not so much the state's well-established formula for the management of Mexico's vast urban and rural working class and peasant sectors. Instead, the system's current difficulties appear to stem from growing deficiencies with the traditional formula for the management of intra-elite relations and elite-middle class relations. The task for the political elite, if it is to ensure its hegemony, is to prevent the coalescing of disaffected middle sector elements with dissident elites. Most critical, however, would be the regime's efforts to achieve a reharmonization of elite interests, a difficult goal given the nature of elite discontent over the nation's economic difficulties and the continuing tendency for the political elite to monopolize increasingly scarce resources. The two issues, therefore, that could serve as a rallying point for a new center-right coalition of opposition supported by disaffected middle sector and elite interests would be first, the apparent erosion of consensus within the broader elite concerning the primacy of the political elite in the management of the nation's economy and the political elite's continuing effort to monopolize resources and second, the problem of the political integration of the dissident middle sectors.

Potentially, then, a center-right coalition could emerge to challenge the traditional political-economic monopoly enjoyed by the political elite. As several contributors in this volume suggest, the middle sectors of Mexico's society have scarcely been placated by the decidedly lackluster commitment made by the regime to its own program of political reform. What benefit might have been obtained by the regime in this regard as a means of offsetting the middle sector's dismay over the regime's record of economic mismanagement has been lost. As in the past, recent reform efforts have come not in response to demands for reform but rather have emerged as elite inspired initiatives designed to assuage middle sector discontent and to direct potentially more disturbing leftist oppositional energies into the electoral channel where they might be managed successfully. Unhappy elements within the ruling coalition of elite interest might also be mollified by the apparent creative initiatives of the political elite.

Previously, the political elite could safely abandon most reform efforts once the propaganda advantage had been won. As both John Booth and Mitchell Seligson have shown, there has been little evidence of support among the urban middle class and urban working class in Mexico for authentic political competition or political pluralism. According to Booth and Seligson's study, only 26.2% of respondents surveyed approved of regime critics seeking public office while fully 51.7% disapproved.[17] And certainly, the non-political elite itself had little interest in such efforts. As there was little insistence observable from any quarter in the system for fundamental political reform, political strategists enjoyed a relatively free hand in fashioning such measures as the *apertura democratica* of the Echeverría period, for example, and then quietly retreating from the pursuit of the initiative.

Yet, as so many political observers have noted over time, one of the most potent stimuli for the erosion of regime legitimacy is continuing economic crisis. While the regime would not otherwise feel pressed to adhere to its strategy of reform in more favorable economic circumstances, the regime's opponents might now seize the opportunity to decry the regime's record on its own reform initiatives as a means of further chipping away at regime legitimacy.

In the long run, the key to the system's future most probably hinges upon the political elite's ability to reach a resolution of inter-elite tensions primarily and secondarily, to resolve the problem of the growing political distance between the corporatist structure that has traditionally shaped non-elite political involvement and the disaffected middle sectors. Likely threats to the political elite, however, should they take on an organizational life beyond anything seen to date, would in all probability have limited impli-cations for most Mexicans in the nearer term. Such implications might, for example include further curtailment, via pressure emanating from a potential center-right coalition of opposition, of the paltry benefits still afforded to those situated at the base of Mexico's corporatist political pyramid.

Change in Mexico's authoritarian system at this historical juncture would appear to be principally a function of elite decision-making and strategy. The political context, despite Mexico's enduring crisis, has not produced what would be labeled a true crisis of participation defined in terms of the expression of popular demands for change. Rather, Mexico appears to be in the midst of a crisis of elites, and for the moment, it is not altogether clear whether the initiative will ever be regained by the existing political elite. A wholly bureaucratized state (an outcome that some suggest looms large in Mexico), which loses its political moorings and fails to resolve major political questions such as those identified earlier, tends not to be sustainable over the longer term and must increasingly resort to the use of force. With the current erosion of an elite governing consensus in Mexico, we may be witnessing the early stages of just such a dislocation. If the political structure reaches a point where its only sustaining components are to be found at the base of society, among the powerless, the regime's prospects appear to be quite difficult. History's record shows that while social movements of enormous import may be stimulated at the grassroots, change in political systems have often been a function of dislocations at the elite level. As such, change in Mexico's authoritarian system appears to be a distinct possibility unless the system restabilizes on the basis of a satisfactory new arrangement for elite integration and the hammering out of a new consensus with Mexico's middle sectors.

The volume's contributors explore contemporary developments in the Mexican authoritarian political framework in light of the ruling party's strategy of political liberalization and consider the performance of the political system within the highly constrained economic context. The first section of the book focuses upon changing contextual factors within the economic and political environment that have bearing upon the performance of the political system. In Chapter 2, Wayne Cornelius examines the program of political liberalization in Mexico initiated in the latter part of the 1970s, assessing its purposes and weighing its long range impact upon the political system. Cornelius argues that the reform effort has run aground and suggests that its failure, while attributable to a complex mix of factors, is primarily due to divisions within the ruling elite concerning the appropriate political strategy to pursue in response to an economic crisis that threatens the regime's political legitimacy and has reduced critical political resources. While Cornelius finds that there is little likelihood of substantial modification to the political system in the near future, he does point to the growing non-affiliated, resentful and discontented middle sector as a serious potential source of political difficulties for the regime and suggests that the ruling Institutional Revolutionary Party, PRI, will have great difficulty in the future in dealing with Mexico's youthful urban middle class.

In Chapter 3, I discuss the regime's political-economic program for the management of the nation's chronic economic crisis and suggest that the policy options that have been favored in the economic sphere directly conflict with the political strategy selected for the reduction of tensions within the system. Prospects for the effective maintenance of regime power in the system appear to be threatened as a result over the longer term.

John Bailey looks at the nature of reform efforts within the structure of the official party, the PRI, in Chapter 4. Bailey explores the role of the PRI in the larger political system, examines the party's concept of democracy, and reviews previous efforts undertaken to reform the political system, in particular, the internal operating procedures of the PRI. Bailey concludes by discussing the party's reform effort in stimulating grassroots involvement in party decision-making activity along with prospects for future party reform.

The second section of the book evaluates the recent performance of the political system, focusing in particular upon electoral conflict, the issue of the integrity of the electoral system and the impact of recent developments upon public opinion and political culture in Mexico.

Joseph Klesner examines the electoral fortunes of the PRI as well as other political parties in the recent period and challenges the argument advanced by some that elections in Mexico's dominant party authoritarian system are meaningless. Klesner suggests that the political reforms of the 1970s, new party mobilization and subsequent electoral contests have had an impact upon the structure of Mexico's party system. Although Klesner does not find that the PRI's hegemony has been critically jeopardized as a result of these developments, he suggests that the PRI now faces potentially injurious challenges to its support among important national constituencies.

Silvia Gómez Tagle's study of post-election challenges to official electoral outcomes in the 1979, 1982 and 1985 federal elections provides a systematic basis for assessing the scope of fraud and abuse in the electoral system. Gómez Tagle's work treats an issue of major concern in considerations of the regime's ability to sustain an aura of legitimacy. The issue of the integrity of Mexico's electoral processes has increasingly gained international attention as National Action party supporters have demonstrated against the ruling party not only within Mexico but have also issued vocal appeals for support in particular to U.S. media and U.S. political authorities.

On the basis of her empirical analysis of electoral practices and post-election challenges, Gómez finds that the scope of fraud and electoral abuse is more substantial than she had originally envisioned. She suggests that ultimately, however, the full range of potentially fraudulent and abusive practices that undercut fair competition can never be fully measured. Gómez concludes that fraud alone will not succeed in tempering the energies of potential regime opponents and maintains instead that the political reforms set in motion in the 1970s have created the expectation of legitimate political competition in the Mexican political community that will be difficult to eradicate, posing difficulties for the regime in the future.

In Chapter 7, Miguel Basañez discusses the evolving character of political culture in Mexico on the basis of his analysis of public opinion survey data. Basañez's principal goal is to discover to what extent, if any, the Mexican political regime has suffered a loss of legitimacy as a result of the continuing economic crisis and to establish whether any such loss of legitimacy is sufficient to lead to a breakdown of the system. In addition, Basañez seeks to compare the distribution of public opinion on key issues relating to regime legitimacy with official electoral outcomes in order to evaluate the reliability of polling data and to assess the predictive capability of such data in Mexico. Basañez concludes that the political system continues to enjoy substantial popular legitimacy and that suggestions concerning the imminent collapse of the system cannot be substantiated.

In Chapter 8, Martin C. Needler considers the character of the current crisis in terms of its potential for generating certain types of changes in the political system. Needler's assessment builds upon several key factors including the current economic juncture, developments in the perspectives of regime leadership, the role and disposition of Mexico's military establishment and the electoral climate. Needler concludes that the regime will most probably be able to successfully weather the difficulties it now faces and that fundamental alterations in the political structure are not likely in the near future.

In the final section of the volume, contributors consider the character and status of the political opposition in Mexico. As an indicator of the extent to which the regime's program of political liberalization has led to substantive political change and as a measure of adjustments to the structure of authoritarian rule, the experience of the political opposition with the reform is of central concern.

Evelyn P. Stevens assesses the record of Mexico's broad variety of political opposition groups and includes in her examination the nation's experience with protest movements, the protest actions of groups formally integrated into the structure of corporatist organization and the experience of political parties operating within the dominant party system. In Chapter 9, Stevens suggests that while the opposition is certainly multifaceted and arguably gaining in strength, it remains politically fragmented and without real direction. Inevitably, this situation confers important advantages upon the ruling elites as they seek to sustain the legitimacy of the political system.

In Chapter 10, Roderic A. Camp provides a comparison of opposition leadership in Mexico that serves as a basis for considering the directions that might be taken in a modified political environment. Camp's analysis evaluates the strengths and weaknesses of various leadership groups in terms of elite-mass relationships and concludes that political elites from across the political spectrum in Mexico share the common characteristic of having only the most remote associations with the mass of the Mexican population, ideological pretensions to the contrary notwithstanding.

If there is an opposition group that enjoys a political advantage for the moment, it is clearly the National Action party, PAN. In Chapter 11, Dale Story evaluates the thesis commonly advanced that the PAN is the party of Mexico's large business interests and assesses the party's potential for political success in the future. Story analyzes the party's basis of generalized and electoral support and discusses the party's political program. Story argues that in fact, rather than being principally the party of big business, the PAN has gained strength as it has come to be viewed as a viable option for protest voters and dissident citizens on an across-the-board basis. Nevertheless, Story maintains that the party will in all likelihood remain a minority element within Mexico's political system due to its apparent inability to transcend its role as a home for an amalgam of protest voters rather than committed PAN supporters.

The history of the left opposition in Mexico has been one of political fragmentation and ideological contentiousness. As a result, the potential political power of the left has been systematically undercut from within, adding to the difficulties faced by all opposition groups in contending with Mexico's authoritarian system. Barry Carr examines recent developments on the Mexican left and discusses the process of unification that led to the creation of the United Socialist Party of Mexico (Partido Socialista Unido Mexicano or PSUM) in the early 1980s. In Chapter 12, Carr evaluates the PSUM's experience within the electoral arena, weighs the impact of economic crisis upon the left's political future, and assesses the risks faced by the PSUM in its selection of various political options. The choices faced by the PSUM are clearly of a very complex nature and Carr suggests that the road ahead for the PSUM will be quite difficult.

Notes

1. Dale Story, *Industry, the State, and Public Policy in Mexico* (Austin, TX: University of Texas Press, 1986), 81.

2. Juan Linz, "An Authoritarian Regime, The Case of Spain," in Erik Allardt and Stein Rokkan, eds., *Mass Politics: Studies in Political Sociology* (New York, NY:

Free Press, 1970), 251–283; and Wayne A. Cornelius and Ann L. Craig, "Politics in Mexico," in Gabriel A. Almond and G. Bingham Powell, Jr., eds., "Comparative Politics Today," 3rd ed. (Boston, MA: Little, Brown & Company, 1984), 411–465.

3. Lorenzo Meyer, "Historical Roots of the Authoritarian State in Mexico," in José Luis Reyna and Richard S. Weinert, eds., Authoritarianism in Mexico (Philadelphia, PA: ISHI, 1977), 3–22; and José Luis Reyna, "Redefining the Authoritarian Regime," in Authoritarianism in Mexico, 155–172.

4. Cornelius and Craig, "Politics in Mexico," 427.

5. Story, Industry, the State, and Public Policy.

6. John Booth and Mitchell Seligson, "The Political Culture of Authoritarianism in Mexico: A Reexamination," Latin American Research Review, vol. XIX, no. 1 (1984): 119.

7. Thomas J. Bossert, "The Promise of Theory," in Peter F. Klarén and Thomas J. Bossert, eds., Promise of Development: Theories of Change in Latin America (Boulder, CO: Westview Press, 1986), 303–334.

8. Silvio Duncan Baretta and Helen E. Douglass, "Authoritarianism and Corporation in Latin America: A Review Essay," in James M. Malloy, ed., Authoritarianism and Corporatism in Latin America (Pittsburgh, PA: University of Pittsburgh Press, 1977), 514.

9. See James M. Malloy and Mitchell Seligson, eds., Authoritarians and Democrats: The Politics of Regime Transition in Latin America (Pittsburgh, PA: University of Pittsburgh Press, forthcoming); and Guillermo O'Donnell, Phillipe C. Schmitter and Laurence Whitehead, eds., Transitions from Authoritarian Rule (Baltimore, MD: Johns Hopkins University Press, 1986).

10. Fernando Henrique Cardoso, "On the Characterization of Authoritarian Regimes in Latin America," in David Collier, ed., The New Authoritarianism in Latin America (Princeton, NJ: Princeton University Press, 1979), 47.

11. See Rose J. Spalding, "State Power and its Limits: Corporatism in Mexico," Comparative Political Studies, 14, no. 2 (July 1981): 139–161 and Nora Hamilton, The Limits of State Autonomy: Post-Revolutionary Mexico (Princeton, NJ: Princeton University Press, 1982).

12. Cornelius and Craig, "Politics in Mexico," 424.

13. Susan Kaufman Purcell, "The Future of the Mexican System," in Authoritarianism in Mexico, 180.

14. Pablo González Casanova, La democracia en México (México: Ediciones ERA, 1965), 123, cited in Roger Hansen, The Politics of Mexican Development (Baltimore, MD: Johns Hopkins University Press, 1977), 121.

15. Kaufman Purcell, "The Future of the Mexican System," 182.

16. Kevin J. Middlebrook, "Political Liberalization in an Authoritarian Regime. The Case of Mexico," Research Report Series, 41 (La Jolla, CA: Center for U.S. Mexican Studies, University of California, San Diego, 1985).

17. Booth and Seligson, "The Political Culture of Authoritarianism in Mexico," 111.

PART TWO

Political Reform and Economic Crisis in Mexico

2

Political Liberalization in an Authoritarian Regime: Mexico, 1976–1985

Wayne A. Cornelius

Introduction

This chapter analyzes the nature, outcomes, and underlying dynamics of efforts at political liberalization in Mexico during the last ten years.[1] What explains the impulse toward liberalization in a 57-year-old hegemonic party regime, in which the ruling Institutional Revolutionary Party (PRI) has never lost—or been forced to surrender—a single nationally important public office? As of June 1985, the PRI controlled 96 percent of the country's municipal governments, the governorships of all 31 states plus the Federal District (Mexico City and surrounding areas), 75 percent of the seats in the federal Chamber of Deputies, and 100 percent of the seats in the Senate. It has won recent presidential elections with majorities of 70–80 percent. And what explains the halting character and meager outcomes of a decade of "political reform" efforts by the three most recent administrations, in a country where executive centralism—including strong presidential control over all stages of the electoral process, from candidate selection to official recognition of election results—has been the hallmark of the political system?

The first section of this chapter reviews Mexico's principal efforts at political liberalization since 1976 and their historical antecedents. The second section focuses on the political reform efforts made thus far by the administration of President Miguel de la Madrid (1982–1988) and on the challenge posed by the mid-term elections of July 1985, which were widely viewed as a test of the incumbent government's commitment to political reform. The chapter's conclusion analyzes the implications of these elections for the future of political liberalization in Mexico.

In this chapter I use the terms "political reform" and "political liberalization" interchangeably. Both refer to a movement toward a more open and competitive political system, especially in the following arenas: electoral parties and electoral politics; political competition within the ruling party-government apparatus; and relationships between that apparatus and various segments of society (urban labor, peasants, the middle classes, business elites, etc.). The term "political liberalization" as used in this paper does not necessarily imply movement toward a democratic polity, since it is by no means certain that those who have presided over or promoted recent liberalization efforts in Mexico are seeking to transform the political system into a Western-style democracy. Indeed, the likely or preferred "end state" of this process is a matter of lively debate in both official and intellectual circles in Mexico today.

For most would-be reformers within the PRI-government apparatus, liberalization is aimed at stabilizing the regime by restoring the effectiveness of the PRI and the whole system of political parties and elections as a vehicle for legitimation, and at preventing serious challenges to the PRI's monopoly of power at the national and state government levels. Some members of the PRI's left-progressive wing are also concerned about refurbishing the regime's relations with organized labor and other mass support groups, relations which have been damaged by the economic crisis and government austerity policies since 1982. None of the reformist/modernizing elements within the regime is interested in pursuing changes that might put at risk the continued control of the key positions in the political system by the present ruling group.

For the private sector and other elements of the conservative opposition who call for "democratization" of the system, the main goal seems to be unfettered capitalism, to be achieved by dismantling the public sector of the economy, severely limiting the powers of the presidency (especially when they can affect private-sector interests), slashing government spending and attacking corruption and inefficiency in government. For some intellectuals, political liberalization means attacking and weakening authoritarian power relationships at all levels and in all sectors of society, from trade unions to peasant organizations, the PRI-government apparatus, and even the traditional Mexican family. Their primary interest is in transforming state-society relations in a fundamental way. They tend to discount the potential significance of changes in the arena of electoral politics, or at least to argue that changes in this arena, by themselves, are inadequate to bring about thoroughgoing democratization, so long as authoritarian structures and processes elsewhere in the polity and society remain intact.

Despite considerable rhetoric to the contrary (especially among supporters of the principal conservative opposition party, the PAN), none of the groups pressing for political liberalization in Mexico seems intent upon creating a truly competitive two-party or multiparty system with alternation of parties in power, at least at the national level. There is a fairly strong elite consensus that this kind of U.S.-style pluralist system is inappropriate and alien to Mexico, a country lacking a liberal, democratic tradition and political culture. There is also a widespread perception that the government will do whatever is necessary to prevent the emergence of such a system, whatever the cost in terms of its own legitimacy. The real issue, therefore, is not whether Mexico will have a Western-style democratic transformation, but whether the existing political system can move toward greater recognition of legitimate, within-the-system opposition groups—at least at state and local levels, in certain regions of the country—without threatening the PRI's hegemonic position at the national level. As Mexican political scientist Juan Molinar has argued, "It is not a question of whether the PRI can win. In completely free and fair elections, the PRI would still win a majority in most parts of the country. The only question is the *margin* of victory, and what it costs the system to maintain a very wide margin of victory."[2]

The Mexican Political System

Scholars have reached a high level of consensus on the nature of Mexico's inclusionary authoritarian regime.[3] The setting of national priorities and all important public policies emanate directly from the incumbent president and his inner circle of advisors. They consult to a certain extent with key economic and political interest-group leaders (for example, the leader of the government-affiliated national labor confederation, CTM), but hardly at all with opposition groups. Political and administrative decision-making is highly centralized, despite a strong rhetorical commitment to "decentralization" by each of the last four administrations. The president, operating with few constitutional or ideological constraints on his authority, completely dominates the legislative and judicial branches. Courts and legislatures at the state level normally mirror the preferences of their state governors, who themselves are hand-picked by the incumbent president.

At all levels of the system, those elected to public office are, in effect, appointed to their positions by higher-ups within the official party-government apparatus. Those elected on the PRI ticket are primarily responsible and responsive not to the people who elected them but to their political patrons within the regime. There are no primary elections to choose who will run as PRI candidates. Instead, nominating conventions attended by party activists ratify the choices made in secret by officials at higher levels.

Most citizens who participate in the electoral process do so with little or no expectation that their votes will influence the outcome of the election: the winner has been predetermined by the selection process within the PRI. The most the voter can hope to accomplish by voting for an opposition party is to register a protest against government policies or performance. An upsurge in anti-PRI protest voting—especially among the urban middle classes—has occurred since Mexico's economic collapse of 1982. But only in a handful of states and municipalities are opposition parties so broadly supported and well organized that they can occasionally compel central authorities to recognize their electoral victories. Apart from these rare opportunities, people vote as an act of civic duty, of patriotic identification with the nation-state, or compulsion (when they fear the consequences— economic and otherwise—of not voting).

Authoritarian regimes elsewhere share these features of the Mexican political system (limited pluralism of little or no political consequence; low levels of popular mobilization; effective restriction of public office and government benefits to those who support the system; centralized, often arbitrary decision-making by a single leader or a small group; weak ideological constraints on public policymaking; etc.). Mexico's political system, however, is more complex than practically any of the authoritarian regimes that have ruled other Latin American, African, and Asian nations in recent decades.

The Mexican state represents a fairly broad coalition of interests, some within the regime itself, some outside. It strives to be inclusionary, incorporating the broadest possible range of social, economic, and political interests, not only within the official party, but also in its affiliated "mass" organizations (like the CTM), as well as opposition groups whose activities are sanctioned and sometimes even financed by the government. It is not the captive of any particular segment of society, even though some social segments (especially the middle class and entrepreneurs) have usually had disproportionate influence and representation within the ruling political elite. As potentially dissident groups have appeared over the years, the state has responded by co-opting their leaders or by establishing and "licensing" new organizations to serve as vehicles for expressing their interests.

Because of this extraordinary capacity for co-optation, most dissident movements have not evolved into overtly anti-system movements. When opposition leaders who threaten the stability of the system reject co-optation, the state represses them, although it might welcome them into the government bureaucracy if they later prove tractable. In general (with certain conspicuous exceptions, such as the "Tlatelolco massacre" of 1968 in Mexico City and the violent removal of a leftist opposition government in the city of Juchitán, Oaxaca, in 1983), the regime has maintained political control with a minimum of physical coercion. Political repression by the Mexican state has not even remotely approached the sustained waves of state terrorism practiced in recent decades by authoritarian governments in other parts of Latin America. In the Mexican system, officials whose political management skills eliminate the need for armed repression are rewarded, while those whose failures to maintain order necessitate the use of force are severely disciplined.

Despite the obvious strength of the Mexican state, it does not completely envelop or overwhelm civil society. There are enough relatively powerful and autonomous actors (e.g., regional economic elites, the military, the Catholic Church) that the government cannot rule in open defiance of the rest of society (as, for example, the Chilean military regime has done during most of the period since it came to power in 1973). There is still no place in the present Mexican political system for large, national-level opposition parties and dissident movements that are truly beyond government control. Nor will the system tolerate large-scale popular mobilizations outside of the structure of officially recognized parties and organizations, as demonstrated by the government's swift efforts to demobilize neighborhood rescue-and-reconstruction groups that emerged spontaneously in the aftermath of the

September 1985 earthquakes in Mexico City. But the state does not have the ability to manipulate all opposition groups all the time, nor can it compel the cooperation of some key groups (e.g., business elites) with government policies. And at least the strongest opposition groups can try to bargain with the government and pressure it to make concessions.

There is one additional feature of this complex, inclusionary authoritarian regime that is particularly relevant to the phenomenon of political reform. It has always been a regime that is very much in process of evolution. The post-revolutionary Mexican state has never been static or frozen in time, like Franco's Spain or Paraguay under Stroessner. At the national level, at least, the Mexican regime has adapted to social and economic changes that have made some aspects of the political apparatus dysfunctional or have created opportunities that might be exploited by dissident groups. Since 1945 alone, Mexico has had six different electoral codes and seven important reforms of these codes. In response to these and other changes in the rules of the game, the configuration of Mexico's system of political parties has changed repeatedly during this period. Adaptability, not rigidity, has been at the root of Mexico's political stability, including the extraordinary continuity of its electoral processes: elections at all levels have been held without interruption since 1920.[4] The apparently retrogressive way in which the government handled the 1985 elections (to be discussed in detail below) raises questions about whether this capacity for adaptation has been exhausted or at a minimum about the limits on evolution of the political system under today's conditions of economic crisis and uncertainty.

The Political Liberalization Process: Antecedents and Milestones

Since the early 1960s, Mexico's ruling elite has periodically found it necessary to revise the federal electoral laws in order to create a more credible political opposition. Sometimes this meant breathing new life into existing opposition parties that failed to gain adequate representation in the federal Congress. This rationale lay behind the 1963 electoral law reform, which created the so-called *diputados de partido*—Congressional seats to be awarded to any party that received 2.5 percent of the national vote. Each party attaining that requirement would receive 5 seats, plus one seat for each additional 0.5 percent of the national vote.

The 1963 reform failed to achieve its objective, since most opposition parties were unable to attain even the 2.5 percent that would qualify them to receive *diputados de partido*. Moreover, important opposition groups on the left did not benefit from such tinkering with the election laws, since they were excluded from the system. The largest of these groups—the Communist Party of Mexico (PCM)—had been banned since 1946.

All of the steps toward political liberalization taken during the 1970s and 1980s have been responses to political crises, or economic crises that have turned into political ones. The election law reforms of 1973 and 1977 had their origin in the 1968 university student protest movement and the traumatic event that ended it: the massacre of an estimated 400 student demonstrators by army troops and riot police in the center of Mexico City during the 1968 Olympic Games. Much of the country's urban middle class sympathized with this protest movement. While its leaders objected to the excessive concentration of wealth and other distributive inequalities that had accumulated in Mexico during a quarter-century of rapid industrialization, the 1968 movement was fundamentally a reaction to the authoritarian features of the country's political and law-enforcement institutions.[5]

Additional incentives for political reform emerged in the 1970s. A number of short-lived rural and urban guerrilla movements sprang up, as did several new opposition parties (all but one to the left of the PRI) outside of the officially recognized party system. In addition, the principal opposition party on the right, the Party of National Action, or PAN, failed to contest the 1976 presidential election. The PAN's default was caused by a deep internal schism which led to the expulsion of most of the party's moderate-progressive wing. The absence of an opponent for the PRI's presidential candidate, José López Portillo, not only profoundly embarrassed the government but also caused a high rate of voter abstention.[6]

The electoral reforms enacted into law in 1977 under López Portillo enabled opposition parties to qualify for electoral participation by polling only 1.5 percent of the votes cast in a nationwide election or by enrolling at least 65,000 members. By 1982 this change had significantly increased the number of officially sanctioned contenders for the national elections (nine parties, seven of which fielded presidential candidates). It also significantly reduced the voter abstention rate, from at least 50.7 percent in the 1979 congressional elections to 25.2 percent in the 1982 congressional presidential elections. The reforms also provided public financing for campaigns and free radio and television time to all parties. Only the PAN has refused to accept financial assistance from the government, preferring instead to rely upon contributions from its supporters in the business community.

Most importantly, the 1977 reforms had the effect of reincorporating the left into the electoral system. For the first time since the 1930s, the government had recognized the existence of a legitimate political opposition to the left of the PRI.[7] This "opening to the left" actually weakened the left-radical opposition to the regime by channeling its activities into a harmless parliamentary arena. As a prominent Mexican journalist observed, "The Chamber of Deputies . . . is a facade. The attitude here is still 'Nostros somos el gobierno. Tú hablas y yo hago.' (We are the government. You talk, but I do.)"

The 1977 electoral reform created a larger forum in the Congress for all opposition parties. It increased the number of seats in the lower house, the Chamber of Deputies, to 400, 100 of which are reserved for opposition parties under a proportional representation system. A safeguard for the PRI was built into the new system: In the (highly unlikely) event that any opposition party wins more than 90 of the seats contested on the first-past-the-post principle, it will lose its right to half the number of seats it has won through the proportional representation formula. Thus PRI supremacy in the Congress is guaranteed, until another party can win a majority of the first-past-the-post districts.

Despite the "opening to the left" signified by the 1977 reforms, they failed to create a viable electoral opposition to the left of the PRI. The leftist opposition parties, including several new ones created in direct response to the 1977 reforms, have failed to develop a mass base. This applies even to what is now the principal leftist opposition party, PSUM (the Unified Socialist Party of Mexico), a fusion party formed in 1981 to contest the 1982 national elections. After leading the formation of the PSUM, the Communist Party (PCM) formally dissolved itself, but its leaders retained the strongest voice in the new fusion party. In every election since 1979, the leftist opposition parties have actually lost ground to both the PRI and the conservative PAN, despite the political opportunities provided by the economic crisis of the 1980s and the harsh austerity measures implemented by the government to deal with it, including a considerable squeezing of wages and sharp reduction in consumer subsidies.

The reasons for the failure of the left to develop an electoral base that extends much beyond urban, middle-class intellectuals are numerous and complex.[8] Among the most important are the parties' constant internal squabbling (along both ideological and personalistic cleavages), and their inexperience in the electoral arena (most of them emerged after the 1968 protest movement and the regime's subsequent "opening to the left"). Moreover, the PRI through its affiliated labor unions and other clientelistic "mass" organizations has locked up a large portion of the left's natural constituency among the working classes. The government's rigid insistence on political control over unionized workers in strategic industries and key export-oriented agricultural sectors has been a major obstacle to opposition party growth. There is very little remaining organizational space in the society available to opposition parties and movements. The leftist parties' organizational limitations and their inability to shake off a public image which identifies them in the minds of many Mexicans with a frightening, anti-religious, anti-national force—international communism—has enabled the PAN to present itself successfully as the principal standard-bearer of democratization. Indeed, the rightist opposition, particularly the PAN, has benefited most from both the political liberalization process to date and the conditions created by the economic crisis.[9]

While the electoral reforms of the 1970s very effectively co-opted the government's opposition on the left, they were less successful in dealing with the grievances of the right. The Federal Electoral Commission, in 1977 and again in 1984, chose proportional representation formulas that took earned representation away from the larger opposition parties and gave it to the smaller ones, leading to significant underrepresentation of the PAN. Although it received 17.5 percent of the total votes cast in the 1982 Congressional races, the PAN was credited with only one victory by simple-majority voting (out of 300 contested seats). Furthermore, many of the municipal-level victories claimed by the PAN that year were also disallowed by PRI-dominated state electoral commissions. The growing belief that the PAN's representation in the system was not proportional to its real electoral base contributed to the PAN's resurgence at the polls after 1982.

Political Liberalization Under De la Madrid

President Miguel de la Madrid took the political reform process a step further by signalling the government's willingness to tolerate real electoral competition at the local level. In December 1982 (the month of De la Madrid's inauguration), dozens of town halls throughout the central region of Mexico were seized by members of opposition parties (mostly PAN*istas*) as a protest against fraudulent vote counts in the 1982 municipal elections. The new administration responded to these challenges in a very low-key, non-repressive manner. De la Madrid ordered negotiations with the dissidents, rather than the traditional response to such provocations (sending in army troops or federal police to impose a PRI-controlled municipal government).

Even more significantly, De la Madrid established a new policy regarding municipal elections: henceforth, municipal-level victories by opposition party candidates would be recognized, wherever they occurred. During the first ten months of his administration, the PRI conceded defeat in municipal elections held in seven major cities, including five state capitals and Ciudad Juárez, a large city on the U.S.-Mexican border. Virtually no electoral fraud was reported in these key municipal contests of 1983. As one high-ranking PAN official recalled, "It was like Switzerland up there. There was no interference in the voting, and the ballot count was absolutely clean."[10] As in the 1982 national elections, most of the opposition vote cast in these local-level elections went to the candidates of right-wing parties: the PAN and the much smaller, even more conservative Mexican Democratic Party (PDM).

De la Madrid's new policy of respect for the outcomes of local elections represented a calculated risk. Having inherited from López Portillo the worst economic crisis since the Great Depression of the 1930s, De la Madrid desperately needed an outlet for popular frustrations, at a time when austerity measures had left the regime with very few material benefits to distribute. It was also believed that a controlled liberalization of the political system from the bottom up might avoid or postpone a major confrontation between reformers and conservatives within the PRI-government apparatus itself, since the PRI's control of the truly important public offices (the presidency and the state governorships) would not be threatened.

This last expectation turned out to be incorrect. Fraud had become such an integral part of the electoral process over the years that its sudden removal, combined with an upsurge in anti-PRI protest voting for the PAN, produced a shock wave in the Mexican political establishment. State and local PRI bosses, enraged by the string of PAN victories in important cities, heavily pressured the administration to truncate this political opening. The administration apparently caved in. Since the municipal elections held in July 1983—in which the PAN rolled up majorities of 7 to 1, by official count, in cities like Chihuahua and Durango—the government has not recognized a single important electoral victory by any opposition party. Traditional heavy-handed electoral manipulations were used to deny victory to the opposition (mainly PAN candidates) in cities like Puebla and Mexicali in 1983 and several cities in the states of Coahuila and Mexico in 1984.[11]

The 1977 political reform had sought to discourage electoral fraud by permitting all participating parties to designate representatives on the supervisory committee for each polling place and by giving the parties access to documentation regarding election results. However, only the PRI possessed the manpower to supervise all polling places (even the largest opposition parties could cover only about 60 percent of the polling sites in 1982), and the holding of clean elections still depended ultimately upon the will of the President and other top officials.

The electoral debacle of 1983 and the furious reaction to it by PRI leaders exposed both the party's organizational weaknesses (at least in urban areas of northern Mexico) and a conflict of attitudes and interests between Mexico's current modernizing, technocratic government and the old-style politicians who still control the PRI and the machinery of elections at local and state levels, as well as the government-affiliated labor movement. This conflict had been building since 1970, when President Luis Echeverría brought into government the initial group of so-called *técnicos*. The main qualifications for high office among these technocrats were their technical expertise and their loyalty to the incumbent president, rather than long experience in electoral politics or political management. This pattern of political elite recruitment was maintained and intensified during the following two administrations (López Portillo's and De la Madrid's). Increasingly, the traditional political class resented and feared being displaced by young, well-educated technocrats whose proposals for modernizing the country's economy and political system were viewed as directly threatening to their interests.

This simmering tension between career politicians and *técnicos* is critical in understanding what happened after the July 1983 elections—i.e., the abrupt suspension of the political liberalization process. In the words of Alan Riding, the Mexico City-based correspondent of the *New York Times*:

> The provincial ranks of the [PRI] could not disguise their scorn for the technocrats suddenly thrown into the maze of political management . . . In some cases influential local *políticos*, as a sign of their disaffection, even refused to run as candidates in municipal elections. When the worried government resorted to fraud to "win" several provincial elections [later in 1983 and 1984], its maneuvers were, owing to inexperience, clumsily—and too publicly executed. Instinctively, De la Madrid preferred greater democracy to more efficient frauds, but his administration seemed paralyzed by indecision reluctant either to give the PRI some independence and credibility or to recall the old *políticos*

to run it—as the crucial test of the July 1985 mid-term congressional elections approached.[12]

This state of political paralysis—which contrasted sharply with the De la Madrid Administration's decisive handling of the country's economic crisis[13]—continued through 1984. That year brought another abortive attempt to improve the PRI's candidate selection process, in order to make it more responsive to local preferences and break the hold on local public offices by corrupt lower-level party bosses. The power to choose the PRI's candidates was to be taken away from state governors and local congressmen, and placed in the hands of the PRI's central executive committee and personal representatives of the Minister of Gobernación (the government ministry responsible for elections and political control). This plan was implemented on an experimental basis in the state of Nayarit during 1984. Like previous attempts to reform the PRI's candidate selection process from the bottom up, this experiment was quickly abandoned after it drew fire from lower-level PRI chieftains.[14]

In December 1984, the De la Madrid Administration suffered another disaster in the electoral arena. Several apparently very close municipal contests between the PRI and the PAN in the northern border state of Coahuila were decided, by highly questionable procedures, in favor of the PRI. Militant PAN supporters rioted and burned the city halls in two of the cities, and local police responded by firing into a crowd of PANista demonstrators. At least two people were killed and 35 wounded, although some estimates place the casualties at many times those numbers. For the first time since the Tlatelolco massacre of 1968, a large group of political protestors had been fired upon in an urban area by government security forces. The central government was forced to send in the army to restore order in these cities. Both the rioting and the official response were widely reported by the international media.

Some officials privately blamed the failure of political control in Coahuila on an inept, inflexible state governor and/or long-standing feuds between the governor and his enemies within the state PRI machine. Whatever the reason, the breakdown was especially significant because one of the cities involved was Monclova, a working-class industrial city with tens of thousands of residents nominally tied to the regime through their membership in government affiliated labor unions. The ability of a handful of PAN militants to take over the city government by force in such a place was dramatic evidence of erosion in the PRI's capabilities for popular mobilization and political control. The event also suggested that the economic crisis and austerity policies of recent years may have severely damaged the traditional support relationship between the government and the official labor movement, whose local leaders have found it increasingly difficult to call on the rank-and-file to defend the government's interests.[15]

The government regained control of the situation in Coahuila within a few weeks. In the case of Monclova, the PRI opted to negotiate a power-sharing arrangement with the PAN. A newly appointed, supposedly bipartisan mayor now presides over a bipartisan city council, whose membership is divided equally between PRI and PAN supporters. But in the border city of Piedras Negras, a more politically sensitive city where the most serious violence occurred, the PRI cut no deal with PAN leaders, who remain excluded from the municipal government.

The events in Coahuila raised the already high stakes in the 1985 mid-term elections for all 400 Congressional seats, seven state governorships, and hundreds of other state and local offices. In these elections, the PRI for the first time faced a genuinely strong opposition party challenge for control of state governments—most notably the governorships of Sonora and Nuevo León, both strongholds of the PAN. In Nuevo León, where the Monterrey group of industrialists had long been at the center of regional power, the PAN nominated a prominent businessman, Fernando Canales Clariond, to contest the governorship. In Sonora, the PAN selected as its gubernatorial candidate a highly popular agribusiness leader, Adalberto Rosas, who had previously been elected to a term as mayor of Ciudad Obregón, the state's second-largest city. A charistmatic figure who campaigned extensively across the state for nearly three years, Rosas seemed to have a reasonable chance of breaking the PRI's monopoly of control over state governments.[16] To begin with, his PRI opponent was a colorless former Minister of Communications and Transportation in De la Madrid's cabinet who had not lived in the state for 40 years. Various idiosyncrasies of the region's economic and demographic structure, its history, and its political culture also favored the PAN. For example, the concentration of a large portion of the population in two cities and the presence of a strong, independently minded entrepreneurial elite gave the PAN fertile ground for developing an organizational base. Additional factors favoring the PAN were the pervasive influence of the nearby United States economy and mass media, and Sonora's long distance from Mexico City, which promoted resentment of political centralism. This sentiment was reinforced by still-smoldering anger among Sonora's prosperous agribusinessmen over the expropriation of much of the state's prime agricultural land by President Echeverría in 1976.[17]

The 1985 mid-term elections were also widely perceived as a critical test of the De la Madrid Administration's commitment to political liberalization. Since the government's recognition of PAN's overwhelming victories in municipal elections in Chihuahua in July 1983, De la Madrid's political reform project had been on hold. This was due partly to the severity of the economic crisis. Not only was the administration preoccupied with measures to deal with the crisis, but De la Madrid's technocrats sensed that this was no time to be making concessions to opposition groups. The fundamental obstacle to continuing the liberalization process, however, had been resistance to change among the members of the traditional political class. "Local interests are very strong," the PRI's chief official spokesman admitted to a foreign reporter.[18] Yet objections to further political opening were not limited to "local interests." The resistance extended into the upper echelons of both the PRI and the Ministry of Gobernación, where no one wanted to appear weak and ineffective—and thereby risk damage to a political career—by "losing" key offices to the opposition parties.

Regardless of its cause, the lack of movement on political reform, coming after a significant opening during the first six months of the new administration, added to the credibility problems that De la Madrid had inherited from the two preceding administrations. President Echeverría had set sustained economic growth "with redistribution" as his primary policy objective, and López Portillo had promised to make Mexico an economically self-sufficient industrial power, no longer dependent on the United States, through a fast-track, oil-based development strategy. Not only did neither administration achieve its goals, but both left the country in a state of financial chaos and political turmoil.

De la Madrid himself had helped to inflate public expectations for a new style of governance by making the modernization and "moral renovation" of the political system the most prominent theme of his ten-month campaign for the presidency. Among the most significant acts of his first months in office were several landmark legislative changes and the creation of a cabinet-level investigatory agency (the Comptroller General's Office), all designed to combat corruption in government and the police forces. In 1983–1984, a number of powerful political figures, including a former director of the government-owned oil company, the former chief of the Mexico City police, and two incumbent state governors, fell victim to government anti-corruption prosecutors. Corruption in government employees' labor unions also became a target, although little progress was made in this area. As his Secretary of Education, De la Madrid appointed Jesús Reyes Heroles, the aging but highly respected leader of the reform wing of the PRI, and gave him a mandate to break the power of the corrupt public school teachers' union. A notable loosening of press controls (more specifically, a decline in self-censorship by editors and reporters) also occurred under De la Madrid. Even leaders of the most harshly critical opposition parties have admitted that the print media have criticized government performance much more freely since De la Madrid took office, and dissident groups have had far more opportunities to be heard.

The De la Madrid Administration's attempts to create a more open and competitive political environment, especially its short-lived policy of recognizing opposition electoral victories, emboldened the PAN and its supporters. For the first time in memory, the government's opponents in the business community began to take party politics seriously. Since 1984, prominent businessmen have been financing the campaigns of PAN candidates and running for office themselves (for both Congressional and gubernatorial posts) on the PAN ticket.

This new development caused considerable concern, not only in official and intellectual circles but among former leaders of the PAN itself. Those leaders warned that the PAN was being captured by ideological extremists of the right (men who had publicly accused the De la Madrid Administration of being "a government of the extreme left") and by entrepreneurs whose only interest in the PAN was to use it to pressure the government for concessions on economic policy.

The post-election disturbances in Coahuila in December 1984 signalled the emergence of a new generation of aggressive, militant PAN leaders who refused to play by the traditional rules of the game. These leaders and their followers were no longer willing to go through the charade of winning elections that PRI-dominated electoral commissions would nullify or refuse to recognize, and then after verbally protesting the fraud, steal away into silence and powerlessness until the next election, when their participation would once again help to legitimize the government that they sought to change.

As the 1985 elections approached, PAN spokesmen began to warn ominously about the possibility of violence, especially in places like Sonora, if the party's victories were not respected. When government and PRI officials accused the PAN leadership of condoning and even fomenting the use of violence as a political tactic, the PAN's national leader, Pablo Emilio Madero, responded by stating the party's position on this issue in a personal meeting with De la Madrid. In the event of election-related violence in 1985, he said, "the responsible party will be the one which violates the popular will, not the one that protests."[19]

In spite of these rumblings, the government and PRI officials confidently predicted tranquil and clean elections in Sonora and all other states where elections were to be held in July 1985. They also predicted sweeping victories for their candidates. PRI officials based their predictions in large measure on the party's overwhelming organizational strength; the party claimed to have 540,000 promoters working in the country's 300 federal electoral districts, each of whom had been "asked to invite 30 citizens to vote for the PRI."[20]

They were also counting on the party's continuing strength among rural voters (even if it had been deserted by significant portions of the more affluent, urban electorate). Even in states like Sonora, where the opposition was well organized in the cities, the PAN's challenge to the PRI would be blunted by its weak representation and limited appeal among *campesinos* and the urban poor. Finally, PRI leaders pointed to the failure of the PAN to articulate an alternative set of economic policies or, in fact, any platform beyond condemnation of official corruption and poor government performance in recent administrations.

The mid-term elections of 1985 did prove to be a milestone in recent Mexican political history, but they were neither the precedent-setting breakthrough predicted by the PAN nor the clean and convincing reaffirmation of popular support for the regime promised by the PRI. On the basis of very partial, unofficial returns, the PRI immediately claimed victory in all 300 Congressional races and all seven gubernatorial contests. While 11 of the PRI's 300 claimed Congressional seats were subsequently awarded to opposition party candidates as a result of successful challenges of the results in the electoral college, all of the PRI's gubernatorial victories were certified. In the state of Sonora, the PRI claimed to have won not only the governorship (by a 3 to 1 margin) but all of the 69 municipal races and 100 percent of the seats in the state legislature. In Ciudad Obregón, the city where the PAN's gubernatorial candidate had served as mayor from 1979–1982, the PRI claimed that its candidate for governor won in all but 1 of the city's 39 precincts. Four of the city's precincts reported tallies of 350 to 1, 400 to 3, 320 to 0, and 1,000 to 20 in favor of the PRI's gubernatorial candidate. In Pueblo Yaqui, the home town of the PAN's candidate for governor, unofficial vote counts showed that in 5 out of the town's 6 precincts, he lost by the astonishing margins of 400 to 0, 320 to 0, 400 to 140, 128 to 55, and 90 to 53. (He was credited with victory in the sixth precinct, by a count of 800 to 100.) PAN leaders were stunned, and even some higher-level PRI officials expressed shock and disbelief when asked by foreign reporters about these results.[21]

What had occurred, especially in Sonora, was one of the dirtiest elections in recent Mexican history. Both the PRI and the PAN had used every possible means, legal and illegal, to try to control the electoral process. On July 4, for example, it was revealed that registration lists prepared by PRI-dominated electoral commissions had been inflated with millions of "phantom" voters, supposedly to permit multiple voting by PRI sympathizers, while hundreds of thousands of PAN supporters had been dropped from the rolls. The government blamed "computer error" and promised to purge the lists in time for the July 7 elections, but that was a physical impossibility. In addition, the PRI employed its full range of traditional election chicanery— from ballot box stuffing and theft to arbitrary disqualification of opposition candidates and poll-watchers on minor technical grounds, including having received a traffic citation. PRI-dominated state electoral commissions func-tioned in an irregular manner, with officials frequently unavailable to receive opposition party complaints.

For its part, the PAN, which saw the whole election machinery as being controlled by the PRI and working against its interests, seemed less concerned on election day with mobilizing its supporters to vote than with sabotaging and discrediting the electoral process. Both PRI and PAN militants committed acts of provocation and intimidation, and no one seemed much concerned about violating electoral laws. A Mexican social scientist who observed the July 7 elections in Sonora concluded that there were so many irregularities that there is no way of ascertaining whether the PRI or the PAN would have won in clean elections.[22]

Government spokesmen were quick to point out that, in most parts of the country, the July 7 elections were tranquil and not marked by blatant fraud. But where it really counted, in hotly contested races such as those in the states of Sonora and Nuevo León, the voting was marred by serious irregularities and, in a few places, violent confrontations between PANistas and government security forces, as well as between PRI and PAN militants. Numerous instances of collusion between the PRI and federal judicial police were observed.

Both during and after the elections, the government mounted a massive show of armed force in areas where PRI-PAN competition was most intense. The highly visible presence of more than 20,000 soldiers in the state of Sonora, for example, was cited by PAN leaders and some Mexican social scientists as one of the factors that depressed voter turnout in the elections and intimidated PAN supporters who might otherwise have taken to the streets to protest election irregularities. The abstention rate in these elections was very high: at least 49.5 percent nationally, in Congressional races, according to official statistics; an estimated 60–70 percent in the state of Sonora. This represents a sharp increase in abstention over the previous (1982) elections, when only 34.3 percent of the electorate failed to vote (again, according to government statistics). Abstention in the 1985 elections nearly equalled the 50.7 percent recorded in the 1979 Congressional elections, the first in which non-voters outnumbered voters.

Another factor that undoubtedly depressed voter turnout in the 1985 elections was the widespread fear of election-related violence. PAN leaders, government and PRI spokesmen, and the U.S. media all contributed to this climate of fear. The expectations of large-scale violence or nonviolent protest demonstrations in the aftermath of the elections were not realized, however. As noted above, a few instances of election-day violence occurred, most notably in the Sonoran city of San Luis Río Colorado; but for the most part supporters of PAN and the other opposition parties suffered their defeats in silence. Only in Monterrey, Nuevo León, was a significant protest demonstration held, attracting an estimated 40,000–50,000 supporters of the defeated PANista gubernatorial candidate, Canales Clariond. The absence of more widespread and more militant protests signalled to many observers that PAN lacked a post-election strategy, and the party suffered a certain loss of credibility both among its supporters and opponents.

The underlying rationale for the PAN's strategy in contesting the 1985 elections was obvious enough. PANistas wanted to provoke the government to undertake more fundamental political reforms and create more space in the political system for their party. However, the sorry spectacle of the 1985 elections raised difficult questions about the government's objectives. The mid-term elections of 1985 took place as the President's highly touted anti-corruption campaign was running out of steam. The economy continued to languish after the debacle of 1982, and only a few days before the elections, the government had ordered another sharp devaluation of the peso. The De la Madrid Administration needed clean elections to help restore its credibility (especially in middle-class eyes) and rebuild support for the system. The President had put his personal prestige on the line by repeatedly promising clean elections and by publicly ordering his state governors to conduct the 1985 elections "with strict adherence to legality." In the aftermath of election-related violence in Coahuila the previous December, the international press was present in large numbers to cover the July 7 elections in Sonora.

Most well-informed observers had not expected the government to relinquish control of any state governorship, and certainly not in a politically sensitive border state like Sonora. Yet the extent and heavy-handedness of election manipulation by PRI officials, especially with so much foreign media attention focused on the event, was truly surprising. The PAN's statewide campaign coordinator in Sonora was guilty of only slight hyperbole when he accused the PRI of resorting to "the fraudulent methods they were using 40 years ago." How can such tactics be explained? Why was the De la Madrid Administration willing to pay such a high cost, in terms of its international image and domestic legitimacy, in order to avoid giving up a few token congressional and municipal offices? Why was it necessary not just to defeat but to crush and humiliate the opposition?

Explaining the Outcome

No single-factor explanation for the government's handling of the July 1985 elections will suffice. But most of the probable contributing factors are rooted in the country's profound economic distress and its impact on the Mexican political elite. The handling of the 1985 elections demonstrates that there is not just a difference in "style" between the high-level technocrats now running the Mexican government and the career politicians running the PRI, but also a basic conflict of interest between these two segments of the ruling elite. The party bosses and their lieutenants in Mexico's villages, urban slums, labor unions and other "mass" organizations may have lost their capacity to influence public policy and national priorities, but they have not lost their capacity to organize and carry out electoral fraud.

Would-be reformers and modernizers in the Mexican government are now confronting the reality that in too many places, the official party is run by men whose distaste for losing an election—any election—is comparable to that of precinct captains in Mayor Daley's Chicago. These políticos have an independent interest in perpetuating their power and increasing their personal clout within the political establishment, whatever the cost. This characterization applies not only to state and local-level PRI leaders whose future mobility within the party structure may depend upon their success in engineering favorable electoral outcomes, but also to nationally significant leaders of the PRI's labor sector, which has become the most resistant to the idea of changing the rules of the political game. It is also the most militantly anti-PAN segment of the ruling political elite. Such motives are often sufficient to explain electoral fraud in Mexico. As PSUM leader Rolando Cordera has observed,

> The PRI commits fraud not only to reverse unfavorable results, but when they win as well. Why? To be able to show absolute dominance, and also to continue the internal competition within the PRI hierarchy, within the PRI delegation in Congress, and in the sectoral organizations (CTM, CNC, etc.). Winning a larger share of the vote than one's rivals [in the PRI] determines the pecking order, the power relations among members of the PRI elite.[23]

The members of this traditional political class were enraged at being forced to recognize the string of PAN victories that took place in the first half of 1983. Academics present at the PRI's annual convention in August 1984 noted among the *políticos* a high level of hostility toward De la Madrid's *técnicos*, who were bitterly criticized in several speeches that went unreported in the press. Twenty months into the De la Madrid *sexenio*, malaise and even demoralization had spread throughout the ranks of career politicians, who feared that they were in jeopardy of being cast aside or sacrificed to the electoral liberalization and anti-corruption projects favored by the technocrats. The extensive ballot rigging of July 1985 might therefore be seen as a concession to the traditional political class.

De la Madrid may have acquiesced in this outcome at least partly in order to avert an open rupture in the national political elite that might destabilize the entire system. The string of opposition victories in 1983 seems to have provoked a confrontation between political reformers and hard-liners, although it was well concealed from public view. The De la Madrid Administration has remained concerned about the possibility of serious internal strife within the PRI-government apparatus. The regime has not had to confront a national election in which the ruling group had any serious internal divisions since 1952. At that time, the split resulted in the poorest showing by a presidential candidate of the official party since its founding in 1929. In 1985, De la Madrid may have chosen a course of expediency: to let the PRI keep all (or nearly all) of its victories rather than risk conflict within the ruling elite itself, especially at a time of considerable economic uncertainty and stress on the regime's relationships with organized labor and other support groups run by old-style political leaders. For this government, a crisis originating in a violent uprising by defeated PAN*istas* in Sonora would be more manageable than a crisis stemming from an intra-regime split.

Another, equally plausible interpretation of the De la Madrid Administration's approach to the 1985 elections discounts the significance of tensions between technocrats and more traditional political leaders within the PRI-government apparatus. In this view, the handling of the 1985 elections was not a sign of weakness on the part of the technocrats (i.e., a concession to restive traditional politicians, or a loss of control by the federal executive over its local and state-level operatives), but rather, an attempt to convey an image of firm control at a time when the government needed to sustain its austerity program and implement some highly controversial economic restructuring policies (e.g., trade liberalization, through entry into the GATT; privatization of many state-owned enterprises). Thus the government's bare-knuckle tactics in places like Sonora and Nuevo León were intended to send a strong signal to its opponents in the business community, the Church, and other elements of the anti-statist coalition that supported the PAN in the 1985 elections. De la Madrid and his advisors may have concluded that in order to keep the anti-government right at bay, its electoral ambitions must be denied. Blatant electoral fraud, however embarrassing and repugnant, was therefore regarded as an acceptable tradeoff.

Other analysts seriously question the commitment of the now-dominant *técnicos* to the goal of political liberalization, regardless of the circumstances operating in July 1985. In their view, the government was never serious about a political opening, and foreign critics had wildly exaggerated expectations about the prospects for clean elections. Thus, the De la Madrid administration's handling of the July 7 elections is proof of the low priority assigned by this government to continuing the political reform process and cutting a new deal with the opposition. This interpretation gains strength from the apparently extensive rigging of local elections held in several states, especially those in San Luis Potosí and Guanajuato, during the last two months of 1985. Still other observers, believing that De la Madrid and his modernizing technocrats "instinctively" prefer political reform, point to the persistence and deepening of Mexico's economic crisis during 1985. As they see it, the economic crisis has sapped the commitment of the current ruling group to political liberalization and made them increasingly dependent upon anti-reform political bosses in order to maintain control of the population.

Critical analysis of the 1985 elections within Mexico quickly became mired in nationalistic reactions to the uniformly negative foreign media coverage of the elections, to persistent U.S. government pressure on Mexico to change its policy toward Nicaragua, and to the prospect of further austerity measures needed for Mexico to keep servicing its huge external debt. Mexican intellectuals as well as government spokesmen criticized the foreign critics for launching a "campaign against Mexico" and drawing a false parallel between democratization movements in South America and what is needed to reform the Mexican political system.

Implications for the Future of
Political Reform in Mexico

The manipulations of local election outcomes at the end of 1985, as well as the violent protests that they elicited from supporters of conservative opposition parties in eight states, signified a hardening of the government's stance toward the opposition as well as the adoption of a more militant strategy of resistance to electoral fraud by the rightist opposition parties. The stage was set for a new round of confrontations in 1986, especially in the northern state of Chihuahua, where the PAN already controlled 60 percent of the municipalities, including the state capital, and was determined to hang on to them.

The elections of 1985 demonstrated that the PAN is now firmly controlled by a new generation of leaders who are unwilling to settle for the traditional role of an opposition party in Mexico ("You can be a party, but not a government") and who are increasingly committed to a strategy of delegitimizing the regime. As they confront a PRI that continues refusing to give up anything of importance, the cost of each future election, in terms of both the government's treasury and its legitimacy, will be progressively higher. If nothing is done, there could be serious conflicts during the presidential succession of 1987–1988.

But what is to be done? The experience of the past decade, and especially the elections of 1985, show that the regime can no longer rely simply upon changes in the electoral laws as the principal vehicle of orderly political change. The opposition parties bolstered by or created in response to these periodic revisions in the electoral rules have failed to become credible alternatives to the PRI. The PAN is the only opposition party that, after nearly a half-century of existence, has succeeded in developing a mass base; and even it continues to serve primarily as a receptacle for anti-PRI protest votes. As even its staunchest supporters admit, the PAN has yet to develop a viable grass-roots organization that could eventually serve as the basis for a serious national-level challenge to the PRI.

Most importantly, Mexico's experience shows that political reforms which serve mainly to create additional space within the political system for opposition parties do not really promote the democratization of the system. And the more competitive elections made possible by liberalized election laws do not even necessarily help to legitimate the government, so long as the basic authoritarian features of the system (i.e., the PRI itself and its affiliated "mass" organizations) remain intact. The De la Madrid Administration's only major political liberalization measure to date—the decision to recognize local-level opposition victories wherever they occurred in 1983— has been criticized on precisely these grounds:

> De la Madrid's early offer to hold clean elections ran head-on into the strong resistance of authoritarian political institutions still alive and functioning, especially the official party . . . Up to that point, elections had served to stabilize national political life by channeling some of the noisiest social tensions. But the recent pledge by the government to recognize the electoral victories of the opposition, while maintaining intact an institutional framework that was essentially [authoritarian and] centralizing, transformed elections into a source of destabilization . . . The relatively high level of participation registered in the border states, Durango, Puebla and others had a flavor of 'electoral insurrection' about it . . . a feeling of challenging the government: 'Let's see if they dare to count the votes!' . . . And when the government can't make good on its initial promise of an electoral opening, its political credibility and claims to legitimacy are sacrificed.[24]

This problem acquires particular seriousness and urgency in light of the continuing revolt of Mexico's middle classes. Still furious about official corruption during the López Portillo and Echeverría administrations, members of the Mexican middle class became even angrier when their standard of living began to drop precipitously, starting with the economic crisis of 1982. Most of the middle-class protest voters in recent elections seem to have been apolitical until they were adversely affected by the economic crisis. Even now, most of them do not consider themselves affiliated with any party or other political organization. Many are public employees who used to vote for the PRI without even thinking about alternatives. Now, they vote for the most vocal critics of the government and of the economic debacle, whose electoral instrument is the PAN.

The De la Madrid Administration recognizes this constituency—the largely unorganized, disaffected, mostly young and relatively well-educated urban middle-class—as its number one political problem. The rural poor and most of the urban working class have not yet deserted the PRI. Most of those still linked to the PRI through one of the party's mass organizations have not wanted to risk abandoning these clientage relationships, which in the past have provided material benefits. However, rebuilding middle-class support for the ruling party and the political system that it is supposed to legitimate will be a long, arduous task. As Hector Aguilar Camín, one of Mexico's most influential political commentators, observed recently, "The hegemony of the PRI at the national level is not in question [in the foreseeable future]. What these [1985] elections signify is a battle for the country's middle class."[25]

In this battle, the government cannot hope to win unless it gets on with the business of rejuvenating and reforming the PRI itself. Without serious internal reform, the PRI will be unable to appeal to the alienated, unorganized middle-class opposition and thereby regain the political space now being occupied by the PAN. In fact, the government's ability to continue using the electoral process as a means of legitimating itself in the future may depend on such internal reform. Another change in the election laws will not prevent a repetition of the abuses of 1985; the electoral process itself must be sanitized with concrete actions to reduce the likelihood of fraud. The PRI would have to improve radically its candidate-selection process at local and state levels, and some entrenched PRI leaders would have to be forced into early retirement. Further decentralization of political decision-making would have to occur, both to reduce resentment of centralism and to improve the PRI's capacity to defuse local conflicts.

None of these changes would be painless, and all would be conflictual. For this reason, all administrations up to now have chosen the easier route of political liberalization: tinkering with the rules of inter-party competition, offering preemptive concessions to dissident groups and creating more space for them in the political system. The focus has been on altering the terms of competition between the PRI and its opposition and not on changing the way in which the PRI conducts itself. In 1985, De la Madrid promised what he could not possibly deliver, i.e., clean elections in highly contested races like the Sonora governorship, in the absence of a fundamental overhaul of the PRI.

Few informed observers believe that the prospects for a thorough internal reform and modernization of the PRI—even for strategic, competitive purposes—are very high. But while there is little belief in the capacity of the PRI to reform itself, there is even less confidence in the ability of the present ruling group to reach a new accommodation with opposition forces. In the immediate aftermath of the July 1985 elections, it was widely expected that the government would seek to negotiate with the PAN to ensure its continued participation in the electoral process (most importantly, the presidential elections of 1988). Instead, De la Madrid's *técnicos* have eschewed negotiations and pursued an increasingly hard line in dealing with the opposition, often painting it as unpatriotic and beholden to U.S. interests. Nor has the present PAN leadership been easy to deal with. As noted above, ultra-conservatives have gained the upper hand in the PAN during the last ten years, and there is a fanatical quality to their leadership. Another complication which has arisen in recent years is the direct involvement in PAN affairs of big businessmen, at least some of whom have their own agendas to pursue with the government. On the other hand, if the government were to hammer out a new consensus with the business community on economic policy, this would undoubtedly facilitate an accord with the conservative electoral opposition. Whether or not such negotiations would evolve into a full-blown "political reform for the right" (comparable to the "opening to the left" implemented by the administrations of the 1970s) remains to be seen.

From our present vantage point, it is hard to escape the conclusion that the political liberalization process in Mexico—at least as we have known it during the last ten years—has reached a dead end. Would-be reformers within the regime seem paralyzed, both by the deepening economic crisis and by their fear that further political opening is likely to benefit only their anti-statist enemies: big business, the Church, the PAN and other conservative opposition parties. Leftist dissidents within the PRI are concerned more with ameliorating the effects of the economic crisis and austerity policies upon the regime's traditional working and middle-class constituencies, rather than creating a more genuinely competitive political environment. The leftist opposition parties remain mired in intramural ideological debates and have lost most of their credibility as vehicles for opposing government policies. The rightist opposition clamors for a "democratic" transformation and continues to do well at the polls, but few Mexicans take it seriously as a national-level alternative to the PRI, and the more militantly it protests PRI electoral abuses the more it seems to strengthen the hand of those within the regime who oppose political reforms.

Based on Mexico's political history during the past half-century, the safest prediction would be that Mexico will experience further, carefully controlled adaptation of the political system rather than any abrupt shift in regime type. But this projection assumes that sustained economic growth will be restored; that inflation can be reduced to a socially tolerable level; and that the social tensions which have accumulated over the past decade of boom-and-bust in the economy do not erupt into civil disorders that require military intervention or a generalized increase in the level of repression.[26] Should any of these assumptions fail to hold, it is highly unlikely that the ruling elite would risk more extensive political liberalization. The catastrophic drop in world oil prices in late 1985 and early 1986 which will cost the Mexican government more than $6 billion in oil export revenues in 1986 alone—makes it improbable that economic and social conditions conducive to political reform will exist very soon in Mexico.

Under such circumstances, some Mexican academics and journalists foresee a progressive distancing of the state from society, as the state's credibility, legitimacy, and capacity for negotiation continue to erode. These observers do not expect the government to fall or be overthrown; but civil society will go its own way, no longer relying upon the government to mediate societal conflicts and allocate resources. In other words, the state-society links that have been forged since the 1910 Revolution will be broken, contributing to generalized social and economic disintegration.

In another scenario, the state will not relinquish its control over society, but will have to rely increasingly upon coercion to maintain its control. The government may be tempted to suspend traditional electoral contests, at least at the state and local levels, until economic conditions are more favorable to the ruling party. The military probably would acquiesce in such a government-directed rupture of the constitutional order. This scenario has some plausibility, as the government confronts a succession of elections that can only weaken rather than strengthen the state, because of high abstentionism, militant resistance by the conservative opposition to fraud, adverse foreign media attention, and so forth. If no further reforms are undertaken, the most important opposition parties can be expected to intensify their attacks on the legitimacy of the regime, and the danger of destabilizing splits within the ruling elite will increase. As the political and financial costs of holding elections continue to rise, the government at some point may opt to "pull the plug."

Mexico's system of political parties and elections is, indeed, malfunctioning. It has lost much of its credibility and mass support. The government must somehow solve the problem of how to keep winning without driving the opposition out of the system. If the "*aparato*" cannot be fixed through some sort of overhaul that is acceptable to all the major power contenders, the state would have to devise a new legitimating mechanism; and many experts believe that elections are the only possible legitimating device in Mexico—there is no alternative! Finding a way out of this impasse will require a high degree of political creativity, on a level that very few governments in Mexico's post-revolutionary history have attained, and none of the more recent administrations have demonstrated.

Notes

1. I wish to thank Arturo Alvarado, professor of political sociology at the Universidad Autónoma Metropolitana (Mexico City) for his valuable field observations and insights on the 1985 elections in Mexico. I also benefited from the insights of the 22 Mexican social scientists and political leaders who participated in a workshop on the 1985 Mexican elections held at the Center for U.S.-Mexican Studies, University of California, San Diego, November 7-9, 1985. I, of course, am solely responsible for the interpretations presented in this paper.

2. Comments at the research Workshop on Electoral Patterns and Perspectives in Mexico, Center for U.S.-Mexican Studies, University of California, San Diego, November 7-9, 1985.

3. For overviews of the contemporary Mexican political system, see: Wayne A. Cornelius and Ann L. Craig, "Politics in Mexico," in Gabriel A. Almond and G. Bingham Powell, Jr., eds., *Comparative Politics Today*, 3rd ed. (Boston, MA: Little

Brown & Co., 1984), 411–465; and Evelyn P. Stevens, "Mexico in the 1980s: From Authoritarianism to Power Sharing?" in Howard J. Wiarda and Harvey F. Kline, eds., *Latin American Politics and Development*, 2nd ed. (Boulder, CO: Westview Press, 1985), 403–445.

4. For a fuller elaboration of this theme, see: Juan Molinar Horcasitas, "The Mexican Electoral System: Continuity by Change," paper presented at the Conference on Electoral Change in the Americas, 1980–1985, University of California, San Diego, February 1985.

5. The most detailed account in English of the 1968 protest movement and government's responses to it is Evelyn P. Stevens, *Protest and Response in Mexico* (Cambridge, MA: MIT Press, 1974).

6. Only the Communist Party, which was not legally recognized as a party at that time, fielded a candidate to run against López Portillo in 1976.

7. See Kevin Middlebrook, "Political Liberalization in an Authoritarian Regime: The Case of Mexico," Research Reports Series, no. 41 (La Jolla, CA: Center for U.S.-Mexican Studies, University of California, San Diego, 1985).

8. The best analyses bearing on this question are Barry Carr, "Mexican Communism, 1968–1983: Eurocommunism in the Americas?" Research Report Series, no. 42 (La Jolla, CA: Center for U.S.-Mexican Studies, University of California, San Diego, 1985); and Barry Carr, ed., *The Mexican Left, Popular Movements, and the Politics of Austerity, 1982–1985*, Center for U.S.-Mexican Studies monograph no. 16 (La Jolla, CA: University of California, San Diego, forthcoming). Nevertheless, as Rolando Cordera, one of the founders of the PSUM, recently observed, "There is no good explanation for why the leftist parties in Mexico aren't linked more closely to 'mass' groups. It is a problem of sociology" (statement at the Research Workshop on Electoral Patterns and Perspectives in Mexico, Center for U.S.-Mexican Studies, University of California, San Diego, November 7–9, 1985).

9. PAN's recent success at the polls, especially in relation to the leftist opposition parties, is all the more striking because of its failure to present concrete alternatives to the policies being pursued by the government to deal with the economic crisis. Barry Carr, one of the most acute observers of Mexico's opposition parties, recently concluded that "the right's success is due to its combative style and its radical rejection of the state's woeful performance. It is more a question of the PAN's style than of its actual programmatic offerings. The left, meanwhile, is still caught up in agonizing debates over the merits of statism and over the viability of ties with progressive sections of the PRI . . . The end result is that the left *appears* to be compromised with the hated 'state' while the right flies the flag of democratization" (personal communication with the author, February 5, 1986).

10. PAN Secretary-General Bernardo Batiz, quoted in William Orme, "At Last, a Challenge to Mexico's Ruling Party," *Washington Post*, National Weekly Edition, 18 February 1985, 17.

11. In the state of Mexico, a PAN stronghold which includes much of the Mexico City metropolitan area, the PAN was credited with winning only 1 out of 121 municipal elections.

12. Alan Riding, *Distant Neighbors: A Portrait of the Mexicans* (New York, NY: Alfred A. Knopf, 1985), 81–82.

13. See Wayne A. Cornelius, "The Political Economy of Mexico under De la Madrid: Austerity, Routinized Crisis, and Nascent Recovery," *Mexican Studies* 1:1 (Winter 1985): 83–124.

14. The most notable earlier effort of this type took place in 1965, under the leadership of PRI national chairman Carlos Madrazo. Madrazo attempted to institute

a system of direct primary elections for PRI candidate selection but encountered such vehement resistance from local and state-level PRI bosses that the incumbent President Gustavo Díaz Ordaz not only repealed the system but also dismissed Madrazo from his post. The incident marked the first time since the official party was founded in 1929 that a president had been forced, under fire, to remove his own hand-picked party chair. Shortly afterward, Madrazo was killed in a suspicious plane crash.

15. During most of the period of economic crisis, however, the official labor movement at the national level has supported the De la Madrid Administration and its austerity program. In fact, the wage discipline approved and enforced by CTM leaders has been an essential ingredient of the administration's battle against inflation. Without it, the inflation rate would have been far above the 64–87 percent experienced in 1985 and 1986. This wage restraint at a time of high inflation had pushed real wages down to 1965 levels by the middle of 1986. For an analysis of organized labor's response to the economic crisis, see Barry Carr, "The Mexican Economic Debacle and the Labor Movement: A New Era or More of the Same?" in *Mexico's Economic Crisis: Challenges and Opportunities*, Center for U.S.-Mexican Studies monograph no. 12 (La Jolla, CA: University of California, San Diego, 1983), 91–116.

16. In its entire history, the official party has never conceded victory in a gubernatorial election to an opposition party, although it is highly probable that opposition candidates have won the vote in several of these contests. For example, Jesús Reyes Heroles, a one-time PRI chairman as well as Minister of Gobernación and Education under three different presidents, admitted, a decade after the fact, that conservative candidate Salvador Nava actually won the 1961 race for the governorship of San Luis Potosí, but his victory was not recognized. Alejandro Gascón Mercado, a leftist candidate for governor of Nayarit in 1977, experienced a similar fate.

17. For analysis of the conditions in Sonora during the decade leading up to the 1985 election, see Arturo Warman, "Divorcio en Sonora," *Nexos* 64 (April 1983): 41–46; and an excellent series of 26 articles by Keith Rosenblum, "Election '85: The Campaign for Sonora," in *The Arizona Daily Star* (Tucson, Arizona), 3 February to 9 June 1985.

18. Quoted in Orme, "At Last, A Challenge to Mexico's Ruling Party."

19. Reported in *La Nación: Organo del Partido Acción Nacional*, no. 1685 (15 June 1985), 8. Eugenio Elorduy, the defeated PAN candidate for mayor of the city of Mexicali in 1983, put the matter somewhat more provocatively: "The PAN has spent 46 years avoiding violence. Maybe that's why we've been considered patsies for so long" (interview with Juan M. Vasquez, *The Los Angeles Times*, 7 July 1985, 4).

20. Statement presented by Genaro Borrego (PRI Chief of Staff) at the Fifth Annual Briefing Session for Professional Journalists, Center for U.S.-Mexican Studies, University of California, San Diego, 20 June 1985, 9.

21. For more detailed reports and analyses of the official results of the July 1985 elections, see Juan Molinar, "Composición y patrones del voto en México: 1985" (paper presented at the Workshop on Electoral Patterns and Perspectives in Mexico, Center for U.S.-Mexican Studies, University of California, San Diego, November 7–9, 1985, forthcoming in a volume of workshop papers to be published by the Center for U.S.-Mexican Studies); and Delal Baer, "Mexico's Midterm Election" (Report No. 4, Latin American Election Series, Center for Strategic and International Studies, Georgetown University, Washington, D.C., 1986).

22. Arturo Alvarado, "Sonora: Victoria PRIrrica" (unpublished manuscript, Center for U.S.-Mexican Studies, University of California, San Diego, July 1985).

23. Rolando Cordera, commentary at the Conference on Recent Electoral Changes in the Americas, University of California, San Diego, 22 February 1985.

24. Soledad Loaeza, "El llamado de las urnas: Para qué sirven las elecciones en México?" *Nexos* 90 (June 1985): 14, 19.

25. Héctor Aguilar Camín, commentary at the Fifth Annual Briefing Session for Professional Journalists, Center for U.S.-Mexican Studies, University of California, San Diego, 20 June 1985.

26. For analysis of the conditions under which military intervention in Mexican politics would be most likely, and the probable consequences of such involvement, see David F. Ronfeldt, ed., *The Modern Mexican Military: A Reassessment*, Center for U.S.-Mexican Studies Monograph no. 15 (La Jolla, CA: University of California, San Diego, 1984).

3

Mexico After the Oil Boom: PRI Management of the Political Impact of National Disillusionment

Judith Gentleman

Introduction

Recent economic and political developments in Mexico have raised questions among observers concerning the long-term prospects for the nation's political-economic system. The cumulative impact of a variety of factors including the 1982 economic collapse, the ensuing austerity program, and more broadly, the failure of Mexico's oil development program to have catapulted the nation into a condition of enduring prosperity, has produced a challenge of unprecedented severity to the regime.

This chapter will examine the strategy employed by Mexico's ruling elite to contain the political damage stemming from recent policy failures along with efforts undertaken by the state to regain the initiative in attempting to surmount the nation's developmental impasse. The regime's approach to the management of conflict will be first explored in terms of its initial policy response to the multifaceted crisis situation. The chapter will then focus upon the state's relationship with the private sector and with labor during the recent critical juncture. Finally, the regime's strategy for political and economic stabilization over the longer term will be discussed.

The stability of Mexico's authoritarian regime has stood in marked contrast to the instability of governments elsewhere that have confronted similar economic and political difficulties. The corporatist, authoritarian political structure erected by the governing elites has been credited with facilitating the skillful management of social and economic forces that have destabilized and overwhelmed less sophisticated political structures elsewhere. The structures and strategies traditionally relied upon by the regime to maintain the stability of the system have been well documented by a variety of observers.[1] The centralized, corporatist, cooptative and authoritarian pattern of politics in Mexico has included a highly functional mix of clientelism and cooptative strategies, the skillful use of political symbolism, the corporatist organization of potentially destabilizing interests, and finally, repression, fraud and corruption. While the latter techniques of system maintenance have sometimes proved counterproductive in other contexts, their usage in the Mexican system has been beneficial to Mexico's governing elites due to their prudent and measured application. The increasingly bureaucratically and technically minded political elite has managed to successfully consolidate its dominant position in society and has constituted itself as a self-perpetuating governing class.

Most important, however, for explaining the enduring stability of the system has been the fact that up until the recent period, the regime had at its disposal various means of financing the nation's development program that involved few political costs. Until the early 1980s the state had been able to rely upon domestic resources, foreign financing, and still later, oil revenues to pursue its objectives. While financial difficulties did lead to the imposition of an IMF-inspired stabilization program in 1977, the program was quickly rolled back when domestic policy-makers and their associates in the international community became convinced that Mexico's petroleum sector would provide the nation with the resources required to finance domestic development and to meet external obligations. In sum, then, the corporatist, cooptative and authoritarian pattern of politics, coupled with the state's ability to provide development financing, without the imposition of harsh austerity programs, had enabled the regime for many years to limit damaging manifestations of conflict in the society and to prevent the emergence of a significant, organized political challenge to its leading position in society.

By 1982, however, it had become abundantly clear that the nation's declining economic fortunes had created a substantially modified context for Mexico's political system. According to the official Mexican government view, the nation's oil boom of the late 1970s and early 1980s had held out the promise of sustained economic progress that would ultimately provide a means of overcoming underdevelopment and dependency.[2] While such optimistic predictions were met with a considerable degree of skepticism in many quarters, there were expectations abroad nevertheless, for an improvement in the nation's fortunes as well as for some progress for the mass of the Mexican population.

The financial collapse of August 1982 that triggered a U.S.-led financial rescue effort stood in stark contrast to the buoyant optimism that had characterized the Mexican elite during the boom years. What had resulted instead was a prolonged financial-economic crisis brought about by a variety of structural and cyclical factors. These ranged from the fundamental insolvency of the development model and the pernicious effects of having attempted to develop a major resource within the context of an already profoundly dependent economy, to depression in the world oil market, skyrocketing interest rates, and recession in the central industrialized economies along with such factors as the unprecedented levels of corruption and mismanagement evident during the López Portillo *sexenio*.

The Financial Crisis of 1982

The crisis in the Mexican economy manifested itself most clearly in the following respects: (1) the inflation-driven overvaluation of the peso; (2) an inflation rate by the end of 1982 of 150%;[3] (3) the depletion of foreign exchange reserves; (4) the virtual collapse of non-oil exports due, to a large extent, to the overvalued peso; (5) a shortfall in anticipated oil revenues due to falling world prices and a soft market generally (the earnings shortfall for 1982 amounted to a devastating US$15.5 billion[4]; and (6) a level of indebtedness that along with a crippling capital flight, contributed to the balance of payments crisis. By 1982, the foreign debt had reached US$85 billion and capital outflows exceeded US$9 billion in that year alone.[5]

The state attempted to regain control of the crisis situation in February 1982 by slashing public sector spending and by devaluing the peso. Later, currency restrictions were imposed and finally in late August 1982, Mexico requested a 90-day moratorium on the repayment of loans from major lenders. With a number of leading banks highly exposed in the Mexican crisis (including Citibank, Chase Manhattan Bank and the Bank of America along with six other major U.S. banks that together, according to one report, had 44% of their capital tied up in Mexico)[6] the U.S. mobilized a financial "rescue" operation designed to stave off formal default. The package that was finally hammered out included debt rescheduling, a variety of short term supports and credits, and an IMF facility of US$4.1 billion. The accompanying IMF Stabilization Agreement included standard prescriptions for a restoration of the nation's financial health which the Mexican government incorporated into its own recovery package, the Program for the Immediate Reorganization of the Economy (PIRE.) The crisis also precipitated the nationalization of the domestic banking sector, one of the government's most significant policy initiatives since the nationalization of Mexico's oil industry in the 1930s. The September 1982 nationalization, designed to stem the tide of massive capital outflows and to reestablish equilibrium in the external sector, angered major interests in the private sector[7] and further weakened the deteriorating state sector-private sector relationship.

The government's National Plan for 1983–1988, incorporating the PIRE, sought to stabilize the state sector financially via budget cuts and a reduction in the scope of state activity. Not only was the size of the public sector deficit to be reduced from the level of 18% of GDP reached in 1982 to a targeted 3–4% of GDP by 1985,[8] public sector expenditures overall would be slashed, having risen to 48% of GDP by 1982.[9] Revenues to the public sector would be enhanced via selected price increases, reductions in subsidies, improvements in tax collection, an increase in the value-added tax and rigorous pruning of inefficient state enterprises along with improvements in the management of public sector enterprises notorious for being awash in red ink.

In addition, the PIRE called for a reduction in inflation (to 35% by 1985) as well as a tightening of credit policies. The public sector deficit did initially shrink substantially as a result of the program, falling to 8.7% of GDP in 1983. However, despite cutbacks in subsidies and general expenditures and price increases for energy, certain foodstuffs and a broad range of other goods and services, the state nevertheless fell short of the targeted 5.5% for 1984 and it appeared that there was little chance, without substantial further adjustments, of arriving at the 3–4% figure targeted for 1985.[10] Importantly, as government expenditures were curtailed, debt service constituted an increasing share of those expenditures. Indeed, in the aftermath of the 1982 collapse, interest payments rose by over 40% in real terms, accounting for nearly one-third of all government expenditures,[11] further intensifying the effects of other domestic cutbacks in current spending. To the extent that any political system relies upon expenditures to sweeten its political fortunes, such developments could only serve to damage the regime politically. Capital spending also experienced deep cuts amounting to 30% in real terms. Public sector expenditures for wages dropped as well, falling 20% in real terms.

The balance of payments crisis also generated drastic cuts in imports. In the 1982–83 period, imports were slashed by nearly 50%, rising slowly thereafter. Cuts in imports were severely felt by the private sector and ensuing bottlenecks in supplies caused a slowdown in production and utilization of plant capacity, creating widespread resentment in the private sector.

Mexico's total foreign indebtedness had risen to US$93 billion by 1985, most of it held by the public sector. Estimates of the nation's future indebtedness in the medium term were put at US$120 billion by 1991. Clearly, the economy would remain highly leveraged producing net capital outflow from the country as a result of an increasingly onerous service burden. A refinancing document affecting US$48.66 billion was initialed in March, 1985,[12] with restructuring conferring a fourteen-year maturity. Yet, with over 70% of oil revenues committed to debt service and with new obligations limited by the IMF to US$5 billion per year, the nation's revenue problems remained overwhelming.

The announcement in early 1985 of an intensification of the austerity program of the preceding three years signaled the government's pessimistic assessments of future oil exports, interest rates, inflation rates and the performance of non-oil exports. The new austerity package called for additional cuts of US$500 million beyond original projections for the 1985 budget.[13] Targeted items included job creation programs, employment in the state sector and an array of state subsidies. A variety of investment activities also would be curtailed and in an important initiative, fully 236 companies would be sold, transferred from the state sector, or liquidated.

As a result of these policies, growth in the economy could be expected to slow with unemployment increasing. Real GDP growth had already seen a steady decline since the 1960s and 1970s. In the 1964–1973 period, growth had averaged 7.4% per annum; in the 1974–1984 period, growth measured 4.7% per annum and in the 1984–1985 period, growth measured 3.0–3.5%.[14]

The bitter medicine, from the government's perspective, would deflate the overheated economy, reducing inflation, which was by then raging at an estimated two and one-half times the targeted rate of 35%. Altogether, the intensified austerity package would presumably enable the state to bring the public sector deficit more into line with the IMF target of 5.5%.[15] While the continuing policy of government austerity budgets and contractionist policy was received with mixed reaction in Mexico, the move toward privatization was welcomed by many in the private sector and by many of Mexico's creditors in the international community.

The recovery program would also mean that the shift to an export-led industrial profile would be necessarily delayed forcing the economy to continue to rely upon crude oil exports for the bulk of its exports, perpetuating the vulnerability of the nation's economy to the volatile petroleum market. Mexico's performance in the manufacturing sector, particularly for export, had been lackluster to say the least as shown in Table 3.1. The petrolization of exports, an outcome feared by policy-makers at the outset of the oil boom, had indeed come to pass. As was the case with many other debtor nations, Mexico had improved its current accounts picture by drastically reducing imports and restraining private investment instead of by improving its savings picture dramatically or by increasing exports.[16]

In his annual report to the nation in September 1985, President Miguel de la Madrid drew upon elements of familiar political rhetoric, declaring that "revolutionary nationalism" continued to guide state policies. It was apparent, however, that the substance of the regime's political-economic agenda differed markedly from any revolutionary-nationalist program that could be envisioned. The economic crisis that had initially surfaced in Mexico in 1976 had, by the mid-1980s, become chronic in nature, leaving the Mexican economy continuously reeling from the dislocations produced. Developments in the latter half of 1985 and early 1986 had only aggravated the existing problems and indeed, the precipitous drop in world oil prices in 1986 to a level nearly equal to production costs,[17] along with the contraction in market demand, placed Mexico's economic fortunes in ever greater jeopardy. The halving of oil prices in late 1985 and early 1986 and the dramatic reductions in crude exports in early 1986, forced the government to jettison its 1986 budget and to appeal to the U.S. for assistance with its debt.[18]

In its budget proposal for 1986, the government claimed success in having reduced inflation (down to approximately 60% by 1985—the target had been 35%) and in bringing down the public sector deficit from 18% of GDP to 9.6%. The IMF, however, did not share the De la Madrid government's enthusiasm for its economic management track record and as a result, the failure of the government to meet targeted goals resulted in the suspension of the remaining drawing rights of $900 million in September 1985. (The announcement of the suspension came on the day of the earthquake and $300 million in drawing rights were quickly restored for earthquake relief.)

By early 1986, it had become abundantly clear that Mexico had reached a new and even more serious political-economic juncture. The foreign external debt after 1982 had continued to grow, climbing to nearly US$97 billion by 1986 with US$74 billion owed to commercial banks, a third of which was owed to U.S. banks. In the fall of 1985, the Mexican government unilaterally notified the IMF of its intention to postpone payment of service due lenders in late 1985 and early 1986. As a result, an initial six-month postponement agreement was formulated by the banks, leaving open the question of subsequent "postponements."[19]

The collapse of oil prices in late 1985 and early 1986 undercut Mexico's "new" borrowing projections for 1986 that had been put at US$4.82 billion.[20] Revised projections called for US$9 billion in "new" borrowing for 1986 to cover public sector deficits which were expected to soar in the wake of dislocations in the petroleum sector.[21] Even before the collapse of oil prices, the public sector deficit was expected to have risen well above the figure originally targeted. Even before the full impact of the collapse of oil prices could be measured it had been estimated that the nation's debt service ratio would rise to 49% by 1987, up from the 33% figure registered in 1985. Clearly, the restructuring activities of the 1985 period would have little impact upon Mexico's ability to meet its servicing requirements.[22] The comparatively generous terms of the US-IMF sponsored loan package initiated in mid 1986 provided clear acknowledgment of the severely distressed circumstances in which the economy found itself.

With inflation continuing to overvalue the peso (inflation running at 63.7% in 1985, according to government statistics, private sources arguing that the real figure might be as high as 80+%) and threatening the prospect of a new round of maxi-devaluations and possibly the imposition of even stronger currency controls, capital flight became increasingly problematic. International reserves reportedly dropped from US$8.1 billion in January 1985 to US$3 billion in January 1986.[23] Capital flight in the first six months of 1985 had been estimated conservatively at US$2.5 billion.[24] Such capital movements indicated that the crisis of confidence continued unabated, and in a poll conducted by the Mexican Institute of Public Opinion in late 1985, only 35% of those surveyed expressed confidence in the President's policies while fully 65% did not.[25] Between 1983 and the end of 1985, Mexico had contracted US$9 billion in new external debt obligation and had exported US$16.2 billion via capital flight to banks in the U.S. and Switzerland.[26]

With US$9 billion in interest payments on the external foreign debt due each year, depression in the petroleum sector would prove to be nothing less than catastropic. Domestic credit would be squeezed even further as the government would seek to utilize domestic resources more fully in order to manage the public sector deficit. As a result of the contractionary policy to be pursued, real growth in GDP could be expected to plunge to levels below the growth rate of 0-1% originally mapped out in the 1986 budget proposal—more dramatic contraction having been mandated by rising inflation and the problems of the public sector deficit. Inflation would climb to at least 70–75% it was predicted, and overall spending on items other than interest would continue to shrink.[27] A massive devaluation was likely for 1986 as the peso was argued to have become as overvalued as it had been in 1982. Such projections certainly did little to build the support or confidence of key actors within the political environment.

Competing Perspectives Within the State Sector on the Economy

The Mexican governing elite has been divided on the question of appropriate economic policy throughout the period of crisis. Two distinctive views that have evolved over time have governed the discussion concerning possible alternatives. Proponents of the first approach, identified variously as "radical-nationalists," "nationalist-populists" or those espousing the "Planner" perspective, occupied minority status during the López Portillo and De la Madrid administrations. Those falling within this category generally espoused a nationalist-statist posture, preferring a relatively closed economy and an emphasis upon a "broad popular alliance"[28] or "*desarrollo compartido.*"

Those situated in the opposing camp have been variously labeled "realists," "liberal-rationalists," internationalists or those advocating the "Treasury" view. For this group, key tenets have included support for a somewhat more limited role for the state, liberalization of trade policies, acceptance of selected foreign investment and relatively stronger although unenthusiastic support for the private sector. While it would be difficult to label adherents to this view "liberals" in the classic political-economic sense of the term, they do move further in that direction, particularly in terms of their position on international trade and the need to "open" the economy. On the question of the leading role of the state and consonant views on the issue of political pluralism, however, their credentials as members of the hegemonic ruling group have remained untarnished.

Both groups have enthusiastically supported the concept of an activist state but each group has been wedded to different notions of the economic goals of such involvement. For the so-called "populist" group, resources should be used to enhance demand, thus fomenting growth whereas for the so-called "realists," a supply-side approach is preferable with resources flowing toward capital (in the state and private sector) rather than to labor.

Arguably, the "populist" view had held sway during the Echeverría period and again periodically, but much more marginally, during the López Portillo period. In response to the crisis itself the approach that prevailed was ultimately an eclectic mixture of state initiative, supply-side economic policy and moderation on the question of trade liberalization. While the bank nationalization was hailed as the triumph of "populist" politics, questions were raised suggesting that the initiative was more an act of desperation than an element of cogent strategy and indeed, subsequent to the seizure of assets, the De la Madrid government all but publicly repudiated the measure. Nevertheless, policy-makers became resigned to the measure either because of the political embarrassment a repudiation of the policy would have caused or because of the state's compelling need to regain control over financial resources in the system—most probably a mixture of both. Other features of the López Portillo economic record similarly defy easy categorization. For example, the "on again-off again" General Agreement on Tariffs and Trade (GATT) sequence signaled disagreement and confusion over the most beneficial direction to follow rather than anything else. In the end, the short-lived "populist" victory on the GATT issue proved to be quite hollow as the dismantling of the protectionist system began soon after the 1979 decision to reject GATT membership. Generally, even when the so-called "populist" position appeared to prevail in economic decision-making, it was difficult to see how the interests of the "broad popular alliance" were served, as for example in the case of the *gasoducto* controversy of the late 1970s or in terms of the limitations placed upon exports of crude oil.[29] Certainly an increase in the wage share of national income had not resulted. Indeed, the "populist" position might best be interpreted as statist in content rather than connoting any particular coherent macroeconomic approach or specific distributive emphasis.

Overcoming the Economic Impasse: State Policy

In attempting to evaluate the direction of state policy, we must first explore the state's own analysis of its political-economic dilemma. To begin with, the clearest and most authoritative voices of analysis resonating from government during the crisis have been those from the "orthodox" or so-called "realist" camp. Only with respect to two issues have consistent voices of dissent from the minority camp been heard: on the issue of debt repayment and on the issue of trade liberalization. The financial crisis of the state, purely and simply, appeared to have severely undercut the legitimacy of the "populist" position at the center of the decision-making structure.

During the crisis, majority perspective within the state sector as articulated, for example by former Secretary of the Treasury, Jesús Silva Herzog, viewed for some time as a serious contender for the presidency, maintained that the "imbalance in public finances is our main malady . . . [and] the fundamental cause of the economy's present problem was the excessive growth of public expenditure since late 1983, with all of its unfavorable consequences."[30] According to the Secretary, the government would continue to "direct the economy," but structural changes would have to be brought about because the Mexican economy was "about to arrive at the point of no return" with all other alternatives "exhausted."[31] According to Mexico's financial managers, a "definitive" economic base would have to be established via (1) the strengthening of public finance, (2) reducing inflation, (3) creating a "realistic and stable" exchange market, (4) opening the economy and (5) facilitating the "fuller participation of the private sector in the economy."[32]

The paring down of the state sector proved to be of paramount concern. By 1985, the state's share of total investment had already fallen by 40%

from 1982 levels, but the reductions would continue. Public sector expenditure as a share of GDP had substantially declined by 1984 from the level achieved in 1982 but remained above 1977–1980 levels (see Table 3.2).

The government would not only continue to curtail subsidies and to cut a variety of expenditures, it would also continue to reduce the scope of government involvement in the economy. According to Silva Herzog, the government would continue to eliminate agencies deemed "superfluous" and in his view "the profound meaning of these measures lies in abandoning a trodden path that has failed to lead anywhere for a number of years."[33]

Efforts to trim the state sector included a variety of measures including the liquidation, consolidation and sale of state entities, cuts in subsidies to state enterprises and programs and massive layoffs. Nonetheless, according to one report, with the exception of Petroleos Mexicanos (PEMEX), all of the state's industrial enterprises continued to be deficit-ridden, leading subsidies to state industries to consume nearly 30% of total government expenditure by early 1985,[34] clearly a problem requiring further attention.

State-Private Sector Relations

While the private sector had always been the beneficiary of state largesse, including generous state subsidies and minimal taxation burdens, conflict was endemic to the relationship between the state and key elements of the private sector due to the state's presence in production and its control over major sources of investment capital. Despite the fact that the "boom" had produced healthy profits for the private sector, with declining income returns to labor,[35] the private sector nonetheless expressed considerable unhappiness with the PRI's record of economic management and ultimately sought and received assurances from the government concerning future assistance with development.

While the business community remained skeptical of the De la Madrid government, as evidenced by the drop in private investment in 1982 and 1983 of 45% with only a slim resurgence of 8% in 1984, as well as by its continuing export of capital, the government earned the grudging support of some for its fiscal conservatism and reductions in the state sector.[36]

The most controversial of all recent measures, the bank nationalization, enraged many in the private sector, however, and was viewed alternatively either as López Portillo's effort to simultaneously scapegoat the banks for the economic crisis and to save face, or as a means of reestablishing control over a national financial system that neither effectively encouraged national savings nor provided much in the way of long term investment capital.[37] The measure was subsequently modified to the satisfaction of much of the private sector and contrary to the wishes of the left, bank shares in most of the companies impacted by the nationalization were sold.[38] The banks' insurance companies, brokerage houses, bonding companies and mutual funds among other interests were all restored to the private sector.[39] The state also opened the door to 34% ownership by the private sector in the new Credit Societies, offering a relatively secure investment opportunity to investors.

The state further sought to assist the private sector by establishing the Fideicomiso para la Cobertura de Riesgos Cambiarios, FICORCA, an agency designed to restructure nearly US$15 billion in external debt. Managed by the Banco de Mexico, FICORCA provided private sector interests with a means of covering dollar liabilities with pesos. FICORCA essentially absorbed the difference between the value of pesos on account to cover debts and the cost of the dollars acquired by FICORCA to pay foreign creditors.[40]

The state's emphasis on private sector development was manifested in the privatization measure announced as part of a package of austerity measures in early 1985. The sale, transferral or liquidation of 236 state owned companies represented a substantial departure from recent historical trends and was suggestive of a major reorientation of policy stemming from simple pragmatism.

The program of divestment-privatization in the state sector was begun in 1983 under the leadership of the new Secretaría de Energia, Minas e Industrias Paraestatales (SEMIP), replacing the Secretaría de Patrimonio Nacional y Fomento Industrial (SEPAFIN). In 1983–1984, as a direct result of the public sector deficit rather than as a result of a macroeconomic analysis of the advisability of divesting or privatizing any particular public entity, the state divested 31 industrial enterprises (including enterprises in sugar, shipping, mining, chemical and service).[41] Among early divestments were Vehiculos Automotores Mexicanos and Renault de México.

In February 1985, SEMIP's privatization plans were announced and called for the divestment of a wide variety of "empresas," "fideicomisos," and "organismos." In the state's industrial sector, comprised of 409 entities, SEMIP announced that 83 companies would be eliminated: 44 would be sold, 32 liquidated and 7 sold to state governments. According to data presented in President De la Madrid's Tercer Informe, by the end of 1982, there were 1,115 entities in the entire public sector. By mid-1985, the government had ordered the divestment by fusion, liquidation, transfer or sale of 482 "non-strategic" entities.[42] Nonetheless, according to the President's report, the government remained steadfast in its opposition to the privatization of "strategic" components of the economy. Economic sectors reserved to the state were to include petroleum, basic petro-chemicals, radioactive minerals, nuclear energy, electricity, rails, communications satellites, mail, telegraph and radiotelegraph operations.[43]

In a related measure, plans were also announced to offer minority participation opportunities in over 40 key state companies in order to retire part of the nation's debt. Reportedly, the list of offerings available to major lenders included the government's steel enterprises Lazaro Cárdenas-Las Truchas, Altos Hornos de México, Fundidora Monterrey; the hotel chain Nacional Hotelera and a variety of mining, metal and chemical companies.[44] As many of the affected operations were money losers, the state sought to offset some of its losses and to reduce its level of indebtedness.

1985 saw cutbacks in personnel both in government and in the parastatal sector. To begin with, by July 1985, the state had eliminated over 20% of all positions in the following categories (totalling 690 in 1982): *subsecretarias, oficiales mayores, contralorias, coordinaciones generales and direcciones generales.*[45] Cuts elsewhere were seen although these were of limited import compared to the full scope of public employment. In the agriculture ministry, 20,000 jobs were eliminated. In the urban development and ecology ministry, SEDUE, the staff was trimmed by 20%.[46] At CFE, the state electricity enterprise, 60,000 temporary workers were dismissed. At the state sugar enterprise, 2000 workers were laid off. Even the banking system felt the pinch with losses totalling 40% of their early 1985 staff levels. Altogether, 51,000 full-time jobs were eliminated due to cutbacks.[47]

From a variety of quarters came reports concerning the political difficulties encountered via such initiatives. According to Secretary Carlos Salinas de Gortari (Ministry of Planning and Budget, SPP), "there were problems and resistance" to these changes.[48] In another report, reference was made to several reasons why it had been so difficult to prune the public sector: "(1) inbred inertia; (2) the force of bureaucracy; (3) the unawareness, in many quarters, of the seriousness of the situation inherited in 1983; (4) the appearance of easy progress."[49]

Through it all, however, the policy designed to trim the government sector reflected the financial constraints pressing upon the state. Little overt enthusiasm was observable in any quarter for privatization per se, and there was no evidence to the effect that decisionmakers believed that the measure would benefit the economy in any way other than simply reducing the public sector deficit.

Mexico's policy on its domestic and external public and private debt also reflected the highly constrained context within which decision-makers had been operating. Because the state had taken the position that raising prices and above all, raising taxes had to be avoided (although prices for many basic goods had been substantially increased) the only realistic means available for public deficit financing other than increased foreign borrowing was to raise the level of the state's internal indebtedness. As a result, the government's domestic indebtedness was expected to double in 1985 in real terms. Clearly, the state's reliance upon such financing would raise the cost of credit to private borrowers and substantially reduce the availability of domestic investment capital and operating funds.[50]

Although Mexico had participated in the meetings of the Cartegena group, an association of debtor states seeking a means of multilateral negotiation with international lenders, Mexico maintained a moderate tone, avoiding a "burn your bridges" posture. Domestically, the most militant voices on the issue, those supporting a moratorium on repayment of the foreign debt, were the left and the left wing of the ruling party, the Institutional Revolutionary Party, PRI, union leaders, church leaders and some business leaders along with an array of minor politicians. In early 1986, however, President De la Madrid cautiously advanced the idea to the international financial community that Mexico's payments would have to be tied to the nation's ability to repay its debt and that the interest on the debt would have to be lowered.[51] Specifically, the government seemed to be floating the trial balloon of capping interest payments and tying those payments to export performance. In the wake of the collapse of oil prices in 1986, Confederación de Trabajadores de México (CTM) leader Fidel Velázquez argued "At this time we cannot pay, we simply cannot pay."[52]

In conveying his worrisome appeal to international creditors for a tying of payments to export performance, President De la Madrid took great pains to highlight the package of reform measures being pursued by the Mexican state in an effort to placate critics of Mexico's record of economic management. In late February 1986, President De la Madrid announced that there would be further sales of state enterprises, further budget cuts, a reduction of credit available to private interests and increasing efforts to liberalize trade.[53] The latter initiative, that of trade liberalization represented a shift in policy of great moment. The external sector, of course, had continued to show imbalance for a number of reasons: (1) non-oil exports had not fared well in international markets; (2) imports had risen precipitously; (3) the Mexican economy was increasingly viewed as non-competitive and a clear liability in terms of long term growth prospects; and (4) capital flight continued to drain reserves.[54]

Mexico, according to the government's economic managers, would have to open itself further to international trade and investment. According to former Treasury Secretary Silva Herzog, such measures would "help to strengthen the competitiveness and quality of Mexican products" and help to increase Mexico's "non-oil export capacity." Furthermore, Silva Herzog argued that "competition is the only thing that guarantees prices and quality."[55]

While small and medium-sized industries and inefficient producers would be most vulnerable to new sources of competition in a freer trading environment Silva Herzog maintained that this would be an "inescapable first step" on the road to "competitiveness." Although the "costs and risks" of such a strategy were deemed "obvious," the government proceeded by 1985 to eliminate permits and quotas for 62% of Mexico's imports.[56] Eventually, trade liberalization would encompass all but items classified as being of strategic import.

In late 1985, President De la Madrid announced that Mexico would finally seek to join the GATT. According to the President, "We cannot isolate ourselves from an increasingly interdependent world." Even prior to this decision, Mexico had agreed to come into compliance with GATT rules on the critical issues of subsidies and "dumping" as part of a bilateral trade accord mapped out in 1985 with the U.S.[57] As was the case in 1979 when Mexico had contemplated GATT entry, opposition to the initiative surfaced principally in the left, in the "populist" sector of the PRI, among the official trade unions and in the Cámara Nacional de la Industria de la Transformación (Canacintra) which represents small and medium-sized producers. Among the major business interests supporting the initiative were the Consejo Coordinador Empresarial (CCE); Confederación de Cámaras Industriales (Concamin); Confederación Nacional de Cámaras de Comercio (Concanaco); the Confederación Patronal de la Republica Mexicana (Coparmex); the Consejo Mexicano de Hombres de Negocios (CMHN); and the Asociación Nacional de Importadores e Exportadores (Anierm).[58] In a breakaway move from the national Canacintra leadership, the Nuevo León branch, Cámara de la Industria de la Transformación, Caintra, also supported the initiative. Not only would Mexico proceed with entry into the GATT and a revision of its own trading regime, the nation would also relax restrictions governing direct foreign investment (DFI) in the economy. During 1985, new DFI would rise to US$2 billion.

The government maintained that it continued to be committed to a selective policy designed to encourage investments that would boost employment substantially, offer technical advantages, enhance regional development, improve the nation's export picture or offer access to international markets. Yet it was clear that the state's renewed interest in foreign investment did not reflect a newfound faith in the intrinsic desirability of such investment, but instead viewed DFI as an option that simply had to be accepted due to the financial constraints faced by the nation. In particular, the concentration of DFI in the manufacturing sector and that sector's important foreign exchange earning capability conditioned Mexico's shift in policy. It had also become clear that efforts to attract investment on a minority equity basis had fallen short of the goal.[59] A number of investment rules were eased,[60] and it was apparent that a more relaxed attitude characterized decision-making concerning most investments.

Guidelines issued in 1984 permitted up to 100% DFI in 34 priority sectors where minority equity had been previously required. Areas identified included heavy machinery, electronics, transportation equipment, chemicals and advanced technology. Believing direct foreign investment to be one of the major avenues of escape from the development financing impasse, the government appeared to be committed to growth in this area. Government forecasts for the period 1984 to 1990 predicted a net gain of US$6 billion in direct foreign investment representing an increase of 50% over and above the US$11.7 billion in total direct foreign investment registered in 1983.[61] (See Table 3.3.) Importantly, the decision to pursue enhanced levels of DFI was made despite the fact that DFI had produced a net outflow between 1974–1984 of US$5.3 billion and despite the fact that ten transnational corporations had come to dominate the 100 top selling firms in Mexico. These included General Motors, Chrysler, VW, Ford, Nestle, Nissan, Industrias Xerograficas (US), Anderson-Clayton, a B. F. Goodrich affiliate, and IBM.[62]

Overtures to the domestic private sector have also included an assortment of strategies ranging from accelerated depreciation of capital equipment to wage restraints. Despite these initiatives the complaints emanating from the business community remained substantial. The state was charged with continuing intervention, with unwarranted regulation in pharmaceuticals, autos and computers, with having failed to sufficiently reduce spending or to curtail inflation, and most broadly, with having failed in the last several *sexenios* to have formulated viable development strategies.[63] The perception by the business community appeared to be that the state was continuing to cling to its management role despite its having lost the ability to serve as the financial driving force of development. Thus, while the "recovery" program did in part win favor with the private sector, the relationship between the state and elements of the private sector remained confrontational. Arguably, the regime's adoption of a policy direction more consistent with liberal economy, and its declared intention to engage in "no inappropriate interference with the activities of private individuals,"[64] served to placate disaffected elements within the private sector. These measures also led to a renewal of political activism by the private sector via the National Action party (PAN). Through the PAN, some elements of the private sector sought to further discredit state leadership and to speed the state's retreat from selected economic activities that seemed to be in conflict with certain private sector interests.

In light of these developments, the post–July 1985 election response of the governing elite was predictable. Specifically, charges surfaced following the July elections that business leaders had been subject to verbal harassment and intimidation by high-ranking government officials. In November 1985, Coparmex officials charged that officials of that organization had been warned to stay out of politics and to refrain from opposing the government's policies.[65] The charge of intimidation was placed most especially in the lap of Gobernación Secretary Manuel Bartlett Díaz. With less and less to offer the private sector in terms of financial support or at a minimum, favorable economic outcomes, political authorities have increasingly seen fit to use intimidation as a means of managing its tense relationship with key elements of the private sector. Even the normally docile and successfully coopted media have felt increasing pressure. While there is no doubt that the state continues to occupy the preeminent position in the direction of the economy and enjoys nearly complete control over financial resources within the system, the emergence of chronic economic crisis in the society has made it more difficult for the state to continue to subordinate the private sector's participation in the economy to its own. Political leaders now speak of society's need to "diversify . . . economically, socially and politically," yet they provide little politico-economic rationale of how such liberalization-diversification may benefit society directly, all-the-while proceeding, at least in the economic dimension, in that very same direction.

The State and Labor

While the state maintained that employment and wages would be fiercely protected as the nation embarked upon its recovery program, the recessionary character of the government's policy, coupled with its insistence upon wage restraint, had a damaging impact upon the lives of Mexico's workers.

Even before the economic collapse of 1982, prosperity had eluded most Mexicans. During the period 1974–1976, real wages had declined by 25%; during the period 1976–1979, a 20% decline was registered. The trend continued, of course, through the early 1980s with real wages falling over 30% between 1982 and 1985.[66] Wage agreements were consistently negotiated at levels well below the rate of inflation and increases of 30% in early 1985 and 32% in early 1986, with provisions for midterm adjustments, scarcely defended wages from the ravages of price increases and subsidy reductions.

Labor was hurt not only by declining real income but also by rising unemployment. According to the United Nations' Economic Commission for Latin America (ECLA), open unemployment had risen to 18.8%[67] by the end of 1984. With the economically active population growing by 2.8 million persons per year during 1982–1984, the nation's future employment picture remained quite grim. The government's claims concerning its having "limited the social cost of the crisis" were of dubious validity.

Organized labor's position by and large throughout the crisis was one of dutiful compliance despite the populist oratory of Fidel Velázquez, head of the CTM. Beyond the PRI's crucial relationship to organized labor, critical to the maintenance of labor peace, was the high rate of un/underemployment, the onslaught of nearly 1 million new workers each year into the labor force and the prospect of a 3.8% to 4% growth rate in the labor force throughout the remainder of the 1980s.[68] In addition, divisions within labor ranks and the failure of the independent union movement to have made a serious dent in the structure or orientation of organized labor further undercut labor's position.

Specifically in terms of the apparent competition between the Confederación Regional Obrera Mexicana, CROM, and the CTM for the leading position within the PRI's labor structure, the state garnered a tremendous advantage. Each endeavored to keep workers in line and to comply with the modest increases afforded by the state. The relatively docile response of labor to the wage depression of the past ten years was also evident with respect to price increases and the curtailment of certain subsidies for basic goods including for example, tortillas, fuel and water. In what might be regarded as the state's only overture to labor during this period, efforts were made to maintain remaining subsidies for some basic goods.

De la Madrid spoke openly regarding labor's position in the austerity program. Calling labor "exceptionally responsible and mature," De la Madrid explained labor's cooperation in foregoing serious demands for wage increases as a result of labor's fear that a wage price spiral, triggering an ever higher inflation rate, would generate further contraction in the economy.[69] Velázquez himself, having earlier adopted a confrontational approach, later abandoned the tactic, acknowledging that salary increases are "not possible in current circumstances . . . the economic crisis doesn't allow greater increases."[70] In effect, despite widespread resentment among workers and Mexicans more generally concerning the nation's declining economic fortunes, that resentment was not systematically translated into labor disturbances beyond scattered strikes among, for example, university workers. The state was therefore free to press forward its austerity program without incurring losses on the production side. Damage elsewhere in the system may have been incurred, however, and its is to the subject of governmental initiatives in the political sector that we now turn.

Austerity and the Management of the Political Process

President De la Madrid initiated efforts to stabilize Mexico politically by calling for an array of political reforms designed to shore up the regime's legitimacy and arguably to provide an acceptable outlet for pent up frustrations. A number of observers have maintained that these initiatives underscored the widening gulf separating the traditional political elements of the PRI from reform-minded political-technocratic elements who had increasingly come to occupy key managerial positions within the state. The fact that the regime potentially faced great difficulties politically did little to engender a consensus within the party concerning the reform issue. Further complicating matters was the fact that the more traditional elements within the PRI had opposed De la Madrid's selection as president to begin with and were thus none too well-disposed to accept casual tinkering and experimentation from one who was regarded as something of a political neophyte.

The initiative for party and electoral reform included efforts to bring about internal democratization in part via the implementation of primaries for local and regional officials, initially on an experimental basis in Narayit.[71] Also as part of its formal campaign of reform, the government indicated its intention to implement a policy of consulta popular as a part of the National System of Democratic Planning. The system was to build in consultation concerning development planning with strategic elites including business, media, academia and elements of the political opposition.[72]

The state also attempted at least marginally, to address the critical issue of corruption as a means of recapturing some elements of popular support. The highly publicized prosecution of former Pemex czar Jorge Díaz Serrano, of a former oilworkers' union chieftain, and of former Mexico City police chief Arturo Durazo, among others, did little to persuade observers that a serious effort had been undertaken to address the problem of corruption. While the De la Madrid government insisted that public officials declare their assets upon entry into and upon departure from public office in an effort to avoid a repetition of the free-for-all atmosphere that prevailed during the López Portillo administration, corruption remained an integral feature of political life. Given that such subterranean transfers have traditionally provided much of the cement holding the system together, serious efforts to undercut established mechanisms of political control during a period of crisis would be most unlikely. In light of the state's restricted ability to finance the cooptative process openly due to austerity budgets, the greater probability would be increasing resort to such activity rather than curtailment.

On balance, despite the ambitious character of the project, the political reform yielded few substantive results. Neither in terms of democratic consultation, nor in terms of internal democratization within the ruling party, nor in terms of electoral reform as discussed by Gómez Tagle and others in this volume, was there ultimately any discernible departure by the governing elite from past practices. It is important to note, however, that despite the PRI's failure to do more than to pay lip service to its own "reforms" other actors in the political environment responded to the nominal strategy of "democratic opening" in ways that may ultimately bring change to the system, however unintentioned by the state. In short, while Mexico's governing elites sought to stop the perceptible erosion of system support among the middle sectors and elements of the elite by pursuing "reform," the program's negligible results could only serve to further undermine the system's legitimacy among these groups.

Evaluating the Policy Direction

The economic crisis itself provoked only a modest political response on the part of the populace and certainly one that was not threatening to the system in any immediate sense. The government's ability to meet the crisis from a political point of view stemmed from two key factors: (1) effective control of labor and (2) a "reform" strategy that had facilitated a highly fractured situation on the left and had pushed the debate over regime performance into the electoral arena where it could be handled most easily.

Mexico's governing forces were not forced to resort to exceptional measures to maintain social peace. Modest though consistent attention was paid to social spending. A small emergency employment program was developed at the onset of the crisis but was later dismantled; wages were tightly controlled whereas prices were allowed to rise. Lip service was paid to the concepts of "democratic" and moral reform with little in the way of substantive changes appearing.

The only significant development in terms of austerity politics came in the form of a greater emphasis upon the private sector. This shift did not stem, however, from any discernible change in philosophy on the part of the governing elite, but stemmed instead from the financial exigencies of the period. The renewed declaration of the state's rectorship over the economy in the wake of the state's financial collapse was illustrative of the distaste with which the privatization policy was evidently pursued. By the same token, it was also abundantly clear that the private sector was itself in a weakened economic position and hardly exhibited a willingness or capacity to seriously challenge the state for the leading role in society. Economic policy decision-making in fact appeared to have been reduced to the level of crisis response with major policy innovations (the bank nationalization, GATT entry, trade liberalization, revised approaches to DFI and cutbacks in the state sector) resembling acts of desperation rather than coherent strategy. Nevertheless, what emerged, however much by default, was increasingly a "free market approach" albeit within an inappropriate political-economic framework.

In sum, what is distinctive about the recent crisis is not the occurrence of "crisis" per se, or the resort to political "reform" as a means of curtailing the erosion of political support stemming from the crisis, but rather the regime's clear departure from its longstanding model of political economy. While the regime continues to exercise "rectorship" in the economy, it is forced to pursue a set of policies fundamentally at odds with statism. Coherence is lost as political authorities pursue, in formal terms at least, the goals of economic and political liberalization, on the one hand, and at the same time, maneuver to undercut pluralist tendencies within the constellation of economic and political forces. This contradictory process results from the fact that the regime has been forced to accommodate itself to a virtually externally imposed process of liberalization on the economic side while at the same time endeavoring to maintain a monopoly over economic and political resources in defense of its hegemonic position.

In short, contradictions inherent in a model that purports to be emphasizing and enhancing a decentralized liberal capitalist economy (if only by default) on the one hand, and yet resists decentralization and pluralism in the political-economic sphere, will certainly undermine discrete "remedies" now being applied to the economy. Mexico's model of political economy thus appears to be in disarray and offers little suggestion of potential success in overcoming the current economic impasse.

Notes

1. Of particular recent note are the works of M. Basañez, J. A. Hellman, A. Riding, K. Middlebrook, S. K. Purcell, P. Smith, S. Sanderson, D. Story, N. Hamilton, S. Eckstein, J. L. Reyna, and R. Hansen.

2. Judith Gentleman, *Mexican Oil and Dependent Development* (New York, Berne & Frankfort: Peter Lang, 1984), 5.

3. Miguel de la Madrid Hurtado, "Mexico: The New Challenges," *Foreign Affairs* (Fall 1984): 66.

4. Judith Gentleman, "After the Collapse: The State of State Autonomy in Mexico" (paper presented at the meetings of the New York State Political Science Association, Albany, N.Y., April 6, 1984).

5. "Mexico: Progress and Prospects," Morgan Guaranty Trust, *World Financial Markets* (May 1984): 2.

6. Peter H. Smith, "Mexico: The Continuing Quest for a Policy," in Richard Newfarmer, ed., *From Gunboats to Diplomacy: New Policies for Latin America* (Baltimore, MD: Johns Hopkins University Press, 1985), 46. Specifically, in 1982, for Citicorp, loans to Mexico represented 62% of the bank's primary capital; for Bank of America, 51%; and for the Manufacturers Hanover Trust Company, 52%. Eric N. Berg, "Bankers Cautious Over Rescue Package," *New York Times*, June 11, 1986.

7. See David Colmenares, *La nacionalización de la banca* (Mexico City: Terra Nova, 1982); also see Gentleman, *Mexican Oil and Dependent Development*, 222–223; Nora Hamilton, "State-Class Alliances and Conflicts: Issues and Actors in the

Mexican Crisis," *Latin American Perspectives*, issue 43, vol. 11, no. 4 (Fall 1984): 17–18.

8. *Plan Nacional de Desarrollo 1983–88*, 49.

9. "Mexico: Progress and Prospects," 2.

10. Teresa J. Taylor, "Mexico: Economy Improves, Offers Opportunities for Business," *Business America* (March 4, 1985): 38–39; Richard J. Meislin, "Mexico Tightens Austerity," *New York Times*, February 11, 1985.

11. "Mexico: Progress and Prospects," 3.

12. "Mexico Pact on Debt," *New York Times*, March 12, 1985.

13. "A Surprising Shift to Austerity," *Business Week*, February 25, 1985, 46; Meislin, "Mexico Tightens Austerity"; "Austerity Drive is Launched," *Latin America Weekly Report* (15 February 1985): 8.

14. "Latin America's Trade Policies," Morgan Guaranty Trust, *World Financial Markets* (May 1985): Table 5, 4; "Two Years of Slump are Unavoidable," *Latin America Weekly Report* (24 January 1986): 4; "Strengthening the LDC Debt Strategy," Morgan Guaranty Trust, *World Financial Markets* (September/October 1985): 1.

15. "A Surprising Shift to Austerity."

16. "J. de Larosiere Reviews Problems of Indebted Developing Countries," *IMF Survey* (November 25, 1985): 356.

17. "Oil Prices Cut Yet Again," *Latin America Weekly Report* (21 February 1986): 4.

18. "Oil Prices Cut Yet Again."

19. Economist Intelligence Unit, *Quarterly Economic Review of Mexico, 1985*, no. 4: 9; Peter T. Kilborn, "Oil Slump Delays 'Baker Plan'," *New York Times*, February 25, 1986.

20. *Quarterly Economic Review of Mexico*, 1985: 16.

21. Robert Hormats, "Mexico Needs Special Help," *New York Times*, February 26, 1986.

22. "Mexico Banks Sign Restructuring Arrangement," *IMF Survey* (April 15, 1985).

23. "Two Years of Slump are Unavoidable," *Latin American Weekly Report*: 4.

24. "Crisis of Confidence in Mexico?" *Latin American Regional Reports Mexico and the Caribbean* (November 14, 1985).

25. "Crisis of Confidence in Mexico?"

26. Clyde H. Farnsworth, "U.S. Backs Idea of Aid to Mexico," *New York Times*, February 25, 1986.

27. "1986 Business Outlook," *Business Latin America* (December 31, 1985): 412–413; "Oil Price Cut to Save Market Share," *Latin America Weekly Report* (7 February 1986): 8.

28. The term "nationalist populist" is used in Roberto Newell G. and Luis Rubio F., *Mexico's Dilemma: The Political Origins of Economic Crisis* (Boulder, CO: Westview Press, 1984). The "planner/treasury" distinction is used by E.V.K. Fitzgerald. See, for example, "A New Direction in Economic Policy?" *Bank of London and South America Review*, vol. 12, no. 10/78 (October 1978): 528–538.

29. Rubio and Newell, *Mexico's Dilemma*, 208. Also see my discussion of the nature of the dispute during the López Portillo *sexenio* in *Mexican Oil and Dependent Development*, 130.

30. "The New Economic Policy," Banamex, *Review of the Economic Situation of Mexico*, vol. LXI, no. 717 (August 1985): 229.

31. "The New Economic Policy," 300.

32. Banamex, *Review of the Economic Situation of Mexico*, vol. LXI, no. 718 (September 1985): 331.

33. "The New Economic Policy."

34. "*Paraestatales* on the Block," *Latin America Regional Report Mexico and the Caribbean* (15 November 1985).

35. Gentleman, *Mexican Oil and Dependent Development*, 168-169.

36. Kenneth Labich, "The So-Far So-Good Mexican Recovery," *Fortune*, January 1984, 97-99.

37. Labich, "The So-Far So-Good Mexican Recovery."

38. Riding, *Distant Neighbors*, 53; "More Companies to Private Sector," *Latin America Weekly Report* (22 June 1984): 10.

39. "Mexico: Selling State Assets," *The Banker*, May 1984.

40. "Mexico," *Bank of London and South America Review*, vol. 17 (February 1983): 12, 15; "Mexico," *Bank of London and South America Review* (August 1983); "Mexico's Debt-Payment Plan: Firms Must Grapple With Several Options," *Business Latin America* (May 4, 1983): 137-139; "Mexico's Private Debt Repayment Plan Meets Resistance," *Business International Money Report* (August 26, 1983): 267, 170; Labich, "The So-Far So-Good Mexican Recovery," 97-99. For a report on the first three years of Ficorca's activity, see "Ficorca: Three Years After Its Creation," *Review of the Economic Situation of Mexico*, vol. LXII, no. 723 (February 1986): 84-90.

41. Hector Islas, "Empresa pública: política actual," *Banco Nacional de Comercio Exterior, Comercio Exterior*, vol. 35, no. 7 (July 1985): 651.

42. Miguel de la Madrid H., "Tercer Informe de Gobierno," *Banco Nacional de Comercio Exterior, Comercio Exterior*, vol. 35, no. 9 (September 1985): 918.

43. "Tercer Informe."

44. "Mexico. Capitalisation of Credits," *Latin America Weekly Report* (22 March 1985): 7.

45. "Tercer Informe," 917.

46. "More Jobs Lost than Expected," *Latin America Weekly Report* (13 September 1985): 3.

47. "*Paraestatales* on the Block, Trading Off Jobs for Survival," *Latin America Weekly Report* (9 August 1985): 4.

48. "Medidas reciente de política económica," *Banco Nacional de Comercio Exterior, Comercio Exterior*, vol. 35, no. 8 (August 1985): 776.

49. "The New Economic Policy," 297.

50. "Rescue Package as Surplus Dives," *Latin America Weekly Report* (18 October 1985): 4.

51. Eric N. Berg, "Bankers Expect Mexican Debt Plea," *New York Times*, February 24, 1986; *Quarterly Economic Review of Mexico*, 1985: 17.

52. William Stockton, "Fall in Oil Prices Is Called a Spur to Mexico Crisis," *New York Times*, February 10, 1986.

53. Clyde H. Farnsworth, "U. S. Backs Idea of Aid."

54. Miguel Mancera, "Financial Markets Under Conditions of Economic Instability," Banamex, *Review of the Economic Situation of Mexico*, vol. LXI, no. 717 (August 1985): 315.

55. "The New Economic Policy," 302.

56. "The New Economic Policy."

57. *IMF Survey* (December 5, 1985): 382.

58. "Divisions Deepen in Private Sector," *Latin America Weekly Report* (18 October 1985): 5; "Preparing for GATT," *Latin America Weekly Report* (23 August 1985): 10.

59. *Business Latin America* (December 18, 1985).

60. "Little Has Changed in Mexico's Message on Foreign Investment," *Business Latin America* (February 29, 1984): 66; Riding, *Distant Neighbors*, 153.

61. "Mexico Woos Foreign Investors and Rejects Them," *Economist*, February 9, 1985, 61–62.

62. "Transnationals Back in the News," *Latin America Regional Reports Mexico and Central America* (25 October 1985): 3.

63. "Businessmen Brood on the Future," *Latin America Weekly Report* (24 August 1984): 10.

64. "The New Economic Policy," 300.

65. Fernando Ortega Pizarro, "Líderes empresariales denuncian: las presiones del gobierno por desesperación," *Proceso*, 18 November 1985.

66. "New 'Shock' Bid to Curb Crisis," *Latin America Weekly Report* (13 December 1985): 10.

67. "More Jobs Lost than Expected," *Latin America Weekly Report* (13 September 1985): 3.

68. "La política de financiamiento del desarrollo: límites y estratégia," Banco Nacional de Comercio Exterior, *Comercio Exterior*, vol. 34, no. 9 (September 1984).

69. "Will Mexico Make It?" 79; De la Madrid, "Mexico: The New Challenges," 62–76.

70. "Will Mexico Make It?" 86.

71. "Experts Wary of 'Good Example'," *Latin America Regional Report: Mexico and Central America* (13 July 1984): 6.

72. *Latin America Regional Report: Mexico and Central America* (10 June 1983): 8.

TABLE 3.1
Manufactures as a Percentage of Total Exports, 1980-1982

Hong Kong	91
South Korea	81
Singapore	42
Taiwan	92
Thailand	25
MEXICO	9
Venezuela	1

Source: "Latin America Trade Policies," Morgan Guaranty Trust, World Financial Markets (May 1985): 7, Table 9.

TABLE 3.2
Public Sector Expenditure as a Percentage of GDP

	Total	Capital
1977-1980	32	8.9
1982	46.9	10.7
1984	38	6.4

Source: "Latin America's Trade Policies," 8, Table 13.

TABLE 3.3
New Direct Foreign Investment in Mexico, 1981-1985
(billions of U.S. dollars)

1981	1.7
1982	.626
1983	.683
1984	1.4
1985	2.0

Source: "Transnationals Back in the News," Latin America Regional Report Mexico and the Caribbean (25 October 1985): 3.

4

Can the PRI Be Reformed?
Decentralizing Candidate Selection[1]

John Bailey

This volume addresses trends in Mexico's political development in the wake of the reform efforts of 1977. The contributors avoid the teleological pitfall of viewing Anglo-American style democracy as the natural product of development and assume that one or another form of authoritarianism is a more accurate point of departure. This chapter examines efforts by the dominant Institutional Revolutionary Party (PRI) to implement internal reforms in conjunction with steps toward broader system reform. My particular approach, unfashionable to many, will be to try to view Mexican reality through the ideological and institutional lenses of the PRI, with both sympathy and skepticism.

To structure the discussion, I first try to characterize the PRI's views of Mexican democracy. Then I summarize my understanding of the place of the PRI in the logic of Mexico's presidential system, noting certain inherent problems. The more significant efforts at party and system reform are briefly recounted, emphasizing the Madrazo experiment of 1965 and the Law of Political Organizations and Electoral Parties (LOPPE) of 1977. This is followed by a brief analysis of the current reform effort of "consultation with the grassroots." Finally, I attempt an assessment of the prospects for party reform for the remainder of the De la Madrid sexennium.

Introduction: The PRI's View of Mexican Democracy

Given Mexico's stated commitment to democracy, it is natural to view party competition and mass voting as major forms of participation. This is valid to some extent, but we should recall that the regime claims multiple bases of legitimacy, not limited to procedural democracy. The Mexican Revolution produced three major themes or projects: nationalism, social welfare, and liberalism; and all three are significant legitimating symbols. Nationalism needs little explanation. The overwhelming presence of the United States requires special attention to the forging of a national awareness, which often is expressed in anti-U.S. sentiments. Social welfare implies economic growth, progress, and improved living conditions, especially for the popular classes. Mexican liberalism, however, is a case of deceptive familiarity. While sharing some elements of the Anglo-American tradition, the Mexican version is shaped as well by European notions of a strong, tutelary state which acts to impose the rule of law over society. These notions find a fertile bed in Mexico's tragic history of political disorder, and they are reflected in the thought of that country's foremost liberal ideologist, Jesús Reyes Heroles.

The PRI considers itself to be the law-giving and order-creating embodiment of an historic social upheaval that left massive destruction and more than a million killed over the period 1910–1929. The party is dedicated to the achievement of all three Revolutionary projects. This leads to a particular view of its role in Mexican democracy, as expressed, for example, in party statutes:

The function that corresponds historically to the PRI consists of assuring the permanence of the nationalist revolutionary current in the exercise of state power. [This will be accomplished] through the cohesion of the fundamental forces of the people and the strengthening of the bases of democratic support for the constitutional regime of government.[2] The party will struggle . . . to maintain power to carry out to its ultimate consequences the historic project of the Mexican Revolution, by means of the complete force of the essential principles of democracy and social justice of revolutionary nationalism and the invigoration of the institutions sustained in such principles.[3]

Lest one mistake this for inconsequential party boilerplate, consider the standard rhetoric of two rather different presidents:

. . . the important thing in a democracy is not so much the procedure as the very essence, and the essence of democracy consists in that it is the sum of the majority wills of the people that determines the paths for government to follow in two respects: with regard to the selection of men and with regard to decision-making.[4]

Democracy [is] understood, not in its strict political and much less electoral sense, but rather as it is defined in Article Three of the Constitution which we revolutionaries wrote into the Fundamental Text and which defines [democracy] not just as a juridical regime and a political system, but rather as a sense of life that seeks the constant economic, social and cultural betterment of the people. Democracy is not measured only in votes but rather has been measured in Mexico by the broadening of social justice to a growing number of Mexicans.[5]

The point is that priistas typically adopt a substantive view of democracy over what they often reject as a formalistic view, or one that stresses mere votes and elections.[6] The substantive version of democracy, in turn, employs elections not as popular choices between competing parties, but rather as plebiscites on the continuing legitimacy of the Revolutionary projects and on the PRI's claim to be the "party of the majorities." There is evidence to suggest that this notion of voting as validation rather than as choice between candidates and policies is widely held in the Mexican electorate as well.[7] The PRI's view of democracy allows considerable personal freedom and creates spaces for opposition, but *as minorities* and within the rules set down by the party of the majorities. "Our party is convinced that 'even though the majorities set the rules of democracy, also indispensable is respect for the expression and participation of minorities.' This is the reason that the party of the Revolution has sponsored actions that lead to the broadening of the forms of expression and participation by minorities."[8]

The contradiction between substantive versus formal democracy is reconcilable in theory as long as the PRI persists in its claim to pursue the "perfection" of democracy. It is reconcilable in practice as long as the system can demonstrate progress on the nationalism and welfare projects. Business elites, by and large, are content with secure, hefty profits; and the lower classes gain some sense of satisfaction from the general image of progress.[9] The major dissatisfied stratum in this arrangement is arguably the heterogeneous middle sectors, in which a commitment to procedural democracy is more widespread. Also, middle class families feel much of the consequences of inflation due to their life-styles (private education, consumer durables) and their lesser participation in price-controlled goods and services such as subsidized health, food distribution and public transportation.

Within the substantive formula, other forms of political participation take on greater importance. The notion of "mediated political efficacy" suggests that individuals gain a sense of efficacy from participation in groups that in turn are connected to the PRI system, either as constituent members or as recognized actors. Such activity is situationally rational in the sense of individuals apportioning their loyalty and energy based on a calculus of self-interest and judgment of success.[10] Thus, for example, rural cooperativists (*ejidatarios*) may act through their associations to pressure for land or water claims; businessmen work through their chambers; workers operate through their unions; street peddlers petition through their guilds, and so forth. The results of such efforts, however meager, reinforce the notion that working through state-sanctioned arrangements is preferable to the riskier path of protest.

Substantive democracy, with its corollaries of plebiscitary elections and mediated efficacy, can reconcile the contradictions with procedural democracy so long as the PRI-government system succeeds in generating an image of progress, stability, and nationalism. But even without the spectacular economic dislocations of 1981–1986, secular trends had been at work for some time to undermine support for this notion of democracy. Most pronounced among the middle sectors, in the larger cities, and in the north of Mexico, these trends include urbanization, improved levels of education, and the infiltration of "foreign" notions of democracy as competition between parties to control government.

With gradual erosion of support among the middle sectors suddenly aggravated by economic austerity, Mexico has entered a profound systemic crisis, which has intensified pressures on governing elites to seek solutions. Governments after the mid-1970s have increased emphasis on nationalism and liberalism, as seen for example in more assertive foreign policies and in greater rhetorical emphasis on political reform.[11] Nationalism and liberalism, however, have proven to be a fatal contradiction, as seen most recently in the 1985 congressional elections. In that instance, the PRI government branded its principal opposition, the National Action party (PAN), as disloyal and anti-revolutionary and called on the public to rally to the PRI to defend national sovereignty. The PRI rejected as totally unacceptable the PAN's campaign to reopen the questions of the agrarian reform, status of the Catholic Church, mandatory school textbooks, and state rectorship of the economy. And the PAN's perceived receptivity to U.S. influence was considered simply treasonous.[12] In short, the PRI's resolute rejection of a two-party model of democracy is based on their view of the PAN as an illegitimate contender, one that likely would invite foreign intervention into domestic politics. The priísta view is buttressed in turn by a particular historiography of the nineteenth and early twentieth centuries which stresses the readiness of the United States to intervene, often in collusion with disloyal Mexicans.

To an outside observer, the PRI's strategy to attack and to "satanize" its opposition appears rational and reasonably successful, as was demonstrated in the party's ability to mobilize support in the 1985 elections. But short-term success also undermines an essential feature of procedural democracy: a legitimate opposition. It suggests as well that the PRI-government is not about to cede power through electoral defeats. At least three reasons support this: first, for the system's beneficiaries, the short-term and specific incentives of retaining a monopoly of power far outweigh the long-term and general benefits of reform in the sense of real procedural democracy; second, impressive tensions have accumulated over time and real party competition risks the specter of competing elites mobilizing mass followings which they cannot control; third, there remains an alternative course of reform which some in the present government prefer to revive.

Whereas to some the idea of genuine political reform might suggest honest elections and multi-party competition, it opens other avenues to those who believe that there was once a golden era of an authentic Mexican democracy. That democracy was lost through the gross corruption and mistakes of recent presidents (Luis Echeverría, 1970–1976, and José López Portillo, 1976–1982), but it can be recovered by rejuvenating the party and providing popular, effective leadership. A logic of this sort leads to a reconsideration of the possibilities of reforming the PRI.

For different reasons, not much serious attention has been given to this topic. Party and government spokesmen can hardly be expected to speak or write frankly, especially to a foreign audience, because such candor jeopardizes their careers. Some Mexican scholars find the subject simply barren of interest: "In 1950 the PRI was already set. Whatever later reform would be inconsequential. In practice only those reforms that fine-tuned a system that now would not change in essence would be allowed. Since then not only the shaping of the PRI has ceased but also that of the Mexican political system as it would function for at least thirty years."[13] Other scholars, both Mexican and foreign, work within variations on structuralist or marxist perspectives, which tend to ignore institutions or to subordinate them to more fundamental forces.[14] Furthermore, the Mexican system has an intimidating quality about it which tends to discourage scholarly inquiry into current and potentially controversial topics.[15] We do enjoy, however, an excellent literature on the origins of the party and its evolution to about the mid-1960s. This foundation, supplemented with journalistic pieces, interpretive essays, and interviews permits at least a preliminary exploration of the topic.[16]

My working hypothesis, a bit mechanistic to be sure, is that governing elites act to retain power and to avoid anti-system violence. Political change at the institutional level proceeds along three interconnected tracks: the PRI, the party system, and the federal bureaucracy (the latter taken as a proxy for federal agencies carrying out an overall development strategy). Reformers typically have attempted to use party system reform to bring pressure to bear on the PRI to modify its internal procedures. Anti-system behavior, apathy and violence, acts as the main impetus for reform. As progress along one track encounters obstacles, efforts shift to another track or tracks. Generally, though, while one might argue that system reform has created incentives to select "better" PRI candidates for the national legislature and some governorships, little has been accomplished in the way of internal reform. Among the several reasons, especially important is the role of organized labor in providing support during a grueling crisis; and for reasons of power and policy, labor shows a longstanding preference for a centralized, sectorialized party.

As illustrated in Figure 4.1, labor unrest in the latter 1950s provided the impetus of Adolfo López Mateos' 1963 "party deputy reform,"[17] and Carlos Madrazo's 1965 campaign to rejuvenate the PRI was intended to complement the party system reform. Madrazo's failure reinforced the bureaucracy track, which was pursued vigorously until the economic-political crisis of 1976. That crisis in turn gave rise to the LOPPE in 1977—which, characteristically, was accompanied by another effort—again unsuccessful— to revitalize the PRI. The oil bonanza of 1977-1981 reignited the bureaucracy-development effort, and party system and bureaucratic activity proceeded until the economic collapse of 1981-1982. With enforced economic austerity, the government of Miguel de la Madrid attempted at first to continue with party system reform, but retreated from this after electoral setbacks in 1983. During 1984-1986, emphasis returned to internal reform of the dominant party.

Systemic Flaws: Centralization, Bossism, Corruption

For this static and schematic analysis, it is useful to depict Mexico as a strong presidential system in which the presidency is seen to embody the whole polity. With the sole limitations of the six-year term (the *sexenio*), no reelection, and the incumbent's own interpretation of the rules of the game, the presidency encounters no effective restraint *within* government. Despite reform tinkering, the congress remains unimportant; and the judiciary, while gaining credibility in noncontroversial areas of law, offers no resistance. There are, however, significant "irritating" constraints, such as the inadequate or filtered information that reaches the president and the complex and sluggish federal bureaucracy. Also, one can make a case that the army is carefully consulted on questions of foreign policy (especially toward Central America) and internal order.[18]

In the wider political system, however, the presidency confronts real limitations from several quarters. First, the international setting imposes constraints in areas such as tourism, trade, investment, and even the vague "world opinion." Mexican macroeconomic policy is virtually dictated by oil prices, interest rates, and trade cycles. Second, business elites, both national and foreign, limit presidential behavior, because of the constant—and real— threat of capital flight. Third, as noted above, the Confederation of Mexican Workers (CTM) constitutes the foundation of the PRI and must be negotiated with. Fourth, the mass media enjoy increasing freedom, although the custom of avoiding direct criticism of the president still generally holds. More constraining perhaps is the increased penetration of foreign media, as through cable television or the proliferating satellite antennae.[19] Finally, the deterioriation of the image of the presidency due to the turmoil of the last two *sexenios* has probably constrained the behavior of the present incumbent. On the one hand, without a popular predecessor, Miguel de la Madrid Hurtado (1982–1988) enjoys a freer rein. On the other hand, his government lacks the negotiating space of previous administrations, which were able to steer a course between factions surviving the powerful administrations of Lázaro Cárdenas (1934–1940) and Miguel Alemán (1946–1952). These factors are reflected in De la Madrid's cabinet, which—in breaking with custom— does not seek to integrate representatives of various political factions but rather magnifies the presence of *técnicos* from the Treasury-Bank of Mexico fraternity.

In a narrow, institutional sense, the presidency rests on the PRI and the extensive federal bureaucracy and employs both clusters of organizations as subordinate instruments. The party thus lacks an identity and purpose separate from the presidency and the bureaucracy, giving real basis to the common label, PRI government. Much of daily politics consists of the circulation of numerous teams within and between both pillars, vying for presidential support. The president's general and specific control over career advancement in party and government constitutes the real motor of centralization. The increasing reward for technical competence since the mid-1960s, consistent with greater emphasis on bureaucracy during 1971–1982, has reduced substantially the career opportunities of those who stressed the political skills of building extensive alliances in the party, negotiating directly with constituent groups, and cultivating a rhetoric rich in Revolutionary slogans.

The PRI both reflects and reinforces this centralized presidential system. As Córdova correctly stresses, the party should be viewed as kind of a holding company of groups, themselves organized into peasant, labor, and popular sectors.[20] In this sense, with a present membership of some 14 to 16 million, the PRI has a valid claim as the party of the *organized* majorities. Further, the party can claim genuine national and multiclass representation in a way that no other Mexican party can.

The Mexican presidential system demands discipline, and this depends ultimately on a monopoly of rewards, party and government offices and all the implied perquisites of power, being distributed from above on a basis of loyalty to intermediate leaders who are loyal in turn to the president. This logic substantially changes the significance of votes as a currency of power, either within constituent party groups or in general electoral competition. A genuinely popular and steadfastly loyal leader is, of course, to be welcomed. But votes are less important than control over those below and loyalty to those above. Similarly, satellite parties are rewarded in exchange for system support.[21]

The logic of presidential control also reduces the importance of ideology and militancy at the grassroots as bases of party cohesion. The PRI's "revolutionary nationalism" is a flexibly drawn social democratic ideology that reconciles state rectorship of a mixed economy, promotion of the rights of the poor, and respect for individual liberties. Grassroots activism has not proven a reliable route for mobility, and the party constantly seeks to stimulate greater participation (but without ceding real power from the center).

On the other hand, presidentialism increases the importance of friendships, patron-client ties and corruption, the latter taken to mean the strictly illegal or broadly unethical use of party or government posts for personal enrichment. Strong personal loyalty among friends is essential in a game in which laws may be stretched and which offers no unemployment compensation. Cultivation of protection and support from those favorably placed is the key to upward mobility. And corruption is essential to reward loyalty in the absence of a militant ideology or generalized attachment to governmental and party institutions. This not to suggest, I would stress, that all *priístas* are somehow corrupt by virtue of party affiliation. The point, rather, is that the logic of the presidential system foments corruption.

It is useful to consider (see Figure 4.2) how incentives to the actors in this system reinforce centralization, as a background to understanding the constraints on party reform. First, the president controls the PRI in good part by placing his own loyalists in key positions in the National Executive Committee (CEN).[22] He also uses the CEN-Interior Ministry linkage as the filter to nominate his personal loyalists to state governorships and the national legislature.[23] Political "notables," a diverse collection of cabinet members, governors, interest group leaders, and influential former officeholders, lobby the presidency-CEN-Interior triangle to influence appointments. Most seek merely to protect their own power bases and to advance their loyalists. A few are positioning themselves to "play the big one," the presidential succession. The sectorial leaders (labor, popular, peasant) endeavor to protect or increase their historical shares of offices and to advance their own loyalists among the group leaders. Party activists and government bureaucrats maneuver to establish friendships with notables higher up in the party and government and hope for that bit of luck known as the *dedazo* (literally, the "big finger"), the signal from above to take one or several career steps forward.

A glance at internal PRI politics helps to understand obstacles to party reform. Scott correctly stresses the sectorial organization of the party as impeding internal modernization in the sense of better responding to grass roots interests and to electoral competition at the municipal and district level.[24] The sectors themselves are not watertight compartments. Travelling about, one finds taxi drivers organized in both the popular and labor sectors; public enterprise unions can be found in both of those sectors; and some agribusiness interests belong to the peasant sector. Nevertheless, the sectors do shape party politics.

Labor is the most important sector. This is because the peasants continue to lose influence due to development policy (industrialization), demographic changes (urbanization), and the food crisis. Also, though the rural vote is the core of the party, the peasantry can be fairly well controlled. (See Klesner's chapter in this volume.) The popular sector is quite heterogeneous, though it houses the enormous federal public employees' unions (FSTSE) and its primary affiliate, the National Educational Workers Unions (SNTE), which alone enrolls some 800,000 schoolteachers. The CTM is the best organized, best financed, and most ably led. Benefiting from the mystique of octogenarian Fidel Velázquez, labor has its own professional staff of economists, planners, lawyers, and the like. Its ideologists, notably Enrique Ramírez y Ramírez and Arturo Romo Gutiérrez, have created a coherent version of a public policy consistent with labor interests. Concentrated numerically in a relatively few cities, labor sees its strength based less on votes than on organization and militancy, and thus on the sectorial design. The labor leadership by and large is skeptical about the rise of the technocrats (as we shall see) and scolds nonlabor *priístas* from time to time about being soft on the Revolution.

If we shift now to the perspective of the PRI leadership, the incentives for reform appear at best tepid. Looking inward, the peasants are largely taken for granted, but they are declining in numbers and influence. More important to *ejidatarios* is the government agricultural bureaucracy: Banrural, Conasupo, SARH, and related agencies that link *ejidatarios* directly to government. Furthermore, agrarian reform in the sense of land distribution is no longer a policy option. Popular sector members are probably among the least disciplined, due to their better education and middle-strata status. Organized labor, then, is the solid rock. Looking outward, real electoral competition could mean conceding important positions, especially in the North and certain urban areas, to an opportunistic band of counterrevolutionaries, the PAN. This is partly because the Left cannot coalesce sufficiently around a common leadership or program to offset PAN strength and to attract a larger share of the anti-PRI protest vote.[25] Also, the PRI has succeeded in coopting much of the Left.

The present system excels in reinforcing presidential power and in fine-tuning power relations among party sectors and political notables. But the sectorial and centralized structure does not necessarily mesh well with the territorial organization of the local party base and with municipal and congressional electoral districts. A national party candidate nominated to a specific congressional district to satisfy the labor sector's quota, for example, cannot always generate enthusiasm among local PRI cadres. The local party activist may welcome the bright, attractive and well-connected congressional or gubernatorial candidate from Mexico City; but he may shudder at the prospect of campaigning for an ineffective, perhaps even tainted candidate, selected as the outcome of some national deal. As long as the PRI operated in an environment of optimism and growth, and confronted a divided and ineffectual opposition in largely symbolic elections, discontent at the party base was manageable. The CEN could usually resolve disputes through negotiation and appeal to discipline.

Efforts to somehow dilute sectorial power are fiercely resisted. The first step in this direction came in 1946 with Miguel Alemán who restricted the powers of the sectors and constituted individual membership as the basis of the party. The changes were consistent with Alemán's pro-business, anti-communist emphases. But the effort did not prosper. "After four years of unhappy experimentation with the new system the objections of the labor and agrarian leaders won the day, and the party was reconstituted on a sectoral basis in 1950."[26]

With some minor variations, the current basic features had taken hold by the early 1950s. Subsequently, the national PRI systematically subordinated its local and regional organizations to the center. Bosses (*caciques*) continued in many areas, to be sure, but they survived by subordinating themselves to the center. Over time, the costs of the system became more obvious: apathy at the base, opportunism at all levels, the sacrifice of talent and constructive dissent to discipline and loyalty. These arrangements were basically what Carlos A. Madrazo encountered on assuming the party presidency in December 1964.

Madrazo's Experiment: The Lessons and Questions of Failure

Carlos A. Madrazo was from Tabasco and pursued his early education in Villahermosa before attending preparatory and law school in Mexico City.[27] He was active on the Left as a leader of the Bloc of Revolutionary Youth of the Red Shirts (1933–1935) under Tabasco governor Tomás Garrido Canabal. Madrazo was elected to leadership positions in preparatory school and in national youth organizations. He served as private secretary to Luis

I. Rodríguez in 1937–1938 during the latter's tenure as governor of Guanajuato and in 1938–1939 when Rodríguez moved on to head the Partido de la Revolución Mexicana (the forerunner of the PRI). He served in the Chamber of Deputies during 1943–1946, where he formed a close friendship with Gustavo Díaz Ordaz, and held several other posts in the federal bureaucracy before serving as governor of Tabasco during 1959–1964. Madrazo distinguished himself as an effective politician and dynamic orator. In December 1964, President Díaz Ordaz appointed Madrazo as president of the CEN, with a charge to reform the party.[28] Madrazo's acceptance speech signalled change:

> There are those who think that assuming this position is three years of easy going. They imagine a quiet, inert party, one without a mystique of work; a party whose only purpose is to be available to gear up the electoral machinery for elections in the states or for federal deputies.
>
> Those who think this way don't know the dynamic of a party; they've heard of the people only to take advantage of them; they don't have any political education; and at base they're no more than spiritual cripples or job-seekers (*caza-chambas*) who don't interest us.
>
> Quite to the contrary, I believe these first three years can be the most fertile, the most promising, when we can count on the calm necessary to struggle to make realities of each one of the points that make up our Declaration of Principles.[29]

And he might have sensed from the outset the stakes of the game: "I don't know if I'll last a minute or a lifetime in this job. I do know that each second will find me serving our revolutionary conviction with dignity and conviction."[30]

Madrazo consistently stressed certain themes. The PRI should attract youth by stressing reform and idealism; the party should establish an identity separate from government; "natural leaders" should be identified and recruited (as opposed to the traditional method of *dedazo*); individual party militancy should be rewarded; corruption should be rooted out; the party should take the lead in defining national problems and in pointing the way toward solutions. Another theme stressed was decentralization by revitalizing the "free municipality."[31]

To complement the 1963 party deputy reform, the strategy to reform the PRI was first to reinvigorate the party apparatus and then to introduce internal party primaries for municipal elections. Madrazo sent special groups of delegates from the CEN to each state to look into local-level demands, reinforce militancy, promote programs for women and youth, and renovate local and state leadership.[32] The delegates were to analyze the party from the bottom up.

The first states to receive the party reform were Morelos, Baja California, Michoacán, Chihuahua, Durango, Guanajuato, and San Luis Potosí. Following this, the local party militants were to elect their leaders in free votes in local assemblies all over the country on July 25, 1965. It was not clear how these elections were to be carried out, and in some cases they took on the appearance of ratification of decisions reached earlier. Important to note is that Madrazo used the national CEN to bypass state party structures, presumably to ensure that the reforms were indeed implemented. The more skeptical observers probably noted that this tactic provided Madrazo with additional patronage to distribute among his own followers.[33]

The next step in reform was the institution of primary elections to select the party's candidates for municipal presidents and councilmen. Customarily, the local party supplied the state committee with the names, qualifications and petitions of support of the several candidates. The state committee, after study and comment, passed the nominations on to the CEN where the final slates were drawn up (including at times a presidential approval). Special delegates from the state committee or even from the CEN were dispatched occasionally to verify information or to resolve problems. In reality, the state governors were the primary deciders of municipal nominations. This was due to the plausible assumption that the governors could work more harmoniously with their own municipal presidents, just as the president could best work with governors of his own choosing.[34]

The system of primaries was put into effect in the municipal elections in Baja California. The new procedures generated unusual public interest, and—although it was evident that existing powers could continue to influence the elections—the close race in Ensenada showed that the primaries introduced new elements in local contests. Elections in other states showed the co-existence of the two systems.

The reports of the *elecciones internas* led to the general conclusions that the experiment was successful in the sense that some new elements were being introduced into the game of Mexican politics. In order for the old system to maintain its dominance, it had to develop new methods to subvert the institutional democracy. Although these methods were effective in most areas, the exceptions proved that the old system would have to evolve eventually to accept the change. Madrazo was being pragmatic in allowing some subversion of the *elecciones,* but his pressure for upholding its purpose was being felt, and in some areas CEN control was able to force the regular power structures to reduce their hold on the *municipios.*[35]

Even in the best of circumstances, changing long-established patterns of power would be difficult. Complicating this experiment was Madrazo's willingness to use the power of the CEN and the discipline of the party to override state and local objections. That style would inevitably create opposition. The governor of Sinaloa, Leopoldo Sánchez Celis, a product of the old school of Mexican politics was quite willing to challenge Madrazo. The specifics involved tainted primaries in September 1965 in two cities of Sinaloa. Madrazo overturned the decisions, and the governor then entered his same candidates as independents in the October general elections, winning both races. Madrazo evidently persisted in objecting; the case apparently was decided by Díaz Ordaz; and Madrazo resigned on 17 November 1965.[36]

Clearly, the opposition to Madrazo's reform had triumphed. Certain governors were opposed, including—in addition to Sinaloa—those of Guerrero and Chihuahua, in which the reforms had led to victories by independent *priístas*. But governors of other states also took comfort from Madrazo's fall. Beyond the governors, the cabinet members, and especially Luis Echeverría of the Interior Ministry, could feel some relief, first with the elimination of a rival for the succession, but also with the reaffirmation of presidential dominance and the continued ascendency of the bureaucracy over the party.

The episode teaches several lessons. First, it was clear that Madrazo held ambitions of building a power base of his own in the party, and President Díaz Ordaz was simply behaving logically in firing him. Second, the failure of the effort demonstrated the system's rigidity; young reformers could take little comfort about their prospects of rising in the PRI. Third, the events following showed that reform would come more likely from other quarters, initially through violent protest, as with the student movement of 1968, then through the bureaucratic apparatus, with new programs and interest representation structures, and later through renewed party system reform.

Assuming that Díaz Ordaz really did choose Madrazo for the purpose of party reform, at least three questions remain unanswered. First, President Díaz Ordaz probably encouraged Madrazo's opponents at some point, and did little to defend the party leader once the counterreform got underway. The question, though, concerns the limits on presidential power: Can any Mexican president force a reform on unwilling governors and party notables? Second, it is far from certain that the party base was ready for internal elections, especially if these were to be introduced across the board throughout the country. Have attitudes changed over the past twenty years? Third, as one of the progressive *priístas* formed in the *cardenista* period, was Madrazo the last best hope of reforming the PRI? Did Echeverría's emphasis on youth, bureaucracy, and technocrats eliminate the possibility of party reform?

Madrazo's observation, a year after his fall, is worth remembering:

> Our democracy would be singular and picturesque if its anachronistic proceedings were not provoking large black clouds which cover a people almost without bread, without enough liberty to choose the best rather than that which is commanded. This, sooner or later, will lead us to a dangerous crossroad which we would have been able to avoid with the democratization which was being started in the party.[37]

The LOPPE and "Transparent Democracy"

President Luis Echeverría took office in the aftermath of the 1968 student movement, encountering an economy in recession, university protests and guerrilla movements in different parts of the country, and a rapidly changing international order. His statecraft emphasized the bureaucracy and youth over the PRI and established party politicians, reinforcing in the process the tensions between *políticos* and *técnicos* that continue in somewhat moderated form to the present. A significant reform was adopted in 1969 to lower the voting age from 21 to 18. Also, minor adjustments were made in the party deputy system, increasing the number of seats allocated to minor parties and lowering the percentage vote required to win them.

As president of the PRI during 1971–1975, Jesús Reyes Heroles continued to push for changes in candidate selection that would strengthen the base, but without altering the basic structure of the party. Padgett concludes that "Despite the party reform, the principles of hierarchy and discipline directed from above were maintained. Most importantly, the all powerful role of the CEN was reaffirmed on every level."[38]

Echeverría's effort to revive a populist style akin to something from the Cárdenas era of the 1930s culminated in the political and economic crisis of 1975–1976, which set the stage for the LOPPE. We might summarize José López Portillo's strategy for government by looking at its explicit and tacit components and then noting the different phases of his *sexenio.*

At the time of his selection, López Portillo was not considered a powerful figure in comparison with the other contenders: Mario Moya Palencia (Interior), Hugo Cervantes del Río (Presidency), Augusto Gómez Villanueva (Agrarian Reform), and Porfirio Muñoz Ledo (Labor). Though not the complete *técnico* that he is sometimes labelled, López Portillo pursued his early career in private law practice and entered government in his early forties. He participated only marginally in PRI activities, and had never run for election nor held a prominent party office. The significance of López Portillo's image was that Luis Echeverría was considered both powerful and interested in retaining power in the succeeding *sexenio.*

López Portillo's explicit strategy was ambitious and quite well integrated. He called for an "Alliance for Production," an administrative reform, and a political reform. The first was to create a new pact between labor, business, and government in order to reinitiate investment and growth. The second, of longstanding personal interest, was to bring order to the chaotic public bureaucracy. And the third was to open new spaces for political participation. The reforms fit into a sexennial schedule: Two years for recovery, two more to establish the base for sustained growth, and the last biennium for attaining high growth. The rhythm of the *sexenio* matters, because the received wisdom holds that political changes are best implemented early in the *sexenio.* In the second half of the term, 23 of the 31 governors are chosen, and the maneuvering for the presidential succession gets underway in earnest.

The tacit strategy was to reduce and then eliminate Echeverría's influence in domestic politics, and in foreign policy to continue the main lines of the Echeverría emphasis on Third World issues but in a less confrontational style. Also in foreign policy the new government toyed with the possibility of a "package" arrangement with the United States. Basically, the package involved some combination of assured access to petroleum in exchange for acceptable trade, investment, and immigration policies. It might be argued that the requirements of the tacit strategy prevented the implementation of the explicit.

As events unfolded, however, the *sexenio* divided itself rather differently. During 1977–1978, the president worked to restore confidence in the economy and to demonstrate competence in political affairs. The failure of the package arrangement, foreshadowed in the collapse of the 1977 gas negotiations and then confirmed in the testy exchanges between López Portillo and Jimmy Carter in February 1979, closed off a major avenue. But the vast new petroleum wealth seemed to open to others. In January 1979, the president fired the party president, Carlos Sansores Pérez, and in May of that year three cabinet members "were resigned." Two of their replacements signalled fundamental redirections: Jorge Castaneda in Foreign Relations suggested greater importance for foreign policy; Enrique Olivares Santana in Interior represented an orthodox, institutional approach to domestic politics. Miguel de la Madrid at Planning and Budget showed more the president's continued frustration with implementing new planning arrangements than a substantive policy.[39] From late 1978 until 1981 the government shifted to full growth (achieving 8–9% real growth per year) and to a more assertive foreign policy. Mid-1981, with the first crack in oil prices, until December 1982 was a period that began with critical mistakes and culminated in financial panic and government arbitrariness. The government lost at least a billion dollars in revenues by refusing to lower oil prices, and added several billions more in short-term foreign debt by continuing its high expenditure policies. Also in 1981 the private sector assumed large amounts of foreign debt, as rapid investment coincided with the increasing problem of capital flight.

With regard to political reform, the initial appointment of Jesús Reyes Heroles as Secretary of Interior signalled changes in the overall party system, as was born out in the LOPPE. The initial appointment of Carlos Sansores Pérez to head the PRI, however, showed the continuing influence of Luis Echeverría and the disinterest (if not opposition) with respect to internal party reform. The firing of Reyes Heroles in May 1979 seemed to signal a retreat from the system reform; but the replacement of Sansores in February 1979 by Gustavo Carvajal reflected more the "take charge" attitude of López Portillo than an internal party policy.

The party system reforms of 1963 and 1973 covered basically three aspects: lowering the voting age from 21 to 18 and lowering the minimum age to run for congress; reducing requirements to register parties for national elections; and providing an easier way for them to win seats in the Chamber of Deputies.[40] The 1977 reforms went beyond the previous efforts in promoting the opposition. The principal author of the reform, Jesús Reyes Heroles, had supported the previous efforts first as a national deputy in 1963 and as PRI president during 1972–1975. Reyes Heroles' main concern was to provide legitimate channels for opposition activity to prevent an accumulation of pressure that might explode in violence and reawaken what he often called, "Mexico bronco" (violent Mexico). His consistent rationale was that the PRI needs institutional opposition: "The PRI's main fear is to find itself in an institutional vacuum, of not having parties to debate with. 'That which opposes assists' is what the CEN president constantly likes to proclaim."[41]

The 1977 reforms provided that:

- parties might qualify to run candidates by registering a minimum number of members in states or electoral districts; alternatively, they might seek provisional registration, and if they received at least 1½% of the vote in the subsequent national election, their registration would be made permanent (unless their vote in the future dropped below the minimum 1½%);
- the Chamber of Deputies would set aside 100 of 400 seats to opposition parties, to be won in proportional representation contests in various regions (presently 5) thoughout the country;
- opposition parties would receive free access to media, the postal frank, as well as subsidies for party expenses.

Also important were a general amnesty granted in 1978 to those convicted of political crimes and the government's commitment to allow greater public access to information that previously was kept guarded.

While the purpose of the reforms in 1977 was to encourage citizen participation through legitimate channels, a subsequent goal was to stimulate the growth of the Left so that it might reestablish a degree of equilibrium in electoral politics given the more impressive growth in influence of the PAN on the Right. We can find this notion of the PRI as the center balance between Left and Right as far back as the electoral law of 1946. It might be argued that the reforms succeeded in increasing participation in elections, as was apparent in higher voter turnouts in 1982 (a presidential election year), but abstention reappeared at near-record levels in the midterm elections of 1985. Also, the Left never really achieved coherence, either as a party or as a coalition of parties, and the prospect of bipartisan competition with the PAN in specific regions of the country, so condemned as an exotic and foreign notion by the PRI-government leadership, has increased as a threat.

One might also make a case that the system reform increased the significance of the congress and led the PRI to nominate congressional candidates who are more articulate and adept at parliamentary maneuvering. Certainly a number of prestigious individuals were nominated by the PRI for the 1979 congress. Also, quite apart from electoral politics, one might argue that the major accomplishment of the political reform was to routinize dissent. Under Díaz Ordaz, and to some degree under Echeverría as well, labor strikes and student demonstrations were often seen as direct challenges to government authority. With López Portillo, strikes could more easily be made legal and resolved through routine bureaucratic mechanisms. Further, writers and intellectuals enjoyed greater freedom of expression. Little, however, was accomplished with respect to internal party reform. This was evident from the outset of the López Portillo *sexenio* with the appointment of Carlos Sansores Pérez, an old-line party regular whose primary alliances were formed with the labor sector. Sansores Pérez might be considered a successful, disciplined *priísta* of the old school. He entered national politics with Miguel Alemán in 1946, serving as a national deputy. Subsequently, he was elected to the chamber on three occasions, to the senate twice, and to the governorship of his home state of Campeche. He also held several party posts before his appointment as president of the CEN in December 1976.[42] If one is to believe the critics, Sansores' alliance with Echeverría dates at least from the Madrazo episode and includes Echeverría's valuable support as Secretary of Interior in reaching the governorship of Campeche in 1967.

López Portillo's selection of Sansores to head the PRI probably involved a number of calibrations of power arrangements. Reyes Heroles at Interior was certainly no *echeverrista*, having feuded with then-president Echeverría in 1975, and appointing Sansores as a counterweight to Reyes Heroles might have seemed useful. Also, the courting of business interests in the early stages of the Alliance for Production implied debts to organized labor. With respect to political reform, labor was apprehensive, fearing a reduction of its influence within the PRI as well as difficult challenges for control over unions by Left opposition parties. Sansores could reassure both Echeverría and labor, and his appointment could contribute to a smooth transition. But Sansores was clearly out of step with the reform project, and his confirmation at the IX Party Assembly in January 1978 left the reformers frustrated:

> Even though they refuse to admit it publicly, *priístas* who are partisans of renovation feel frustrated by the decision to ratify Sansores Pérez as PRI president: they know that their party will remain in the rear guard of social change
> . . . with the ratification of Sansores, those who prevail are the unmoveables (*inmovilistas*). Thus, the happy ones are the Fidel Velázquez', the Enrique Cárdenas Gonzáles', the Manuel Bernardo Aguirres', the Joaquín Gamboa Pascoes', and all those who oppose change within or outside the government.[43]

Even so, Sansores sponsored internal party reforms that came to be labelled "transparent democracy" (*democracia transparente*), which appear similar in some respects to Madrazo's program, and which will reappear in 1984–1985 in a later iteration as "consultation with the militant base" (*consulta a la base militante*).

Party statutes (e.g., Article 142, 1983; Article 148, 1984) call for internal nomination processes to be congruent with the varying levels of political, social, and economic development of the various regions of the country. Thus, the particular nominating mechanism (*auscultación*, party assemblies, primary elections) for the varieties of elections in each state is left to the decision of the party president, who generally consults with the party delegate, the state governor (invariably a *priísta*) and other political notables.

Transparent democracy, thus, was more a style of nomination than a rigid statute.

In a July 1977 press conference, Sansores characterized the policy as a flexible process being implemented gradually, in which nominations for local-level offices were chosen by secret ballot in party assemblies. As to the success of the nominees in the general elections, he claimed that some 20,600 municipal posts had gone up for election by that time, and—with the exceptions of Puebla and Oaxaca—the PRI had won them all. Counting the three additional states that would hold elections by the end of the year, general elections would be held in 1,489 municipalities. Furthermore, he believed that the new nominating process worked to fortify internal democracy and to lessen voter abstention in the general elections.[44]

How much of these claims should be accepted is questionable. We lack a serious study of the effort.[45] It was also clear in the reporters' questions, though, that tensions were apparent between Sansores and Reyes Heroles. The press had been carrying attacks on Sansores and raising doubts about his continuing as party president. The association-by-question of Sansores with Carlos Hank González, the popular mayor of the Federal District and contender (though constitutionally ineligible) for the presidential succession, must have been damaging as well.[46]

Whatever the case, Sansores and transparent democracy disappeared from the scene in February 1979 with the selection of Gustavo Carvajal Moreno, López Portillo's own man, to head the PRI. With midterm elections only five months ahead and the second half of the sexenio thereafter, Carvajal— and his two successors—needed to emphasize stability and control. Internal party reform would have to await a new sexenio.

Moral Renovation and Consultation with the Grassroots

Miguel de la Madrid inherited even a worse economic crisis and a more debilitated political system than did José López Portillo. The bank nation-alization of 1 September 1982 jolted many, but the measure won the outgoing president considerable short-term popular support. The currency controls which froze dollar accounts, however, sent shock waves throughout the middle and upper classes. The old rules of the game had been shattered. López Portillo lashed out against disloyal business interests that had enjoyed enormous profits for many years; some businessmen replied that the pres-idential system no longer worked and that the time had come to impose checks on presidential power. As with López Portillo, we might consider the explicit and tacit strategies attempted by the new government.

The explicit strategy, President de la Madrid's complicated "seven theses" of government might be reduced to two imperatives: economic recovery ("new economic realism") and combating corruption ("moral renovation of society"). The tacit program involved working toward international trade and investment liberalization, moving away from confrontation with the United States on the Central American issue, and maintaining the party base while controlling organized labor. There was no apparent calendar for this. The changes would require the whole term, and the government might be considered successful if it set the direction and managed a smooth succession in 1987–1988.

Both economic realism and moral renovation act to undermine the existing party-government system. This is because trade and investment liberalization threatens many of the less efficient industries and associated labor unions that prospered during the long period of import-substitution industrialization. Opposition to Mexico's entry into the GATT is therefore most pronounced in the CTM and the CANACINTRA. Too, greater efficiency will require changes in the public sector (including elimination of some agencies and substantial job lay-offs). Thus, the material benefits that create incentives for loyalty will be reduced.[47] Subsidies to the middle and lower classes, such as public education and nutrition programs, will have to be cut back or eliminated. To the extent such policies might foment the private sector, they would promote centers of power outside the government and beyond Mexico City. Such new centers might in turn be attracted to the opposition PAN. Foreign investment and "economic realism" antagonize the nationalist Left, which exercise influence less through numbers than through their ability to legitimate the present order. Moral renovation of society would imply eliminating the forms of corruption that are essential to maintain control over groups, as in the labor unions.

As subsequently implemented, economic realism has fared somewhat better than moral renovation. Though with many delays and detours, the government announced in November 1985 the initiation of negotiations for Mexico's accession to the GATT. Even so, the campaign to win back the confidence of investors has fallen short, and capital flight remains a serious problem. The effort to reduce corruption in the public administration may have produced some improvements in the middle levels, but it has failed to impress a skeptical public opinion.

The banner of moral renovation was carried into the electoral arena as well, where it met with further setbacks. The 1982 presidential elections produced the desired result for the PRI: a plausible claim that it still represented the majority.[48] But the state and local elections of 1983 produced some surprising setbacks: the opposition won seven major cities, including five state capitals. Particularly striking was the PAN's apparent strength in the North, where it won the capital cities of Sonora, Durango, and Chihuahua, and in the central states of Guanajuato and San Luis Potosí. Not until Baja California Norte in September of 1983 did the PRI halt the opposition. There, amid the typical claims and counterclaims of fraud, the PRI held the state governorship, thus preserving intact its monopoly of governorships since 1929.

In the sexennial election calendar, 1984 was a relatively quiet year with no governorship up for election. But in 1985, the President and Secretary of Interior repeatedly invoked the symbol of moral renovation in the context of assuring the opposition that the July elections of seven state governors and 400 national deputies would be clean. But the official fraud perpetrated against the PAN in Sonora and Nuevo León (and to some extent in Chihuahua and Baja California Norte) was of a scale and style of the 1940s, and the fragile credibility of moral renovation suffered further, especially in the eyes of foreign observers.

Of the various explanations offered to account for the apparently deliberate fraud in the North, the most convincing is the need to choose the lesser evil. President de la Madrid possibly concluded at some point in 1983 that honest elections would produce serious setbacks for the PRI, that such would create even more insecurity in an already difficult situation, and that the party needed to maintain the support of its labor constituency, the CTM, and of its local party bosses. This especially was the case if the government were committed both to austerity and economic opening on the one hand and to a more accommodative posture toward the United States on the other. Political reform was thus the victim of political necessity.[49] Also important to the retreat from party system and electoral reform is the President's strained relations with the PRI.

The selection of Miguel de la Madrid in September 1981 as the PRI's presidential candidate provoked tensions not seen since at least 1952. The PRI president, Javier García Peniagua, openly indicated his irritation with the selection; and Fidel Velázquez conditioned labor's support on the candidate's agreement to a series of demands. During the campaign, rumors abounded of tensions between party regulars under PRI president Pedro Ojeda Paullada and the candidate's own team. Throughout 1983 the new administration dealt harshly with the CTM, occasionally supporting a rival block, the Revolutionary Confederation of Mexican Workers and Peasants (CROC). Tensions persisted into 1984 and complicated the timing and agenda of the PRI's XII Ordinary Party Assembly.

Under PRI statutes, the party assembly is the maximum organ, even though in real terms the CEN dominates virtually all other organs. An assembly is to be called at least once every six years, or more frequently if the National Council deems it necessary. The first assembly convened under a new administration is especially important because personnel changes are ratified and ideological and programmatic directions are announced. The XII Ordinary Assembly was postponed until August 1984 reinforcing rumors of discord and the possibility of dramatic changes. One rumor had it that the sectors would be eliminated and the party renamed. In the event, the assembly produced no dramatic change, but did reassert—among several planks—a commitment to revitalize direct participation of party militants in the nominations process.

What came to be called "direct consultation with the militant base" originated in July 1983 from problems with a specific city: Salina Cruz, Oaxaca. There, several factions struggled to control nominations to municipal posts. The recommendation of the PRI's Director of Assemblies, Maximiliano Silerio Esparza, was to attempt a direct vote of party members, which produced an acceptable candidate. Another experiment was conducted in

May 1984 in the state of Nayarit. This state was significant because the governor, Emilio M. González Parra, is of the labor sector. The results were sufficiently encouraging that the idea was adopted by the XII Party Assembly. The cumbersome name eventually given the process was to distinguish it from previous reform efforts, such as those of Madrazo (internal elections) and Sansores Pérez (transparent democracy).

Though with some experimentation and flexibility in application, the basic process of direct consultation involves six steps: (1) convocation of municipal party members (including sectors and sections) to explain procedures; (2) circulation of petitions by those seeking nomination to office; (3) study of the petitions by the national PRI's Coordinator of Assemblies to ascertain that the pre-candidates fulfill legal and party qualifications; (4) random assignment of candidates (name and photograph) on ballots; (5) establishing voting tables at the sectional level, each with representatives of the three sectors, the pre-candidates, and CEN; (6) collection and tabulation of the vote, with appeals processes stipulated.[50]

The principal formal requisite for the implementation of direct consultation is that the CEN's Secretary of Organization certify that the municipality's sectional committees have been restructured, that the party rolls are complete, and that credentials—which are required for the vote—have been issued to party members. Table 4.1 shows the record of implementing the direct consultation in local elections after Nayarit.

Direct consultations confront the many vested interests at the local level. Though with variations, municipal governments are frequently controlled by cliques or families, party sectors, labor unions, business interests, or some combination of these. Furthermore, the state governors seek to control *at a minimum* the capital city as well as their own particular power bases in the state. Gubernatorial ambitions often exceed the minimum.

The diversity of the various states complicates the analysis, but two hypotheses might be suggested to explain the pattern of direct consultations: gubernatorial style and opposition strength. Despite the notion of presidential omnipotence, the state governors enjoy considerable autonomy on political matters. The Secretary of Interior and party president are reluctant to impose policies; and governors retain power as long as they contain problems within state boundaries.[51] Thus, the governor's decision on consultations is paramount. Where opposition party strength is considerable, direct consultation *might* weaken the PRI in the general elections. (However, one can conceive of situations in which consultations might strengthen the PRI.)

Keeping in mind that the analysis is highly subjective, Table 4.2 shows how these considerations might group the states.[52] Box 6 is that happy situation in which governors support the reform and face debile opposition. Even here we have governors retaining control over the capital city (e.g., Yucatán) or trying to cope with entrenched fiefdoms (e.g., Hidalgo). Box 1 represents the other extreme: skeptical governors, whose opponents exercise appreciable power. Lack of space prohibits an analysis of each state, but two "limiting" cases, Tabasco and Nuevo León, reveal conditions that facilitate or limit reform.

In the oil-rich Gulf state of Tabasco, the PRI received on average over 86% of the congressional vote during 1970–1982. Governor Enrique González Pedrero is considered a progressive and holds ambitions to someday become PRI president. The consultations for the state's 17 municipalities of 10 September 1985 produced surprises: four of the candidates supported by the governor were defeated. Interestingly, the outgoing mayors exercised influence in the selections, which led some to speculate that if the reform continued, the mayors might become the key actors at the municipal level. "Normal" politics seemed to hold in other cases. A candidate in Cárdenas was able to use the governor's endorsement to deter opponents, and in Paraíso the local section of the Oil Workers Union used money and PEMEX vehicles to bring workers in from other areas to secure the nomination of its candidate. In the state capital of Villahermosa a former congressman faced no opposition after PRI members learned he had the support of Interior Secretary, Manuel Bartlett Díaz.[53]

Nuevo León presents stark contrasts. There, the PRI won an average of 71% of the congressional vote during 1970–1982, but opposition has increased in recent years. The gubernatorial elections of 7 July 1985 produced strong protests and minor violence due to the PAN's claim that the PRI had resorted to extraordinary levels of fraud. Outgoing governor Alfonso Martínez Domínguez is a leading figure of the "old school" of the PRI and is thought to seek a leadership role in strengthening the hand of the *político* faction of the party. The PRI's candidate for mayor of Monterrey, Luis M. Farías, is a party veteran cut from the same cloth as the outgoing governor. In a surprisingly low turnout in the October municipal elections, Farías won easily, but amid strenuous protests about official fraud.

In a year-end speech, PRI president Adolfo Lugo Verduzco summed up the party's policy on direct consultations: the commitment to the process remains firm; consultations will be attempted flexibly, according to the specific conditions in each state; the indispensable conditions are unity and internal discipline; the process will proceed gradually with political realism; and "despite the great deal that has been accomplished in deepening democratic life in the heart of the party, that—due to the survival of local fiefdoms (*cacicazgos*)—we encounter obstacles and resistance."[54]

Party officials stress the success of the direct consultations in producing candidates that in turn can win in general elections. A recurring problem, though, is that the consultations appear in some cases to divide the party internally and to reduce voter turnout in the general elections. Losers in the consultations may not give full support to the willing candidate, and there have been cases of losers defecting to opposition parties. In a way similar to the Democratic party in the Old South of the United States, the important decisions are taken in the primary with the general election held merely as ratification. This puts the PRI in jeopardy in cases where an opposition party has strength, and one finds repeated exhortations to *priístas* to turn out and vote.[55]

What Future for Party Reform?

The easiest conclusion about party reform is skepticism. Certainly, the complaint by a disgruntled PRI official in San Luis Potosí makes one leery: ". . . we can't show our faces. No one believes us. Everybody listens to us with a smirk (*sonrisa burlona*). One wants to convince the people—the way I was—that there is a different, democratic attitude, but one ends up thinking they were right: the PRI doesn't evolve, it's always the same."[56]

More interesting, however, is to make the cases both for and against party reform and then consider the likelihood of each. Affecting both cases is the fact of the second half of the *sexenio* in which there likely will be some circulation of people among posts, including perhaps the PRI presidency. Also, the attitude of the party's presidential candidate, who will emerge in the last quarter of 1987, will affect party policy.

In support for party reform is that President de la Madrid needs a political banner in the face of almost universal skepticism about moral renovation and widespread criticism of the governor's inept response to the earthquake of September 1985. The continuing hardline rejection of the PAN works against another effort toward party system reform. Also, the consultations process is limited to the municipal level and is implemented flexibly. Over time, as perhaps the Tabasco example suggests, support for continuing the consultations might acquire a certain momentum. Conceivably, some set of circumstances might reduce labor opposition, either a passing of the present leadership or a tradeoff in some other area.

Arguing against reform is the conventional wisdom that the party returns to its foundations during the second half of the *sexenio*. Fifteen states hold gubernatorial and/or local elections in 1986, including cases in which the opposition counts (Chihuahua, Baja California Norte, Durango, Sinaloa, Tamaulipas) or which have especially conflictive histories (Guerrero, Oaxaca, Puebla, Veracruz). One searches the list in vain for a case hospitable to consultations. Even in terms of limited personnel resources, the party would be hard-pressed to implement consultations in most cases. Furthermore, the government has committed itself to renew the austerity program, which can only mean more difficult relations with labor. Complicating matters further is the November 1985 decision to initiate talks to enter the GATT.

Thus, some skepticism seems warranted indeed. But that skepticism should be tempered with the knowledge that significant reform currents remain alive within the party and that the rhythm of Mexican politics will provide opportunities for a renewal of the effort.

Notes

1. I want to acknowledge my gratitude to the U.S. Department of Education for a Fulbright-Hays Faculty Study Abroad grant that supported my research in Mexico from January to June 1985, to the Colegio de Mexico's Center for International Studies, which hosted me during that time, and to Georgetown University for additional financial support. In addition to the editor, Bruce Bagley, Jorge G. Castaneda,

and Gabriel Székely provided helpful comments. The usual disclaimers of responsibility hold. Unless otherwise noted, the translations herein are done by me.

2. PRI, *Documentos básicos* (México: Talleres Gráficos de la Nación, 1984), 63.

3. PRI, *Documentos básicos*, 76.

4. Gustavo Díaz Ordaz, quoted in Instituto de Capacitación Política (PRI), *Historia documental del Partido de la Revolución PRI, 1963-1968* (México: Offset Altamira, S.A., 1984), vol. 8, 16.

5. Miguel de la Madrid, *Ideología y partido* (México: PRI, 1984), 106-107.

6. The subordination of formal to substantive democracy is frequently encountered in varieties of Latin American populism. See Guillermo O'Donnell, "Tensions in the Bureaucratic Authoritarian State and the Question of Democracy," in David Collier, ed., *The New Authoritarianism in Latin America* (Princeton, NJ: Princeton University Press, 1979), 288-291.

7. See Ann L. Craig and Wayne A. Cornelius, "Political Culture in Mexico: Continuities and Revisionist Interpretations," in Gabriel Almond and Sidney Verba, eds., *The Civic Culture Revisited: An Analytic Study* (Boston, MA: Little, Brown & Co., 1980), 365; Soledad Loaeza, "El llamado de las urnas: para qué sirven las elecciones en México?" *Nexos*, 90 (June 1985): 13-19; and L. Vincent Padgett, *The Mexican Political System*, 2nd ed. (Boston, MA: Houghton-Mifflin, 1976), 115.

8. Secretaría de Divulgación Ideológica (PRI), *Textos revolucionarios* (Mexico: 1985), vol. 25, 51.

9. See the discussion in Craig and Cornelius, "Political Culture in Mexico."

10. Craig and Cornelius, "Political Culture in Mexico," 363-371.

11. Students have long noted the importance of foreign policy as a factor in domestic politics. The failure of Mexico's effort to assume the status of a regional power and of the Contadora process subsequently further complicates internal politics. See Jorge G. Castaneda, "Don't Corner Mexico," *Foreign Policy*, 60 (Fall 1985):75-90; and Bruce Bagley, "Mexican Foreign Policy: The Decline of a Regional Power?" *Current History* (December 1983): 406-409, 437.

12. The drama involved such allegations as the PAN's accepting support from the U.S. Republican party and the U.S. ambassador's meddling in domestic politics, most notably in his mother's home state of Sonora.

13. Pablo González Casanova, *El estado y los partidos políticos en México* (México: Ediciones Era, 1982), 62.

14. This is hardly a completely fair statement, because some scholars in this school do an excellent job of linking broader context to specific institutions and behavior. The tendency, however, is to dismiss "mere politics" as epiphenomenal and inconsequential.

15. The point is more subtle than my comment. Both academic and journalistic criticism has long been tolerated but within understood limits and in an esoteric, almost aesopian language. This is changing, too, since Daniel Cosío Villegas, *El estilo personal de gobernar* (México: Cuadernos de Joaquín Mortiz, 1975) opened new possibilities of scholarly criticism. See, e.g., Gómez Tagle's chapter in this volume.

16. On historical background, see Arnaldo Córdova, *La formación del poder político en México* 8th ed. (México: Editorial Era, 1980); Robert K. Furtak, *El partido de la revolución y la estabilidad política en México* (México: UNAM, 1974); Luís Javier Garrido, *El partido de la revolución institucionalizada: la formación del nuevo estado en México (1928-1945)* (México: Siglo XXI, 1982); Gloria Leff, "El partido de la revolución: aparato de hegemonía del estado mexicano," in Jorge Alonso, coord., *El estado mexicano* (México: Editorial Nueva Imagen, 1981); and Robert

Scott, *Mexican Government in Transition* (Urbana, IL: University of Illinois Press, 1964). More current analyses include Evelyn Stevens, "Mexico's PRI: The Institutionalization of Corporatism?" in James M. Malloy, ed., *Authoritarianism and Corporatism in Latin America* (Pittsburgh, PA: University of Pittsburgh Press, 1977), 227-258; Robert Scott, "Necesidad de actualizar el sistema político mexicano," in PRI, *Perspectivas del sistema político mexicano* (México: Editorial Madero, 1982), 49-52; Soledad Loaeza, "Comentario," in *Perspectives del sistema político mexicano*, 57-59; and Jacqueline Peschard, "Los escenarios del PRI in 1985," *Revista Mexicana de Ciencias Políticas y Sociales*, 31: 120 (nueva epoca) (April-June, 1985): 49-64. I interviewed PRI and opposition party activists in the Federal District, Morelos, San Luis Potosí, Tabasco, Nuevo León, and Sonora during January to May and November 1985.

17. The party deputy reform granted minority parties seats in the National Chamber of Deputies based on a formula of 5 seats each to parties winning at least 2.5% of the total national vote plus an additional seat for each .5% of the vote, up to a maximum of 20 seats.

18. David Ronfeldt, "The Modern Mexican Military: Implications for Mexico's Stability and Security" (Santa Monica, CA: RAND Corporation, A Rand Note, N-2288-FF/RC, February 1985) provides a recent assessment of the army in politics. Some would interpret the government's decision to minimize the army's role after the 19 September 1985 earthquake as reflecting concern about granting additional power and visibility to the armed forces in the midst of a difficult political situation. Others argue that the problem concerned how to invoke and then remove the legal mechanisms of emergency power.

19. Daniel Levy, "What Are the Political Consequences of Changes in Elite-Mass Socialization?" in *Mexican Trends: The Next Five Years* (papers presented at a conference held at the Department of State, Washington, D.C., December 12, 1985), 85-114, comments on recent trends in Mexican media.

20. Arnaldo Córdova, "El desafío de la izquierda mexicana," *Nexos*, 18 (June 1970): 3-15.

21. Gabriel Zaid, "Escenarios sobre el fin del PRI," *Vuelta*, 103 (June 1985): 16, sums the point up by noting that in Mexico, unlike countries with freely elected legislatures, public spending creates rather than responds to votes. Satellite parties, the Partido Popular Socialista, Partido Socialista de los Trabajadores, and the Partido Auténtico de la Revolución Mexicana, typically support the PRI on broad ideological issues and have generally endorsed the party's presidential candidate.

22. With about 23 members at present, the CEN is the most significant decision body of the party, with the resources to manage other organs (the Council, party assembly) as well as state and local organizations.

23. The Interior Ministry (Gobernación) is the key political agency, which during the heyday of the *políticos* (c. 1940-1970), served as the main pathway to the presidency. Though it varies with personalities, the Interior Minister is generally seen to "outrank" the party president. As one might imagine, complicated and ambitious agendas are brought to the negotiations on nominations to offices.

24. Scott, "Necesidad de actualizar el sistema político mexicano."

25. One should note, however, the significance of the Left in some areas of the South—for example, Juchitán, Oaxaca.

26. Martin C. Needler, *Politics and Society in Mexico* (Albuquerque, NM: University of New Mexico Press, 1971), 27.

27. In popular lore, *tabasquenos* are noted for frankness and spontaneity. Some find it convenient to dismiss Madrazo's failure as inevitable given his outspoken and impulsive character.

28. Roderic Ai Camp, *Mexican Political Biographies, 1935–1981* (Tucson: University of Arizona Press, 1982), 182–183; interview material.

29. PRI/ICAP, *Historia documental del Partido de la Revolución PRI, 1963–1968*, 418–419.

30. PRI, *Historia documental del Partido*, 419.

31. Much of the following discussion draws on Thomas J. Bossert, "Carlos A. Madrazo: The Study of a Democratic Experiment in Mexico" (senior thesis, Department of History and the Woodrow Wilson School of Public and International Affairs, Princeton University, 1968), 21–31 and *passim*. The idea of the free municipality has roots both in the Spanish colonial and modern liberal traditions. Establishing a municipality gave Cortez the legal basis for continuing the conquest, and the municipality figured in the liberal emphasis on federalism. Madrazo emphasized it as a strategy to combat hypercentralization and the loss of what he valued in Mexican vitality.

32. The CEN of the PRI employs several types of delegates to carry out party policy. A general delegate is assigned to each state on a continuing basis. In addition, the party sectors may assign delegates to oversee activities in their organizations. Finally, the CEN may assign special delegates to attend to specific problems on an *ad hoc* basis. In addition, the state party usually assigns delegates to particular municiplities. Designation as a CEN delegate carries status, since it is the party's recognition of ability and prestige. A primary assignment for the delegate involves consulting the party sectors and a variety of interests (sometimes including opposition parties) in recommending PRI nominees for elections. Called *auscultación* (roughly how the doctor listens with a stethoscope) this function is essential to the successful working of a centralized party. For many, the "union card" as a *político* as opposed to a *técnico* is successful service as a delegate. The job offers many possibilities for failure, since the delegate is frequently subjected to conflicting pressures from the various "pre-candidates" and their patrons. In this case, sensitive to the sectors' apprehensions, Madrazo assigned to each state a general delegate as well as delegates from each of the sectors.

33. Bossert, "Carlos A. Madrazo," 51–54.

34. Bossert, "Carlos A. Madrazo," 60–62.

35. Bossert, "Carlos A. Madrazo," 75–76.

36. Bossert, "Carlos A. Madrazo," 100.

37. Translated by Bossert, "Carlos A. Madrazo," 66. By way of epilogue, Madrazo hovered at the edge of party activity during 1966–1969, toying at times with the idea of forming an independent party. He died in an airplane accident at Monterrey, Nuevo León, in September 1969.

38. Padgett, *Mexican Political System*, 88.

39. But here the removal of Ricardo García Sáinz, formerly the head of a business chamber, might have sounded faint alarms in some quarters of the private sector.

40. The discussion draws on Kevin Middlebrook, "Political Change and Political Reform in an Authoritarian Regime: The Case of Mexico" (prepared for delivery at the conference on "Prospects for Democracy: Transitions from Authoritarian Rule," sponsored by the Latin American Program of the Woodrow Wilson International Center for Scholars, October 1982); and Octavio Rodríguez Araujo, *La reforma política y los partidos en México* (México: Ediciones Era, 1982).

41. Rafael Segovia, "La reforma política: el ejecutivo federal, el PRI y las elecciones de 1973," in Centro de Estudios Internacionales, *La vida política en México (1970–1973)* (México: El Colegio de México, 1974), 57.

42. Camp, *Mexican Political Biographies*, 281–282.

43. Elias Chávez, "Acatamiento en público, cuestionamiento en privada," *Proceso*, 86, 26 July 1978, reprinted in Elias Chávez, et al., *50 anos de PRI* (México: Editorial Posada, 1980), 262–271.

44. PRI, *Historia documental del Partido*, vol. 10, 301–307.

45. Certainly Fidel Velázquez' joke to the effect that transparent democracy is so transparent that no one can see it plants a seed or two of doubt.

46. PRI, *Historia documental del Partido*, vol. 10, 308–313.

47. The elimination of some 30,000 administrative positions in July 1985 must have sent shock waves throughout the system, whose strength had derived in good part from constant expansion.

48. De la Madrid won roughly 75% of the vote of a nearly 75% turnout of those registered. *Reform política, gaceta informativa de la Comisión Federal Electoral, Tomo IX, Acuerdos, indicadores de opinión pública y estadistica electoral* (México, D.F., 1982), 128–129.

49. This is the position argued in Delal Baer and John Bailey, "Mexico's 1985 Midterm Elections: A Preliminary Assessment," *LASA Forum* (Fall 1985), 7–8.

50. Information on the direct consultations is based on interview material as well as Comisión Coordinadora de Convenciones (PRI), "Consulta directa a la base militante" (Secretaría de Divulgación, 1985); and PRI, "Proceso interno de consulta a la base militante" (mimeo, 1985).

51. Under President de la Madrid "only" four governors had been removed by the end of 1985 (Yucatán, Guanajuato, Coahuila, and Chihuahua). Removing a governor may antagonize state residents, who typically prefer some latitude in managing their own affairs. The case of Guanajuato is especially interesting.

52. Two states present special circumstances and ought to be excluded. Veracruz has long suffered a history of disorder, and the situation has apparently worsened over the past few years. Chiapas has at times resembled a military zone, given the tensions on the border with Guatemala.

53. This account draws on an article from *Excelsior*, 11 September 1985, "States" section, p. 4, translated in JPRS-LAM—85-092, 86–88.

54. Adolfo Lugo Verduzco, "Intervención del presidente del Comité Ejecutivo Nacional del Partido Revolucionario Institucional, en la sesión del Consejo Nacional Extraordinario correspondiente a 1985" (Mexico, 10 December, mimeo), 12.

55. Adolfo Lugo Verduzco, "Intervención"; also, Rodolfo Echeverría Ruíz, "Los adversarios, situados a la derecha," conferencia nacional de análisis ideológico sobre la Revolución mexicana 1910–1985, 7–8 August (supplement to *Excelsior*, 18 August 1985).

56. Quoted in Elias Chávez, "En el PRI la lealted se entiende como servilismo," *Proceso*, 480, 12 January 1986, 12. One ought perhaps to note that San Luis Potosí was going through difficult times as the center worked both to break the grip of a powerful *cacique*, in this case the leader of the Vanguardia faction of the SNTE, and also to overcome recent local inroads by the PAN.

FIGURE 4.1 Alternative Routes for Political Change in Mexico, 1963-85

Reform Route	Significant Events						
System Reform							
PRI	1965 Madrazo "internal elections"				1978-79 Sansores Pérez "transparent democ."	1983-86 "Consultations with the grassroots"	
Party system	1963 "Party Deputy reform"	1970 Voting Age Lowered	1973 Expanded "Party Deputy"	1977 "LOPPE"	"Moral Renovation"		
"Bureaucracy"	"Stabilizing Development," 1955-71	1971 "Shared Development"	1976, Economic Collapse	1979-81 Full Growth	1982 Collapse	1983-86 Austerity	
Anti-System Behavior							
Violence	1958 teachers' and railroad workers' strike	1968 Student Movement	1971 "Corpus Cristi"	(sporadic protest & violence)			
Apathy							
Presidencies	Adolfo López Mateos, 1958-64	Gustavo Díaz Ordáz 1964-70	Luis Echeverría, 1970-76	José López Portillo, 1976-82	Miguel de la Madrid, 1982-88		

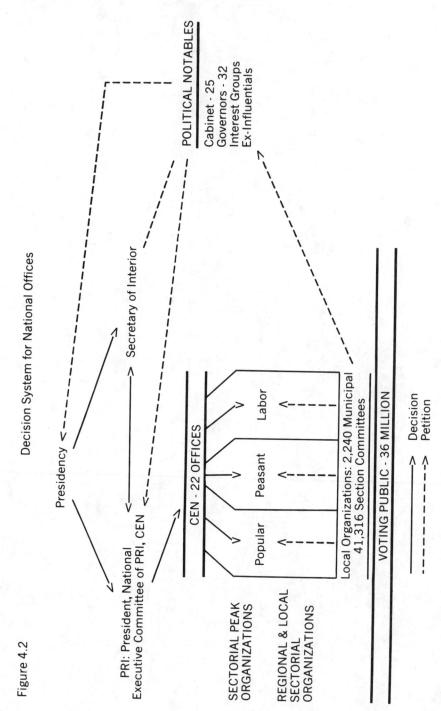

Figure 4.2

Decision System for National Offices

TABLE 4.1
Mexico 1984-85: PRI's Implementation of "Direct Consultations"
in Choosing Municipal Candidates

State	Date of General Elections	Number of Municipalities	Number of Consultations
Nayarit	May 1984	19	12
Yucatán	November 1984	106	104
México	November 1984	122	11
Coahuila	November 1984	34	12
Hidalgo	December 1984	84	33
Morelos	March 1985	33	0
Querétaro	July 1985	18	0
Sonora	July 1985	69	39
Vera Cruz	October 1985	203	57
Tlaxcala	October 1985	44	39
Nuevo León	October 1985	51	0
Tabasco	November 1985	17	17
Colima	November 1985	10	10
Chiapas	November 1985	111	0
Campeche	November 1985	8	7
Guanajuato	December 1985	46	0
Jalisco	December 1985	124	10
Zacatecas	December 1985	56	55
San Luis Potosí	December 1985	56	55

Source: Interview material, CEN/PRI, November 1985, Mexico
City.

TABLE 4.2
Factors Affecting Successful Implementation of PRI Consultations With the Grassroots
Governors' Support for Consultations

		Weak	Strong
Opposition strength	General	(1) Nuevo León Jalisco	(2) Coahuila Sonora
	Limited to capital or very few muni- cipalities	(3) México Guanajuato	(4) San Luis Potosí Yucatán
	Low	(5) Morelos Querétero	(6) Nayarit Tabasco Colima Campeche Hidalgo Tlaxcala Zacatecas

PART THREE

Recent Performance in the Political System

5

Changing Patterns of Electoral Participation and Official Party Support in Mexico[1]

Joseph L. Klesner

Introduction

A critical component in the interpretation of the current Mexican regime is the role played by the electoral system.[2] Mexico holds elections at regular intervals for executive and legislative positions at all three levels of government: national, state, and local (*municipio*). In these elections political parties from a broad ideological spectrum present candidates. At least two parties have competed for most electoral positions for over thirty years. However, the Partido Revolucionario Institucional (PRI) has won nearly every election held since 1929, including every presidential and every gubernatorial race, and all but one senatorial contest. Thus, Mexico has the constitutional and institutional appearance of a multiparty democracy, yet its electoral positions, including the nearly all-powerful presidency,[3] are in fact monopolized by one party.

This may lead an observer to conclude that elections in Mexico are meaningless since the PRI always wins the elections that count and that thus Mexico is a one-party state.[4] However, I will argue that elections are *not* meaningless in Mexico. Further, I will suggest that the single-party nature of the Mexican regime is passing. At the same time, though, I will argue that the PRI is far from dead, perhaps is even far from losing its hegemony, as the elections of 1985 have shown.

Those in the opposition within Mexico have been very divided about how to intepret the electoral process. Whether or not to actually participate in elections which one is likely to lose while at the same time legitimating the rule of the PRI is a question which has created divisions within both the left and the right and forced opposition groups to think hard about their strategy of opposition. This debate came to a head especially after José López Portillo's electoral reform initiative in 1977.[5] The opposition, both left and right, seems to have arrived at a position similar to that

95

expressed by Pablo González Casanova: "The political reform (and the political struggle) is not 'just a trap of the bourgeoisie' as some groups of the left fear; it is also the possibility of opening a field of ideological and revolutionary struggle, intending to broaden and consolidate the political space of workers, the middle classes, and the country."[6]

Theoretically and comparatively, the role that these traditionally democratic institutions, elections and a (at least formally) multiparty system, have played and now play in maintaining in power what has been described by many as an authoritarian regime should be explored. The theoretical discussion of the role of parties and party systems in authoritarian regimes is not very extensive and reaches ambivalent conclusions.[7] Yet that the Mexican regime, a regime with parties and elections, is authoritarian is a frequent conclusion of scholars.

The two major aspects of an authoritarian regime, or any regime, are decision-making and political participation. The decision-making dimension of a regime refers both to how public policy decisions are made and to what the content of those policies is. In authoritarian regimes, public policy decisions are made without the direct (and perhaps not even the indirect) input of the various social groups that make up the society. Frequently, and depending upon the political and ideological orientations of those making the decisions within such a regime, the output of this restricted decision-making process affects different social groups in highly unequal ways.

Given these restrictions on decision-making and the often inequitable results of its policies, the appearance of control over political participation in an authoritarian regime can be understood as the response by those who control the state which most effectively protects them from challenges. This control can take two forms: exclusion or incorporation.[8] If those who control the state fear that extensive participation will challenge the existing order, control of participation will take the form of exclusion, especially through suppression. Exclusion is usually the form of control seen in regimes in which the regime's major effects are detrimental to the majority of the population, the popular classes and perhaps parts of the middle classes. On the other hand, if the elite controlling the state fears other strategic elites as much as it does the lower classes, participation is more likely to be used by those controlling the state against their opponents within the elite. This form of participation is an incorporating, channelling method of control. In this situation, those in command of the state use displays of participation to assure themselves that they can control the masses for their own purposes and to indicate to their actual or potential opponents that they could direct these masses against them. Mexico's authoritarian regime as it has developed since the Revolution is an example of this latter use of participation. In this respect, the electoral system is a key component of the Mexican political regime.

Those controlling the Mexican state originally mobilized the masses for armed movements against their opponents within the "Revolutionary Family."

Presidents Obregón, Calles, and Cárdenas all used this strategy against dissident revolutionary generals and *caudillos*.[9] The mobilized masses were also used to oppose counterrevolutionary movements[10] and pressures from foreign capital.[11] Eventually this incorporation came within the institutional control of the official party of the Revolutionary elite, at first called the Partido Nacional Revolucionario (PNR) and later renamed the Partido de la Revolución Mexicana (PRM).

Madero's revolutionary rallying cry of "effective suffrage and no re-election" dictated legitimation by elections in post-revolutionary Mexico. The PNR was initially founded to facilitate Calles's control of the electoral process which the Revolution had made necessary. The incorporated working class and *campesinos* became effective guarantors of electoral success for the candidates of the PNR and later for the PRM, especially to oppose those who rebelled against the hand-picked successors of Calles and Cárdenas.[12]

While the incorporation of unionized labor and the peasantry brought these groups material gain under Cárdenas,[13] under his successors incorporation into the official party (renamed and reorganized as the PRI by Alemán) became exclusion from the benefits of economic progress. The development policies of Presidents Alemán and Ruiz Cortínes created rapid economic growth in Mexico during the late 1940s, 1950s, and into the 1960s. However, this development program was predicated upon the ability of the state to hold down wages and to direct investment funds to the industrial sector. Its distribution policy can be summarized as "trickle down."[14] The channelling of participation through the electoral process then became a method of assuring that the masses were controlled and that discontent with this development policy had not reached an intolerable level. Elections became a trienniel manifestation of the regime's legitimacy and its continued mobilizational power.

Paradoxically, as this development policy succeeded it became apparent that the growing segments of the population fostered by development could not be controlled as effectively as the traditional rural sectors. The growing middle classes could not be incorporated as completely as were the working class and the *campesinos*. Non-unionized labor, especially in the services sector, was not well controlled either, although it manifested less electoral discontent than the middle class. The student unrest of 1968 and guerrilla movements and urban terrorism in the early 1970s indicated that new modes of political expression existed which were explicitly anti-regime in character. In addition, growing abstentionism showed an implicit withdrawal of legitimacy for the regime and thus a lessening ability on the part of the regime to mobilize the masses against its opposition. The channels of participation as control were failing.

To overcome these challenges, the state sponsored a partial political reform in 1977 designed to bring political participation back within the manageable electoral channels but permitting wider expression of political preference through opposition parties. I will present data to show that, since then, even broader expression of opposition to the regime has developed;

that is, control over electoral participation and the basic freedoms of expression have diminished. However, the PRI has mobilized even greater numbers of voters to support the continued rule of the current ruling elite and has shown an ability to still use its old techniques of electoral fraud if necessary to win an important race. Thus, even though the opposition's voice has strengthened, the regime's base has been refortified, at least for now.

The remainder of this chapter is divided into four parts. First, a brief history of changes in electoral rules sets the institutional context. Second, the development of the parties and the ideological spectrum of the party system is presented. Third, the social bases of the PRI and its opposition are analyzed with the use of state-level electoral data. Fourth, trends in participation, especially in the period since the 1977 political reforms, are examined.

Evolution of Electoral Rules

Because electoral participation and party competition are constrained by the existence or absence of legal electoral institutions and legal regulations, the evolution of participation and competition, or their converses, abstention and control, is structured to a great extent by the parallel development of electoral legislation. Without trying to explain this legislation's change over time,[15] this section will trace electoral legislation since the Revolution in order to set the legal context within which the evolution of participation and competition must be explained.[16]

The first post-Revolution electoral law, passed by the Congress in 1918, granted the vote to literate, married males over eighteen years of age and to literate, unmarried males over twenty-one years of age. Political parties could easily be formed[17] but were not permitted to be affiliated with religious denominations. Presidential elections were to be held every four years with no re-election. Deputies were to be elected to the Chamber of Deputies from single-member districts in a winner-take-all system. Until 1946 this system remained essentially unchanged except for the changes proposed by Calles in 1928 to effect the election of the president. These reforms lengthened the president's term of office to six years and allowed re-election, although not immediate re-election, of the president. The latter provision was rescinded after Obregón was assassinated and the PNR was founded.

A new electoral law was enacted in 1946 which made it more difficult for opposition parties to operate legally: any party had to have certified registration of at least 30,000 members, 1,000 or more of them being distributed in at least two-thirds of the federal entities (states and territories) at any time. This law forced the nation's oldest registered party, the Communist party, underground because it could not meet these requirements. The 1946 electoral law also gave the government and the PRI complete control over the electoral process by giving government, therefore PRI, personnel controlling positions in the Comisión Federal Electoral and by giving formal confirmation of both presidential and congressional election results to the two chambers (Chamber of Deputies and Senate) of Congress. The 1946 electoral law therefore contributed to the PRI's hegemony in electoral politics by stifling the opposition's legal opportunities to compete in elections.

Between 1946 and 1977, when the electoral reform proposed by the López Portillo administration was passed, a number of less comprehensive electoral laws were enacted which produced minor changes in the electoral process. One group of these changes concerned the extension of the franchise. In 1954 women were granted the right to vote and in 1970 the franchise was extended to the eighteen-to-twenty age group.

The other major group of changes concerned the representation of opposition parties in the Chamber of Deputies. In 1963, the regime adopted a combined winner-take-all and proportional representation system for the election of deputies (but not senators). Under this system, opposition parties were granted five seats in the Chamber of Deputies if they received at least 2.5 percent of the national vote and up to fifteen additional (twenty in all) deputies, one for each additional 0.5 percent of the national vote. In 1973 the threshhold for representation in the Chamber was lowered from 2.5 to 1.5 percent and the maximum number of seats available to an opposition party under this "party deputy" system was increased to twenty-five. This greatly improved the opposition's opportunities to win seats in the Chamber but also decreased the PRI's need to allow the opposition to win some district elections as a means of indicating the competitiveness of the political and electoral systems.

A significant, comprehensive electoral law was enacted in 1977. The Chamber of Deputies was enlarged from about 200 deputies (the exact number depending upon how many minority party deputies were elected) to 400, 100 of which were reserved for minority parties which won fewer than 60 seats in the 300 winner-take-all single-member district races. In practice to date, this has meant that all of the opposition parties have shared these 100 seats in a proportional representation scheme, the exact formula used being chosen from between the "formula of minimum representivity" (a Hare-Andrae system) and the "formula of first proportionality" (a Hagenbach-Bischoff system), the former favoring larger parties, the latter smaller parties. There may be from two to five proportional representation districts used in any election, the number and composition of each being chosen by the Comisión Federal Electoral.

Barriers to the formation and registration of political parties were lowered by the 1977 law. There are now two methods of achieving legal status as a political party. One method is to apply for conditional registration and thereby participate in national elections. Upon attainment of 1.5 percent of the national vote the party becomes "permanently" registered; failure to reach this threshold in three elections after achieving permanent registration was to lead to loss of registration. In 1982 the latter provision was altered so that failure to reach 1.5 percent of the national vote in one election leads to loss of registration. The second method is to provide the Comisión Federal Electoral with a copy of the statutes and principles of the party plus evidence of at least 65,000 party members distributed in one of two ways: 3,000 or more in one-half plus one of the federal entities or 300 or more in one-half plus one of the federal electoral districts. In addition, the 1977 electoral law granted free radio and television time each month to all legally registered parties. The 1977 law greatly enhanced the abilities of smaller opposition groups to participate in elections and to at least take seats in the Chamber of Deputies.

The Emerging Party System

The Mexican party system has been called an established, one-party system,[18] a hegemonic-pragmatic party system,[19] a competitive single-party system,[20] among many other labels. The dominant party, the PRI, has been likened to a pluralist interest aggregator within the party system[21] and to a political machine along the lines found in cities in the United States.[22] Today Mexico maintains the appearance of a multiparty system which represents the full spectrum of political ideologies from traditionally conservative *sinarquistas* on the right to Trotskyists on the left. However, the PRI remains the hegemonic party in Mexico; even if the party merely functions as the electoral arm of the elite that controls the state, nonetheless most of the top decision-makers in the Mexican state apparatus and three quarters of the members of the Chamber of Deputies belong to the PRI. Yet, it cannot be said that the PRI and the government make their decisions without regard to the expressed opinions of the minority opposition parties. The very decision to expand the party spectrum through the 1977 electoral law, a decision initiated by the López Portillo government through Minister of Gobernación and former president of the PRI, Jesús Reyes Heroles, indicates that the PRI was forced to respond to the legally unrecognized emergence of opposition groups and to the growth of the PAN's electoral strength. The following description of the political parties of contemporary Mexico will, to the extent possible, set them in the political and ideological spectrum of modern Mexico so as to help clarify the electoral analysis to follow.

The Parties

The *Partido Revolucionario Institucional (PRI)*. The PRI has dominated the electoral system of Mexico since its inception as the PNR in 1929. Its candidates allegedly come from one or the other of its three functionally-based components, the *campesinos*, organized labor, and the popular sector.[23] A general consensus among observers is that the popular sector has been more successful in getting its candidates nominated by the PRI than either of the other two sectors.[24] Once the candidates have been chosen, the party begins its massive electoral campaign effort which includes rallies, seminars among professionals (especially lawyers), intellectuals and *políticos*, and extensive coverage in the media. This effort is nearly always successful, although whether there is any direct causal link between the PRI's campaign and its seemingly inevitable victories is unclear.

The PRI is usually considered to occupy the center of the political spectrum. Although its rhetoric is usually revolutionary and often radical, its policies are not. Being the party in power for as long as it has dictates that the PRI fill the political center if for no other reason than that it allows those who are more conservative than it to formulate policy platforms and ideologies that are to the right of those of the PRI and those who are more liberal than it to formulate platforms and ideologies to the left of it. A frequent assertion that the PRI itself has a left, a right, and a center, the left associated with Cárdenas (and later Echeverría), the right with Alemán (and later Díaz Ordaz), and the center with those who have succeeded them and tried to steer a middle course.[25] The PRI's left wing is not considered as far to the left as those radical groups not associated with the PRI and its right wing is not considered as conservative as other traditional groups unassociated with the PRI.[26] If this is correct, then the PRI can in fact be considered to occupy the political and ideological center of Mexican party politics.

The Partido Auténtico de la Revolución Mexicana (PARM). The PARM is sometimes considered to be slightly to the right of the PRI although its ideology is basically the same as that of the PRI. It was founded in 1952 by retired revolutionary generals who considered themselves *carransistas* and who were alienated from the PRI because of the corruption of the Alemán administration.[27] Since then, however, many of its complaints have been remedied, and it has generally supported the presidential candidates and policies of the PRI. It has only given the PRI serious electoral competition in legislative and local races, especially in the state of Tamaulipas, particularly in Nuevo Laredo, where it expresses local discontent with Mexico City. In 1982 it failed to get the minimum 1.5 percent of the vote required to maintain its legal status and thus lost its registration. It regained registration in 1984, allegedly because the PRI and the government wanted another voting member of the Comisión Federal Electoral to support their side.[28]

The Partido Demócrata Mexicano (PDM). The PDM is the most conservative party with registration in Mexico. Its support is based among the followers of the Unión Nacional Sinarquista (the UNS), originally founded in 1937 by conservative Catholics who had been defeated in the Cristero rebellion of 1926 to 1929 but had not been eliminated by any means.[29] *Sinarquista* means, literally, "without anarchy," or "with order" in Spanish; the UNS's ideology has been strongly against anarchism and communism and in support of an "intransigent social Catholicism."[30] Unlike the PAN, which is also a Catholic party, the UNS (and the PDM) has its roots in the countryside, mostly in the areas of the Bajío region (the states of Guanajuato, Jalisco, Querétaro, San Luís Potosí, and Michoacán) where the UNS directed its missionary-type efforts at the landless *campesinos* in the 1930s and 1940s.[31]

The UNS has run candidates for office under many political parties since its founding, including supporting PAN candidates and more recently those of the Partido Nacionalista de México (PNM), a minor party which folded after the 1961 elections.[32] The PDM was founded in 1972 and received registration in 1978 so that the UNS could legally participate in electoral politics. Although the PDM claims to be completely separate from the UNS, the leadership of the PDM is composed of former UNS leaders and there is circulation of individuals between the leaderships of the two organizations. Ideologically, the PDM is critical of both capitalism and Mexico's mixed economy. It is strongly pro-family and pro-church.

The Partido Acción Nacional (PAN). The PAN was founded in 1939 by a group of traditionally Catholic professionals who enlisted the support of some Mexican businessmen who opposed the economic policies of Cárdenas. In Mexico, the PAN has been considered as the major party of the right. It is usually depicted as the party of Mexican business, although during at least the 1950s and 1960s the PAN did not support the policies of big business, as Mabry argues, but rather followed a Christian Democratic line.[33]

The PAN began supporting legislative candidates in 1943 and ran its first presidential candidate in 1952. Since then its electoral strength has grown steadily except for a setback in 1976 which was caused by its own failure to nominate a presidential candidate after a very divisive national convention. The division within the party at that time was expressed in a conflict between those who wished to participate in the electoral arena and those who preferred to abstain, thus removing the mirage of democratic competition.[34] While the lack of agreement at that time led to abstention in 1976, the faction in favor of participation is now dominant. The PAN is without doubt Mexico's strongest opposition party.

Ideologically, the PAN has consistently supported certain abstract political principles: the dignity of the human person, the essential liberties of man, the consideration of the family and the *municipio* as man's principal social units, and the necessity of active participation by all citizens to achieve an authentic democracy.[35] Founded partly to counter trends toward socialistic education introduced by Cárdenas, one of the PAN's most prominent early goals was to broaden educational opportunities at the primary and secondary levels so that Catholic education could take place alongside "state indoc- trination." As this is now an accomplished fact (whether the PAN was at all influential in achieving it is unclear), it has ceased to be a major issue of the PAN.[36] While the PAN flirted with international Christian Democracy in the late 1950s and early 1960s, it abandoned this trend toward overt religious affiliation under PAN presidents Aldolfo Christlieb Ibarrola and Manuel González Hinojosa after 1962. Instead, it became a secular social reformist party to the point of being accused of sharing traditional PRI rhetoric.[37] Yet, analysis of the PAN's platforms reveals that they closely parallel the Catholic reformism called for in the papal encyclicals of Pope John XXIII and Pope Paul VI, a parallel that the PRI's ideological statements cannot claim to share.[38]

Reflecting the growing polarization within Mexican society regarding Mexico's future development path which appeared during Echevarría's term,[39] divisions developed within the PAN also. Under PAN president José Angel Conchello the party became more outspoken concerning specific policies of reform, abandoning its usually more general, reformist pronouncements.[40] This alienated the PAN's more intellectual and philosophical former leaders. In addition, Conchello wished to lead the PAN to the right toward the Manchester liberalism espoused by the Monterrey group.[41] This caused a conflict to develop between the PAN's social reformist element and Conchello's followers over the 1976 nomination for president of Pablo Emilio Madero, Conchello's choice. As Madero was not able to obtain the 80 percent majority necessary for the nomination, the PAN did not present a presidential candidate in 1976. Madero (grandson of the "apostle of the Mexican Revolution," Francisco Madero) became the 1982 candidate of the PAN and the president of the party in 1984, demonstrating that a movement toward the Conchello-Madero position has taken place within the PAN, moving it definitely to the right of the PRI. A number of former leaders of the PAN, including González Hinojosa and Efraín González Morfín, have left the party since 1976 in protest of its rightward movement.

The Partido Popular Socialista (PPS). Radical intellectual and labor organizer Vincente Lombardo Toledano founded the PPS as the Partido Popular in 1947, during the presidential term of relatively conservative and pro-capitalist Miguel Alemán, to provide an electoral option for leftists. Initially supported by alienated unions, Lombardo's labor movement, and leftist intellectuals, the PPS lost its labor support rather quickly.[42] Its intellectual support also deserted it when the PPS moved closer to the PRI (endorsing the PRI presidential candidate since 1958) and as other options become available to intellectuals in the 1960s and 1970s.[43] Many of its followers joined the Communist party after the PCM regained its registration in 1978 while others broke away to form the Partido del Pueblo Mexicano (PPM), which later joined with the PCM to form the Partido Socialista Unificado de México (PSUM).

Ideologically, the PPS is in favor of greater state intervention in the economy and strongly opposes American imperialism.[44] Unlike many other sectors of the Mexican left, however, the PPS does not find it necessary to oppose the regime. Because the PRI is generally anti-imperialist in rhetoric and favors state intervention, the PPS usually allies with the PRI electorally and legislatively, occasionally exhorting the state to take a more radical line on these issues. This alliance has often favored the PPS electorally as the government gives it more legislative seats than it ordinarily would deserve.[45]

The Partido Socialista Unificado de México. The Partido Comunista Mexicano (PCM) was founded in 1919, a decade before the PRI's earliest embodiment, the PNR. After it lost its registration in 1946, the PCM remained underground until 1978, when it received conditional registration. The PCM was traditionally a revolutionary Marxist-Leninist party which followed the dictates of Moscow. However, a number of controversies within the PCM about following orders from Moscow, particularly concerning Stalin's order to assassinate Trotsky, weakened the party. While the PCM had had approximately 30,000 members in 1939, by 1960 membership had dwindled to 1,500. The PCM leadership, especially led by Arnoldo Martínez Verdugo, abandoned its close alignment with Moscow in the 1960s. Since then, the PCM has drifted into a more reformist line, one that looks very much like Eurocommunism, although the party carefully denied that it was Eurocommunist.[46] In the process it has lost the support of some radicals who have broken away to form more radical parties.

The third strongest electoral force in the 1979 elections, the PCM called for a unified leftist front for the 1982 elections, but only succeeded in getting four Marxist-Leninist groups, the PPM (a PPS faction); the Partido Socialista Revolucionario (PSR), which originated in 1974 as a faction within the Partido Socialista de Trabajadores (PST); the Movimiento de Acción y Unidad Socialista (MAUS), a group which had broken from the PCM in the early 1970s; and the small Movimiento de Acción Popular (MAP) to join it as the PSUM.[47] The PSUM was again the third strongest electoral force in both 1982 and 1985. In general, though, its electoral showings have been disappointing, causing the PSUM to be open to offers from other parties of the left for joint electoral efforts and unification. To date, this unification has not taken place. In fact, division within the party has led many to leave it, including Roberto Jaramillo of the PSR and Alejandro Gascón Mercado of the PPM (the latter taking many of his followers with him). Despite their electoral weakness, the PCM and the PSUM, led by Congressional leader Rolando Cordero, have used the forum provided by their inclusion in the Chamber of Deputies to gain public respect as critics of the government and the regime.

The Partido Mexicano de los Trabajadores (PMT). The PMT was founded in 1974 by Heberto Castillo, a leader of the 1968 student uprising, with the help of Demetrio Vallejo, leader of the 1958–59 railroad workers' strikes, other university activists, and old members of the Movimiento de Liberación Nacional (MLN), an opposition movement of the early 1960s. Castillo, Vallejo, and others traversed the country in the early 1970s seeking support for a new opposition party.[48] Some members of the group have since departed to join other parties of the left, including Vallejo, now a member of the PSUM. Castillo's control of the party and his own ego are sometimes attributed to be causes of the party's weaknesses. Efforts by the PCM to bring the PMT into the PSUM in 1981 failed due to differences between Castillo and PSUM leaders over the name, emblem, hymn, and composition of the leadership organ of the new party.[49]

Radical, nationalist, and anti-imperialist, but not strictly Marxist-Leninist, the PMT's ideological positions are not dogmatic, but rather eclectic: Castillo has particularly opposed the state's petroleum development policies. The PMT decided not to participate in elections as it did not trust the regime and did not consider the 1977 electoral reform to be truly democratic. It thus did not apply for conditional registration until 1981. Conditional registration was granted in 1984. This delay in joining the electoral game has probably lost the PMT much of its potential electoral support. It finished eighth out of nine participating parties in the 1985 deputy race.

The *Partido Socialista de Trabajadores.* The PST was founded in 1975 by members of the group affiliated with Heberto Castillo who wished to fill the electoral space of the declining PPS. This meant that they were willing to "seek alliance with democratic and progressive forces in general, including those in the government."[50] In other words, the PST was looking to fill the PPS's space as a collaborator with the PRI. In this effort, it was supported by left-wing *priístas* who wished to protest certain aspects of government policy but could not do so within the PRI and did not want to do so from within an established left-wing group. The PST received registration in 1978. It is a socialist party, but not overtly Marxist-Leninist. Electorally it has been favored by the PRI and the state. In the 1985 elections, for example, CTM members were instructed to vote for the PRI in majority deputy races but then for the PST in the plurinominal deputy races. Consequently, the PST finished fourth, just behind the PSUM, in the plurinominal race and received twelve deputyships, the same number as the PSUM.[51]

The *Partido Revolucionario de los Trabajadores (PRT).* The PRT was founded in 1976 as a union of Trotskyist groups which had been kicking around Mexico since the late 1950s. It is the Mexican section of the Trotskyist Fourth International.[52] Its general policy proposals and strategy do not differ significantly from the other leftist parties.[53] However, it has become an important organization for protesting repression and political imprisonment, especially since its choice for presidential candidate in 1982, Rosa Ibarra de la Piedra, a well-known critic of the government's politics regarding political prisoners, has brought many of her followers to the PRT. The PRT was granted registration by the Comisión Federal Electoral in 1982 after having successfully received the 1.5 percent of the 1982 presidential vote which was necessary for registration. In the 1985 election, the PRT received deputy seats for the first time.

The Party Spectrum

The foregoing suggests that the ideological and political spectrum in Mexico is formed from two issues. The first is religion and state control of education, which caused the right, the PDM and the PAN, to be distinguished as more conservative than the rest of the parties. The second is socioeconomic development policy, which distinguishes the PAN as being somewhat to the right of the PRI, and the leftist parties as being more radical than the PRI. Within this latter group can be distinguished reformist socialists (PMT and PST), Marxist-Leninists (PPS and PSUM), and Trotskyists (PRT). It should further be noted that the PPS, and the PST, and the PARM have cooperated electorally with the PRI in the past. The evolution of the left-to-right arrangement of the electorally relevant parties would look something like Figure 5.1

The Social Bases of Support for and Opposition to the PRI

The Growth of Opposition to the PRI

The traditional strength of the PRI, its monopoly at the electoral polls, is shown in Table 5.1. As this table illustrates, the organized opposition (that is, candidates of other than transitional parties, such as those parties established by mavericks from the PRI) did not push the PRI's national electoral share in presidential elections below 90 percent before 1964 and not below 80 percent until 1982. It is small wonder that scholars observing the Mexican situation in the early 1960s concluded, as did Huntington, that "other parties may exist . . . but they have little effect on the course of events"[54] and thus looked inside the PRI to find political competition in Mexico.[55]

The PRI's share of the vote has been falling ever since the PAN began competing in elections, however. This is even clearer when one observes the party shares in Chamber of Deputies races,[56] shown in Table 5.2. Except for the election of 1976, when the PAN did not present a candidate for president and thus lost support in the legislative races through a coattails effect, the PRI's share of votes in races for Chamber of Deputies has been falling since 1961. The PRI's percentage fell below 70 percent for the first time in 1982.

This deterioration of the PRI's monopoly occurred even earlier and more rapidly in urban areas than in the nation as a whole.[57] Figure 5.2 compares the decline in the vote for the PRI in urban states and in rural states through the 1982 election.[58] The PRI's share of the vote in urban areas has been consistently lower than the national average, and dramatically lower than the average for rural states. The decline in support for the PRI in urban areas has been rapid, especially up to 1979. This decline in support for the PRI in cities is especially critical because of the rate in which the nation as a whole is urbanizing. The PRI is losing its hold on precisely those areas which are growing most rapidly. The potential for the opposition to seize an important source of new electoral support is thus great. While in 1982 the support for the PRI in urban areas actually grew by a small percentage, reflecting efforts by the party to reinvigorate itself in areas where it was weakest, in 1985 the electoral challenge to the PRI was concentrated in the urban areas of northern and western Mexico.

The PAN has been the main beneficiary of this deterioration of the PRI's hegemony, building its percentage of the total vote in deputy elections from 7.6 percent in 1961 to 16.5 percent in 1973 and to 17.5 percent in 1982 after its 1976 collapse (see Table 5.2). In 1985, the PAN's official share of the vote was down from its 1982 share, but the extent of fraud reported in 1985 indicates that the PAN's total probably had increased. In addition, the independent organized left (the PSUM, the PMT, and the PRT), since becoming registered after the 1977 political reform, gained 4.9 percent of the vote in 1979, 5.7 percent in 1982, and 6.0 percent in 1985 (see Table

5.2). The PDM has also taken better than 2 percent of the vote since registering. Despite the appearance and limited success of these new parties, however, it appears that the PAN, reinvigorated since 1976, remains the principal opposition to the PRI.

The Social Bases of Electoral Support for the Parties[59]

The social bases that might support political divisions reflected in the modern Mexican party system include (1) religion, (2) the factors which together are referred to as modernization and industrialization, and (3) regional issues.[60]

Church-state conflict. The first, religion, a source of struggle in Mexico since the Wars of Independence, has been a struggle over the relationship between the church and the state. Most recently, this struggle took the form of the Cristero rebellion against Calles, his secularization policies, and his persecution of the church in the late 1920s.[61]

The strongest religiosity in Mexico is found in the west central region known as the Bajío where traces of traditional Spanish colonial society persist and the traditional Catholic Church is strong.[62] The Cristero rebellion found its home here in the 1920s. Jean Meyer's research shows that the number of Cristeros under arms was most concentrated in Michoacán, Jalisco, Aguascalientes, Colima, Guanajuato, Querétaro, Nayarit, and the southern part of Zacatecas.[63] Following the Cristero rebellion, the UNS was very active among the *campesinos* in this region, preaching its militant brand of Catholicism.[64] If there is to be found a relationship between religiosity and political party support, it should be found in this region. Those parties which should do relatively well among traditional Catholic elements are the PAN and the PDM, the PAN because of its general accordance with Catholic social and political philosophy and the PDM because of its militant and traditional Catholicism.[65] The PRI, on the other hand, should do relatively less well in this region because of its historical association with repression of the church.

Figure 5.3, which indicates the relative strength of the PRI in the various federal entities in the 1982 Chamber of Deputies race, shows the Bajío region (especially Jalisco, Michoacán, and Guanajuato) to be one of the areas of the PRI's weakest electoral showing, along with the north in general and the central core region. As noted above, the PAN's appeal to Catholic elements was probably strongest in the 1950s and 1960s when it was debating the idea of joining the international Christian Democratic movement. Figure 5.4 illustrates the areas of strongest support for the PAN in the 1964 race for Chamber of Deputies. The west central area clearly was a strong source of PAN support.

With the appearance of the PDM, the PAN has been challenged for its Catholic base. This is especially true among the more traditional Catholics and rural Catholics. The west central region as a whole is less important to the PAN now than it was two decades ago, although Jalisco (especially Guadalajara) and Guanajuato remain important. Undoubtedly the PDM has cut into the PAN's base of support. Figure 5.5, again based on the 1982 Chamber of Deputies race, shows that the PDM has already done well in this region. Its 7.8 percent showing in Guanajuato in 1982, its 5.0 percent finish in Michoacán, and its 4.0 percent showing in Jalisco must have cut into the PAN's base, although the PDM probably mobilized some of this electorate from among non-voters. In 1985, the PDM further strengthened its showing in these states with finishes of 15.7, 5.6, and 5.7 percent respectively.

It seems clear, then, that religiosity is correlated with voting for the right in Mexico. While the church-state conflict has subsided in Mexico, historical memories of the Cristero conflict have left a greater voting preference for pro-Catholic parties in the areas of greatest conflict. Indeed, the simple bivariate correlation coefficient between a measure of *sinarquista* concentration in 1940 and the PDM's vote share in 1982 is .50.[66] The missionary efforts of the UNS in the 1930s and the 1940s in the Bajío appear to continue to pay off for the UNS's current electoral arm, the PDM. It seems unlikely, however, that this social base of support for the PAN or the PDM can be expanded too dramatically in the future, since conflict between the church and the state, especially between the traditional, conservative church hierarchy and the state, is no longer divisive.

Industrialization and Urbanization. A basic premise of both types of developmental thought—Marxist and liberal modernization theories—is that changes in the realm of the economy lead to changes in the social structure which lead to changes in political behavior. A generally accepted version of the impact of industrialization and modernization, or changes in the mode of production, on the party system has the working class gravitating toward parties of the left; the business community, professionals, and middle classes supporting liberal and/or conservative parties; and traditional social groups—the increasingly marginalized lower middle class such as artisans and shopkeepers (the petty bourgeoisie) and rural sectors such as small farmers and at times the peasantry—forming the basis for radical right parties. Thus a socially pluralistic society, such as that of Mexico, should develop a broad spectrum of political parties unless strong political structures stand in the way. In Mexico, the PRI is that structure, combining as it does revolutionary legitimacy and an ideology of class coalition (at a level below that of the bourgeoisie, of course). This deters the development of competing class-based parties, especially those of the working class and *campesinos*. Meanwhile, the control of the electoral processes and the mechanisms of suppression and repression effectively constrain the growth of those which do spring up. The PRI has incorporated organized labor of the *campesinos* into the "center" through a combination of populist and corporatist measures, thus weakening the mass bases for the parties of the left and the right. Parties of the left and the right have developed, but their mass bases have been weak when compared to those of the PRI, at least until recently.

As the PRI is basically able to control the political activities of the rural masses through *caciques* and limitations on the diffusion of information, we might expect that migration to cities would free the migrating portion of these rural masses from *cacique* control, subject them to more sources of information, and in that way channel them away from the PRI to opposition parties.[67] As shown above, the more urban states have been the locations of the growth of the strongest opposition to the PRI. Table 5.3 complements those data with simple bivariate correlation coefficients for the relationship between the vote for the PRI in deputy elections since 1961 and urbanization, using two different measures of urbanization. While the correlations are by no means perfect, they are quite strongly negative for all eight elections since 1961. Furthermore, they are, if anything, becoming stronger.

Table 5.3 also shows the correlations between voting for the major opposition party, the PAN and urbanization. Clearly, the more urban states tend to vote more strongly for the PAN. This supports notions that the PAN has been relatively successful in Mexico's larger cities, but has been unable to penetrate the rural areas, which remain controlled by the PRI.

These data support the findings of statistical analyses of the urbanization-opposition voting relationship based on aggregate data from the 1960s.[68] (Lacking a time-series study, it is not possible to argue that higher rates of urbanization are associated with more rapid growth of the opposition.)[69] In support of this argument, Cornelius found that migrants tend to vote for the PRI more strongly than those born in the city, even those of the same class and income characteristics.[70] So, growing political support for the opposition does not come from migrants. Rather, it comes from their children, and even more so from the sons and daughters of the urban middle and upper classes, who are perhaps several generations removed from the migrant generation.[71]

Thus, the PRI dominates rural areas and the PAN is relatively more successful in urban areas. While in the pre-1976 period this opposition strength in urban areas was nearly monopolized by the PAN, this is no longer so. The organized left is also strong in urban areas.

Table 5.4 illustrates the correlations between left support and urbanization in the 1982 deputy race. Both the PSUM and the PRT seem to do well in urban areas, while it is difficult to conclude much about the PST's and PPS's support. If anything, these parties do better as cities grow larger, and they do especially well in Mexico City. The PSUM does disproportionately well in urbanized states, but less consistently so than the PAN. This is because the PSUM has not yet conquered, or even made a strong presence felt, in the urbanized northern states. In Baja California Norte, Nuevo León, Coahuila, Tamaulipas, Sonora, and Chihuahua, all among the most urbanized states in Mexico, the PSUM did not achieve its national average in 1982.

The urbanization phenomenon reflects the movement of the labor force from the primary (agricultural) sector to the secondary (industry and construction) and tertiary (commerce and services) sectors. Thus, one would expect to find that voting patterns identified with reference to rural-urban differences would be replicated in a division between states whose labor forces are principally engaged in agriculture on the one hand and those whose labor forces are incorporated into the secondary and tertiary sectors on the other hand. Figure 5.6 is a scatter diagram of the relationship between the size of the agricultural sector and the degree of support for the PRI in the 1982 deputy elections. The conclusions regarding the rural-urban division of the vote are bolstered by the relationship shown in this figure: states with a disproportionately large rural agricultural workforce vote very strongly for the PRI. Displayed in Table 5.5 are the simple bivariate correlations between the sectoral distribution of the workforce and PRI and PAN voting in all eight deputy elections since 1961. The strong and positive correlation between PRI support and large agricultural labor forces lends evidence to the suggestions of Figure 5.6. Support for the PAN is as weak in agricultural states as support for the PRI is strong there. The PAN does much better in industrialized states, while the PRI shows weakness in industrialized areas. If anything, this weakness is growing more pronounced. This contributes further evidence to the suggestion that the peasantry and rural workers vote nearly unanimously for the PRI, either by choice or by force, while those living in more industrial settings are much freer to vote as they choose.

But, is there any difference between how the secondary sector workforce and the tertiary sector workforce vote? Both live in urban settings. But, do those working in industry vote differently than those working in services?

The industrial sector can be divided into roughly two groups: those in manual jobs and those in non-manual jobs. As organized labor is associated with the PRI through the CTM and the Congress of Labor, it is usually assumed that manual workers vote for the PRI. However, as of 1972, only 38.8 percent of the industrial sector workforce was unionized.[72] This means that the PRI has the mobilizational aid of the CTM among at most 40 percent of the workforce in industry; at least 60 percent is not subject to CTM electoral mobilization. Thus, the vote of this sector is far less subject to control than is the vote of the agricultural sector. Furthermore, those in white-collar positions in the industrial sector are probably apt to be anti-PRI because of tensions between the public and private sectors. Those manual workers who are unionized are probably highly controlled by the PRI, but the rest of this sector is likely to be free to vote as it will. A high correlation between industrial concentration and relatively low voting for the PRI is thus not surprising. The high negative correlations in Table 5.5 between PRI voting and industrial sector workforce support this hypothesis.

Because the services sector is a diverse sector which includes full and part-time sales workers, those in transportation and communications, and domestic servants as well as highly paid white-collar employees in non-manufacturing settings, such as government jobs, finance, and education, one would expect quite diverse voting behavior on the part of those in this sector. The services sector is not highly unionized, so this source of control over those in lower-class occupations is not available. However, this sector includes both teachers and government employees, groups very likely to be strong supporters of the regime. As a result, a strong private sector-public sector antagonism is not likely to exist as is the case with the industrial sector white collar workforce. Thus, a weaker correlation between voting for either party and the percent of the workforce in the services sector, at least since 1970, as demonstrated in Table 5.5, is not unusual. The similarity in the direction of the correlation with that of the industrial sector probably reflects the fact that the workforces of the two sectors live in the same urban locations. Note that the 1982 partial correlation between PRI vote and services sector workforce, when controlling for industrial workforce, is only −.22, compared to −.41, the correlation coefficient for when industrial workforce is not held constant. In contrast, holding services sector workforce constant only reduces the correlation between industrial sector workforce and PRI voting from −.77 to −.73. This suggests that the services sector workforce does not seem to vote strongly in favor of the PRI or its opposition. In fact, it might not vote much at all. Meanwhile, the industrial sector workforce, despite CTM control of manual laborers, does not seem to vote strongly for the PRI. The opposition, especially the PAN, apparently exploits PRI weakness here.

The following profile of the social bases of electoral support for the PRI emerges: the PRI's strength is in the relatively backward, rural, agricultural areas of Mexico. This suggests that the social classes that back the PRI are those that it can most completely control through fear, violence, and economic pressure, the rural lower classes: the *campesinos,* especially *ejidatarios,* and the landless proletariat.[73] The correlation coefficients relating social class and vote for the PRI displayed in Table 5.6 strongly support this view. Moreover, the PRI's strength in areas populated by this rural lower-class has not weakened over time; if anything, it has increased, as shown by the especially strong correlation coefficient for 1979.

Meanwhile, states populated by the modern sectors of Mexico more strongly back the PRI's opposition: areas inhabited by the urbanized, non-primary sector, wealthier groups. The class bases of each of the various other opposition parties is less clear from the use of these aggregate data, as the correlations between class and support for the opposition parties other than the PAN are largely insignificant. From this, one might conclude that the opposition parties mobilize heterogeneous support (even the PDM receives support from outside its constituency of agrarian Catholics in the Bajío) from among urban white-collar groups and the urban lower classes.

Given that the recently arrived migrants that become urban marginals tend to be PRI supporters, and given that the middle and upper classes can only form 30 to 35 percent of the urban class structure at most, some of whom vote for the PRI (especially state employees), some of the urban support for the opposition must come from the industrial working class. The 330,000 votes for the PSUM in the Distrito Federal in 1982 could not have come from intellectuals and disaffected members of the middle class alone, especially considering that many of the latter vote for the PAN.

The PAN undoubtedly receives substantial working-class support as well. In the highly industrialized state of Nuevo León, home of Monterrey, the PAN received 24.4 percent of the vote in 1982—over 200,000 votes, almost all of them in Monterrey and its suburbs; the PSUM only received 5,600 votes. It is doubtful that the middle and upper classes alone could have sustained that level of PAN support. As the CTM has not successfully conquered the Monterrey workforce, and as the ideological environment is not healthy for the left, it is not surprising that some members might channel their vote outside both the PRI and the leftist opposition. Thus although a majority of working-class *voters* probably vote for the PRI, the left and the PAN no doubt also receive support from this group. In sum, the political support of the working class seems to be relatively less firm than that of the white-collar or peasant classes. This is probably even more true of those working-class groups in the burgeoning services sector than in the industrial sector. This points to the existence of a large group of not completely incorporated urban residents which could become the bulwark of a political movement, but which to date has not.

The areas in which the PAN does particularly well are inhabited by the urban middle and upper classes (see Figure 5.7). As the PAN evolved from a party of reformist professionals and intellectuals with a goal of criticizing the government to a vote-seeking party, its appeals became more middle-class oriented. Mabry argues that the "PAN derives most of its electoral support from protest voting . . . One reason for middle-class votes for PAN is the belief that the government favors the rich and the poor."[74] Walton and Sween's study of voting in urban *municipios* in the 1960s found the highest correlations between socioeconomic indicators and PAN support with the indicators "percent nonagricultural labor," "percent nonmanual labor," and "percent professional-technical labor."[75] The correlation coefficients between PAN voting and class membership in Table 5.6 support that conclusion.

Thus, the social class bases of Mexico's parties seem to be something like the following (of course, these conclusions could be subject to the ecological fallacy): the PRI receives almost all rural lower-class votes, perhaps a majority of working-class votes, especially unionized working-class votes, and a large percentage but not a majority of urban middle and upper-class votes. The PAN does very well among the urban middle and upper classes, receives some but not much working-class support, and does very poorly in the countryside. The PSUM's base is among intellectuals and disaffected middle-class members, but probably receives some lower-class support as well. The PDM does very well among the very religious *campesinos* of the Bajío region and receives some support from urban marginals. The social class bases of the PPS, the PST, the PARM, and the PRT are not clear.

The foregoing has identified a number of important sociological aspects of support for the PRI and its opposition, especially the PRI's principal opposition, the PAN. However, it is difficult to determine from these analyses which factors are most important for understanding how the vote will be distributed among the parties in any particular state. For this purpose, a multivariate analysis is appropriate, but in this case it is difficult to perform one using all of the variables previously discussed because of the high degree of intercorrelation among the potential independent variables. This is because most of these variables are indicators of the same underlying dimensions. The underlying dimensions which might be uncovered here are probably two (although a factor analysis has not been undertaken to verify this): (1) industrialization and (2) urbanization. That is,

Distribution of the vote = f (industrialization, urbanization).

Table 5.7 displays the results of ordinary least squares regression estimation of this multivariate model for the distribution of the vote to the PRI. The share of the total variance in the vote for the PRI explained by these two factors (as shown by R^2) is relatively high, especially considering that only two independent variables are being used. Furthermore, the ability of these two factors to explain the variance in the vote, especially for the PRI, grows stronger over time, suggesting that the PRI's base of support in non-industrialized, non-urbanized states has become more and more important to it over the past twenty-five years.[76] Table 5.7 also illustrates how important these two variables are relative to each other in explaining variance in the distribution of the vote (see the beta-weights in parentheses). A conservative conclusion is that the levels of urbanization and industrialization are equally important for explaining the shares of the vote that the PRI and its opposition receive, and have been so for the past two-and-a-half decades.

Regionalism. It is common to argue that a large part of the parties' bases of support is regional. Because of disenchantment by the northern states against Mexico City's centralism, and therefore against its electoral organ, the PRI, the PAN does well there. At the same time, the opposition parties have not penetrated the distant Gulf region and have done poorly in the agricultural south. A glance back to Figure 5.3 will verify the regional bases of support for the opposition: the north, the west central (the religious element discussed above being important), and the central core states vote least strongly for the PRI. Figure 5.4 shows that these same areas have been the PAN's major bases of electoral support. Figure 5.5 shows the PDM's strength in the west central region, which reflects religiously based regionalism.

This regionalism, however, may be a product of the effects of the two factors discussed above, religion and modernization/industrialization. The north, the central core, and Jalisco in the west are the most developed parts of the country. The west is the most religious part of Mexico. However, because of the relatively concentrated nature of these two phenomena, probably some organizational economies are enjoyed by the PAN and the PDM in these regions, thus contributing to their organizational strength and their ability to mobilize voters at a level higher than would be expected given the industrialization and religiosity variables alone. For the PAN, these organizational economies seem to spill over into higher levels of support than would be expected in the states lying between the core and the west on the one side and the north on the other. The PRI may enjoy the same economies in the backward areas of the Gulf and southern Mexico, where it faces no opposition. There also may be some feedback effect in operation here: regionally based protest voting leads to government attempts to quell the opposition by increased state contributions to economic development, which leads again to the modernization phenomena, which further contributes to opposition voting.

Table 5.8 shows the results of analyses of variance performed on the residuals of the multiple regression equations estimated in Table 5.7. That is, it examines the variance in the PRI's electoral shares not explained by the urbanization and industrialization variables. This procedure tests the null hypothesis that the PRI and its opposition actually do no better in any one region than in the others, controlling for the effects of urbanization and industrialization. These analyses of variance seek to determine how much of the variation (from state to state) in the vote for either party can be attributed to between-region differences, as opposed to within-region differences, after the effects of urbanization and industrialization have been accounted for. (The regional breakdown used is that of Smith.)[77] Table 5.8 shows that there is some regionally based variance in the electoral success of the PRI and its opposition, especially in 1970, 1979, and 1982. While not analyzed here, the results of the 1985 election would suggest that this regionalism is growing stronger. This may indicate that regional differences in the vote for the PRI and for the principal opposition are growing greater, not weaker, as time passes.

The data and statistics presented above show that, within Mexico's authoritarian regime, opposition to the regime via electoral means has expanded during the last two decades. This broadened expression of opposition has resulted from the long-term development of the PAN as a voice for expressing opposition and from the explicit encouragement of other opposition parties through the government-sponsored political reform of 1977. This opposition comes from the more advanced, urbanized, industrialized areas of Mexico, from religiously alienated rural areas, and from the northern states. Within the urban areas that support opposition groups, the upper and middle classes probably most strongly support the opposition, especially the PAN, while the working class and urban marginals are probably much less supportive of those who oppose the PRI.

Trends in Electoral Participation

Given the one-party hegemony experienced by Mexico since 1929, participation trends can provide as much evidence concerning popular support for the regime as can trends in the distribution of the vote. Those not participating in elections form the party of those not actively supporting nor incorporated into the PRI nor actively supporting the opposition. This party of non-voters represents those dissatisfied with the electoral alternatives and those who do not feel that their vote will matter because of the PRI's long-standing monopoly on electoral victories. The existence of this group creates a challenge to the legitimacy of the Mexican regime because it demonstrates the existence of a large body of potential voters who choose neither to indicate their approval for the government by voting for the PRI nor to indicate approval for the system by which the political elite maintains itself in power, by elections. Furthermore, it is threatening to Mexican political stability because it demonstrates the existence of a large number of Mexicans who are not incorporated into the PRI nor channelling their political expressions via the electoral system. This unincorporated group is available for mobilization into non-electoral patterns of political expression, such as guerrilla movements and mass political demonstrations. As Przeworski asserts, "incorporation into existing institutions is a strategy that serves to keep things as they are."[78] This is exactly the role played by Mexico's electoral system. Mexican observers also recognize the importance played by participation in a one-party hegemonic system. This concern with turnout and abstension became very pervasive during the 1976 presidential election when the PAN failed to contest the presidential race.[79] This concern was one important factor leading to the *Reforma política* in 1977 which included provisions to discourage nonparticipation by the PAN, thus to avoid in the future the situation of a race between the PRI candidate and abstention.

Figures 5.8 and 5.9 illustrate trends in participation in the period from 1961 to 1985. Note that there is a significant and apparently growing divergence between presidential-year participation rates and off-year participation rates, which is not terribly different from the experience of the United States. At the national level, the rate of participation by the potential electorate grew steadily up until 1970. This is a continuation of a trend begun with the first post-Revolution election in 1917.[80] After 1970, perhaps as a reverberation of discontent associated with the student rebellion in 1968, the rate of participation by eligible voters declined; the large declines between 1970 and 1976 and between 1973 and 1979 were dramatic given the previous growth of the participating share of the potential electorate.

The rate of participation by the potential electorate tells an important story about how well the electoral system has performed in incorporating the population into electoral channels. The Mexican electoral system was effective at this up until 1970. The rate of participation by the registered electorate tells another important tale, this one about how well the electoral system and the parties perform in actually controlling those who have been incorporated. Figure 5.9 shows that the PRI had begun to fail in this effort as early as 1964. By 1970 there was little doubt that there was a growing politically unincorporated sector of the population and a growing group of previously incorporated but uncontrolled voters.

This decline in participation was serious enough in 1973 and 1976 that it was a major source of debate during the formation of the political reform of 1977 and a probable cause of this reform.[81] The rate of participation declined still further in 1979, although its importance should not be overestimated.[82] 1982 witnessed a dramatic increase in participation, or an increase of almost 8 million voters. However, in 1985 participation was again off, to 45 percent of the potential electorate. Whether the political reform's sponsors were mistaken in their view that increased party competition would increase electoral participation or not is unclear. The role of the presidential campaign in bringing out voters and the anti-abstention campaign in 1982 may have caused an abnormal turnout in that election year. Whatever the cause, the mobilization for the 1982 election was very striking and will be analyzed below.

As with the case of opposition voting, electoral participation has been correlated with the degree of urbanization and industrialization of the states: more urban, industrial states have seen lower rates of participation, more rural states have seen higher rates of participation.[83] However, this relationship is much weaker than that for the direction of the vote, as illustrated by the relatively low correlation coefficients in Table 5.9 compared to those in Table 5.3. It is likely that some of the correlation, especially in the earlier part of the period being studied here, is only due to fraud: since the PRI faces less opposition in rural states, it was freer to inflate participation figures because no one who would protest was available to observe the practice of ballot-box stuffing. That this relationship washes out after the 1977 electoral reform is probably in part a testament to the effectiveness of the reform's provisions for poll watching.

As I previously mentioned, the most striking aspect of electoral participation in Mexico in the past twenty years was the mobilization that took place for the 1982 election. Participation by eligible voters increased nationally by 18.3 percent between the 1979 and 1982 elections, returning to the level of 1970. Table 5.10 illustrates the mobilization of voters between 1973 and 1982 (in 1979 the PAN was still recovering from its catastrophe in 1976, when it only ran a partial list of deputy candidates, so 1973 was chosen as the most recent representative year). Certain rural states stand out for low rates of mobilization of new voters: Campeche (10.9 percent growth), Guerrero (−7.8), Michoacán (21.7), Oaxaca (14.8), and Yucatán (18.7) are illustrative. Veracruz (80.9), Tabasco (80.4), and Durango (106.8) are important exceptions. In the industrialized, urban states, on the other hand, great numbers of new voters were mobilized; the rates are striking for Baja California Norte, México, and Nuevo León. Clearly a great degree of mobilization took place among the urban sectors of the population. While is is true that some of the growth of the voting electorate is simply due to the large influx of migrants, and thus a growth of the potential electorate, it is nonetheless also true that the rates of participation have evened off among the states, regardless of their degree of urbanization (see the correlation coefficient for 1982 in Table 5.9).

Who effected this mobilization and who benefited from it? The answer is, in large part, the PRI. Table 5.10 shows that the PAN's rate of mobilization of new voters was larger than that of the PRI; however, in absolute numbers, the PRI's totals dwarf those of the PAN since a 40 or 50 percent increase of 75 percent of the total votes is far larger than a 100 percent increase of 15 percent of the total votes. As Table 5.10 illustrates, the PRI's percent of the total change was larger than the PAN's percent of the total change in 24 of the 32 federal entities. Furthermore, the major portion of this mobilization of new voters took place between 1979 and 1982, after the PRI had lost an important segment of its voters in the 1973 to 1979 period. What seems to have happened is that the PRI lost a good share of its electorate between 1973 and 1979, perhaps some of it due to its inability after 1977 to produce as many fraudulently obtained votes. However, in the 1979 to 1982 period, the PRI recouped its previous loss, at least temporarily. Table 5.11 illustrates these trends. Note the preponderance of negative numbers in column 2 and of positive numbers in column 5. The other parties were definitely mobilizing many new voters, but compared to the PRI, relatively few.

The last three columns of Table 5.10 shows the magnitude of the PRI's mobilization effort: in many states 60 to 80 percent of the new voters went to the PRI (and this is assuming that no conversion of PRI voters to the opposition took place; if conversion did take place, the PRI's mobilization of new voters takes on even larger proportions). The PRI's new votes as a share of the whole potential electorate in 1982 was in the 20 to 30 percent range in several states.

An equally important question concerns where this mobilization took place. Tables 5.12 and 5.13 provide two answers. The massive mobilization seems to have taken place in those states where there were the most voters available to mobilize, that is, in the states which previously had the lowest rates of participation by both registered and eligible voters (see Table 5.12). This relationship seems particularly strong for the crucial 1979 to 1982 period, when the greatest mobilization took place. The social group which was earlier identified as the least incorporated or alienated group, those in the services sector, seems to be the only social group among which a significant relationship with mobilization can be found. Thus, the PRI seems to have mobilized voters from states with concentrations of precisely the groups which were most ripe for incorporation, those which had previously not participated in elections, particularly those working in the services sector.

The second answer to the question of where mobilization took place is that it took place in the areas where the PRI had previously faced the greatest competition. Table 5.13 shows a relationship between the change in participation rates and locations of strong PAN voting before the growth in participation. This is not a strong relationship, but it is the strongest that exists for explaining change in participation rates. This suggests that the PRI made efforts to mobilize voters for the 1982 election in precisely the areas where it faced its strongest competition from the PAN. If the proponents of the 1977 reforms actually did intend that they have the effect of invigorating the PRI, to spur it to greater efforts to incorporate the unincorporated, they must have been pleased with the results of the 1982 election.

In 1982, then, the regime's problem of low participation, thus weak incorporation, seemed to have been overcome. The political reforms of 1977 encouraged at least enough competition from opposition parties that the PRI seems to have been spurred on even to the point of mobilizing new voters in some areas where it faced little competition. The government's anti-abstention campaign in 1982 encouraged many to come out to vote who previously had not. There has also been some evening out of the discrepancies in participation rates between rural and urban areas.

Whether participation can be pushed on to any higher levels or even maintained at the 1982 levels, though, is unclear. The 1985 election results suggest not, that it is in fact hard to maintain high levels of participation. The narrowing or disappearance of the gaps between rural and urban areas as a result of mobilization in urban areas and lessening of fraud in the countryside suggests that perhaps a limit has been reached of somewhere between 55 and 65 percent of the potential electorate. If so, this could have important consequences for future electoral competition. The increased numbers of votes for the various parties in the 1982 race seem to have come largely from mobilization of previous non-voters. Conversion was important in few places (Coahuila and Guerrero most significantly). If no new voters can be mobilized other than the young, future electoral competition must be fought out over converting current voters, especially from among the PRI's majority. Even mobilization of Mexico's enormous youth population involves conversion of a sort: conversion from family and/or social group preferences. This type of electoral competition will be much more bitter and costly for the opposition, and dangerous for Mexico's vaunted political stability if the PRI becomes intransigent. The 1985 elections provided an indication of this competition between a PAN intent on converting PRI supporters, especially in the north, and a PRI willing to return to its old methods of maintaining hegemony. The PRI is already ahead of its opposition in one important area: mobilizing Mexico's huge services sector workforce. The parties of the opposition face a tough future if the PRI wins the battle for the electoral loyalty of this group.

Conclusion

The decision-making process in Mexico is highly authoritarian. The executive initiates and implements policy with little consultation from outside groups, especially the lower and middle classes. In this system, the means of expression must be controlled and channelled to assure that it is supportive or at least not erosive to the power of the policy makers. In Mexico, because of the heritage of the Revolution, "effective suffrage and no re-election," the major means of mass expression is electoral participation, which has been highly channelled in the past.

The inability of the PRI to attract the total potential electorate, especially those living in Mexico's more modern cities, led to a decline in electoral participation and increased voting for the PAN since the mid-1960s or so, in that way undermining some of the legitimacy and some of the control enjoyed by the Mexican regime. It is significant that the Mexican regime chose to try to restore this legitimacy and to try to regain control by inclusionary methods, not exclusionary means. This reflects the fact that the Mexican regime relies on the electoral system both to legitimize itself and control the masses.

As long as the PAN and the newer opposition parties do not achieve too much success among the PRI's main bases of electoral support, the urban and rural lower classes, this expansion of electoral means of expression can provide legitimacy to the regime (if not the government) without increasing political conflict. However, the experience of 1985 suggests what the ruling elite, especially the *políticos* within it, will do when their hegemony is effectively challenged. Undoubtedly, the López Portillo government expected that the results of its political reform project would be to incorporate various non-participating discontented elements within the electoral system. Conversion of the PRI's supporters was probably not expected. To this point those expectations have been borne out, although the most recent election points to this danger for the PRI. However, the new parties' organizations and the PAN have been strengthened and improved by being forced to develop candidates for three hundred federal electoral districts and thousands of state and local posts while at the same time building electoral organizations. These parties, especially the PAN, are developing the capacity to challenge the PRI for its own supporters. The competition for the PRI's supporters holds the promise of a greater opposition impact on the decision-making process, as the PRI may have to make and keep promises to the lower classes if it is to hold their loyalty. However, it also holds the threat of the kind of partisan conflict which could lead the regime to clamp down on opposition and increase control over participation. Perhaps this is the lesson of the 1985 legislative elections. As such situations develop, the style of the opposition's expression of discontent and the ability of both the government and the opposition to learn from the experiences of the countries of the Southern Cone will be important determinants of the continuation of Mexico's political opening.

Notes

1. I would like to thank Peter H. Smith, Walter Dean Burnham, Kevin Middlebrook, and Miguel Basañez for their comments on previous drafts. William Stanley and Kimberlee Klesner provided valuable comments on technical questions. Some of the information presented here was collected while I was in Mexico under a Fulbright grant, administered by the United States Information Agency. I would also like to thank the Department of Political Science of the Massachusetts Institute of Technology and Kenyon College for their support. A previous draft of this paper was presented on the panel "Politics and Political Parties in Contemporary Mexico,"

XII International Congress of the Latin American Studies Association, Albuquerque, April 18, 1985.

2. For interpretations of Mexican politics that stressed the pluralist aspect of the Partido Revolucionario Institutional's rule, despite its nearly complete dominance of electoral victories, see Robert E. Scott, *Mexican Government in Transition* (Urbana, IL: University of Illinois Press, 1959); Martin Needler, "The Political Development of Mexico," *American Political Science Review* 55, 2 (1961); and L. Vincent Padgett, "Mexico's One-Party System: A Reevaluation," *American Political Science Review* 51, 4 (1957) and *idem, The Mexican Political System*, 2nd ed. (Boston, MA: Houghton Mifflin, 1976). Early exponents of a view of Mexican politics that stressed the authoritarian nature of the political system, especially focusing on the electoral hegemony of the PRI, included Frank Brandenburg, *The Making of Modern Mexico* (Englewood Cliffs, NJ: Prentice-Hall, 1964) and Pablo González Casanova, *Democracy in Mexico* (New York, NY: Oxford University Press, 1970; Spanish version, 1965). Stronger statements about the authoritarian nature of the Mexican regime came especially after the 1968 massacre of students at Tlatelolco; see especially Roger D. Hansen, *The Politics of Mexican Development* (Baltimore, MD: Johns Hopkins University Press, 1971); Kenneth F. Johnson, *Mexican Democracy: A Critical View* (Boston, MA: Houghton Mifflin, 1971); Evelyn P. Stevens, *Protest and Response in Mexico* (Cambridge, MA: MIT Press, 1974); Susan Kaufman Purcell, *The Mexican Profit-Sharing Decision: Politics in an Authoritarian Regime* (Berkeley, CA: University of California Press, 1975); Wayne A. Cornelius, *Politics and the Migrant Poor in Mexico City* (Stanford, CA: Stanford University Press, 1975); José Luis Reyna and Richard S. Weinert, eds., *Authoritarianism in Mexico* (Philadelphia, PA: Institute for the Study of Human Issues, 1977); and Peter H. Smith, *Labyrinths of Power: Political Recruitment in Twentieth-Century Mexico* (Princeton, NJ: Princeton University Press, 1979). Current interpretations are more mixed. Daniel Levy and Gabriel Székely conclude that "our analysis of political freedom, political equality, and political change suggests mixed and variable patterns of authoritarianism and pluralism." *Mexico: Paradoxes of Stability and Change* (Boulder, CO: Westview Press, 1983). A recent attempt to go beyond the democracy-authoritarianism typology is Miguel Basáñez, *Mexico: La lucha por la hegemonía* (Mexico City: Siglo XXI, 1981). See also the essays collected in Tommie Sue Montgomery, ed., *Mexico Today* (Philadelphia, PA: Institute for the Study of Human Issues, 1982).

3. On the presidency and its power, see Brandenburg, *The Making of Modern Mexico*, Ch. 6 ("The Liberal Machiavellian").

4. Mexico figures heavily in the discussion of one-party systems. E.g., see Samuel P. Huntington and Clement H. Moore, eds., *Authoritarian Politics in Modern Society: The Dynamics of Established One-Party Systems* (New York, NY: Basic Books, 1970).

5. On the electoral reform and the opposition's reaction to it, see my forthcoming dissertation, "Electoral Politics and Political Change in Mexico's Authoritarian Regime" (M.I.T., forthcoming).

6. Pablo González Casanova, "Las alternativas de la democracia," in Pablo González Casanova and Enrique Florescano, eds., *Mexico hoy* (Mexico City: Siglo XXI, 1979), 370.

7. E.g., see Juan J. Linz's seminal article "An Authoritarian Regime: Spain," in Erik Allardt and Stein Rokkan, eds., *Mass Politics: Studies in Political Sociology* (New York, NY: Free Press, 1970), especially 259–266. The problem of explaining the role of parties in authoritarianism leads Fernando Henrique Cardoso to categorize Mexico as being different from the military authoritarian regimes. "On the Characterization of Authoritarian Regimes in Latin America," in David Collier, ed., *The*

New Authoritarianism in Latin America (Princeton, NJ: Princeton University Press, 1979), especially 43–49. The other contributors to the Collier volume have little or nothing to say about political parties or elections in bureaucratic-authoritarian regimes while continuing to at least call Mexico authoritarian and bureaucratic. Huntington, "Social and Institutional Dynamics of One-Party Systems," in Huntington and Moore, eds., *Authoritarian Politics in Modern Society*, however, suggests that "the fate of authoritarianism in modern society depends upon the viability of the one-party system in modern society" (p. 4) and suggests that revolutionary one-party regimes which evolve into institutionalized one-party regimes will become stable and lasting. Yet, Mexico's party system is expanding and changing, even though it fits his modal pattern. In general, studies of authoritarianism have either focused on the role of the state bureaucracy and the military or upon the methods of controlling interest articulation through corporatism. Political parties, party systems, and electoral politics receive little attention.

8. Guillermo O'Donnell, *Modernization and Bureaucratic-Authoritarianism: Studies in South American Politics* (Berkeley, CA: Institute of International Studies, University of California, 1973), 51–53; Alfred Stepan, *The State and Society: Peru in Comparative Perspective* (Princeton, NJ: Princeton University Press, 1978), 73–81.

9. Edwin Lieuwin, *Mexican Militarism: The Political Rise and Fall of the Revolutionary Army, 1910–1940* (Albuquerque, NM: University of New Mexico Press, 1968).

10. Such as the Cristero rebellion in the Bahío; see Jean Meyer, *The Cristero Rebellion: The Mexican People between Church and State, 1926–1929* (Cambridge: Cambridge University Press, 1976).

11. Such as during Cárdenas's expropriation of the oil industry; see Nora Hamilton, *The Limits of State Autonomy: Post-Revolutionary Mexico* (Princeton, NJ: Princeton University Press, 1982); Lorenzo Meyer, *México y los Estados Unidos en el conflicto petroleo* (Mexico City: El Colegio de México, 1972); and Wayne Cornelius, "Nation-Building, Participation and Distribution: The Politics of Social Reform under Cárdenas," in Gabriel Almond, Scott C. Flanagan and Robert J. Mundt, eds., *Crisis, Choice, and Change* (Boston, MA: Little, Brown and Co., 1973).

12. The elections of 1929 and 1940 were particularly strongly contested: Philosopher and educator José Vasconcelos opposed Calles's choice, Pascual Ortiz Rubio, in 1929 and undoubtedly had greater popular support than the 5.3% of the vote which he was granted. In 1940 General Almazan opposed Avila Camacho in an election marked by political violence throughout the country. His 5.7% official showing clearly understated his popularity, especially given the violence of the election. On both elections see Lorenzo Meyer, "La revolución mexicana y sus elecciones presidenciales, 1911–1940," in Pablo González Casanova, ed., *Las elecciones en México: evolución y perspectivas* (Mexico City: Siglo XXI, 1985).

13. Cárdenas distributed over 20 million hectares of land to *campesinos* and greatly increased the amount of credit available from the Banco Ejidal. Steven E. Sanderson, *Agrarian Populism and the Mexican State: The Struggle for Land in Sonora* (Berkeley, CA: University of California Press, 1981), Ch. 5. Organized labor in the Confederación de Trabajadores de México was given aid in organizing urban industrial workers. Strikes greatly increased and wages improved. Hamilton, *The Limits of State Autonomy*, Ch. 5.

14. See Hansen, *The Politics of Mexican Development*.

15. For one such effort, see Francisco José Paoli Bolio, "Legislación electoral y proceso político, 1917–1982," in González Casanova, ed., *Las elecciones en México*.

16. This review is based on Paoli Bolio, "Legislación electoral"; John Foster Leich, "Reforma Política in Mexico," *Current History*, 80, 469 (1981): 361–364, 392–393;

and Luis Medina Peña, *Evolución electoral en el México contemporaneo* (Mexico City: Comisión Federal Electoral, 1978).

17. A party had to have governing rules and had to publish a party newspaper or magazine. Many parties formed; Rafael Segovia states that over 3,000 party groups (parties and their factions) supported Obregón's candidacy in 1928. "Elites, Masses, and Parties," in Montgomery, ed., *Mexico Today*: 67.

18. Huntington, "Social and Institutional Dynamics of One-Party Systems" and Robert E. Scott, "Mexico: The Established Revolution," in Lucian W. Pye and Sidney Verba, eds., *Political Culture and Political Development* (Princeton, NJ: Princeton University Press, 1965).

19. Giovanni Sartori, *Parties and Party Systems, Vol. 1: A Framework for Analysis* (Cambridge: Cambridge University Press, 1976).

20. Ronald H. MacDonald, *Party Systems and Elections in Latin America* (Chicago, IL: Markham Publishing, 1971), 235–259.

21. Scott, *Mexican Government in Transition*; Needler, "The Political Development of Mexico"; and Padgett, "Mexico's One-Party System."

22. John F.H. Purcell and Susan Kaufman Purcell, "Machine Politics and Socio-economic Change in Mexico," in James W. Wilkie, Michael C. Meyer and Edna Monzón de Wilkie, eds., *Contemporary Mexico: Papers of the IV International Congress on Mexican History* (Berkeley, CA: University of California Press, 1976).

23. The fourth sector of the party, the military sector, was dissolved by Cárdenas in 1940 as part of his effort to break the power of conservative revolutionary generals. Its membership was to become included as individuals within the popular sector. Cornelius, "Nation-Building, Participation, and Distribution." See Padgett, *The Mexican Political System*, 1–9 for a description of bargaining between the PRI and its functional organizations over the nominating process at the local level. Padgett also provides a discussion of the PRI's organizational structure (see 73–92). See also Davis Schers, "The Popular Sector of the Mexican PRI" (Ph.D. dissertation, University of New Mexico, 1972).

24. Judith Adler Hellman, *Crisis in Mexico* (New York, NY: Holmes and Meier, 1978), 50–51; Smith, *Labyrinths of Power*, 217–221. One suggestion for why this is so concerns the state's ability to control each of the sectors: the state has little sanction over members of the popular sector and there is little to force them to join the CNOP so to get this sector's electoral and political support it is necessary to buy it (through offices for its leaders or more favorable policy for its members).

25. Basañez, *La lucha por la hegemonía*, Ch. 1, surveys a number of studies which have reached this conclusion using different approaches. See especially Brandenburg, *The Making of Modern Mexico* and Martin Needler, *Politics and Society in Mexico* (Albuquerque, NM: University of New Mexico Press, 1971), 46–49.

26. Brandenburg, *The Making of Modern Mexico*, 119–140.

27. Pablo González Casanova, *El estado y los partidos políticos en México* (Mexico City: Ed. Era, 1981), 79; Luz María Silva Ortiz, "Partido Auténtico de la Revolución Mexicana," in Antonio Delhumeau Arrecillas, ed., *Mexico: realidad política de sus partidos* (Mexico City: Instituto Mexicano de Estudios Políticos, 1970), 311–313.

28. This allegation was made by both PAN and PSUM leaders in personal interviews, June 1984.

29. On the Cristero rebellion, see Meyer, *The Cristero Rebellion*. As Meyer shows, the Cristeros cost the federal forces many lives lost and only a diplomatic settlement ended the fighting. On the UNS, see Jean Meyer, *El sinarquismo: un fascismo mexicano?* (Mexico City: Joaquín Mortiz, 1979).

30. Meyer, *El sinarquismo*, 136.

31. Meyer, *El sinarquismo*, 152-197. See the table Meyer presents on p. 47 for an appreciation of the regional concentration of UNS activity.

32. The relationship between the PAN and the PDM is described by Franz Alfred von Sauer, *The Alienated "Loyal" Opposition: Mexico's Partido Acción Nacional* (Albuquerque, NM: University of New Mexico Press, 1974) and by Donald Mabry, *Mexico's Acción Nacional: A Catholic Alternative to Revolution* (Syracuse, NY: Syracuse University Press, 1973), especially 29-30, 43-44, 52-53.

33. von Sauer, *The Alienated "Loyal" Opposition*; and Mabry, *Mexico's Accion Nacional*.

34. Carlos Arriola, "La crisis del Partido Acción Nacional (1975-1976)," *Foro Internacional*, 17, 4 (1977): 542-546; Octavio Rodríguez Araujo, *La reforma política y los partidos en México* (Mexico City: Siglo XXI, 1982), 125-135; Kenneth F. Johnson, *Mexican Democracy: A Critical View*, rev. ed. (New York, NY: Praeger, 1978), 146-148.

35. Jaime González Graf and Alicia Ramírez Lugo, "Partido de Acción Nacional," in Delhumeau Arrecillas, ed., *Mexico: realidad de sus partidos*, 183-188.

36. See von Sauer, *The Alienated "Loyal" Opposition*.

37. On the evolution of PAN ideology up to 1972, see Mabry, *Mexico's Acción Nacional*, 50-95.

38. González Graf and Ramírez Lujo, "Partido de Acción Nacional."

39. See Rolando Cordera and Carlos Tello, *México: la disputa por la nación* (Mexico City: Siglo XXI, 1981).

40. Arriola, "La crisis del Partido Acción Nacional," 545.

41. See the statements by ex-PAN secretary general Jesus González Schmal in Johnson, *Mexican Democracy*, rev. ed., 146-148.

42. MacDonald, *Party Systems and Elections in Latin America*, 250.

43. The *Movimiento de Liberación Nacional* (MLN) in the early 1960s was a rallying point for leftist intellectuals. In the years after 1968, a number of other leftist groups formed, some of them becoming parties. A relatively exhaustive list of these groups, with some description of them, is given in Rogelio Hernández and Roberto Rock, *Zócalo rojo* (Mexico City: Ed. Oceano, 1982).

44. González Casanova, *El estado y los partidos políticos en México*, 78-79; Tatiana Galván Haro and Susana Ralsky de Cimet, "Partido Popular Socialista," in Delhumeau Arrecillas, ed., *Mexico: realidad de sus partidos*, 258-265.

45. The party deputy system initiated in 1963 did not lead the PPS to receive more than the 2.5% necessary to receive party deputies until 1973 yet it (and the PARM) received party deputies anyway in accord with the "spirit" of the law.

46. Barry Carr, "Mexican Communism 1968-1981: Eurocommunism in the Americas?" *Journal of Latin American Studies*, 17, 1 (1985): 201-228.

47. Chronologies of Mexican parties, including where they originated as factions, can be found in Alejandra Lajous, *Los partidos políticos en México* (Mexico City: Premia, 1985) and in Hernández and Rock, *Zócalo rojo*.

48. Castillo and Francisco José Paoli Bolio describe early efforts by the PMT in *El poder robado* (Mexico City: Edamex, 1980).

49. Hernández and Rock, *Zócalo rojo*, 310-311.

50. An unnamed PST leader quoted by Rafael Junquera, *La reforma política* (Jalapa, Mexico: Universidad Veracruzana, 1979), 51.

51. Delal Baer and John Bailey, "Mexico's 1985 Midterm Elections: A Preliminary Assessment," *LASA Forum*, vol. XVI, no. 3 (Fall 1985): 4-10.

52. Rodríguez Araujo, *La reforma política y los partidos en México*, 205-210.

53. For example, see "Programa de los partidos sin registro," *Proceso*, May 9, 1977.

54. "Social and Institutional Dynamics of One-Party Systems," 5.

55. Padgett, "Mexico's One-Party System"; Scott, *Mexican Government in Transition*; Brandenburg, *Making of Modern Mexico*, for example.

56. This is not to suggest that Chamber of Deputies races are as important as presidential races. Since the president has clearly been both the policy initiator and implementor in Mexico, the selection of the president is the most important decision made through the electoral process. However, Chamber of Deputies races are held twice as often as presidential contests (every three years as against every six) and thus provide a greater number of cases for analysis. Furthermore, when elections are held simultaneously for president and deputies (every six years), the results by party are usually very similar between the two races (as well as the elections for senators and party deputies), seldom differing by more than 10 percent. This is especially clear at the district level. For example, see the results for the elections for president, majority deputies, party deputies, and senators in 1982 printed in *Excelsior*, July 12–19, 1982. Thus, these legislative races do seem to offer a measure of public electoral support for the various parties.

57. This drew the attention of Mexicanists by 1970. See Barry Ames, "Bases of Support for Mexico's Dominant Party," *American Political Science Review*, 64, 1 (1970): 153–167 and José Luis Reyna, "An Empirical Analysis of Political Mobilization: The Case of Mexico" (Ph.D. dissertation, Cornell University, 1971, especially ch. 5).

58. Urbanization is measured here by the percent of the population living in communities over 2,500 inhabitants in 1980.

59. The problem of fraudulent official voting figures suggests that care be used in the analysis of electoral patterns. I am not arguing that an individual's vote for the PRI indicates that he or she would support the PRI in non-electoral ways, such as publically demonstrating for it or taking up arms on its behalf in the event of a political crisis. As long as elections determine the final selection of presidents, governors, mayors, and legislators, though, a vote for the PRI (even a fraudulent one) is support for it because it permits PRI candidates to accede peacefully to office. If peaceful selection of rulers ends, the patterns of support for the PRI shown here may very well end. Thus, it is important to the PRI and the political elite which it sustains to maintain peaceful political competition.

Statistically, the results of fraud would depend upon how it is perpetrated. Three possibilities are (1) that fraud is relatively random, which should not bias statistical estimation of regression and correlation coefficients (the basic regression model assumes randomly distributed error); (2) that fraud is carried out in some proportional manner (the same number or same percentage of votes are added to the PRI's total in all districts), which might affect the regression coefficients but should not dramatically change correlation coefficients (there would still be variance which can be explained statistically); or (3) that fraud is carried out selectively, in areas where the PRI is weak and the local party organization must perpetrate fraud in order to maintain control (or the appearance of control) of the district, in which case correlation coefficients would usually be weakened (provided that the regression model is accurate) and suggestions of the instances of fraud may be found through analysis of regression residuals. The latter case will at least not lead to conclusions based on artificially inflated correlation coefficients.

60. The data used here are aggregate data at the level of the 32 federal entities (states and territories, including the Federal District), for which it is impossible to

determine differing patterns of political behavior of women and those of different age cohorts. They are thus not discussed here.

The use of aggregate data, of course, raises the possibility of the ecological fallacy. This is even more serious considering the high level of aggregation used herein. Survey data would obviously be preferable for determining the propensity of certain religious, occupational, educational, or regional backgrounds to vote for or against the PRI. Unfortunately, no nationwide sample survey seeking answers to these questions has been done since the Almond and Verba study in the late 1950s. (The PRI itself has probably done such surveys, but these data are not available for public use.)

To minimize the problem of the ecological fallacy, it would be advantageous to further disaggregate the state-level data. That is being done in my forthcoming dissertation "Electoral Politics and Political Change in Mexico's Authoritarian Regime," Department of Political Science, Massachusetts Institute of Technology. The level of analysis there is the federal deputy district, of which there are now 300 and were about 200 before 1977.

61. See Meyer, *The Cristero Rebellion*; Robert E. Quirk, *The Mexican Revolution and the Catholic Church, 1910–1929* (Bloomington, IN: Indiana University Press, 1973).

62. Martin Needler, *Mexican Politics: The Containment of Conflict* (New York, NY: Praeger, 1982), 44–45.

63. Meyer, *The Cristero Rebellion*, 85.

64. Meyer, *El sinarquismo, passim.*

65. Three of the PAN's five presidential candidates (Efraín González Luna in 1952, his son Efraín González Morfín in 1970, and José González Torres in 1964) came from Michoacán or Jalisco. Needler, *Mexican Politics*, 45.

66. See Meyer, *El sinarquismo*, 47, for data on *sinarquista* membership.

67. For explication of this hypothesis in various forms and evidence from both aggregate data analysis and survey analysis for the case of Mexico, see (for aggregate data analysis) Reyna, "An Empirical Analysis of Political Mobilization"; Ames, "Bases of Support for Mexico's Dominant Party"; and John Walton and Joyce A. Sween, "Urbanization, Industrialization and Voting in Mexico: A Longitudinal Analysis of Official and Opposition Party Support," *Social Science Quarterly*, 52, 3 (1971): 721–745. A recent effort is Rogelio Ramos Oranday, "Oposición y abstencionismo en las elecciones presidenciales, 1964–1982," in González Casanova, ed., *Las elecciones en México*; (for survey analysis) Wayne A. Cornelius, "Urbanization as an Agent in Latin American Political Instability: The Case of Mexico," *American Political Science Review*, 63, 3 (1969): 833–857 and idem, *Politics and the Migrant Poor in Mexico City*, 53–108.

68. See the studies by Reyna, Ames, and Walton and Sween noted in the previous note.

69. Ames found "no evidence that rapidly urbanizing states are becoming less strong for the PRI," in "Bases of Support for Mexico's Dominant Party," 166. Time series analysis of voting patterns will be found in my forthcoming dissertation, "Electoral Politics and Political Change in Mexico's Authoritarian Regime."

70. Cornelius, *Politics and the Migrant Poor in Mexico City*, 63–65, especially Table 3.5.

71. Among his sample of residents of poor urban neighborhoods, Cornelius found that the sons of migrants were less likely than their fathers to support the PRI. The sons of natives of Mexico City were even less likely than the sons of migrants to support the PRI. Cornelius, *Politics and the Migrant Poor in Mexico*

City, 65–67. Using survey data from 1969 and 1973, Charles L. Davis and Kenneth
M. Coleman located the greatest gains of the PAN among the young and the upper
class (their response sets were broken only into lower and upper class—at any rate,
the PAN gain was most noticeable among urban white-collar elements). "Electoral
Change in the One-Party Dominant Mexican Policy," *Journal of Developing Areas,*
16, 2 (1982): 523–542.

72. Raúl Trejo Delarbe, "El movimiento obrero: situación y perspectivas," in
Pablo González Casanova and Enrique Florescano, eds., *Mexico hoy* (Mexico City:
Siglo XXI, 1979), 124.

73. The position of the rural middle and upper classes is less clear, but electorally
their weight is small: the rural lower classes made up about 83 percent of the
population of the countryside in 1960. (Calculated from Smith, *Labyrinths of Power,*
Tables 2, 3, and 4, 43.) The position of these rural middle and upper classes is
important, however, to the extent that they are the party cadres and *caciques* that
force the lower classes to vote for the PRI.

74. Mabry, *Mexico's Acción Nacional,* 181.

75. Walton and Sween, "Urbanization, Industrialization and Voting in Mexico,"
Table 3, 732–733. See also Davis and Coleman's survey findings from 1969–1973.
"Electoral Change in the One-Party Dominant Mexican Polity."

76. Note that the measure of urbanization used here is the percent of the
population of the state living in localities of over 50,000. This is used in preference
to the 5,000 threshold because the intercorrelation with the other independent
variable, percent of the workforce in industry, is lower for the 50,000 measure of
urbanization than for the 5,000 measure. Thus multicolinearity in the model is
reduced. For instance, for 1970, the Pearson's r between urbanization ($<50,000$) and
industrialization is .46 while r between each of these two independent variables and
PRI vote is $-.58$. This is more than a statistical trick. Conceptually one can think
of industrialization occurring in localities with less than 50,000 population—that is,
localities here defined as rural—but this is much less likely to happen in localities
of less than 5,000. This means that two different dimensions can be tapped by these
two variables. Also, the 50,000 threshold measures a locality in which many of the
political and social aspects of urbanism can really take place: congestion, existence
of mass media, and existence of intellectuals.

77. *Labyrinths of Power,* 68.

78. Adam Przeworski, "Institutionalization of Voting Patterns, or Is Mobilization
the Source of Decay?" *American Political Science Review,* 69, 1 (1975): 66.

79. The editorial pages of Mexico's newspapers were full of this topic. E.g., see
Carlos Pereyra, "El peligro del abstencionismo," *Excelsior,* Feb. 16, 1976; Abelardo
Villegas, "Oposición domesticada y abstensionismo," *Excelsior,* June 28, 1976; Renato
Leduc, "Ya no piden PAN," *Novedades,* February 6, 1976; Gaston García Cantu,
"Abstencionismo o referéndum," *Excelsior,* January 30, 1976; Enrique Maza, "Ab-
solutismo o abstención," *Excelsior,* February 25, 1976.

80. See González Casanova, *Democracy in Mexico,* Table 18, 221, for pre-1964
figures.

81. Kevin Middlebrook, "Political Change and Political Reform in an Authoritarian
Regime: The Case of Mexico," (Woodrow Wilson Center for International Scholars,
Washington, D.C., Latin America Program, Working Paper No. 103). The issue of
abstention was extensively discussed in the editorial pages of Mexico City's newspapers
during the uncontested 1976 campaign. For a sampling, see Javier Marquez, ed.,
Pensamiento de México en los periodicos: paginas editoriales (Mexico City: Ed. Tecnos,
1977).

82. Rafael Segovia, "Las elecciones federales de 1979," *Foro Internacional*, 20, 3 (1980): 398, states that the decline in participation reflects as much an increase in electoral honesty owing to stricter control enacted with the new election law in 1977 as a decrease in actual voting. A couple of examples support this: participation in Guerrero, long known as a bastion of PRI and government corruption, fell from 72.1 percent in 1976 to 34.1 percent in 1979; similar declines took place in other rural areas of PRI control (Campeche, from 80.7 to 49.2 percent; Tlaxcala, from 82.8 to 44.2 percent).

83. Walton and Sween, "Urbanization, Industrialization and Voting in Mexico," Table 4, 736.

FIGURE 5.1 Evolution of the Mexican Party System

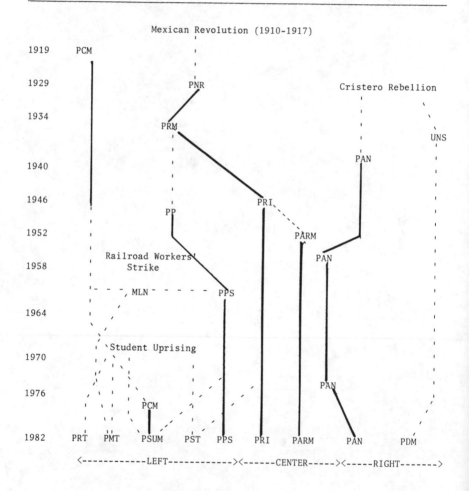

TABLE 5.1
Presidential Election Results Since 1929

| | Percentage of Total Vote | | | | |
	Organized Left	PRI	PAN	Other Right	Others
1929	1.1	93.6	---	5.3	---
1934	0.7	98.2	---	---	1.1
1940	---	93.9	---	---	6.1
1946	---	77.9	---	---	22.1
1952	2.0	74.3	7.8	---	15.9
1958	---	90.6	9.4	---	---
1964	---	88.6	11.4	---	---
1970	---	85.5	14.0	---	0.5
1976	1.3	98.7	---	---	---
1982	7.0	74.3	16.4	2.3	---

Sources: Mario Ramírez Rancaño, "Estadísticas electorales: presidenciales," Revista Mexicana de Sociología (1976); Daniel Levy and Gabriel Szekeley, Mexico: Paradoxes of Stability and Change (Boulder, CO: Westview Press, 1983), 69; Excelsior, July 16, 1982, 9A.

TABLE 5.2
Federal Deputy Election Results, 1961-1985

YEAR	PAN	PRI	PPS	PARM	PDM	PSUM	PST	PRT	PMT
1961	7.6	90.3	1.0	0.5	---	---	---	---	---
1964	11.5	86.3	1.4	0.7	---	---	---	---	---
1967	12.5	83.8	2.2	1.4	---	---	---	---	---
1970	14.2	83.6	1.4	0.8	---	---	---	---	---
1973	16.5	77.4	3.8	2.0	---	---	---	---	---
1976	8.9	85.2	3.2	2.7	---	---	---	---	---
1979	11.4	74.2	2.7	1.9	2.2	5.3	2.2	---	---
1982	17.5	69.3	1.9	1.3	2.3	4.4	1.8	1.3	---
1985	16.3	68.2	2.1	1.7	2.9	3.4	2.6	1.3	1.6

Annulled votes have been excluded as have votes for two minor parties, the
PNM in 1961 and the PSD in 1982, to facilitate greater comparability of party
shares from year to year.

Sources: Comisión Federal Electoral, Reforma política: gaceta informativa
de la Comisión Federal Electoral, tomo IX: acuerdos, indicadores de opinión
publica y estadística electoral (Mexico City, 1982): 128-129; Latin America
Regional Reports: Mexico and Central America, August 16, 1985, 4.

Figure 5.2

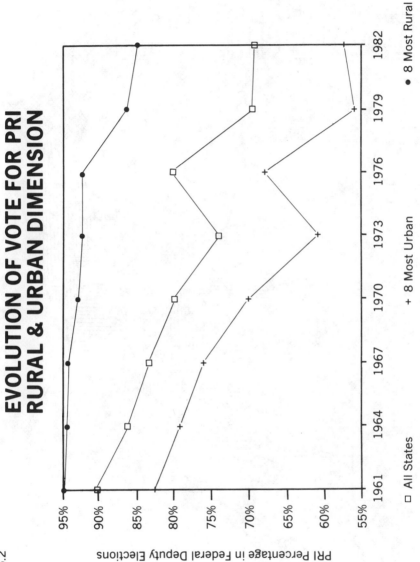

EVOLUTION OF VOTE FOR PRI
RURAL & URBAN DIMENSION

PRI Percentage in Federal Deputy Elections

□ All States   + 8 Most Urban   ● 8 Most Rural

132

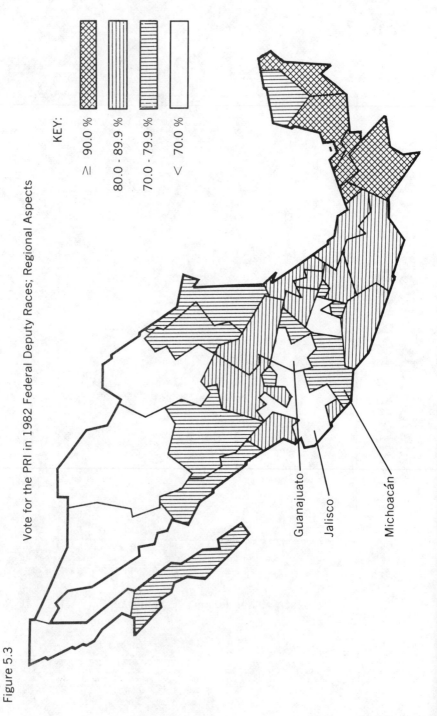

Figure 5.3

Vote for the PRI in 1982 Federal Deputy Races; Regional Aspects

KEY:

≥ 90.0 %

80.0 - 89.9 %

70.0 - 79.9 %

< 70.0 %

Guanajuato

Jalisco

Michoacán

Figure 5.4

Vote for the PAN in 1964 Federal Deputy Races; Regional Aspects

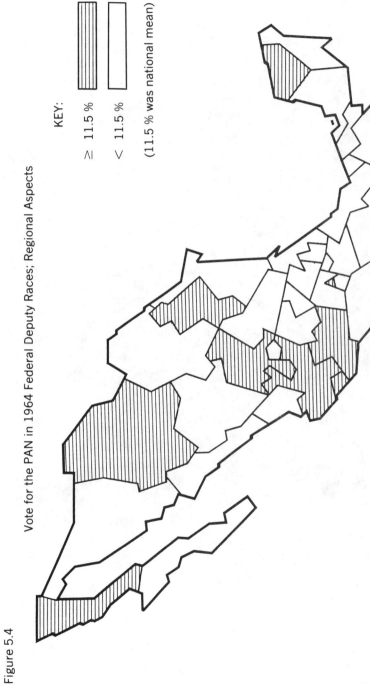

KEY:

≥ 11.5 %

< 11.5 %

(11.5 % was national mean)

134

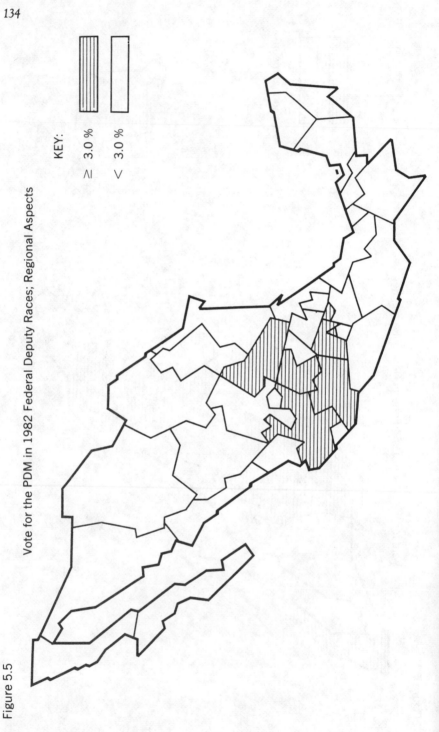

Figure 5.5

Vote for the PDM in 1982 Federal Deputy Races; Regional Aspects

KEY:

≥ 3.0 %

< 3.0 %

TABLE 5.3
Correlation Between Direction of Vote and Urbanization in Federal Deputy
Elections, 1961-1982

	1961	1964	1967	1970	1973	1976	1979	1982
				VOTE FOR PRI				
PERCENT URBAN (≥50,000)	-.49	-.63	-.57	-.57	-.52	-.71	-.79	-.72
PERCENT URBAN (≥5,000)	-.62*	-.69*	-.56	-.61	-.55	-.68	-.78	-.71
			VOTE FOR PAN					
PERCENT URBAN (≥50,000)	.55	.63	.68	.65	.38	.63	.67	.69
PERCENT URBAN (≥5,000)	.62*	.69*	.70	.63	.46	.63	.72	.68

*For 1961 and 1964, percent urban measured by $\geq$ 2,500 in 1960.
For 1961, urbanization data is from 1960; for 1964 and 1967, interpolated
for 1965; for 1970, from 1970; for 1973 and 1976, interpolated for 1975;
for 1979 and 1982, from 1980.
Sources: 1960, 1970, and 1980 Mexican census; Comisión Federal Electoral,
Reforma Política IX (1982).

TABLE 5.4
Correlation Between Left Vote and Urbanization in 1982
Federal Deputy Election

	PSUM	PPS	PST	PRT	TOTAL LEFT
PERCENT URBAN (>50,000)	.23	.14	.16	.40	.33
PERCENT URBAN (>5,000)	.23	.09	.14	.41	.31

Source: See notes for Tables 5.3. Total Left is PSUM,
PPS, PST, and PRT.

Figure 5.6

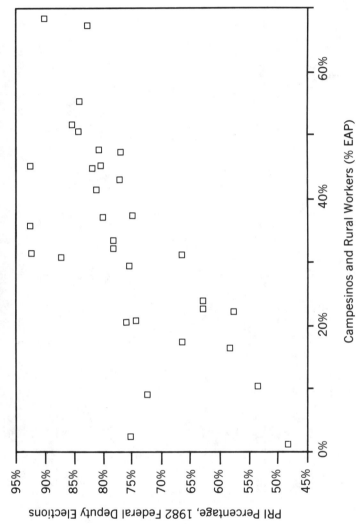

TRADITIONAL SECTOR AND PRI VOTE
IN 1982 FEDERAL DEPUTY ELECTIONS

TABLE 5.5
Correlation Between Direction of Vote and Sectoral Distribution of Workforce
in Federal Deputy Elections, 1961-1982

	1961	1964	1967	1970	1973	1976	1979	1982
				VOTE FOR PRI				
AGRICULTURE	.58	.62	.57	.60	.55	.74	.78	.73
INDUSTRY	-.47	-.57	-.49	-.58	-.65	-.73	-.79	-.77
SERVICES	-.63	-.59	-.57	-.52	-.35	-.60	-.50	-.41
				VOTE FOR PAN				
AGRICULTURE	-.64	-.57	-.67	-.63	-.52	-.69	-.75	-.72
INDUSTRY	.54	.57	.63	.68	.71	.73	.70	.71
SERVICES	.67	.51	.64	.50	.25	.51	.54	.48

Shown are zero-order Pearson's r correlation coefficients. N=32 states.
$r \geq .30$ is statistically significant at the .10 level, $r \geq .45$ at the .01 level.
For 1961, sectoral data are from 1960; for 1964 and 1967, data are interpolated
for 1965; for 1970, from 1970; for 1973 and 1976, interpolated for 1975;
for 1979 and 1982, from 1980.
Sources: 1960, 1970, and 1980 Mexican census; Comisión Federal Electoral,
Reforma Política IX (1982).

TABLE 5.6
Correlation Between Direction of Vote and Occupational Distribution of Workforce in Federal Deputy Elections, 1961–1982

	1961	1964	1967	1970	1973	1976	1979	1982
VOTE FOR PRI								
URBAN WHITE COLLAR	-.62	-.65	-.62	-.64	-.56	-.74	-.78	-.69
Urban Upper Class	-.63	-.61	-.60	-.59	-.53	-.72	-.75	-.64
Urban Middle Class	-.62	-.66	-.62	-.67	-.57	-.74	-.78	-.70
URBAN LOWER CLASS	-.54	-.58	-.51	-.53	-.48	-.66	-.63	-.59
RURAL LOWER CLASS	.59	.62	.57	.59	.52	.72	.76	.69
VOTE FOR PAN								
URBAN WHITE COLLAR	.66	.58	.70	.62	.47	.64	.64	.61
Urban Upper Class	.64	.53	.64	.55	.45	.63	.62	.57
Urban Middle Class	.66	.60	.72	.65	.47	.64	.63	.62
URBAN LOWER CLASS	.61	.53	.63	.59	.52	.62	.60	.58
RURAL LOWER CLASS	-.65	-.56	-.67	-.61	-.50	-.65	-.66	-.64

Zero-order Pearson's r correlation coefficients. N=32 states.
$r > .30$ is statistically significant at the .10 level, $r > .45$ at the .01 level.
For 1961, occupational data are from 1960; for 1964 and 1967, data are interpolated for 1965; for 1970, from 1970; for 1973 and 1976, interpolated for 1975; for 1979 and 1982, from 1980.
Sources: 1960, 1970, and 1980 Mexican census; Comisión Federal Electoral, Reforma Política IX (1982).

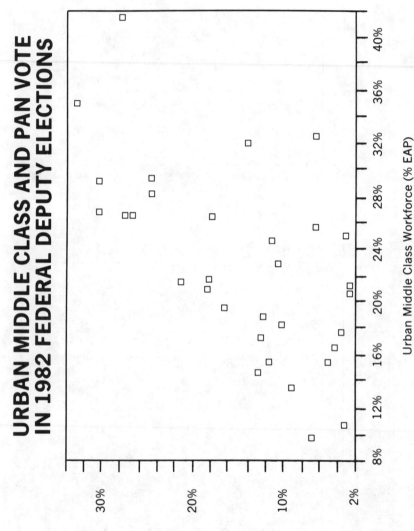

Figure 5.7

TABLE 5.7
Industrialization, Urbanization and Voting for the PRI: A Multiple Regression
Model, Federal Deputy Elections,1961-1982

| YEAR | INDEPENDENT VARIABLE REGRESSION COEFFICIENTS | | | |
	INDUSTRIALIZATION	URBANIZATION	CONSTANT	R^2
1961	-0.30 (-0.23)	-0.15* (-0.32)	99.5***	.27**
1964	-0.26* (-0.25)	-0.21*** (-0.51)	98.4****	.48****
1967	-0.24 (-0.19)	-0.22** (-0.46)	96.0****	.36****
1970	-0.49*** (-0.39)	-0.17*** (-0.40)	100.9****	.47****
1973	-0.87* (-0.37)	-0.19 (-0.18)	111.0****	.26**
1976	-0.58*** (-0.50)	-0.16** (-0.32)	104.3****	.58****
1979	-0.47*** (-0.43)	-0.23*** (-0.45)	96.6****	.69****

(Continued)

TABLE 5.7 (Cont.)

| | INDEPENDENT VARIABLE REGRESSION COEFFICIENTS | | |
YEAR	INDUSTRIALIZATION	URBANIZATION	CONSTANT	R^2
1982	-0.58***	-0.15*	95.6***	.63***
	(-0.54)	(-0.30)		

***Significant at .01 level.　　　N=32 states.
**Significant at .05 level.　　　 Standardized Regression
*Significant at .10 level.　　　　Coefficients in parentheses.

　　Dependent variable is percent of vote to PRI, annulled votes excluded. Industrialization is measured by percent of the workforce in industrial occupations (secondary sector). Urbanization is measured by the percent of the population living in cities of greater than 50,000 inhabitants. Constant is percent of vote of a state which would go to PRI if there were no cities of greater than 50,000 and if there were no workers in the industrial sector. Regression coefficients measure percent of change in PRI vote for a 1 percent change in the independent variable. (E.g., in 1982, 1 percent change in percent of workforce in industry would cause a .58 percent drop in PRI percent.)

TABLE 5.8
Analysis of Variance of Residuals of Regression of Industri-
alization and Urbanization on PRI Vote Using Region as
Treatment Effect

YEAR	F-ratio	eta^2
1961	1.29	0.20
1964	1.22	0.19
1967	0.98	0.16
1970	2.94**	0.36
1973	1.39	0.21
1976	0.82	0.14
1979	2.47*	0.32
1982	2.61**	0.33

**Significant at .05 level.   N=32 states.
*Significant at .01 level.
A significant F-ratio indicates that PRI vote share varies
by region even allowing for the effects of urbanization
and industrialization. [One-way analysis of variance
on residuals of the equation: PRI% = B_0 + B_1 *%EAP in
industry + B_2*%Urban (>50,000)].
Eta^2 is a proportional reduction in error (PRE) statistic
analogous to R^2.
Region is defined as by Smith, Labyrinths of Power, 68.

Figure 5.8

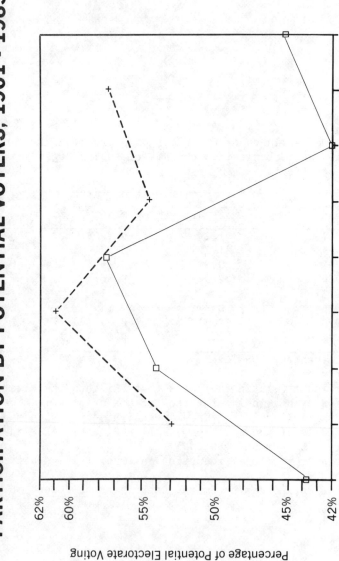

PARTICIPATION BY POTENTIAL VOTERS, 1961 - 1985

Percentage of Potential Electorate Voting

1964   1970   1976   1982

□ Off-Year Elections   + Presidential Years

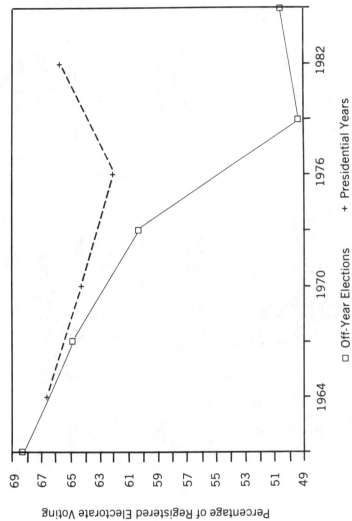

PARTICIPATION BY REGISTERED VOTERS, 1961 - 1985

Figure 5.9

145

TABLE 5.9
Correlation Between Participation By Registered Voters and
Urbanization, Chamber of Deputies Elections, 1961-1982

1961	1964	1967	1970	1973	1976	1979	1982
-.27	-.44	-.38	-.44	-.36	-.22	-.01	-.03

Urbanization statistics are, for 1961 and 1964, % of
population in localities $\geq$ 2,500 in 1960; for 1967 and
1970, % of population in localities $\geq$ 5,000 in 1970; for
1973 and 1976, % of population in localities $\geq$ 5,000 in
1975 (estimated by interpolation); for 1979 and 1982, % of
population in localities $\geq$ 5,000 in 1980.
Sources: 1960, 1970, and 1980 Mexican censuses; Comisión
Federal Electoral, Reforma Política IX (1982).

TABLE 5.10

Mobilization of Voters, 1973-1982: TOTAL, PRI AND PAN

State	Increase in Participation		Increase PRI Vote		Increase PAN Vote		%Total Change		PRI Change as % of potential vote
	number	% change	number	% change	number	% change	PRI	PAN	
Aguascalientes	88,361	96.6	59,854	81.0	17,260	115.9	67.7	19.5	22.4
Baja California Norte	239,786	102.3	58,873	30.2	did not run in 1973		24.5	---	8.5
Baja California Sur	50,916	155.7	33,439	114.2	9,046	363.9	65.7	17.8	26.5
Campeche	10,524	10.9	2,311	2.4	6,085	512.6	22.0	57.8	1.2
Chiapas	203,937	47.5	155,416	37.4	14,439	250.1	76.2	7.1	14.1
Chihuahua	167,406	46.2	54,214	19.0	93,036	151.1	32.4	55.6	5.2
Coahuila	45,150	16.6	-32,266	-13.2	67,200	341.6	-71.5	148.8	-3.9
Colima	52,780	92.5	42,495	79.7	4,181	138.8	80.5	7.9	24.1
Distrito Federal	973,586	40.5	389,424	31.3	5,026	0.5	40.4	0.5	6.9
Durango	187,350	106.8	121,905	81.2	55,520	518.3	65.1	29.6	21.9
Guanajuato	262,396	45.7	61,008	12.3	111,937	175.8	23.3	43.0	4.0
Guerrero	-41,021	-7.8	-93,917	-18.7	9,640	80.4	228.9	-23.5	-8.3
Hidalgo	167,208	42.5	127,996	36.8	20,881	71.6	76.5	12.5	16.9
Jalisco	395,730	42.6	105,858	16.1	125,858	56.7	26.8	31.8	4.7
México	1,294,710	111.6	630,776	79.1	300,285	100.6	48.7	23.2	15.6
Michoacán	129,088	21.7	35,018	6.7	32,616	59.6	27.1	25.3	2.2
Morelos	145,888	95.4	113,409	101.2	1,586	5.2	77.7	1.1	22.6
Nayarit	112,338	150.4	107,244	246.5	1,130	27.6	95.5	1.0	29.1
Nuevo León	467,611	117.7	305,639	95.6	143,780	213.2	65.4	30.7	22.8
Oaxaca	87,787	14.8	57,716	11.4	-15,828	-10.0	65.7	20.3	4.3
Puebla	512,004	78.0	488,506	107.3	28,958	278.7	95.4	-3.1	29.2
Querétaro	96,742	67.5	57,631	44.4	3,012	1506.0	59.6	29.9	16.0
Quintana Roo	57,291	158.4	50,683	142.4	4,976	17.6	88.5	5.3	44.0
San Luis Potosí	100,505	31.0	61,155	20.9	51,306	350.4	60.8	5.0	7.1
Sinaloa	315,438	135.6	253,947	125.0	112,188	812.8	80.5	16.3	26.2
Sonora	186,028	89.0	57,184	30.3	3,026	30.6	30.7	60.3	6.9
Tabasco	141,154	80.4	131,243	80.6	12,437	49.6	93.0	2.1	23.3
Tamaulipas	168,148	41.8	99,651	30.2	11,305	98.0	59.3	7.4	9.5
Tlaxcala	45,068	32.7	21,675	18.2	12,513	23.7	48.1	25.1	7.8
Veracruz	823,356	80.9	615,853	69.3	38,036	191.4	74.8	1.5	21.7
Yucatán	50,183	18.7	8,538	3.5			17.0	75.8	1.5
Zacatecas	71,968	26.8	39,739	16.1	20,100	107.5	55.2	27.9	6.9

Sources: 1970 and 1980 (preliminary returns) censuses; potential electorate estimated as number of residents aged 18 and over. Diario de los Debates de la Cámara de Diputados (Mexico City), August 1982; Franz A. von Sauer, The Alienated "Loyal" Opposition: Mexico's Partido Acción Nacional (Albuquerque: University of New Mexico Press, 1974).

TABLE 5.11
Mobilization and Demobilization of PRI Supporters

	CHANGE IN PRI PERCENTAGE OF POTENTIAL ELECTORATE*				
STATE	(1) 1970-1976	(2) 1973-1979	(3) 1976-1982	(4) 1970-1982	(5) 1979-1982
AGUASCALIENTES	-10.17	-16.12	8.31	-1.86	22.39
BAJA CALIFORNIA NORTE	-3.69	-3.70	-3.04	-6.73	3.60
BAJA CALIFORNIA SUR	-12.42	-19.08	5.13	-7.29	24.34
CAMPECHE	6.89	-16.86	-59.78	-52.89	-26.47
CHIAPAS	-11.03	-12.54	1.58	-9.45	10.24
CHIHUAHUA	-8.53	-16.22	-6.63	-15.15	4.85
COAHUILA	-6.07	-31.32	-26.63	-32.70	5.90
COLIMA	-3.14	-15.69	14.98	11.84	33.04
DISTRITO FEDERAL	-3.67	-9.13	-6.18	-9.84	4.12
DURANGO	5.05	-2.80	1.59	6.64	12.58
GUANAJUATO	2.43	-6.18	-8.72	-6.30	4.69
GUERRERO	11.46	-21.59	-37.84	-26.38	2.20
HIDALGO	-10.23	-19.22	0.38	-9.85	14.78
JALISCO	-6.96	-17.69	-8.00	-14.97	7.64
MÉXICO	-4.10	-2.36	-2.27	-6.36	6.24
MICHOACÁN	1.95	-14.31	-16.10	-14.15	5.68
MORELOS	-17.57	-9.91	9.69	-7.89	10.09
NAYARIT	4.71	-24.02	-12.30	-7.58	21.69
NUEVO LEÓN	-16.54	-12.85	-22.57	6.03	24.36
OAXACA	-18.34	-29.55	-4.67	-23.01	12.05
PUEBLA	-1.35	-10.02	13.81	12.46	26.38

QUERÉTARO	-9.43	-14.47	2.67	-6.76	15.80
QUINTANA ROO	-18.52	5.00	16.85	-1.68	17.67
SAN LUIS POTOSÍ	-5.68	-15.86	-4.67	-10.35	10.77
SINALOA	-9.01	-21.21	12.48	3.47	30.99
TABASCO	-14.58	-26.60	-1.79	-16.38	20.31
TAMAULIPAS	-9.70	-20.47	-0.13	-9.84	16.35
TLAXCALA	21.49	-15.62	-29.71	-8.22	13.11
VERACRUZ	-11.20	-9.05	9.12	-2.09	13.71
YUCATÁN	9.05	-2.13	-14.33	-6.28	4.78
ZACATECAS	-7.05	-19.70	-3.80	-10.85	16.91

*e.g., 1982 PRI % of potential electorate less 1979 PRI % of potential electorate.

TABLE 5.12
Determinants of Voter Mobilization, 1973-1982

	GROWTH OF THE ELECTORATE (PERCENT CHANGE IN TOTAL NUMBER OF VOTERS)		
	1973 TO 1979	1973 TO 1982	1979 TO 1982
Participation by Eligible Voters 1973	-.23	-.45	---
Participation by Registered Voters 1973	-.02	-.09	---
Participation by Eligible Voters 1979	---	---	-.49
Participation by Registered Voters 1979	---	---	-.56
Urban White Collar	.33	.22	.10
Urban Lower Class	.30	.13	-.07
Rural Lower Class	-.33	-.19	-.01
Agricultural Sector	-.37	-.23	-.08
Industrial Sector	.21	.04	-.07

Services Sector   .41   .35   .22

Zero-order Pearson's r correlation coefficients. N=32 states.
$r \geq .45$ is statistically significant at the .01 level, $r \geq .35$ at the .05 level,
$r \geq .30$ at the .10 level.
Note: Percent Change in Total Voters, in Votes for PRI, in Votes for PAN,
in Registered Electorate defined as the difference between the total for
Year 2 minus the total for Year 1, divided by the total for Year 1. It is
not a change in percentages from Year 1 to Year 2.

TABLE 5.13
Correlation Between Change in Participation Rates and Vote for PRI and PAN

	CHANGE IN PARTICIPATION RATE OF ELIGIBLE VOTERS	CHANGE IN PARTICIPATION RATE OF REGISTERED VOTERS
	1979 TO 1982	1979 TO 1982
PRI VOTE 1979 (%)	-.04	-.11
PAN VOTE 1979 (%)	.20	.20
	1973 TO 1982	1979 TO 1982
PRI VOTE 1973 (%)	-.15	-.23
PAN VOTE 1973 (%)	.10	.24

Zero-order Pearson's r correlation coefficients. N=32 states.
Change in Participation Rate defined as Participation Rate Year 2 minus Participation Rate Year 1.

6

Democracy and Power in Mexico: The Meaning of Conflict in the 1979, 1982, and 1985 Federal Elections

Silvia Gómez Tagle

Due to its peculiar features, the Mexican political system has been the subject of many discussions and controversies.[1] The political regime is defined in the Constitution as a federal, representative democracy; however, in everyday political practice, it has functioned very differently. The country has been governed since 1928 by the same political party; the president has gained power over democratic structures such as the Federal Congress, and elections have had a dubious meaning. As a result, one may conclude that many of the features of western democratic models are not present in the Mexican political system. In spite of all this, Mexico has been one of the Latin American nations that has maintained one of the longest periods of political stability and economic development in the capitalist system. In this chapter I will discuss the meaning of democracy in relation to specific features of the Mexican political system.

Formal Democracy and the State

Because the term *democratic* is ambiguous, several problems arise when we apply it to a given political system. Therefore I will try to differentiate the two ways in which the term is most frequently used. The first is "formal democracy," which addresses the features of the electoral system itself and provides for the unrestricted participation of all the members of a society in the election of government and representatives in law-making processes. The second is "democracy" in a more general sense (frequently attached to a marxist theoretical orientation), whereby the participation of the members of the society at large, in organizations, social benefits, education, decisions, and political power is provided for.

With regard to the first conceptualization, "formal democracy," Hermet identifies at least three criteria for establishing the degrees that may exist in the practice of democracy in a given political system. The first criterion refers to the *freedom to vote*, which presumes the absence of pressures on, or reprisals against, the voters in order to induce them to vote one way or another. This also means

> that their vote will not be broken down into categories or electoral bodies which nullify the idea of popular sovereignty . . . and it is taken for granted that the ballot will be computed in a non-fraudulent manner, even when it does not correspond to the wishes of those in power, or to the people in charge of counting the votes; the falsification of elections denies, *de facto*, the voter's freedom.[2]

Another characteristic of "formal democracy" would be *competitiveness*. Even though perfect competition is practically impossible because there always exists a larger party or one with more economic resources, and so forth, there are situations opposed to pluralism, in which there is only one candidate or a single list of candidates for whom to vote. (The author places Mexico in one of these alternatives.)

Finally, a third criterion used to evaluate the degree of democratic practice in a political system is the importance, in terms of power, of what the elections decide or, in other words, whether the distribution of power is really decided by the voters. In those elections Hermet calls "classical" the center of power is normally involved in the final determination of electoral results.[3] Thus political leaders are replaced peacefully through the electoral process and the opposition has the opportunity to rise to power by way of elections.

According to Hermet, the intersection of these three variables—the degree of the voter's freedom, competition among candidates and what is at stake in the elections—permits the classification of political systems in those countries in which the classical formal democratic model is not in place. Hermet classified Mexico, Senegal in 1976 and Brazil in 1966 as having "formally competitive and pluralistic elections, manipulated by a central power."[4]

Hermet's approach is interesting in terms of the analysis of the Mexican political system in its formal aspects, but I believe that the discussion of a political system presupposes a more general conception of power and of the political system as a whole, which would enable us to take other aspects of democracy into account. The differentiation of the basic form of the state, capitalist or socialist, must be taken into consideration in order to analyze the problem of democracy. With this, I do not intend to avoid the problem of democracy in the countries of "real socialism," but I do not agree with Hermet's position, insofar as he does not make any differentiation among states, assuming implicitly that the three variables he defines can adequately characterize democracy in a socialist as well as a capitalist system.

In a capitalist country the problem of democracy cannot be seen only as the participation of an undifferentiated population in an electoral process. More, it is the concrete expression of a form of political representation of social classes in that society. That is to say, given that a population has been divided into differentiated sectors or groups with regard to possession of the means of production and with regard to power, the problem of democracy is not exhausted in the formalism of the political system. Rather, the electoral process should be viewed as the expression of a more complex system of political and economic relations among social classes or fragments of social classes that are capable of the organized expression of political interest. As Alonso appropriately pointed out, "although conflicts arising about the electoral question do not, as a rule, correspond directly to a process of class struggle, placing the exploited on one side and the exploiters on the other, elections usually cross over classist sectors with different articulations."[5] But at the same time, it must be borne in mind that democracy is not expressed only through the electoral process. To understand what Mexican democracy is, therefore, Alonso suggests that the focus should be placed upon the participation of the citizens in the sphere of public power in a more general sense, as such involvement has remained a constant goal that has been expressed differently in accordance with socio-economic changes.[6] Formal democracy, understood as one of the expressions of political representation of social classes, is very important, but it certainly is not the only expression of democracy and sometimes not even the main one.[7]

Historical Roots of the Mexican Political System

In order to understand the role that the electoral process, with its peculiar characteristics, has in the Mexican political system, it is essential to be mindful of its historical genesis. The Revolution of 1910 was sparked by the slogan "effective suffrage and no re-election," and this principle and others more pertinent to substantive rather than formal democracy (as for example Article 3 of the Constitution relating to public education, Article 123 to labor rights and Article 27 to ownership of natural resources by the nation) became cornerstones of the new political order.

The no re-election principle has been carefully observed, permitting the constant renewal of political personnel; the only president who planned on being re-elected was Obregón, who was assassinated in 1928 before having the opportunity to realize his plan. Since then presidential succession, if not democratic in a formal sense, has at least been orderly and peaceful. No other president, high-ranking official or candidate for the presidency has ever been the victim of violence (in contrast with what has occurred in the United States, for instance). However, the same cannot be said about leaders of important movements (nor about candidates for political parties); one need only recall the assassination of the agrarian leader, Ruben Jaramillo, in the 1960s or the many years that Vallejo, the railroad union leader, suffered imprisonment. Thus while it is clear that the political system in Mexico has kept order in the sense of transmitting power from one member of the official political party to the next, and though no other very significant political party has competed for power, it cannot be said that the system has been free of political repression.

The question could, however, be raised as to whether this system of transmitting power from one member of the official party to another is necessarily anti-democratic, insofar as the PRI (Institutional Revolutionary Party) has been a party with a broad popular base and an ambiguous relationship with different social classes, so as to allow its classification as a pluralistic party. Is not the difference between a president like Cárdenas (1934–1940) and another like Avila Camacho (1940–1946), or between a president like Díaz Ordaz (1964–1970) and one like Echeverría (1970–1976) as great, if not greater, than the difference between Carter, a Democratic president of the United States, and Reagan, a Republican president?

In the Mexican political system there is a process of negotiation for power among political elites and with interest groups such as labor, peasants, entrepreneurs and foreign powers (the United States, for example) that serves as a substitute for electoral democracy in the alternation of individuals in power. However, this does not solve other important problems of democracy, since there does not exist an autonomous political opposition capable of competing for power, hence providing for only limited criticism within the system.

In the Mexican system, the president enjoys enormous power at least in part due to having been selected for the office via a complex process of negotiation. The president is not only the most powerful political figure in the system, but is also the most sensitive to the demands of different social forces and has been able to promote some of the social reforms that have legitimated the system, in the broad substantive sense of democracy, despite the lack of formal democracy.

It was Calles who, in 1928, promoted the creation of the governmental party, which would facilitate the settling of differences between the revolutionary leaders who controlled the country by regions, and the establishment of rules permitting the institutionalization of political relations. It was also Calles who organized the first primary elections, in which a "competitive" opposition participated. José Vasconcelos was the candidate for the opposition, and for the first time, the election took on a truly national, pluralistic character with the involvement of groups ranging from the Catholic extreme right to sectors identified with the left.[8]

The fraud committed on election day in 1929 was obvious, and in that first competitive election, a pattern was created from which subsequent electoral contests have deviated little. However, official election returns would lead one to think that the Partido Nacional Revolucionario (PNR) had not really been on the verge of losing the presidency and that, therefore, the fraud had been rather useless: 1,825,732 votes (93.58%) for Pascual Ortiz Rubio, the official candidate, and 105,655 votes (5.42%) for José Vasconcelos, the opposition candidate.[9]

When Cárdenas was nominated as the PNR candidate in 1934, there was no conflict; the actual struggle occurred within the group in power in the official party. Upon the conclusion of Cárdenas' presidential period, a large dissident sector emerged in 1940, unsatisfied with the candidate proposed by the official party (Partido de la Revolución Mexicana—PRM). This group organized an electoral movement of great proportions, headed by General Juan Andrew Almazan. On this occasion also, the groups that supported the opposition came from the right as well as from popular social forces, such as electricians, miners, streetcar-line employees, and so forth. The PCM (Mexican Communist Party) backed the PRM candidate, and according to Paoli's observations,

> the leading social forces, not in number but in actual power, had adhered to Avila Camacho, the official candidate, and supported him. Regional and local political bosses (caciques), farm laborers, domestic and foreign entrepreneurs of great importance, a majority of the armed forces and important labor groups upheld Avila Camacho's victory regardless of the votes."

However, the fraudulent practices during the elections were obvious; once again, the election returns were apparently out of proportion with the violence surrounding the process, what would suggest either a monstrous or an entirely useless fraud: Avila Camacho 2,476,641 votes (93.89%), Almazan 151,101 votes (5.72%).[10]

Something similar occurred in 1952 when a significant opposition, the "Henriquist Movement" (the supporters of Henríquez), arose. The Federación de Partidos del Pueblo (Henríquez) obtained 579,745 votes (15.8%); Ruiz Cortínes, the official candidate, 2,713,419 votes (74.31%); the Partido Acción Nacional (PAN), 285,555 votes (7.82%); and Partido Popular (PP, Socialist), afterwards PPS, 72,482 votes (1.98%).[11] As had happened on previous occasions, the opposition pointed out a variety of fraudulent acts of violence that had occurred during the electoral process, although the protest was perhaps milder as the figures seemed less exaggerated than in the two previous elections to which I referred.

But two years later, shortly after a modification in the electoral legislation and at the request of the Institutional Revolutionary Party (PRI), the registration of the Henríquez Party was cancelled. This act can only be interpreted as repression against the real opposition, since the registration of less important parties, such as the PAN and the PP, was not cancelled.

After 1952 the electoral opposition declined to such an extent that the government itself, despite the contradiction with its own party, decided on various occasions to stimulate the democratic system in order to activate actual participation in the electoral process. This can be seen in the 1962 reform that launched the innovation of the "party representatives" (deputies). This reform conceded minority parties a number of representatives according to the votes they had received at the national level: five deputies for the parties that would have reached 2.5% of the national votes and an additional deputy for each additional 0.5% of votes, up to a total of 20 representatives or deputies per party.

In 1973 President Echeverría initiated further reforms in the electoral arena in order to stimulate the participation of the existing parties: PPS, PARM and PAN, of which only the last one may be considered real opposition. These measures proved failures, and in the 1976 presidential election the situation went as far as to have a single registered candidate: José López Portillo, nominated by the PRI. The Mexican Communist Party launched an electoral campaign, but it was not granted the right to register so its participation was not legally recognized.

Certain general characteristics of the opposition can be derived from Paoli's work. On the three occasions he considers, the opposition candidates— Vasconcelos, Almazan, as well as Henríquez—were political personalities who, in some way, had been shaped within the government party or the group in power. Essentially they were members of the Revolutionary Family. They did not represent an alternative national project, with regard to the one proposed by the Mexican Revolution; instead, they offered criticism of the way in which the government, in each period, was "interpreting the principles of the Revolution." Among these criticisms, corruption was a notable constant. The organization of these political movements revolved around a single political figure, and no permanent opposition political party was ever created. The political leader defined the ideology of each movement in speeches without supporting documentation that would have provided further detail as to the movement's precepts. Finally, like the official party, the most important opposition movements also represented a wide diversity of social classes.

There are two types of considerations to be made in this regard. The first concerns the nature of the opposition, and the second concerns the response of the State to the electoral opposition. With respect to the first consideration, it seems to me that the 1910 Revolution provided the nation with such a hegemonic national project that no other political group, right or left, has ever been able to represent a significantly popular opposition. After several attempts to raise an independent opposition, the PCM (Mexican Communist Party) finally decided to join the official party in 1938 and become part of the popular national front, organized by the Party of the Mexican Revolution (Partido de la Revolución Mexicana—PRM). The right has thus far been equally unable—although this may change in the future— to organize the alternative of a "counterrevolution" as a national project.

The official party, because of its status as heir of the Revolution, has enjoyed this great hegemony that has not only been maintained as an ideological image, but has also been renewed through the exercise of power, thanks to some limited material achievements. This could explain why the most significant movements of the opposition, at a nationwide level, have been the work of leaders who have fallen out of the ruling group itself. The political space occupied by the official party, under its successive names—PNR, PRM, PRI—has been so great that the opposition has only existed as its subordinate and in many ways has derived life from the latter's mistakes.

Regarding the government, one must remember that the Revolutionary Family came to power through armed struggle, not by election, and that this group has remained in power by resorting to force if necessary, although it has managed to preserve the hegemonic project of the Revolution as its own heritage. This project has secured for the official party great popular support that has given the system a broad democratic character in the sense of the participation of organized social forces in the benefits of society. Unfortunately, these benefits do not extend to the masses of poor, unemployed urban and peasant non-organized workers or Indian groups, for example, thereby creating a highly unequal distribution of income.

I am not sure if one can say that in a system where there is a formal democracy, there is less repression, but I think that the lack of formal democratic mechanisms in the Mexican political system very often inclines political leaders to respond to their opposition with repression. This has been the case even though sometimes the system has also been capable of granting some of the demands made by such political forces.

The electoral system and the official party were designed from the beginning (1928) to provide an institutional course for the political struggle, but the government does not seem to have, or to ever have had, any intention of allowing the popular vote to decide who will rise to power. The same mechanisms of control and "clientelism," which are characteristic of the political system as a whole, also prevail within the party.

But one must not forget that the scope of democracy is not limited to the formal practices within the official party (PRI) or to formal practices and institutions in the broader society. Otherwise the stability and hegemony enjoyed by the Mexican state that emerged from the 1910 Revolution would be inexplicable. Therefore, characterizations of the Mexican state as authoritarian are, in my opinion, inadequate. It is essential to keep in mind the entire historical problem of the Mexican state when analyzing electoral conflicts and fraud in recent Federal Deputy elections, so as not to remain focused only upon the pure formality of democracy.

The 1977 Political Reform

Although no radical change has occurred in the Mexican state since the 1930s, the relationship among the social forces that constitute the State has been substantially modified. By 1976 the weakened nature of the political system, unable even to carry out the function of curbing the decisions made by key political officials and pressure groups, was quite evident. The absence of opposition and high rates of abstention were the passive expressions of how the system had been repudiated; these, in conjunction with an economic crisis that jeopardized the social pact that had been sustained by the State, stimulated a search for deeper and more far-reaching changes than the ones attempted by previous electoral legislative reforms. During this critical period of strong national and extranational pressures, government officials decided to look for an institutional solution to the crisis. Nevertheless, a full eight years later, the crisis continues to threaten the foundations of the political system.[12]

It appears that the political reform was never intended to offer the opportunity of a complete change in the governing group by means of the electoral process. Rather, as has been repeatedly stated, the political participation of minority groups would be promoted insofar as they remained minorities. This is why Reyes Heroles, in the speech proclaiming the political reform, expressed the chief executive's willingness to broaden the possibilities of political representation so that the organs of representation might embrace "the complicated national ideological mosaic composed of a vast *main political current* and several *small political currents* which, differing widely from the major one, nevertheless form part of the Nation."[13] It must also be borne in mind that this decision was not gratuitous, since those democratizing and popular currents have always been present in Mexican society, and it would be those social movements, and not only the chief executive in power, who would bear the responsibility for the advance of the political reform begun in 1977. A great deal has been written concerning the political reform, and as a result, I shall limit myself to citing two outstanding aspects of the issue germane to the current discussion. First, the reform provided for the conditional registration of political parties wishing to participate in elections. The condition for obtaining permanent registration was to obtain 1.5% of the total vote in one of the elections for which the party had been granted conditional registration.[14] Second, minority parties would have the right to obtain deputies on the principle of proportional representation. One hundred of the four hundred federal deputies who make up the Lower House would be elected on this principle, according to the votes they obtain in each of the major subdivisions in which the country is divided, called *circumscripciones.*

In short, the political reform modified two aspects of the democratic panorama. Political competition was considerably enhanced by granting the possibility of participation to parties whose registration had been cancelled at previous times, such as the Mexican Communist Party (PCM) or the Mexican Democratic Party (PDM), the electoral organization of the Unión Nacional Sinarquista, as well as to new organizations, both left-wing and right-wing: the Partido Socialista de los Trabajadores (PST), the Partido Revolucionario de los Trabajadores (PRT), the Partido Social Demócrata (PSD) and the Partido Mexicano de los Trabajadores (PMT), all of which have been permitted to participate since the 1979 federal elections. Since the seats that the opposition obtains by direct election are very few, the political reform also made possible wider participation in the Lower House, as it guarantees at least one-fourth of the seats to the opposition through the election of deputies on the principle of proportional representation.[15] The modifications in the electoral system introduced by the 1977 political reform were limited at first to federal elections for members of the Lower House. In the elections for president and senators, parties with "conditional registration" were also allowed to participate, though not on the principle of proportional representation. This fact limited the opposition to a governmental sphere considerably distant from actual power, insofar as the Lower House has functioned as a sounding board for the president rather than as an autonomous legislative power.

As can be seen in Tables 6.1A, 6.1B, 6.1C (for 1979, 1982 and 1985), the total number of votes increased following the reform (up 29.19% in

1985 over 1979). 1982 stands out as the year with the highest level of electoral participation. This could be because the elections in 1979 and 1985 were only for representatives to the Lower House, but the 1982 elections were also for president and senators; this can also be observed in the record of the electoral process prior to the political reform of 1977. Clearly, the difference between the votes obtained by the official party and those cast for the opposition is so great that the opposition's chances to win an election by "general majority" are very slim. The PAN is the only party with increasing opportunities: in 1979 it had won three districts, in 1982 only one, but in 1985 it won nine districts. The other exception is the PARM, which won two districts in 1985 to everyone's surprise, since in 1982 it had lost its registration due to the scant votes obtained. This fact, together with the ideological and political position of this party, often very close to the government and the PRI, has aroused suspicion as to the cause of such triumphs.

The conclusion easily drawn from these figures is that a pluralist system can only be installed through elections by proportional representation. In this kind of election the total number of votes cast for each majority party is taken into account within each one of the major electoral regions into which the country is divided. (There were three regions or *circumscripciones* in 1979, four in 1982 and five in 1985.) A minority party is defined as one with less than sixty general majority representatives.[16]

Hardly eight years after the political reform introducing new electoral procedures passed, many signs indicate that electoral authorities and the PRI are negotiating with the political parties of the "friendly opposition" the number of representatives that they will have by the principle of proportional representation, rather than obtaining representatives according to the number of votes received. Since the information on how many votes were obtained by each party at the district level has never been given, one may assume that the figures have been altered. It appears then that lately the election by proportional representation of deputies for the opposition has often been the result of a particular negotiation between the opposition parties, the government and the PRI, more than the direct result of the number of votes cast. Such a method permits a decision as to not only who will be the majority in the Lower House, but also as to in what proportion each opposition party will be represented.

After the reforms to Article 115 of the Constitution, promoted by President Miguel de la Madrid, the political reform gradually made its way to other electoral levels: governors, deputies and senators in the federative entities' chambers and, finally, municipal authorities. However, the process is slow and faces serious obstacles from local pressure groups.[17]

Conflict and Fraud in the 1979, 1982 and 1985 Electoral Process

It is an increasingly more conscious citizenry that, motivated to participate politically in order to shake off the yoke of an often arbitrary and corrupt power hidden in the official political party, promotes political reform and will perhaps prevent the system from sinking into bureaucratization. In this context, the fight for the respect of the vote and strict legality in the electoral process is a fundamental question, in which all the opposition political parties, regardless of their right- or left-wing tendency, have participated as standard bearers. Only the wider participation of opposition parties has been able to give gradually—in a process that as yet cannot be considered complete—an image of legitimacy to the Mexican elections, which up to now have been suspect, especially in rural areas.[18]

The electoral process begins with the registration of candidates and the nomination of electoral authorities at the local level and ends with the actual computation of the votes cast. During the long period that begins almost one year before an election, officials at the polls are designated, representatives of candidates and parties are incorporated, the lists of voters are compiled, equal opportunity to campaign is offered to the opposition parties, the votes are cast on election day and finally, votes are computed.

The only way the legality of this process can be evaluated is through the experience of the independent opposition parties (those that are not supported by the government). However, such experience is difficult to document, insofar as the political parties themselves often lack a documented record of their participation in the elections or of the conflicts and the struggles in which they took part. In some instances, they even lack proper records of the elections they won. Furthermore, political parties are not monolithic entities: the leaders change; groups clash or hold different criteria. The views and information offered by the ruling national press provide certain clues, but in a piecemeal fashion and always colored by the political interests represented. Local press reporting on elections, offering a more comprehensive view of the process, has yet to be studied due to limited research resources.

As a result, at least in this first approach to the problem, the most direct source of information about the electoral process—the sessions of the Lower House—were examined. In these sessions, 100 future deputies (already elected, but not yet confirmed) assemble as an Electoral College and judge, one by one, the 300 electoral districts in which deputies are elected by general majority. The analysis of Electoral College proceedings was restricted to this type of election, because these are the only cases in which results are discussed at the level of the electoral district and where the parties of the opposition have some possibility of winning. An analysis was made of the Electoral College sessions relative to elections in these 300 districts for 1979, 1982 and 1985. Such sessions generally take place in August of the election year, although in some cases they extend into later months (if, for instance, there is a conflict or an election has been annulled and new primaries have to be convened). The minutes of the sessions, published in the *Diario de Debates de la Cámara de Diputados* (Debate Records of the Lower House) were analysed for 1979 and 1982. For 1985, a personal observation of the entire evaluation process was undertaken, from the first session of the Federal Electoral Commission following the election of July

7 through the two-week session of the Electoral College. Additional documents relating to vote tabulations were also consulted.

Qualitative information concerning events in the 300 districts during those three years was classified according to the following criteria: *qualification of the election, types of conflicts arising during the electoral process and legal action taken by complaining parties and questioning parties.* The information was classified according to a conventional numerical code, with the purpose of processing it statistically and developing a comparison for the three elections in question.

As soon as the political reform bill was submitted for discussion in 1977, several of the political parties in the opposition and various personalities who participated in the deliberation pointed out that the fundamental problem in the Mexican electoral system had so far been the absence of an independent and unbiased court able to pass judgment on the legality of the elections. This problem has remained unsolved, insofar as the Upper and Lower House still constitute themselves into an Electoral College, which determines whether or not Federal Deputy and Senatorial elections are valid. As there is an overwhelming prevalence of official party members in both Houses, it is logical to suppose that all of the fraud and irregularities committed by this party, generally with the support of government officials, are looked upon with leniency and that the complaints presented by the opposition are rarely addressed.

As a rule, the procedure is as follows: the Federal Electoral Commission is the highest authority on the subject until the computing of the votes is completed, at the end of July. The returns are then turned over to the Electoral College for its final decision on the matter. As we said, the 100 deputies that form the college are at the same time elected deputies. All the political parties are represented in that instance; yet, for example in 1985, the opposition only had 40 seats in the Electoral College. During the first two weeks of August there are no electoral activities; the Electoral College meets only after August 15 and sits every day, sometimes including Sundays, from 10 A.M. until 2 A.M. or 3 A.M. the following day. Such pressure is due to the fact that by August 28 the 300 representatives elected by general majority principle and the 100 representatives elected by proportional ballot must have been "confirmed." If the Electoral College's decision is unsatisfactory in the opinion of a political party, it may appeal to the Supreme Court. Besides the fact that this represents a notoriously complicated legal procedure, it must be noted that the Supreme Court has no authority over the Electoral College and can only make suggestions. In the case of presidential or senatorial elections, the Senate has the power to issue the final verdict.

Qualification of the Electoral Process

Two extreme alternatives can present themselves in the elections of each district: (1) a majority has been attained by the winning candidate and the result has been "approved without debate"; or (2) the election is annulled because evidence exists that proves the returns were altered and new elections must be held. Between these two extremes, there are various alternatives, that have been separated into three general categories according to different situations: the first category, "approved with debate," involves those instances when the decision was approved after a brief debate and little evidence was presented to support the claim that the election returns had been altered or another type of conflict had arisen. In this case, complaints may even have been presented and conflicts may have arisen, requiring the annulment of votes in one or more polls; however, these problems were attended to satisfactorily and there were no further claims raised to the Electoral College by the opposition. Such may also have been the case in the first category, "approved without conflict." The second category, "approved with serious conflict," denotes those cases in which the ruling of the Federal Electoral Commission has been approved but has given rise to a lengthy process of argumentation pursued by one of the opposition parties, generally supported by others, with arguments presented that cast doubt as to the legality of the electoral procedure. The third category, "approved with very long debate," includes those cases in which the ruling has been discussed at length and abundant evidence of fraud has been presented by one or several parties.

The criteria presented for qualifying the electoral process in each district enable us to summarize the various aspects of conflict that may present themselves in an electoral process and render the outcome suspect. Ultimately, it is difficult to draw definitive distinctions between the categories "approved with debate," "long debate" and "very long debate," and additional information may prove necessary, in the future, to modify this categorization. Yet, in spite of such limitations, one can confidently state that, at least in the districts where results were subject to very long debate, the official party majority in the Electoral College imposed a decision of approval, disregarding the legitimate complaints of the parties in the opposition and often dismissing those complaints with insignificant pretexts, such as the fact that they had been filed one or two hours after the time stipulated by law. To be able to determine which of the parties—the opposition or the official party— was right, it would be necessary to embark on a thorough investigation of each case with facts drawn from sources unrelated to the conflict. However, one can say that it is in these districts where the electoral procedures should have been reconsidered.

All the documents relative to each district election are contained in an "electoral package" which includes the ballots, the official report of each voting booth, the official reports of the district computation, as well as the complaints and evidence of fraud presented by the opposition parties. No thorough examination of the evidence was made for any of the districts questioned by the opposition parties in 1985 (I do not know if the same happened in 1979 and 1982), although this demand would have been easy to satisfy. The only problem would have been to ask the Commission in charge of the case to examine the documents stored in the same building in which the sessions took place. The PRI's systematic denial of such requests may be interpreted as a tactical move to cover up electoral fraud.

Surprisingly enough, for the three years under study, in more than two-thirds of the districts the elections were not questioned at the Electoral College and were classified as "approved without debate." Some conflicts might have existed in those districts, but they were solved in time at the level of local authorities. It may also be possible that, regardless of the existence or not of fraud in those districts, the opposition parties had no information on the electoral process because they had no representatives present at the poll. Or it is possible they had no interest in fighting for a district that, in any event, they had no chance of winning. (See Table 6.2.)

In fact, my experience at the Electoral College in 1985 leads me to suspect that electoral fraud is a much more extended practice than an outside observer might first think. However, since the opposition parties do not question these practices, it is impossible to measure their impact on the electoral results.

It is clear, however, that conflict over electoral fraud is increasing significantly, if we take into account those districts where the opposition really fought in order to modify the results the Electoral College considered legitimate. In 1979 those districts (which gave rise to extended debate) amounted to only 2% of the total; by 1985 they had reached 7%. Since those districts are too few to constitute a real threat to the PRI majority, one wonders why the PRI is so unwilling to recognize a few triumphs for the opposition. We find here again the same disproportion between the opposition's limited forces and the extraordinary efforts displayed by the official party to defeat the opposition, as we observed in the 1929, 1940 and 1952 elections.

The "annulled election" category shows a negative trend in the governmental party's response to conflict, since in 1979—yet a year with limited conflicts—five districts were annulled; in 1982 only one was annulled, and in 1985 none were annulled. In that last year a new practice was instated: in three districts, instead of annulling the election and having to call for a new one, the commission that analyzed the documents pertaining to the electoral process in those districts, changed the figures (taking votes away from the PRI to add them to the PAN), so that the results of the election turned out differently, with the PAN candidate the new victor. This also suggests that negotiation concerning electoral results is a practice that the government and the PRI rely on to avoid facing direct electoral competition. However, the increased conflict in electoral activities also shows that real opposition parties (PAN, PDM, PSUM, PRT and PMT) are fighting harder to defend true democratic practices in the electoral process.

Another aspect that was analyzed was the type of conflict arising in different instances, regardless of the qualification assigned to the district. Several types of conflicts were identified. The first type concerns the eligibility of the winning candidate, depending upon whether the candidate has a criminal record or, more often, whether the candidate was born in the electoral district and has resided there the length of time stipulated by law. It must be made clear that the opposition parties generally question the eligibility of the winning candidate because they hope to take advantage of the legal stipulation that, if the winner is not qualified to fill the position of representative, the second-place candidate will be elected. The number of questioned PRI candidates was 15 in 1979, 13 in 1982 and only 8 in 1985. (See Table 6.3.) This shows that the PRI officials have been more careful in choosing their candidates for deputies.

The electoral registration lists have been subject to many criticisms because they have been intentionally manipulated to allow the PRI to increase its votes directly at the urns, to allow its sympathizers to vote several times, to exclude the opposition's sympathizers or simply to make it difficult for them to vote. In 1979 there were 13 cases of protest for such causes, 23 in 1982 and 32 in 1985. In 1985 there was much complaint because in some places whole lists of false names (in alphabetical order and starting with the same number) were introduced into the registration list. On the other hand, evidence was also brought to the College that showed that members of opposition parties had been excluded and not allowed to vote. Nevertheless, as only a few of the complaints were backed with evidence, the PRI majority argued that they would not modify the election results, so, in their view, it was not worthwhile lodging such complaints.

Campaign abuse by the authorities is another current cause of conflict. Electoral officials were accused of adopting a more accommodating attitude toward the official party than to other parties—allowing, for instance, the use of hillsides for campaign advertising and permitting the use of government employees and equipment to carry out electoral campaign activities. The opposition also pointed out that their candidates and supporters had been victims of repression while carrying out their campaign. Destruction of their propaganda was most common, although physical violence and imprisonment were also used in some cases. In 1979 this type of conflict was formally protested in 28 districts, in 1982 in 32 districts and in 1985 in 40 districts.

Conflicts also appear related to other activities carried out before the election day. These refer, for instance, to the locating of electoral booths, to the verification of the credentials of candidates' or parties' representatives at the booths, and to the timely reception at the voting station of the full array of official documentation (including the voter registration list, paper ballots, various supervisory and verification sheets and so forth) required for the legal conduct of the election. In 1979 conflicts of this type occurred in 23 districts; in 1982 the number rose to 47 and in 1985 to 50 districts.

Conflicts on election day involve the opening and closing of booths before or after the indicated hours. They may also result from the fact that opposition representatives were not admitted into the booths, that voters were not able to cast a secret vote, that there was propaganda placed inside the booths in order to sway the voter to the official party and, in an extreme case, that the urns were "refilled" or stolen. These were, in general, the most frequent cases of conflict. In 1979, 67 districts reported irregularities, decreasing to 53 in 1982, but increasing to 89 cases in 1985.

Once the voting is over and the centers closed, a complicated computing process starts. It begins with the computation made by the booth officials on the same election day and concludes with the assembling of an "electoral package" that includes the votes cast and the corresponding record signed by all the parties' and candidates' representatives and the officials at each booth. This "package" must be turned over to the Electoral District Committee, which meets one week later and verifies the computation records of each booth before issuing its majority dictum. This dictum is then turned over to the Federal Electoral Commission and finally to the Electoral College. In the course of this first week, which starts with the closure of the election day and finishes with the issuing of the majority dictum, many irregularities may occur that give the opposition parties good reason to suspect that the computation has been inaccurate. In 1979 refutations on this matter were presented for 48 districts; in 1982 the number increased to 56, but in 1985 it decreased to 37.

Conflicts also arose because the Catholic Church took an active part in the political campaign, supporting the right-wing parties, the PAN and the PDM. Such activities are illegal since the Constitution clearly states that the Church should not use religious activities to engage in political propaganda. Although the Church's political action was directed not only against the government, but also against the left-wing opposition parties, the complaints on this matter generally came only from the PPS and the PST and could therefore be interpreted as a tactic to undermine the strongest opposition party prestige, that of the PAN. In 1979 this type of conflict occurred in 2 districts, increasing to 8 in 1982 and to 11 in 1985.

Finally there are districts where we know conflicts existed because in the final dictum some kind of complaint is mentioned; however, we lack any information about the type of conflict in question because these districts were approved without debate, or frequently, in the complaints presented by the opposition, no specific reference was made to the type of conflict.

It is necessary to keep in mind that several conflicts may occur simultaneously in the same district; that is why their sum is not equal to 300. Rather what generally happens is that in the very conflictive districts, many types of conflicts arise simultaneously. In Table 6.4 it is evident that in the districts qualified as having "very long debate," many of those conflicts are concentrated. Moreover, the number of conflicts per district tends to increase from one election to the next: in 1979, 14 conflicts were registered in 6 districts; in 1982 the number increased to 50 conflicts in 14 districts (over 3 on the average per district) and in 1985, 101 conflicts were registered in 21 districts, an average of almost 5 per district). When comparing the three election years, one can conclude that conflict has been increasing significantly, not only as to the number of districts classified as approved after "very long debate," but also as to the number of conflicts simultaneously found in each district.

The questioning of the candidates' eligibility and of the district vote tabulation are the only two types of conflict that have decreased, whereas all other types have increased.

Legal Remedies

The law provides for five different types of remedies that may be used should any problem arise in the electoral process—remedies ranging from the location of the voting booths to the Electoral College's final dictum.

Sequence and timing requirements related to the submission of such challenge petitions must be strictly adhered to. Compliance with the complex procedures required by law is extremely difficult and serves to reduce the opposition's chances for successful achievement of legal redress. In fact, due to the burdensome requirements, many complaints have been invalidated simply on procedural grounds despite the well-founded character of the petitions.

Legal remedies may be considered only in the instances of formal "protest" and "complaint." Formal "complaints" not properly adjudicated in the Electoral College may be appealed, by the political party in question, to the Supreme Court as a last resort. An election will be declared null when returns from 20% of the voting stations are invalidated.[19] The protest recourse is valid against violations outlined in the law that affect results contained in the final tally of votes from the booths. This protest petition can be filed at the booth itself on election day, or with the Electoral District Committee concerned, within the following 72 hours and is attached to the final tally. This protest petition will be submitted for the District Committee's consideration on the day it checks the final tally, and if approved, the result of contested booths will not be computed.

The complaint petition is presented, according to the law, as a challenge against the results shown in the District computation record of the election and the majority dictum issued by the Committee itself. This is designed to strengthen the annulment process.[20] The complaint petition must be filed with the committee officials themselves at the end of the computing session or within 24 hours following the conclusion of such a session.[21] In both cases, a time limit is established for the formal submission of challenges to electoral outcomes. Importantly, however, as the deadline for submission varies as a function of the hour at which the vote tally document "was signed" at the voting booth or when the District Committee session concluded, there has tended to be considerable difficulty with the submission of such complaints. In both situations, if the official party representation constitutes a majority, its members can agree to defer those legal petitions with the argument that they were not presented on time.

It often happens that, in the same districts where the booths have been the subject of a protest, the opposition lodges afterward a complaint affecting the whole district, in order to attempt to obtain the annulment of the election. As the "complaint" petition is specifically to be processed by the Electoral College, it is no surprise that this has been the petition more often mentioned and discussed: 64 times in 1979, 80 in 1982 and 117 in 1985. (See Table 6.5.) But it is rarely successful, since in 1979 only five districts were annulled, one in 1982 and none in 1985.

The "protest" petition questioning the results of one booth is more frequently successful, and it is also used more often, but since it is generally attended to before reaching the Electoral College, we are not informed on all the cases in which such a petition has been presented, nor for those districts in which it has been successful. Nevertheless, we can conclude that the opposition tends more and more to process its claims through legal channels. Yet, the PRI's and the government's response tends to deny any chance of success to the opposition.

The last recourse is to appeal to the Supreme Court. The PAN appealed the Electoral College dictum on four occasions in 1985, but without success.[22]

Parties and Procedural Challenges to the Electoral Process

We finally turn our attention to the identity of those political parties that have challenged the electoral process. It is clear that true opposition rests in the PAN, the more active party, as well as in the PCM/PSUM, the PRI and the PMT on the left. The PDM, although less active, has also been increasing its critical intervention. (See Table 6.6.) In contrast, the PPS, the PARM and the PST have decreased their activity. Evidence from the 1985 election indicates that the PPS, the PARM and the PST rarely acted as a real opposition since they supported PRI's proposals most of the time.

Surprisingly enough, however, the PRI challenged three times more electoral outcomes in districts in 1985 than in 1979. This seems to be a new tactic since the PAN has turned into a stronger competitor. In 1985, for example, the PRI undertook all possible efforts to annul two districts in Chihuahua where the PAN had won. But later, in the negotiations held at the national level, it was decided that none of the elections would be annulled, so that the majority dictum was approved even though the votes of many booths had not been computed because of the PRI's protests. (In the Third District of Chihuahua, the PAN won with 1656 votes against 919 for the PRI, with only ten booths computed out of a total of 116.)[23]

Conclusions

Although this analysis only covers Federal Deputy elections, for which it was possible to obtain detailed information at the district level, one can nevertheless extrapolate from it that electoral fraud in senatorial and presidential elections must be similar, since voting for president, senators and deputies takes place on the same day, in the same booth, and with the same electoral authorities.[24]

In this preliminary analysis of conflicts in the electoral process, it is not possible to go into further details concerning qualitative information, which would give a more complete version of what has occurred in each case. Nonetheless, two tendencies are evident. On the one hand, the party in power, the PRI, with the support of the governmental authorities at all levels, makes an exaggerated defense of its triumphs, a pose that frequently dissolves into assuming a right to commit abuses during the whole electoral process and could well be deemed electoral fraud. On the other hand, the opposition parties show a tendency to exaggerate at times the effects of such abuses on the election results, which could in a certain way appear to be a means of justifying the scarcity of the votes cast in their favor.

The Mexican political system has not complied with the three variables defined by Hermet as characteristic of democracy: freedom of the vote, because the possibility of fraud nullifies the freedom of the vote; competitiveness, because opposition political parties are not sufficiently strong and because the support that the PRI receives from the government makes the political competition unfair; and what is decided in the electoral process, because it seems that power has never been decided through the electoral process, being, instead, negotiated in other quarters.

If the criterion of the degree of debate in an electoral district has a certain objectivity, which I think it does, then we can make a fairly accurate evaluation of the weight that conflict has at a national level in federal elections. But this does not mean we can measure fraud, since all the peculiar procedures used in the elections, which I have described, seem to be far more generalized than expected at first. Instead, what I have measured is the conflict that surrounds the traditional practices of the electoral process inasmuch as fraud itself, in its fullest dimension, cannot be measured. My impression is that, often, what the opposition is questioning in the electoral process of a district is not only possible fraud, but rather a more general problem of government legitimacy, perhaps because at the local level the PRI is identified with unpopular groups (*caciques,* corrupt union-leaders, entrepreneurs willing to support foreign investments and interests, and so forth).

So the problem of formal democracy is not always the only question raised in the electoral conflicts. The problem of democracy, understood in a wider sense, is sometimes more important. One possible reason why electoral conflict increases in times of economic crisis may therefore be, not so much the increasing fraud, but rather the fact that the Mexican state is not able to carry on an economic policy that can absorb some of the major social dissatisfactions. There has been a contradiction between the hegemony enjoyed by the official party as heir of the revolutionary project and the need to use repression and electoral fraud to exclude opposition, a problem that cannot be resolved here. But the increasing level of conflict in the electoral process shows that Mexican society is changing and that the PRI's traditional practices, such as responding to the opposition with limited concessions during negotiation, are no longer satisfactory.

This is why the political reform of 1977 is so important. Even if it was never designed to afford the opposition the opportunity to reach power through elections, it has nonetheless opened a new democratic space. In the elections that I have analyzed, the opposition political parties are fighting to participate in the electoral contest on a formal democratic basis, as an expression of a process of self-identification of autonomous political forces that cannot be reversed. It appears that the official party and the government have not yet developed an adequate response to this changing situation, as they have continued to try to restore old political practices.

Notes

1. This chapter is part of my research project "Perspectives on Political Reform in Mexico." Alejandra Fernández Wong, sociologist, and Javier Rodríguez from the Centro de Computo of El Colegio de México took part in the research, for which I am very grateful. Research results were presented for the first time at the Twelfth International Congress of the Latin American Studies Association. This is a revised version of the paper presented at those meetings.

2. Guy Hermet, "Las elecciones en los regímenes autoritarios," in Guy Hermet, Alain Rouquie y Juan J. Linz, eds., *Para qué sirven las elecciones?* (Mexico City: Fondo de Cultura Económica, 1982), 23.

3. Hermet, "Las elecciones en los regímenes autoritarios," 26.

4. Hermet, "Las elecciones en los regímenes autoritarios," 28.

5. Jorge Alonso, "Elecciones y lucha de clases: apuntes para elaborar un proyecto de investigación sobre procesos electorales" (CIESAS, 1985) mimeo, 2.

6. Alonso, "Elecciones y lucha de clases," 7.

7. I have discussed this issue elsewhere and mention it only in brief for the purposes of this discussion. See Silvia Gómez Tagle, "La Reforma Política en México y el problema de la representación política de las clases sociales," in *El Estado Mexicano* (México, DF: CIESAS, Nueva Imagen, 1982); "Estado y Reforma Política: interpretaciones alternativas," *Nueva Antropológia*, vol. VIII, no. 25 (October 1984).

8. Francisco Paoli Bolio, "Legislación electoral y proceso político 1917–1982," in Pablo González Casanova, ed., *Las elecciones en México: evaluación y perspectivas* (México, D.F.: Siglo Vientiuno, 1985), 135.

9. Paoli Bolio, "Legislación electoral," 137.

10. Paoli Bolio, "Legislación electoral," 145.

11. Paoli Bolio, "Legislación electoral," 151.

12. González Casanova, *Las elecciones en México.*

13. Jesus Reyes Heroles, "Discurso pronunciado por . . . Chilpancingo, Gro., 1 de abril de 1977," in *Reforma Política, Gaceta Informativa de la Comisión Federal Electoral*, num. 1, Audiencias Publicas, Comisión Federal Electoral, México, 1977, xii. The emphasis is mine.

14. Ley Federal de Organizaciones y Procesos Electorales y su Reglamento (LFOPPE) (México, Editorial Porrua, 6a. ed., 1985), 50.

15. For a more detailed explanation, see Kevin J. Middlebrook, "Political Liberalization in an Authoritarian Regime: The Case of Mexico," Research Report 41, (La Jolla, CA: Center for U.S.-Mexican Studies, University of California, San Diego, 1985).

16. LFOPPE, 79.

17. Regarding this problem, see the collection organized by Carlos Martínez Assad, *Municipios en conflicto* (México: UNAM-G.V.Editores, 1985) which includes a number of very revealing cases.

18. Hermet, "Las elecciones," 25.

19. LFOPPE, articles 222 and 223.

20. LFOPPE, article 223.

21. LFOPPE, article 229.

22. Session of the Lower House, October 22, 1985.

23. See Dictamen del Tercer Distrito de Chihuahua, Colegio Electoral, 1985.

24. For further reference in the 1979 and 1982 election see Cámara de Diputados del Congreso de los Estados Unidos Mexicanos, 1979, *Diario de Debates*, LI Legislatura, Primer Periodo Ordinario, ano I, tomo I, 15 al 31 de agosto, nums. 1 al 14, México. Cámara de Diputados del Congreso de los Estados Unidos Mexicanos, 1982, *Diario de Debates*, LII Legislatura, Primer Periodo Ordinario, ano I, tomo I, 15 al 31 de agosto, nums. 1 al 14, México. Comisión Federal Electoral, Registro Nacional de Electores, 1979, *Estadística Electoral*, Elecciones para Diputados segun el principio de Mayoria Relativa, México. Comisión Federal Electoral, Registro Nacional de Electores, 1979, *Estadística Electoral*, Elecciones para Diputados segun el principio de Representación Proporcional, México.

TABLE 6.1A
Federal Deputies Election, 1979: Votes and Deputies Elected
by Political Party

POLITICAL PARTY	VOTES	%	DEPUTIES ELECTED	%
PAN	1,487,242	10.78	3	1.0
PRI	9,608,742	69.68	297	99.0
PPS	358,920	2.60	---	---
PARM	249,726	1.81	---	---
PDM	285,040	2.06	---	---
PCM	688,947	4.99	---	---
PST	293,511	2.12	---	---
C.N.[1]	9,824	0.07	---	---
V. Annulled[2]	806,453	5.84	---	---
Total	13,788,432	99.95	300	100.0
Total ballot	27,937,237	49.53[3]		

1) Unregistered candidates (votes annulled).
2) Annulled votes.
3) Electoral participation: percentage of votes with respect to the total number of persons inscribed in the electoral ballot.
Source: Gaceta informativa de la reforma política num. IX, and Diario de Debates de la Cámara de Diputados, 1979.

TABLE 6.1B
Federal Deputies Election, 1982: Votes and Deputies by
Political Party

POLITICAL PARTY	VOTES	%	DEPUTIES ELECTED	%
PAN	3,676,091	17.46	1	0.33
PRI	14,598,026	69.33	299	99.67
PPS	393,989	1.87	---	---
PARM	282,711	1.34	---	---
PDM	483,865	2.29	---	---
PSUM	925,841	4.39	---	---
PST	376,493	1.78	---	---
PRT	265,570	1.26	---	---
PSD	40,454	0.19		
C.N.[1]	97	0.00	---	---
V. Annulled[2]	10,661	0.05	300	100.00
Total	21,053,798	99.96		
Total ballot	31,526,386	66.78[3]		

1) Unregistered candidates (votes annulled).
2) Annulled votes.
3) Electoral participation: percentage of votes with respect
   to the total number of persons inscribed in the electoral
   ballot.
Source: Gaceta informativa de la reforma política num IX,
   and Diario de Debates de la Cámara de Diputados,
   1982.

TABLE 6.1C

Federal Deputies Election, 1985: Votes and Deputies Elected
by Political Party

POLITICAL PARTY	VOTES	%	DEPUTIES ELECTED	%
PAN	2,769,433	15.54	9	3.00
PRI	11,575,742	64.97	289	96.33
PPS	350,300	1.96	---	---
PARM	295,344	1.65	2	00.67
PDM	484,407	2.71	---	---
PSUM	574,945	3.22	---	---
PST	425,603	2.38	---	---
PRT	225,529	1.26	---	---
PMT	276,592	1.55	---	---
C.N.[1]	11,922	0.06		
V. Annulled[2]	824,752	4.62		
Total	17,814,569	99.92	300	100.0
Total ballot	35,196,525	50.61[3]		

1) Unregistered candidates (votes annulled).
2) Annulled votes.
3) Electoral participation: percentage of votes with respect
   to the total number of persons inscribed in the electoral
   ballot.
Source: Session acts of the Electoral College of 1985 and
          Comisión Federal Electoral.

TABLE 6.2
Qualification of Electoral Districts

QUALIFICATION	1979		1982		1985	
	No.	%	No.	%	No.	%
Districts approved without debate	233	77.7	232	77.3	216	72
Districts approved with debate	31	10.3	13	4.3	32	10.7
Districts approved with long debate	25	8.3	40	13.3	28	9.3
Districts approved with very long debate	6	2.0	14	4.7	21	7.0
+Elections annulled	5	1.7	1	0.3	3	1.0
TOTAL	300	100	300	100	300	100

+Elections annulled or results changed.
Source: Diario de Debates de la Cámara de Diputados, 1979 and 1982, and field work, documents and session acts of the Electoral College for 1985.

TABLE 6.3
Federal Deputies Election 1979, 1982, 1985: Types of Conflict in Each Electoral District

TYPES OF CONFLICT	1979		1982		1985	
	No.	%	No.	%	No.	%
CANDIDATE	15	5.00	13	4.33	8	2.66
ELECTORAL POLL	13	4.33	23	7.66	32	10.66
REPRESSION AND ABUSE OF POWER	28	9.33	32	10.66	40	13.33
CONFLICTS BEFORE ELECTION	23	7.66	47	15.66	50	16.66
CONFLICTS ON ELECTION DAY	67	22.33	59	19.66	89	29.66
VOTES COMPUTATION	48	16.00	56	18.66	37	12.33
CHURCH POLITICAL PARTICIPATION	2	0.66	8	2.66	11	3.66
WITHOUT DATA	11	3.66	29	9.66	44	14.66

NOTE: There are simultaneous alternatives for each district, so the total number by row does not correspond with the total number of districts. The percentage has been calculated with respect to the total number of electoral districts: 300.
Source: Diario de Debates de la Cámara de Diputados 1979 and 1982, and field work documents and sessions acts of the Electoral College of 1985.

TABLE 6.4
Federal Deputies Election 1979, 1982, 1985: Districts Approved With Very Long Debate

TYPES OF CONFLICT IN EACH ELECTORAL DISTRICT	1979 No.	1979 %*	1982 No.	1982 %*	1985 No.	1985 %*
CANDIDATE	1	.33	2	.66	2	.66
LIST OF ELIGIBLE VOTERS	1	.33	7	2.33	10	3.33
REPRESSION AND ABUSE OF POWER	2	.66	7	2.33	13	4.33
CONFLICTS BEFORE ELECTION	3	1.00	9	3.00	16	5.33
CONFLICTS ON ELECTION DAY	4	1.33	12	4.00	18	6.00
VOTES COMPUTATION	3	1.00	10	3.33	12	4.00
CHURCH POLITICAL PARTICIPATION	---	---	3	1.00	3	1.00
WITHOUT INFORMATION	---	---	---	---	---	---
TOTAL NUMBER OF CONFLICTS	14		50	0	101	---
TOTAL NUMBER OF DISTRICTS	6	2.00	14	4.66	21	7.00

NOTE: There are simultaneous alternatives for each district, so the total number by row does not correspond with the total number of districts. The percentage has been calculated with respect to the total number of electoral districts: 300.
Source: Diario de Debates de la Cámara de Diputados 1979 and 1982, and field work documents and sessions acts of the Electoral College of 1985.

TABLE 6.5
Federal Deputies Election 1979, 1982, 1985: Legal Remedies

LEGAL REMEDIES	1979		1982		1985	
	No.	%*	No.	%*	No.	%*
PROTEST	43	14.33	58	19.33	95	31.66
COMPLAINT	64	21.33	80	26.66	117	39.00
APPEAL TO THE SUPREME COURT	---	---	---	---	4	1.33
OTHERS	3	1.00	7	2.33	11	3.66

NOTE: There are simultaneous alternatives for each district, so the total number by the row does not correspond with the total number of districts. The percentage has been calculated with respect to the total number of electoral districts: 300.
Source: Diario de Debates de la Cámara de Diputados 1979 and 1982, and field work, documents and session acts of the Electoral College of 1985.

TABLE 6.6
Federal Deputies Election 1979, 1982, 1985: Political
Parties Petitioning for Legal Remedy

POLITICAL PARTIES	1979		1982		1985	
	No.	%*	No.	%*	No.	%*
PAN	73	24.33	82	27.33	105	35.00
PRI	4	1.33	3	1.00	12	4.00
PPS	24	8.00	7	2.33	22	7.33
PARM	15	5.00	3	1.00	9	3.33
PDM	9	3.00	10	3.33	17	5.66
PCM/PSUM	35	11.66	47	15.66	39	13.00
PST	15	5.00	9	3.00	9	3.33
PRT	**		5	1.66	28	9.33
PSD	**		24	8.00	**	
PMT	**		**		20	6.66

**Party did not take part in the election.
NOTE: There are simultaneous alternatives for each district,
so the total number by row does not correspond with the total
number of districts. The percentage has been calculated with
respect to the total number of electoral districts: 300.
Source: Diario de Debates de la Cámara de Diputados 1979
and 1982, and field work, documents and session
acts of the Electoral College of 1985.

7

Elections and Political Culture in Mexico

Miguel Basañez

The political sociology of elections in Mexico is virtually unexplored territory, and the use of public opinion polls to identify preferences and trends is in the earliest stages of development and thus is viewed with some skepticism. The rapidly changing conditions of recent years and the spread in Mexico and abroad of an increasingly negative view of Mexico's present and future, force us to search for new tools to use in a more detailed, empirically based analysis of the nation's circumstances, in general, and of sociopolitical events, in particular.

The origin of this essay was an attempt to test the usefulness and reliability of opinion polls in Mexico. The essay presents the analysis of two surveys conducted by the author[1] and presents the predictions that were made of electoral behavior in the July 1985 elections.[2] Finally, official results are compared with the forecast.

One school of thought currently in vogue in North America is reflected in Newell and Rubio's comment that "as a consequence of the erosion of the political system's legitimacy, Mexico's government has resorted more and more frequently to populism in order to try and restore its debilitated political status."[3] Wayne Cornelius quotes—and rejects—a similar image, when he says that "Mexico's economic crisis . . . caused concern in the United States about the possibility of a breakdown of the Mexican political system."[4]

The questions that necessarily arise are: Just how deep is this alleged "erosion of legitimacy"? How real is the possibility of a "breakdown of the system"? An analysis of the July 1985 elections can help to produce a clearer picture of the strength or weakness of the system and of the possibilities— or lack of feasibility—of current political practices and parties.

As will be seen later, the data obtained from opinion polls do not support the rather facile inference of the inevitability of "erosion and breakdown." Instead, one might argue that the work of Silvia Gómez Tagle and of Joseph Klesner, found elsewhere in this volume, supports the view that the PRI

(Institutional Revolutionary Party) has hardly lost its hegemonic status in society and that elections in Mexico may, as Gómez Tagle suggests, have a meaning quite different from their conventional significance in other countries.[5]

The importance of these new studies lies further in the fact that they may help to stimulate a shift away from the conventional authoritarian-corporatist framework toward a more open-ended empirical approach to political research,[6] closer to the social plane, for explanations as to why and how Mexican society has produced a system of political practices and parties that has endured with relative stability for almost sixty years, in clear contrast to the rest of Latin America.

Much has been said in academic circles about the scope and limitations of surveys as primary tools to explore and describe social phenomena. The July 1985 elections were, unquestionably, an occasion for Mexican and foreign intellectuals and politicians to update their interpretations about Mexico's future. In this context, the interest in opinion polls as elections drew near may be considered a first step forward. Moreover, interesting studies were published that examined the historical trends of the forces engaged in the struggle for power in Mexico, such as the works by Pablo González Casanova[7] and David Torres.[8]

Projections as to electoral outcomes also appeared at this juncture such as the report published by Gómez Tagle[9] which suggested interesting methodological approaches in this area. Gallup/Mexico provided national level data generated through opinion surveys on party preferences.[10] Other useful material was included in Granados Chapa's "Paradox of Suspicions" (Paradoja de la Suspicacia).[11] Nonetheless, Rodríguez Araujo[12] concludes that surveys in our political system "are no good," as there is no guarantee as to the quantitative accuracy of forecasts of electoral results. Before dismissing survey data as having little utility, however, one may argue that such predictive exercises are primarily useful in qualitative terms as tools of electoral sociology despite the fact that the results are expressed in eminently quantitative terms.

Survey and Elections

The lines of analysis that served as the basis for the exploration of current political culture and for an attempt to predict the outcome of the elections were: (1) party sympathies and perceptions of the legitimacy of government; (2) public opinion about public works and services (education, health, police), as well as about the respondent's own personal situation; (3) the distribution of radical, moderate and conservative political attitudes among occupational groups; and (4) opinions about important principles and issues in Mexico (the Church's participation in politics, non-reelection, the right to strike, land distribution, foreign debt).

According to the 1983 survey,[13] party preferences were distributed as follows: PRI, 55%; PAN, 10%; (National Action party) PSUM, 4% (Mexican

Unified Socialist Party), other parties, 5%; and none, 26%. These data agree, in general, with those obtained in a poll carried out by the author in 1982,[14] as well as with Gallup polls.[15]

The three polls were then compared with the results of votes for Federal deputies in 1982. Especially outstanding is the support for the PRI by all strata of the population. For each PAN follower, there are 5.5 PRI sympathizers, and 14 for each person who favors the PSUM. Even among students, who exhibit the greatest skepticism toward political parties, 42% of students favor the PRI, as compared with 10% who support the PAN, and 4.6% supporting the PSUM.

What is striking in Table 7.1 is the extremely high level of sympathy for the PAN reported by the 1985 Gallup polls as compared to the other results reported in Table 7.1. The discrepancy is probably explained by the ways in which the answers were elicited. In the author's surveys, the interviewer asked a direct question and noted the answer; in the Gallup polls the interviewee was given a piece of paper on which he marked the party of his choice and then dropped it into a closed container, simulating actual election proceedings.

The difference in the data seems to indicate some reluctance or timidity about openly admitting support for the PAN. If this hypothesis is correct, it might be important to investigate the correlation between such timidity and possible inactivity, reflected in voting abstentions, as borne out by the results of the 1982 elections.

Table 7.2 shows the distribution of opinion concerning public works, government schools, state health services and the police as well as about the personal situation of the persons interviewed. This last item is very important because it reflects, to a certain extent, the people's range of expectations, a central issue in the Mexican political system. More than measuring the objective situation of the country, it indicates Mexicans' optimism or pessimism about the future.

As can be seen, the educational system definitely confers legitimacy, especially considering that 79% of the respondents refer to public schools and 21% to private schools. Similar results are seen in response to the question on health services although they are not as pronounced as the results on the education survey item. These data represent empirical evidence of people's views of the degree of achievement of two objectives of the Mexican post-revolutionary state.

Opinions about the police differed markedly from the answers to the questions on health and education services. This issue is gaining in importance and has become a factor that detracts significantly from government's legitimacy. Suggestive of the severity of the problem is the fact that of all variables tested, "middle class status" and "poor opinion of police" most strongly correlate with "government rejection." If the two conditions are disaggregated, the correlation weakens.

Government legitimacy is enhanced among those who view public works positively, especially in the case of those projects that are readily and continuously in the people's sight. In this regard, the implementation of small projects for community service seems to play a more important role than massive public works projects that for the majority of the people are difficult to comprehend.[17]

Given the country's economic difficulties, it is somewhat surprising that the people interviewed have such a favorable opinion about their personal situation: 78% believe that it is similar to or better than the previous year. This in itself requires exploration in greater depth, which falls outside the scope of this essay. However, certain lines of reasoning are worthy of note.

First; what is the subjective origin of this optimism? An immediate answer might be found in the Catholic-Latin values of self-denial, sacrifice and resignation. Secondly, who benefits from this expression of satisfaction with current circumstances? Which political parties benefit? Initial analysis would indicate that the PRI and the government would be the principal beneficiaries. Thirdly, in view of these data, can the thesis of "erosion and breakdown" be easily maintained? In an initial review, subject to analysis in greater depth—the thesis would seem difficult to substantiate.

In Table 7.3, the respondents' views on five major issues are reported: Church participation in politics, non-reelection, right to strike, agrarian land distribution, and the foreign debt. The survey items attempted to solicit opinion on issues that were long ago resolved (the Church and reelection) and on issues now the subject of dispute (strikes, land distribution, and foreign debt).

As Table 7.3 indicates, 80% feel that the Church should participate very little or not at all in politics; 76.4% of those surveyed believe the current foreign debt is bad or very bad; 70.4% believe the principle of non-reelection is good or very good; and 56.6% support the right to strike as very good and good. This clearly defined majority only breaks down in the case of land distribution, which is considered just and very just by 36.4%, as opposed to 28% who believe it to be unjust and very unjust.

Party Sympathies

The data in the tables shown above demonstrate the potential utility of surveys for predicting overall election results. However, the theoretical and practical benefit of such a rough exercise is doubtful, unless further disaggregation can be accomplished. In order to achieve this it is necessary to identify the distribution of sympathies by occupational strata. These are the basic data upon which to develop vote predictions, after correcting disproportions in the sample by weighting, according to data from the Demographic Census.

The data reveal a strong correlation between party sympathies and occupational categories.[18] By contrast, Ivan Zavala argues that "for electoral purposes, Mexicans are divided into three groups of political parties . . . defined . . . by their ideological sympathies rather than demographic or economic characteristics."[19] In fact, however, the two arguments, rather than contradicting each other, are supplementary, and both illustrate the additional correlation between ideology and occupation which will become more evident further on.

Table 7.4 shows that in 1983 the PRI demonstrated its greatest strength among public officials (76.5%), political leaders (73.3%), bureaucrats (67.1%) and peasants (64.5%); the PAN among business interests (15%), blue-collar workers (14.9%), farmers (13.9%), industrialists (13.8%) and housewives (13.3%); the PSUM, among white collar workers (5.8%), political leaders (5.7%), bureaucrats (5.3%), business interests in the service sector (5.3%) and professionals (5.1%). Finally, among those larger segments of the population exhibiting no sympathy for any particular party were students (34.1%), business interests (26.3%) and marginals, or the extremely poor (26.1%).

By and large, the results shown in Table 7.4 agree with conventional knowledge of Mexican politics (with the exceptions discussed further on) and confirm the ranges found by the author in the 1982 poll, although there are certainly some discrepancies. What is particularly improbable is the extent of business support for the PSUM, which may be due to an error of definition in the survey's original design.

It is not surprising to find that the highest percentage of PRI sympathizers is mainly drawn from groups more directly linked to the public sector, that PAN followers, in turn, are found in greater numbers in the private sector, and that the highest percentage of rejection of political parties is among students and the marginals.

What is striking, however, is the presence of white-collar workers and business interests, as well as the absence of students and blue-collar workers in the composition of PSUM support; it is also peculiar that there is a relatively high rate of blue-collar worker support for the PAN, although only 14.9%, as compared to 52.7% for the PRI. It should be noted that this group accounts for 10.5% of PAN sympathizers, while business, with greater relative weight, represents 15.0%, only 0.1% more.

As to the strange spectrum of support for the PSUM, it should be stressed that in the 1982 poll the composition found was just as unexpected: 13% students, 8% each for professionals, officials and bureaucrats, and only 4% blue-collar workers. These discrepancies cannot be clarified at present, but it is important to note them for future research.

Blue-collar support for the PAN seems to have its origins in other factors, also brought out by the survey.[20] First of all, these workers, like the "marginals" or people totally without resources, along with students, housewives and businesspeople, are the ones who express the least favorable view of the government. (See Table 7.5.) In the second place, blue-collar workers are surpassed only by peasants in their minimal opposition to Church participation in politics, followed by housewives and marginals. (See Table 7.6.) Thirdly, as a social stratum, blue-collar workers exhibit the highest proportion of conservative tendencies, followed by peasants, farmers and housewives. (See Table 7.7.)

It is understandable that the unfavorable opinion blue-collar workers may have of the government, especially in times of economic difficulties and wage restrictions, should be expressed in greater rejection of the PRI, and it would seem logical that this feeling be directed toward support for leftist parties that promote and defend their interests. Contrary to expectations, it seems that discontent among workers is giving a slight edge to the PAN. The explanation may perhaps be found in the low level of opposition to the Church's participation in politics and in the conservative tendencies of the workers, which are consistent with PAN principles.

What remains to be presented are party sympathies by states, for further disaggregation of results. Table 7.8 shows the electoral behavior of at least three groups that match three relatively compact geographic regions: North, Center and South. Particularly outstanding is the lower percentage for the PRI and higher for the PAN in the North, and the better position for the PSUM in the South.

Examined in greater detail it is interesting to find that the states where the PRI has the greatest sympathies are Hidalgo, Sinaloa and Nayarit, and the least in Sonora, Chiapas and Tlaxcala. The PAN has its greatest support in Sonora, Nuevo León, Jalisco, Chihuahua and Coahuila, and the PSUM in Jalisco, Tlaxcala and Chiapas. Seen in this context, there were two states—Sonora and Nuevo León—that may cause some concern to the PRI.

Electoral Forecast

Based on the data and material presented, an attempt was made to develop a forecast of the outcome of the July 1985 elections. This prediction was based on Table 7.4, "Party Sympathies by Occupational Strata," with changes and adjustments drawn from an analysis of the other tables, and disaggregated by states. The Appendix explicitly describes the bases and criteria utilized in the procedure, with the purpose of submitting the methodology employed to critical review. Table 7.9 below compares the forecast with actual election results.

It is important to note that the government form for election reports does not include the category "abstention." Therefore, in order to render the forecast presented in Table 7.9 more comparable with official results, the category of non-voters is given outside the total, which is composed of the four columns of parties. A "repercenting" process was required for the figures assigned to each party, in order to develop figures comparable to Table 7.8, thus resulting in 53.3% for the PRI, 12.5% for the PAN, 4.8% for the PSUM, 3.3% for others and 26.1% for non-voters (none), as shown in Tables 7.1, 7.4 and 7.8.

As can be seen in Table 7.10 a comparison of the data shows 98% accuracy for the PRI and 83.5% for PAN. The forecast tended to overestimate returns for the PRI, PAN, PSUM and for Abstentions, while it tended to underestimate returns from "others."

The scope of abstentions proved to be the greatest area of discrepancy between the forecast and actual returns—25.9% in absolute terms. This may have two explanations which should be borne in mind for future exercises: (1) it may be that when questions are asked about party sympathies, the person's answer may not imply any intention of expressing this opinion by voting; and (2) answering an interview question requires substantially less effort than does the act of voting.

We can see that, except for abstentions, the lower the proportional weight of votes for each party, the greater the difference between forecast and results. This is explained by the quantitative narrowness of ranges and the sample quota of the survey.

A more painstaking evaluation by states shows that the forecast was more accurate in Michoacán, Puebla, San Luis Potosí, Zacatecas, Chihuahua and Colima, with less than 5% difference in the four groups (PRI, PAN, PSUM, others). In second place are Durango, Guerrero, Jalisco, Oaxaca and Querétaro, with differences under 10%. In summary, by states we found 11 accurate predictions, 12 that were acceptable, and 9 that were discrepant.

Moreover, the prediction of regionally distinctive electoral behavior in the North, Center and South, was virtually confirmed: (1) in the North, lower support for the PRI and higher support for the PAN; (2) in the South, while the PSUM did poorly, in 4 of the 5 states where the PRI had the highest percentage of votes (Campeche, Chiapas, Guerrero and Tabasco), the PAN had the lowest number of votes; and (3) the Federal District and the state of México demonstrated the highest degree of political plurality, while the states of Baja California, Chihuahua and Sonora showed great bipolarity between the PRI and the PAN.

The hypothesis we are proposing—that Mexico's current political situation shows no signs of a major crisis, and that it still seems to be organized around the four great pillars of the existing hegemony, education, the labor movement, agrarian reform and non-reelection[21]—seems to be empirically borne out by election data. While the Mexican political system clearly faces a great variety of problems, elections demonstrate that the system has not begun to approach catastrophic breakdown, solvable only by force, as some have argued.

Notes

1. The 1983 survey included 7,051 anonymous interviews, with equal quotas for 15 occupational groups in the 32 states, according to population. The questionnaire had 46 closed questions. The 1985 survey had 3,102 interviews divided into the same 15 groups, in 31 municipalities in the state of Mexico, using a questionnaire of 28 questions; 24 closed and 4 open-ended.

2. Miguel Basáñez, "México 1985: Un pronóstico electoral," Nexos, no. 91 (July 1985).

3. Robert Newell G. and Luis Rubio F., Mexico's Dilemma: The Political Origins of Economic Crisis (Boulder, CO: Westview Press, 1984), 6.

4. Wayne Cornelius, "El mexicano feo: México y Estados Unidos en la decada de los ochentas," Nexos, no. 89 (May 1985): 24.

5. For a more extensive discussion of the meaning of elections, see Soledad Loaeza's article "El llamado de las urnas: para qué sirven las elecciones en México?" Nexos, no. 90 (June 1985.)

6. A shift that would arrive at the logical corollary of this school of thought that gives excessive weight to "dysfunctions" of political systems when comparing them with the U.S. model and that pays particular attention to issues like cooptation, clientelism, corruption, and fraud.

7. Pablo González Casanova, ed., *Elecciones en México: evolución y perspectivas* (Mexico, D.F.: Siglo XXI, 1985).

8. David Torres, "México 1985: elecciones, partidos y reforma política," *Revista Mexicana de Ciencias Políticas y Sociales*, no. 120, UNAM, Mexico (1985).

9. Silvia Gómez Tagle "La derecha, avance y retroceso," *La Jornada*, 2 July 1985.

10. Gallup/Mexico, "Las Elecciones del 7 de Julio," Mexico, June 1985.

11. Miguel Angel Granados Chapa, "Plaza Pública," *La Jornada*, 1 and 2 July 1985.

12. Octavio Rodríguez Araujo, "Del pronóstico electoral a la inflación de votos," *La Jornada*, 21 July 1985.

13. In the 1983 survey, 66% of the people interviewed were men and 34% women; 40% were between 18 and 30 years of age; 30% between 31 and 40; 19% between 41 and 50, and 11% over 50; 5% with no schooling, 28% with some elementary schooling, 17% with secondary, 18% with preparatory schooling, 29% with professional studies and 3% with graduate studies; 18% stated they had no income, 17% had less than the minimum wage, 26% had 1 to 2 times more than the minimum wage, 24% from 2 to 4 times; 11% between 4 and 8 times and 4% more than 8 times the minimum wage.

14. Miguel Basáñez and Roderic Camp, "La nacionalización de la banca y la opinión pública en México," *Foro Internacional*, no. 98 (October-December 1984): 212.

15. Gallup/Mexico, 3.

16. Important for discussion of the concept of "non-sympathizers" used in the table; that is, voting for none of the parties (28%), because the phenomenon differs from simple abstentions. The former is obtained by dividing the number of non-voters between the total of citizens enrolled on the voters' list (29% or 25%, as the case may be), while the latter is calculated by dividing non-voters by the sum of voters and non-voters.

The figure used in the above calculation is 7.9 million "listed voters" that did not vote, instead of the 28% shown on the table, because the number of citizens is subject to major corrections due to migratory movements and margination of Indian zones. See Banamex, *México social, indicadores seleccionados* (1982), 374.

The range of this adjustment is equal to 1.7 million persons, the difference between the number of citizens in the census (33.2) and the number on the voters' list (31.5 million). Even so, it should be noted that even if 32% abstained, this compares well with levels found in other countries. In the United States the level of abstention was 38% in 1960, 39% in 1964, 40% in 1970 and 44% in 1972.

17. In the 1985 survey by the author (with the questions about public works and personal situation) 64% of the people interviewed were men and 36% women; 44% were between 18 and 30 years of age, 29% between 31 and 40; 14% were between 18 and 30 years of age, 29% between 31 and 40; 14% between 41 and 50; and 13% over 50; 16% without schooling, 29% with some elementary school, 17% with secondary studies, 17% with preparatory studies, 20% with a professional degree and 1% with graduate studies. 21% stated they had no income. 16% received less than the minimum wage, 31% between 1 and 2 times that amount, 19% between 2 and 4 times, 10% between 4 and 8 times and 2% more than 8 times the minimum wage.

18. Basañez and Camp, "La nacionalización de la banca," 215.
19. Ivan Zavala, "Las ideas irán a las uranas," *La Jornada*, 12 May 1985, 5. Three groups are presented: Marxists (PPS, PST, PRT and PSUM), moderns (PRI, PAN and PSD), and traditionals (PDM and PARM).
20. The sample of 450 blue-collar workers included 72% men and 28% women; 49% were between the ages of 18 and 30, 30% between 31 and 40, and 21% over 40. 7% had no schooling, 55% had some elementary schooling, 24% had secondary schooling and 14% with preparatory school; 23% received an income lower than the minimum wage; 54% received between 1 and 2 times that figure, 16% receive between 2 and 4 times the minimum wage and 7% receive no income.
21. Miguel Basañez, *La lucha por la hegemonía en México, 1968–1980* (Mexico: Siglo XXI, 1981), 176.

Appendix

Votes for the PRI were given a "premium" of 4 percentage points for favorable opinions of public works, education, personal situation and health and are "demerited" 5 points for unfavorable opinions about the police. 3 points are given for opinions about the Church, non-reelection, right to strike, and 4 are subtracted for the foreign debt and lines 2, 3 and 4 in the next paragraph. 2 points were added for the legitimacy declared in Campeche and Quintana Roo, but 4 were subtracted for attitudes in favor of the Church in Coahuila, Chihuahua, Sonora and Zacatecas. In brief, adding 9 and subtracting 13, there was a 4% reduction for the PRI, leaving it at 69.6%.

An additional 7 percentage points were given to the PAN in national voting: (1) for unfavorable opinions about the police; (2) for the uncritical attitude of factory workers and campesinos regarding the Church's participation in politics; (3) for the slight acceptance by housewives of this participation (Table 7.6); (4) for the slightly conservative trend observed in factory workers and campesinos (Table 7.7); and (5) for Puebla's support of the Church. Moreover, 3 points are subtracted for rejection of the Church in the states of Aguascalientes, Campeche and Colima. In short, 4% was added to the PAN, to give it a total vote of 19.4%.

The nation's votes for leftist parties, mainly the PSUM, goes up by 2 points for the radical campesinos and marginals (Table 7.7), as well as because of current economic difficulties, but was decreased by 1 because of the left's lack of political cohesion. In this way they would have a total of 6.5% of votes. The ratio of non-sympathizers is increased by 1 point for campesinos with no opinion of the government (Table 7.5), but is decreased by 1 because of intensive use of mass media, and thus remained at 26%. The residual percentage 4.5% remained as votes for other parties.

TABLE 7.1
Comparison of 1982 Federal Deputy Election Results and
Opinion Polls for 1982, 1983, 1985

	1982 Federal Deputy Elections[1] (%)		Author's Survey 1982 (%)	Author's Survey 1983 (%)	Gallup Poll 1985 (%)
PRI	14.4	51	54	55	47
PAN	3.6	12	12	10	18
PSUM	0.9	3	6	4	4
OTHERS	1.8	6	6	5	5
NONE	7.9	28[2]	23	26	27
TOTAL	28.6	100	101[3]	100	101[3]

[1]Millions of voters
[2]Names on the voters' list who did not vote;
"non-sympathizers"[16]
[3]Does not add to 100, because numbers are rounded off.

TABLE 7.2
Opinion About Public Services, Public Works and Personal Situation,[1] 1983 and 1985

	GOOD	FAIR	POOR	DON'T KNOW	NO ANSWER	NOT APPLICABLE	TOTAL
Public Works[2]	61.8	27.4	5.9	3.7	1.2	---	100%
Education[3]	66.2	19.5	2.6	1.1	6.0	4.6	100%
Health[4]	25.5	36.8	15.7	1.4	3.0	17.6	100%
Police[5]	13.7	31.7	49.4	2.2	3.0	---	100%
Personal Situation[6]	42.1	36.1	19.6	1.2	1.0	---	100%

[1]Answers were grouped under good, fair and poor, to make them comparable (see notes 2 to 6). The questions on public works and personal situation were taken from the 1985 survey, and the remainder from the 1983 study.

[2]Question 2: Do you think the government's public works projects are of great benefit? of benefit? fair? of little benefit? of very little benefit? do not know - no answer - not applicable.

[3]Question 3: Do you think the school attended by your children (or brothers and sisters) is very good? good? fair? poor? very poor? do not know - no answer - not applicable.

[4]Question 4: Do you think the health center, clinic, hospital or medical unit you go to provides good service? fair? poor? do not know - no answer - not applicable.

[5]Do you think that the police service is very good? good? fair? poor? very poor? do not know - no answer - not applicable.

[6]How would you rate your personal situation in comparison with last year? much better - better - the same - worse - much worse - do not know no answer.

TABLE 7.3
Opinions On Principles and Important Issues, 1983

	VERY GOOD	GOOD	FAIR	POOR	VERY POOR	DON'T KNOW	NO ANSWER	TOTAL
CHURCH[1]	0.0	3.7	6.6	14.2	65.8	5.1	4.6	100%
NON REELECTION[2]	38.5	31.9	11.2	3.8	2.8	6.7	5.1	100%
STRIKING[3]	21.0	35.6	17.2	7.6	4.9	6.4	7.4	100%
LAND DISTRIBUTION[4]	10.8	25.6	23.2	20.5	7.5	6.9	5.5	100%
FOREIGN DEBT[5]	0.8	2.8	8.4	25.5	61.9	5.0	5.6	100%

[1]Question 1: What do you think about Church participation in politics? very good? good? fair? bad? very bad? do not know - no answer.
[2]Question 2: What do you think about non reelection and the change of the people in government office? very advisable? advisable? sometimes advisable? inadvisable? very inadvisable? do not know - no answer.
[3]Question 3: Do you think the right to strike is very good? good? fair? bad? very bad? do not know - no answer.
[4]Question 4: Do you believe that agrarian distribution is very just? just? indifferent? unjust? very unjust? do not know - no answer.
[5]Question 5: What do you think about Mexico's current foreign debt? very good? good? fair? bad? very bad? do not know - no answer.

193

TABLE 7.4
Party[1] Sympathies By Occupational Strata, 1983

	PAN	PRI	PSUM	PST	PRT	PDM	PMT	PARM	NONE	NO ANSWER	TOTAL
Officials	3.2	76.5	2.6	0.4	--	0.2	1.0	0.2	11.1	4.7	100
Business Execs.	11.9	50.8	2.4	0.7	0.5	1.7	0.7	1.4	21.0	8.8	100
Pol. Leaders	7.7	73.3	5.7	1.7	1.0	2.2	0.7	1.7	3.5	2.5	100
Farmers	13.9	59.4	2.0	0.9	0.2	0.2	0.2	0.9	15.4	6.9	100
Industrialists	13.8	50.6	1.0	0.5	0.2	1.2	0.2	1.0	22.8	8.8	100
Business	15.0	46.5	3.4	1.2	2.0	0.6	0.6	0.4	26.3	4.0	100
Service[2]	12.9	47.1	5.3	1.9	1.0	1.0	0.5	0.5	25.6	4.3	100
Professionals	8.5	53.7	5.1	1.3	0.2	0.9	0.6	0.4	24.7	4.7	100
WC Workers	9.4	50.2	5.8	2.6	2.4	1.4	0.4	1.2	22.8	3.8	100
Bureaucrats	5.3	67.1	5.3	0.2	0.6	0.4	0.4	0.2	15.6	4.8	100
Housewives	13.3	51.6	2.0	1.2	0.8	0.4	--	0.8	23.9	6.0	100
Students	10.0	42.2	4.6	0.8	1.0	1.2	0.2	0.6	34.1	5.4	100
BC Workers	14.9	52.7	4.7	2.0	1.1	1.3	0.4	0.4	18.0	4.4	100
Peasants	7.3	64.5	2.8	0.9	0.4	0.9	0.2	1.1	12.6	9.4	100
Marginals	10.9	44.8	4.6	3.6	0.6	2.3	0.8	0.6	26.1	5.5	100
Total	737	3902	270	93	57	73	33	52	1442	392	7051
Percentage Total	10.5	55.3	3.8	1.3	0.8	1.0	0.5	0.7	20.5	5.6	100

[1]Parties include Partido Acción Nacional (PAN), Partido Revolucionario Institucional (PRI), Partido Socialista Unificado de Mexico (PSUM), Partido Socialista de los Trabajadores (PST), Partido Revolucionario de los Trabajadores (PRT), Partido Democrata Mexicano (PDM), Partido Mexicano de Trabajadores (PMT), Partido Auténtico de la Revolución Mexicana (PARM.)

[2]Data regarding service sector business interests should be taken with reservations due to deficiencies in the survey.

QUESTION: What political party do you like?

TABLE 7.5
Government Legitimacy By Strata, 1983

	VERY GOOD	GOOD	FAIR	POOR	VERY POOR	DO NOT KNOW	NO ANSWER	TOTAL
Public officials	19.8	45.3	26.5	4.9	1.2	---	2.2	100.0
Business Executives	10.3	31.3	34.1	12.9	4.3	1.7	5.5	100.0
Political Leaders	26.2	38.1	20.8	8.9	2.7	0.7	2.5	100.0
Farmers	7.8	32.5	34.7	9.5	2.2	8.2	5.0	100.0
Industrialists	8.3	37.1	35.2	7.8	3.8	3.6	4.3	100.0
Business	6.1	30.1	43.2	12.3	3.4	2.4	2.6	100.0
Service business	7.4	37.1	40.0	7.4	2.9	1.7	3.6	100.0
Professionals or technicians	8.9	39.0	37.5	10.7	2.3	0.8	0.9	100.0
WC workers	8.4	29.8	42.2	10.4	3.6	3.8	1.8	100.0
Bureaucrats	13.3	38.4	33.3	7.7	4.4	1.6	1.4	100.0
Housewives	6.0	32.5	41.4	8.0	3.2	6.4	2.4	100.0
Students	6.0	29.5	45.4	10.0	4.8	3.2	1.2	100.0
BC workers	6.4	29.3	40.4	12.2	3.3	6.4	1.8	100.0
Peasants	11.1	38.7	28.6	4.3	1.3	8.5	7.5	100.0
Marginals	5.1	32.2	39.6	10.7	4.6	4.8	2.9	100.0
Total	701	2448	2567	648	225	253	209	7051
Percentage Total	9.9	34.7	36.4	9.2	3.2	3.6	3.0	100.0

QUESTION: What is your opinion of the state government's functioning?

195

TABLE 7.6
Church Participation in Politics, 1983

	YES	LITTLE	VERY LITTLE	NO	DO NOT KNOW	NO ANSWER	TOTAL
Public officials	2.0	3.0	11.7	79.1	1.8	2.2	100.0
Business executives	2.1	7.6	15.3	65.4	2.6	6.9	100.0
Political leaders	4.0	5.0	9.2	74.3	3.2	4.5	100.0
Farmers	1.5	5.0	10.8	67.7	9.3	5.6	100.0
Industrialists	3.1	5.7	11.9	69.6	3.3	6.4	100.0
Business	4.4	8.7	15.0	63.8	5.0	3.2	100.0
Service business interests	3.1	5.3	16.7	65.1	5.7	4.1	100.0
Professionals or technicians	4.0	6.4	14.1	71.0	1.7	2.8	100.0
White collar workers	3.2	6.4	16.6	66.8	4.8	2.2	100.0
Bureaucrats	4.2	4.4	11.7	72.1	3.4	4.4	100.0
Housewives	5.6	7.0	19.1	58.6	5.8	3.8	100.0
Students	3.4	6.6	12.7	69.9	4.2	3.2	100.0
Blue collar workers	3.6	8.4	20.7	54.2	7.8	5.3	100.0
Peasants	5.6	10.9	11.1	48.5	11.8	12.2	100.0
Marginals	5.7	8.2	16.0	60.4	5.9	3.8	100.0
TOTAL	262	464	1002	4640	357	326	7051
Percentage Total	3.7	6.6	14.2	65.8	5.1	4.6	100.0

QUESTION: Do you think the Church should participate in politics?

TABLE 7.7
Political Tendencies By Strata, 1983

	VERY RADICAL	RADICAL	MODERATE	CONSERVATIVE	VERY CONSERVATIVE	TOTAL
Public officials	11.9	25.5	55.3	5.9	1.4	100.0
Business executives	15.0	32.7	43.4	6.7	2.1	100.0
Political leaders	13.4	30.0	50.0	5.2	1.5	100.0
Farmers	15.2	29.3	40.3	11.3	3.9	100.0
Industrialists	11.9	39.2	39.2	6.7	3.1	100.0
Business	15.6	30.9	38.4	10.1	5.0	100.0
Service business	13.9	26.1	48.6	8.1	3.3	100.0
Professionals or technicians	8.5	34.1	49.7	5.5	2.3	100.0
WC workers	13.6	29.0	42.2	10.2	5.0	100.0
Bureaucrats	11.3	32.5	45.1	8.9	2.2	100.0
Housewives	15.3	25.9	44.2	11.2	3.4	100.0
Students	12.2	27.9	51.2	6.6	2.2	100.0
BC workers	11.1	28.0	41.3	12.2	7.3	100.0
Peasants	15.2	34.2	31.4	12.6	6.6	100.0
Marginals	17.7	31.6	37.7	9.7	3.4	100.0
Total	945	2144	3097	617	248	7051
Percentage Total	13.4	30.4	43.9	8.8	3.5	100.0

QUESTION: What should we do now? Change things radically? Change things slightly? Change some things and retain others? Retain as much as possible? Keep everything as now?

TABLE 7.8
Party Sympathies By States, 1983

	PAN	PRI	PSUM	PST	PRT	PDM	PMT	PARM	DO NOT KNOW	NO ANSWER	TOTAL
Aquascalientes	15.0	68.3				1.7			13.3	1.7	100.0
Baja California Norte	11.1	47.8	3.3	2.2	0.6	0.6			30.6	3.9	100.0
Baja California Sur		60.7	7.1						21.4	10.7	100.0
Campeche	6.7	73.3	4.4						13.3	2.2	100.0
Coahuila	16.3	49.0		14.3					18.4	2.0	100.0
Colima	8.7	65.2							21.7	4.3	100.0
Chiapas	9.9	37.9	7.5	2.5	0.6	3.1	1.2	1.2	32.3	3.7	100.0
Chihuahua	16.4	45.6	2.0	0.4		0.8	0.4		29.6	4.8	100.0
Distrito Federal	13.4	41.3	7.1	3.2	1.5	0.9	1.2	1.4	25.3	6.1	100.0
Durango	15.8	54.4	4.4					1.8	17.5	4.7	100.0
Guanajuato	8.6	62.8	3.3	2.6	1.5	2.6	0.4	0.4	14.5	3.3	100.0
Guerrero	3.6	60.0	4.0	2.4	3.2	1.2	0.4	0.8	20.4	4.0	100.0
Hidalgo	1.2	80.7	0.6	0.6	0.6	1.2		0.6	9.6	4.8	100.0
Jalisco	17.3	45.8	8.8	0.4		2.9	0.2	0.4	21.7	2.4	100.0
México	9.0	50.8	2.1	0.6	1.0	0.2	0.5	0.5	24.2	11.1	100.0
Michoacán	9.4	58.8	3.4	1.1	2.2	0.7	0.7	2.2	16.9	4.5	100.0
Morelos	13.3	39.2	4.2	1.7	1.7	0.8	0.8		30.8	7.5	100.0
Nayarit	1.2	78.3	4.8					1.2	9.6	4.8	100.0
Nuevo León	22.0	47.9	2.8			1.0		1.4	16.1	8.0	100.0
Oaxaca	6.5	58.3	1.5	0.7	1.0	1.0	0.5	2.0	21.1	8.0	100.0

(Continued)

TABLE 7.8 (Cont.)

	PAN	PRI	PSUM	PST	PRT	PDM	PMT	PARM	DO NOT KNOW	NO ANSWER	TOTAL
Puebla	11.8	65.3	3.4		0.8	2.3	0.4	0.4	13.0	2.7	100.0
Querétaro[1]		55.0	10.0						25.0	10.0	100.0
Quintana Roo	1.7	75.0		1.7					16.7	5.0	100.0
San Luis Potosí	5.5	69.9	1.1		1.1	1.6		1.1	14.2	5.5	100.0
Sinaloa	4.1	78.6	1.0		0.3		0.3		11.7	3.8	100.0
Sonora	30.6	37.6	2.9	0.6					24.1	4.1	100.0
Tabasco	5.8	59.4	1.4	2.2			0.7		29.7	0.7	100.0
Tamaulipas	5.4	57.3	2.9	1.3	0.4	0.4	0.4	1.7	22.6	7.5	100.0
Tlaxcala	10.0	38.3	8.3			10.0			28.3	5.0	100.0
Veracruz	4.3	75.2	2.9	1.0	0.4	0.4	0.4		10.5	4.9	100.0
Yucatán	10.7	52.5	0.8	1.6		0.8		0.8	27.0	5.7	100.0
Zacatecas	3.8	70.8	4.7						5.7	15.1	100.0
Total	737	3902	270	93	57	73	33	52	1442	392	7051
Percentage Total	10.5	55.3	3.8	1.3	0.8	1.0	0.5	0.7	20.5	5.6	100.0

1Querétaro should be discarded because of deficiencies in the survey.

TABLE 7.9
Prediction and Results of Voting, Federal Deputies Elections, July 1985

	P R I		P A N		P S U M		OTHERS		OTHERS TOTAL	NON-VOTERS	
	Prediction	Result	Prediction	Result	Prediction	Result	Prediction	Result		Prediction	Result
NAL	69.6	68.2	19.4	16.2	6.5	3.4	4.5	12.2	100%	26.1	52.0
AGS	78.0	75.0	20.0	16.6	1.2	0.6	0.8	7.8	100%	15.0	34.9
BCN	67.5	52.9	22.5	29.4	6.5	2.7	3.5	15.0	100%	34.5	49.5
BCS	86.5	70.8	--	18.3	11.9	1.8	1.6	9.1	100%	32.1	50.9
CAMP	82.4	94.2	10.2	3.2	6.3	0.3	1.1	2.3	100%	14.6	37.6
COAH	56.5	69.5	25.5	22.7	--	1.4	18.0	6.4	100%	20.4	68.9
COL	83.3	83.3	14.2	10.0	1.3	1.1	1.2	5.6	100%	25.1	49.3
CHIS	56.1	90.2	18.6	3.6	13.3	1.1	12.0	5.1	100%	36.0	41.8
CHIH	59.5	55.7	35.0	38.5	4.6	1.7	0.9	4.1	100%	34.4	67.6
DF	53.7	47.3	24.5	24.2	11.6	7.8	10.2	20.7	100%	30.0	50.2
DGO	68.6	67.5	23.3	26.6	7.1	1.5	1.0	4.4	100%	23.6	55.6
GTO	74.0	60.1	12.9	19.2	5.2	0.8	7.9	19.9	100%	17.8	59.7
GRO	76.7	88.3	7.4	3.6	6.6	3.1	9.3	5.0	100%	24.4	58.9
HGO	91.9	82.9	3.7	5.4	1.9	1.3	2.5	10.4	100%	14.4	46.0
JAL	55.3	58.3	27.9	24.0	12.9	4.2	3.9	13.5	100%	24.1	53.1
MEX	69.8	59.9	13.2	17.4	8.7	5.5	8.3	17.2	100%	18.7	43.7
MICH	72.3	71.6	14.5	15.3	5.6	1.8	7.6	11.3	100%	21.4	64.6
MOR	60.3	73.7	24.8	11.4	8.4	2.6	6.5	12.3	100%	38.3	56.2
NAY	89.1	82.3	3.7	3.1	6.8	7.8	0.4	6.8	100%	14.4	52.8
NL	60.5	74.1	31.6	23.8	5.0	0.5	2.9	1.6	100%	24.1	42.3
OAX	79.4	82.8	12.0	3.9	3.5	1.8	5.1	11.5	100%	29.1	41.6
PUE	75.1	79.1	16.4	13.6	5.2	1.5	3.3	5.8	100%	15.7	48.3
QRO	81.5	79.7	--	15.3	16.9	0.7	1.6	4.3	100%	35.0	38.0
QR	93.2	90.9	4.7	2.5	1.3	0.9	0.8	5.7	100%	21.7	31.5
SLP	84.6	82.5	9.3	11.4	2.6	0.8	3.5	5.3	100%	19.7	49.8
SIN	90.6	73.5	4.8	18.7	2.4	3.8	2.2	4.0	100%	15.5	56.5
SON	49.4	69.9	45.2	25.9	5.4	0.7	0.4	3.5	100%	27.9	59.0
TAB	82.5	88.7	11.2	2.4	3.4	0.8	2.9	8.1	100%	30.4	47.6
TAMPS	79.1	71.6	10.6	7.5	5.6	2.2	4.7	18.7	100%	30.1	55.0
TLAX	54.4	84.9	18.0	4.3	13.9	1.3	13.7	9.5	100%	33.3	33.4
VER	84.0	65.8	9.9	7.1	4.6	4.8	1.5	22.3	100%	15.4	60.4
YUC	75.0	84.8	18.9	13.3	2.7	0.5	3.4	1.4	100%	32.7	46.8
ZAC	84.3	85.3	7.2	8.3	7.1	3.5	1.4	2.9	100%	19.7	46.2

TABLE 7.10
Comparison of Vote Forecast and Electoral Results, 1985

	Prediction	Result	Result Difference	Relative Difference
PRI	69.6%	68.2%	+ 1.4%	+ 2.0%
PAN	19.4%	16.2%	+ 3.2	+ 16.5%
PSUM	6.5%	3.4%	+ 3.1%	+ 47.7%
OTHERS	4.5%	12.2%	- 7.7%	-171.0%
ABSTENTIONS	26.1%	52.0%	-25.9%	- 99.0%

8

The Significance of Recent Events for the Mexican Political System

Martin C. Needler

I

Mexico, Pablo González Casanova tells us, is in crisis.[1] Judith Hellman had the country in crisis in 1978.[2] The crisis came some years earlier for Manuel Moreno Sánchez.[3] Numberless commentators, observers, and ordinary Mexican citizens spoke of crisis when they witnessed the terrible massacre at Tlatelolco in 1968, when troops shot down peaceful protesters; or when Lázaro Cárdenas came out of retirement in 1961, leading massive street demonstrations in support of the government of Fidel Castro. But for Emilio Portes Gil Mexico was already in crisis in the 1950s.[4] Is crisis continuous or intermittent in Mexico? And are these crises serious enough to presage fundamental change in the country's political system, or are they like Italy's parliamentary "crises," simply part of the normal functioning of the system? Is it true, that is, as M. Delal Baer writes, that "the Mexican political system is at a crossroads"?[5] The present writer thought the political system was "at the crossroads" fifteen years ago.[6] Are the crossroads really there or are they a mirage produced as the blurred eyes of Mexico-watchers peer across the arid wastes of commentary into the hot air of political rhetoric?

Put more directly and less extravagantly, the question is the following: Can the difficult economic and political circumstances through which the country has been passing be handled within the norms of the hitherto existing political system, or is its remarkable resilience no longer equal to the challenges facing it? And if that system is forced to change, not just cosmetically or in minor questions of degree, will it change in the direction of greater openness and responsiveness to popular opinion—that is, will it become more democratic—or will it change in the direction of becoming more repressive, more militarized, less tolerant of dissent?

Now in fact no commentator, no matter how well informed or subtle his analysis may be, knows the answers to these questions. There are too many possibilities in the system, too much room for variation; most importantly, it is never clear whether some accommodation to new circumstances will turn out to mark a genuinely new direction, the first step that begins the journey of a thousand miles, or whether it will fade into a merely nominal or cosmetic change as it is circumvented by forces unwilling to yield privileged positions. The apparent crossroads may then turn out to have marked only a minor detour which brings one shortly back again to the main highway. While it is thus not possible at this point to answer the major questions about the direction of future evolution with any degree of certainty, however, one can indicate the possibilities, describe the forces tending in different directions, and draw up a balance of the conflicting pressures. We will examine here the lines of development suggested by the state of the economy, the president's most recent "state of the nation" report, some recent commentary on the Mexican military, and the legislative elections of 1985.

II

How serious is the present crisis in Mexico? Will it simply necessitate marginal adjustments that will then permit everything to go on as before, or does its impact imply a fundamental change in the nature of the political system?

We have to acknowledge, first of all, that the extraordinary political stability that Mexico enjoyed from 1940 until the middle 1970s was due, in part, to its unparalleled economic growth during that period. After all, if the economy is growing steadily at a dependable six or seven percent a year, statecraft is relatively simple. It is merely a question of distributing benefits and co-opting different class and sectoral interests by gratifying their demands, at least in part. Those days are clearly over, not to return within the foreseeable future.

The Mexican system was subverted in the first instance by plenty rather than scarcity, however. Rates of spending and indebtedness established when oil was close to $40 a barrel cannot be sustained as its price slips to $20 and below. There is no reason to believe that the current decline in oil prices is a temporary phenomenon that will be reversed. At the time of writing, the standard price for the benchmark grade of Isthmus Light crude is $26.50 a barrel; although the price may perhaps turn upward temporarily in response to crisis in the Middle East—always to be expected—aided by a little psychological manipulation of the market in the usual manner of the major companies, there seems no reason to think that there is any firm sticking place for oil prices in their long-range decline above an equilibrium figure probably closer to $15 than to $20.[7] Of course, in a declining market, Mexico must be concerned not only over the price of oil, but over its market share. However, this should be rather easier to protect, given Mexico's closeness to the U.S. market.

Meanwhile, the break in the petroleum market—after the boom had led to a decline in non-petroleum exports because of the overpricing of the peso—has had its secondary and tertiary effects on the Mexican economy in the form of the disruption and hardship caused by the collapse of the peso; capital flight; the colossal burden of debt and the ensuing austerity; permanently negative expectations about economic performance; a quantum jump in distrust of the honesty and capacity of national leadership; and diminished ability to resist economic and political pressures from the United States. The terrible earthquake that struck Mexico City in 1985 merely added the finishing touches to this dismal picture.

One may thus be justified in believing that the weathering of previous crises does not in itself guarantee that the present crisis may not be of a new magnitude, which forces a mutation in the political system. The strongest way of putting the case would be to say that for almost forty years the economic performance of the regime was a factor contributing to its legitimacy, the third factor along with its revolutionary pedigree and its claim to be the issue of democratic elections. For a time, at least, economic performance has become instead a delegitimizing factor for the regime. De la Madrid and his successor must work mightily with both the substance and the appearance of economic policy and with measures of "moral renovation" so as to identify the failures of economic policy as due solely to acts of commission and omission of the Echeverría and López Portillo administrations, and not to faults in the system itself. The difficulty will be that, given the softness of the oil market and of the U.S. economy, external economic realities will not prove cooperative, certainly not in the short term.[8]

III

One of the most interesting documents for assessing the regime's view of how things are going in the political and economic realms and for attempting to discern the lines of future evolution is the annual *informe*, the "state of the union" address delivered by the Mexican president to the Congress at the beginning of September each year. A very nice thesis or dissertation could be written analyzing the changes of theme in presidential *informes* over the years. President de la Madrid's Third Annual *Informe*, delivered shortly before the Mexico City earthquake, provides, along with the obligatory self-congratulation, a few interesting insights into his thinking.

A principal theme in the speech is De la Madrid's insistence on the democratic character of the Mexican political system. "Mexican democracy is free and open."[9] This is said to be true on the whole, despite a realistic acknowledgement of some of the problems. "We must acknowledge that the electoral process still has failings that we must correct, but also that these failings do not invalidate its general legitimacy." And implicitly De la Madrid acknowledges the defects in the democratic character of the system by calling Mexico "a democracy which is continually improving."[10]

If one source of the regime's legitimacy is the holding of elections, the other is its pedigree as the heir of the Mexican revolution, and De la

Madrid took advantage of 1985 representing the one hundred seventy-fifth anniversary of Mexican independence and the seventy-fifth anniversary of the Revolution to give a sketch of Mexican history—in its official, Revolutionary version—concluding with his summary of the provisions of the 1917 constitution. The constitution "enriched the liberal tradition with the postulates of social democracy"; and, in addition to specifying the institutions of a representative and federal republic with division of powers, it posited "leadership of national development by the state, as the representative of the nation; and a mixed economy." This provides a very clear (and, I would say, correct) view of the Mexican Revolution as a liberal and social democratic one, to whose purposes the policies of Mexican governments have, over the years, been broadly faithful. This constitutes an implicit rejection of the left-wing argument that recent Mexican governments have betrayed the Revolution, which was a socialist one. Not so, De la Madrid is saying; the state must take a leading role, but within an economy in which private enterprise coexists with state corporations. This is the blueprint given us by the constitution.

And, very explicitly: "Mexico has a democratic system. Even with the defects and limitations that have been acknowledged and pointed out by the government itself, the facts show that it is relevant and functional. The problems that crop up, the elections that have been annulled, disputed, protested, and heatedly debated have to be weighed in the context of a social life of freedom and of the number of [electoral] processes that have not been questioned." The policy of balance in economic affairs, under which private and state activity co-exist, is analogous to the policy of balance in foreign affairs. Mexico's foreign policy grows out of the interaction between the will for autonomy and the desire to pursue national interests and the necessity of not offending overmuch the United States. This is phrased by De la Madrid as follows: "With the United States, we have sought a relationship that acknowledges two irrefutable facts: the proximity and the diversity that exists between the two countries. The inter-dependence generated by proximity and the asymmetry of development between the two peoples demand mutual respect, respectful treatment, knowledge and understanding of one another, and constant goodwill for broad cooperation." The president's discussion of the economic situation was phrased much less delicately. The only hopeful note in his bleak recital of the facts was the improvement in the inflation figures.

Much of the material in the speech was routine and predictable by anyone familiar with the conventions of the annual *informe*. However, two elements received special stress. One of them was the theme of moral renovation, particularly as it applied to the nation's police forces. This was a question De la Madrid returned to more than once under different rubrics. The other was the theme of increase in municipal autonomy. Amendments that had been made to Article 115 of the constitution, conferring new powers on the municipal governments, were stressed as part of the movement toward greater democracy in Mexico.

The stress on more authority for municipal governments is part of a general decentralization strategy that was pushed by De la Madrid when he was Minister of Planning under López Portillo but which is hardly likely to have much concrete effect.[11] If municipal autonomy were to be given greater content by making available greater financial resources to municipal governments, however, as the *informe* suggested that it would be, then some interesting results could ensue.

The Partido de Acción Nacional, the leading opposition party, has always made municipal autonomy one of the central features of its programs. Although the PAN has tried to present this as a principled position in favor of greater liberty, consonant with its programmatic views on the economy and freedom of religion, the skeptic may be forgiven for noting that while the PAN has been unlikely to win the presidency or indeed any governorships, it has been successful in capturing municipal governments. More authority and resources at the municipal level, apart from what else they might mean, would thus mean a strengthened political base for the PAN. The *informe* showed that De la Madrid was perfectly well aware of this aspect of the municipal reform program. "Today, 82 of the country's municipalities are headed by parties other than the one that is responsible for national level government."

A serious attempt to promote municipal autonomy might thus resemble the electoral reform law of 1977 in providing a political opening for the legitimate expression of opposition views—either a step in the gradual evolution of the country toward a fully competitive party system, or, more likely, as a way of co-opting the opposition into the system, of allowing the opposition to find itself a place which is not without significance but which at the same time does not threaten the national hegemony of the PRI. Municipal governments are after all subject to the authority of the state governments, which would remain safely in the hands of the PRI. However, the municipal reform—like the electoral reform itself—could get out of hand and acquire rather more substance than the regime would like. The northern states in which the PAN has successfully contested municipal elections (albeit with the results sometimes disallowed) have been the states where the opposition party has been able to mount genuinely threatening campaigns for governorships. Of course it is also true that the PAN's attempts to establish fraternal relations with the U.S. Republican party, and the position of northern states on the U.S. border, facilitate the PRI's implying that the PAN is not completely loyal—even that some *panistas* may be conniving in a secessionist movement.

IV

Change will of course occur in Mexican politics, as in everything. As noted above, that change can conceivably be such as to modify the character of the political system itself so that it operates on different principles or, what appears more likely, can be contained within the norms of the current system. If the former, it can also be continuous and gradual or discontinuous and abrupt. A limited amount of discontinuity is inherent in a system which prohibits presidential re-election. The sexennial change from one president to another makes possible an adjustment in policies and personnel to a closer fit with the perceived requirements of changing times. Indeed, it makes such a shift probable, since each president wants not only to succeed in mastering the challenges that face him, but also to distinguish himself from the man who chose him for the role, and to set his own distinctive stamp on the era which historians will record by his name.

Nevertheless, change in political structure might come about in even more abrupt a manner, by means of a successful revolution or a military seizure of power. I don't believe that anyone familiar with Mexico credits the possibility of some kind of successful popular revolution against a united ruling group in any kind of foreseeable future. The military *coup* scenario is regarded as somewhat more likely, although opinions vary as to the degree of its likelihood. But Mexico is after all within the Latin American cultural area, where military *coups* have taken place even in countries where democratic institutions were long thought to be immovably entrenched, such as Chile and Uruguay.[12]

The recent crises have helped to generate new interest in the role of the military.[13] Some of the new research on this issue has provided valuable information and insights into the internal workings of the Mexican armed forces. Nevertheless, I think we know enough about the processes that have led to military seizures of power in Latin America to appreciate that they typically respond not merely to developments internal to the military but also, and more importantly, to the performance of the political system as a whole. Particularly decisive in precipitating a *coup* are three perceptions on the part of the military and of the citizens at large: that the incumbent has failed in performing some important function, such as managing the economy, maintaining order, or successfully prosecuting a war; that the incumbent government lacks legitimacy, because of its extra-constitutional origins, its lack of popular support, or its violation of legal norms and practices; or that a vacuum of power exists, as evidenced by the physical incapacity of the head of government, or of a crisis in the succession.[14] Now one can never assess the possibilities of a military *coup* purely mechanically, for example, saying that a *coup* will occur if Factor X is present and will not if Factor X is absent. A *coup* results from the interaction of a variety of elements in a complex manner. Under such circumstances, it is extremely difficult to predict single events with certainty except in the very immediate future. Nevertheless, one can certainly assess probabilities, which may range from very high to very low.

In the case of Mexico, circumstances have arisen in the past and could well arise in the future which increase the probability of a *coup* occurring, principally poor economic performance and breakdowns in the maintenance of order. Nevertheless, very potent elements reducing the probability of a coup are present and are likely to continue to exist. Primary among these is the system's legitimacy—not in the ideological sense that current governments claim descent from the Revolution of 1910, or that in form they owe their existence to democratic elections—but in the operational or behavioral sense that habits of obedience to constitutional authority have been deeply inculcated in the military. In addition, knowledge that the population at-large is integrated into the system through a multiplicity of organizations owing allegiance not to one man but to the regime as a whole means that a powerful inertial force inhibits any thought of interrupting institutional continuity. Further, it is highly unlikely that a vacuum of power could ever develop. It is perfectly clear in the Mexican system—as it might not always be, for example, in a parliamentary regime with weak multi-party cabinets—who has the power to command. Moreover, the system of succession is so well established, and party discipline with respect to accepting the president's choice of successor has been so firm, that the transmission of the mandate to rule has become smooth and uninterrupted, especially so since authority starts to flow to the president-designate as soon as his identity is revealed, almost a year or so before he actually takes office.

Despite the defects, actual and potential, of the dominant single-party system, its preeminent strength under Third World conditions is that it acts to inhibit the military seizure of power. "In Mexico's case, system viability is the key variable, not physical military power or levels of professionalization."[15] And "es la propia debilidad del Estado en tanto organización formal lo que explica el auge de los militares como fuerza política."[16]

Finally, Mexico lacks another factor increasing the probability of military coups which is generally present in Latin America; that is that the military institution, in most countries of the region, is the ultimate instrument through which hegemony is made effective. If a government violates the norms insisted on by the United States with respect to Cold War alignment or treatment of foreign property and proves resistant to economic and other pressures, in the last analysis United States officials have been known to encourage and even solicit seizures of power by military officers whose cooperative attitudes toward the United States government had long been cultivated. Mexico has purchased some immunity from this possibility by holding aloof from cooperative military relations with the United States and not participating in the aid and training programs through which such relations are fostered. Mexico's aloofness from military cooperation with the United States has been due not only to general principles of policy but to the circumstance that, as a country which borders the United States, out of which situation arise areas of disagreement and friction, Mexico might find herself in a confrontation with the United States as an enemy. Several of the contributors to the Ronfeldt volume cited above express the view that Mexico has been drawing closer to the United States in military cooperation over the last twenty years. I would doubt, however, that Mexican nationalism and historical memories of difficulties with the United States in the past would ever permit the Mexican military to become a tool of United States policy as occurs on occasion elsewhere in the region.

For all of these reasons, the probability of a military seizure of power in Mexico is very low.

V

The electoral scene in Mexico has become more interesting in recent years. There had seemed to be for several decades a long-term decline in the aggregate vote for the PRI, and a gradual long-term increase in the vote for the PAN. Part of this may have been due simply to a greater willingness to acknowledge lower vote totals for the PRI, but part was certainly due to greater popular support for the PAN, especially in the northern states and in the federal district. The measure passed under López Mateos providing for "*diputados de partido,*" subsequently amplified under López Portillo into the electoral law of 1977, was a demonstration of flexibility serving ultimately the maintenance of the system. The tree that cannot bend is the one that breaks; or, to use a more appropriately Mexican metaphor, the building that survives the earthquake is the one that can shift along with movements of the subsoil. Is it not possible that the new electoral law was genuinely intended to facilitate transition to an authentically competitive multi-party system? Hardly. Some individuals involved in the drafting process may have had intentions of this kind, but clearly the thrust of the law is simply to allow greater play for the opposition parties, to relieve some of the pressure built up on their behalf, without jeopardizing control of the government by the PRI. This is made plain by some curious elements in the construction of the law.

The form which the intention to give greater representation to opposition parties took was that of the elector's having a second vote, in addition to the one he casts for a representative from a single-member district, with which he votes for a party list of candidates in a larger electoral region. Seats based on the results of this second-vote election are distributed proportionally, within some limits, among parties which have won fewer than sixty district seats, that is, parties other than the PRI.

The intention of the law becomes clear when we contrast it with the model on which it was based, the system of voting for members of the Bundestag in West German elections. In the West German system, similarly, each voter votes twice, once on each half of a divided ballot. His first vote is for an individual candidate in his district, the second for a party list competing at the state level. Thus, half of the members of the Bundestag are elected in single-member districts; however, the total membership of the assembly is allocated proportionally with the vote received by each party on the second half of the ballot. In other words, the number of representatives elected at large in districts is not itself proportionate to the party list vote; the number considered elected from the party list is added to the seats already won in districts so that the *total* number of seats held by the party is equal to the proportion earned on the party list vote. Thus the Christian Democratic Union (CDU/CSU) won 48.8% of the vote on the second, party-list, half of the ballot in the 1983 elections. This entitled it to 244 of the Bundestag seats. It had already won 180 seats in single-district elections, by the votes on the first half of the ballot. Therefore, 64 people on its party lists were declared elected to bring up its total to the 244 it had earned.[17] This system has the merit of achieving overall proportionality while conserving whatever advantages there may be in individual district elections, in the sense of voters having specific individuals to correspond with on issues, to represent them in dealings with the bureaucracy, and so on.

In contrast with this model, which it could have adopted in toto, the Mexican law displays the following significant features:

1. Proportionality is not characteristic of the total distribution of seats in the Chamber. Arbitrarily, only 100 out of 400 seats are reserved to be distributed in accordance with the results on the second half of the ballot. Arbitrarily, also, not all of those seats are in fact distributed proportionately, since each registered party receives a minimum of one seat out of that number per electoral district. This has the effect of strengthening tiny micro-parties at the expense of any larger parties more likely to approach the status of genuine threat to the PRI.

2. The plurality single-member district elections by which 300 of the 400 seats are filled translate anything over a plurality of the votes, given more than one opposition party, into an overwhelming majority of the assembly seats.

3. The stipulation that a party gaining over 60 seats in district elections does not share in the proportional distribution of the 100 extra seats clearly indicates the expectation that the system will continue to be one of a single dominant party in effective control of the legislature, with a minority of seats earmarked as a concession to small parties in permanent opposition.

4. The provision that parties gaining over 60 seats do not share in the proportional distribution of the vote on the second half of the ballot also means that the PRI sustains no loss if it instructs its voters to opt for insignificant micro-parties on the second ballot, especially micro-parties willing to collaborate with the PRI, thus giving seats to such parties at the expense of the larger, more serious, opposition parties. This was reported to have happened during the 1985 Congressional elections, with members of some PRI unions being asked to vote for the Socialist Workers Party, the Partido Socialista de los Trabajadores or PST, on the second ballot.[18] In fact, the PST, along with the other traditional allies of the PRI, the Authentic Party of the Mexican Revolution, or PARM, and the Popular Socialist Party, or PPS, gained disproportionately on the at-large ballot over their showing in the single-member district elections.[19]

Over the last twenty-five years the vote won by the PRI in national elections has gone down from about 90% to about 65%, a drop of 25%. Under the present system—even with its provision for the representation of opposition parties, and even without allowing for the announcement of fraudulent results—given the division of the opposition between left and right and given the PRI's alliance with, or control of, micro-parties of the center and left, the vote for the PRI could drop another 25%, to 40% of the vote, and still leave the PRI with a clear majority of the seats in the Chamber of Deputies. This is not to say that the electoral system itself is beyond the pale and no more than a deceitful way of providing democratic window-dressing for an authoritarian system. In Britain at present the Conservatives control 60% of the seats in the House of Commons with only 42% of the popular vote, and the British system is less generous to very small parties than the Mexican. Moreover, it is universally the case that electoral laws are designed to maximize the advantages of the party or parties composing the legislative majority that passes them. Nevertheless, it remains true that Mexican electoral law is designed for a political system containing a dominant party and several minor parties of opposition, not for a genuinely competitive system in which an opposition party has a realistic chance of capturing a majority of seats.

VI

Normally one expects changes in the economic substructure to be reflected in the political superstructure. This is true in a long-term sense, as Mexico's evolution towards a more urban, better-educated society has coincided with a decline in the role of military officers and an increase in the proportion of people with advanced university training in leadership roles,[20] and with a "political reform" that, in least in principle, has allowed for greater political participation. The same is not true of drastic short-term economic shifts, such as the petroleum boom and bust and the financial crisis. In this respect, the dynamics of Mexican politics are clearly different, in a curious way, from those in other Latin American countries where short-term economic crisis is the most reliable predictor of the overthrow of the incumbent government. Paradoxically, in Mexico economic crisis has had the short-term effect of stalling long-term political change. This is so because, on the one hand, the crisis has weakened substantial business interests that might otherwise have been expected to give backing to the PAN and instead has forced them to look to the government for assistance, thus putting them in no position to side with the opposition.[21] On the other hand, the crisis has strengthened the role of that constituent of the ruling coalition most resistant to political reform, labor union leadership, by making it impossible for the government to risk strikes that would interrupt production.[22]

VII

One of the interesting aspects of recent political change in Mexico is that, since most Mexican academic commentators are to the left of PRI, greater prominence is given to the left-wing critique of the system, that is, the view that economic policy has erred on the side of neglecting the poor and needy in favor of the middle classes, and national interests in favor of those of foreign business. In electoral terms, however, opposition on the right has always been stronger than opposition on the left, and the results of the 1985 legislative elections do nothing to change that picture. In the party-list voting in the five at-large districts, the vote of the center (PRI and PARM) totaled 67.3% of the vote, the vote of the right-wing parties (PAN and PDM) totaled 19.7%, while the left-wing parties (PPS, PSUM, PST, PRT, and PMT) totaled just 13%. Thus the vote on the right is half again as large as the vote on the left, even if we ignore the fact that almost half the left-wing vote, that won by the PPS and the PST, is in effect disguised voting for the PRI, with which those two parties are permanently linked. This distribution of the vote is extremely interesting. Except for the preeminence of the PRI, it resembles that emerging in newly stabilizing party systems such as Venezuela, the Dominican Republic, and Costa Rica, where the normally largest party is of center-left, social democratic character, challenged by a party almost of equal size on the center-right, while a third party, further to the left, brings up the rear. Like the PRI, Acción Democrática in Venezuela, Liberación Nacional in Costa Rica, and the Partido Revolucionario Dominicano in the Dominican Republic, while social democratic in character, have become compromised by personal corruption, expansion of bureaucratic make-work jobs, and ties with racketeering labor unions. The center-right parties in those countries have given themselves ideological respectability (and access to West German funds) by calling themselves "Social Christian," an option denied to the PAN by the provision of the Mexican constitution that forbids any reference to a religion in a party title.

Comparisons like this help to clarify the nature of the PRI, complicated as it is by the party's status as the permanent party of government. It remains of significance that the PRI has to be accounted as of the center-left in the political spectrum. This remains meaningful not only in terms of its rhetoric, but also in its policy instincts and its greater ability to coopt left-wing intellectuals and university students.[23]

While the apparent weakening of the government and the ruling party as a result of the events of the last few years is a general problem of the system, in point of fact the immediate threat to the continuity of the political system is a regional one, represented by the growing power of the PAN in the northern states. It is true that there are nuclei of opposition sentiment among the voters elsewhere; opposition growing out of the conservative Catholic opposition to the Revolution and finding expression in the PDM, the Partido Demócrata Mexicano, is strong in the Bajío in the center-west of the country; anti-Mexico City sentiment remains strong in Yucatán; dissent is high among the more sophisticated voters in the Federal District. But it is primarily in the northern border states of Baja California, Sonora, Nuevo León, and Chihuahua that the opposition has had its great success in electing mayors, including mayors of state capital cities, and where opposition threatens to break through to a new level of success by capturing governorships. Taken in historical perspective, this is an interesting phenomenon. Since the establishment of the present border with the United States in the middle of the nineteenth century, the northern states have grown in population, wealth, and political significance. The Revolution focused to a great extent on the north, with its cross-border supplies of arms and ammunition, its key battles, and its cowboy cavalry. Of course, great leaders came from elsewhere in the country—Zapata, Felipe Carrillo Puerto—but it was the northerners that emerged victorious: Madero, Carranza, and finally Obregón.

After the adoption of the revolutionary constitution, the presidency was at first dominated by men from the north: Carranza from Coahuila, de la Huerta, Obregón, and Calles from Sonora, Portes Gil from Tamaulipas, and Rodríguez from Baja California; the only exception was Ortíz Rubio, from Michoacán. The next series of presidents was from states closer to the capital: Cárdenas also from Michoacán, Alemán and Ruíz Cortines from Veracruz, Avila Camacho and Díaz Ordaz from Puebla, López Mateos from México. Then finally, we have two presidents, Echeverría and López Portillo, born in the Federal District, and one, De la Madrid, raised there. It is as though power had moved in a gradual but steady wave motion from the north toward the center, and that the strength of the opposition today in the northern states represents the beginning of the next such wave. It would be far too extravagant to base a conclusion, much less a prediction, on a metaphor of this type. What it does mean, however, is that as the most developed region, and as the one most influenced by ideas of political and economic freedom from across the northern border, with concentrations of private capital that provide a continuing political base outside the state sector, the north is a natural arena of opposition to a regime characterized by tight political control and economic *dirigisme*.

It should be noted that there remains tremendous "give" in the system and that a great deal of the pressure generated by growing support for the PAN in the northern states can be accommodated without threatening continued PRI control at the national level. Between now and the end of the century the PRI may judge it politic to accept PAN victories for two or three governorships, which would rightly be regarded as a major breakthrough for the forces of opposition. Yet the example of India shows that a dominant single-party system may continue at the national level even where individual states are from time to time under the administration of opposition parties.

For all of the changes that have taken place under the impact of recent events, therefore, it seems to me that the system remains resilient enough to adapt without changing its basic character, so that the long-awaited systemic change in Mexican politics lies in a future that remains distant.

Notes

1. "Democracia en tiempos de crises," in Pablo González Casanova, ed., *Las eleccions en México: evolucion y perspectivas* (Mexico City: Siglo XXI, 1985).

2. Judith Adler Hellman, Mexico in Crisis (New York, NY: Holmes and Meier, 1978).

3. Manuel Moreno Sánchez, Crisis política de México (Mexico City: Editorial Extemporaneos, 1970).

4. Emilio Portes Gil, La crisis política de la Revolución y la proxima elección presidencial (Mexico City: Ediciones Botas, 1957).

5. M. Delal Baer, "The Mexican Mid-Term Elections" (Washington, D.C.: Georgetown University Center for Strategic and International Studies, November 5, 1985), 27.

6. Martin C. Needler, "Mexico at the Crossroads," Current History, vol. 6, no. 354 (February 1971).

7. "There is simply no chance that the equilibrium price could be any higher than $15," Morris T. Adelman, "The Future of Oil Supply and Demand," in David Howdon, ed., The Energy Crisis: Ten Years After (London: Croom Helm, 1984), 69.

8. Some responsible observers remain cautiously optimistic for the long term. See Robert E. Looney, Economic Policy-Making in Mexico: Factors Underlying the 1982 Crisis (Durham, NC: Duke University Press, 1985). Abel Beltran del Río was cautiously optimistic if the external situation was favorable, in "Problems and Prospects of the Mexican Economy in 1983–1988" in The Mexican Economic Crisis: Policy Implications for the United States, Joint Committee Print 98-11 (Washington, D.C.: Government Printing Office, February, 1984). A less optimistic tone generally characterizes the contribution to the earlier symposium, Donald Wyman, ed., Mexico's Economic Crisis: Challenges and Opportunities (La Jolla, CA: Center for U.S.-Mexican Studies, University of California, San Diego, 1983).

9. Quotations are taken from the English-language version provided by the Foreign Broadcast Information Service. "President Delivers State of Nation Speech," FBIS, Mexico (September 6, 1985).

10. Here and at one or two other points I have corrected obvious errors of translation in the FBIS version.

11. C. Richard Bath and Victoria E. Rodriguez, "Decentralization Policy in Mexico" (paper presented at the meeting of the Pacific Coast Council on Latin American Studies, October 1985).

12. On re-reading this sentence I realized, with a profound sensation of nausea, that I had last made this point before the coups in those countries took place: "Even in the countries which seem to have placed the era of the coup d'etat behind them, such as Mexico and Chile, or Uruguay and Costa Rica, military intervention remains even today a possibility," in "The Causality of the Latin American Coup d'Etat: Some Numbers, Some Speculations" (paper presented at the American Political Science Association meeting, Washington, D.C., September 1972).

13. Edward J. Williams and David F. Ronfeldt have organized symposia on the role of the military on Mexico, and Ronfeldt has also edited a volume of contributed essays: David Ronfeldt, ed., The Modern Mexican Military: A Reassessment (La Jolla, CA: Center for U.S.-Mexican Studies, University of California, San Diego, 1984).

14. For discussion of the evidence on these points, the reader is referred to Samuel E. Finer, The Man on Horseback, 2nd ed. (New York, NY: Praeger, 1983); Eric Nordlinger, Soldiers in Politics (Englewood Cliffs, NJ: Prentice-Hall, 1977); Samuel J. Fitch, The Military Coup d'Etat as a Political Process (Baltimore, MD: Johns Hopkins University Press, 1977); Alain Rouquie, L'Etat Militaire en Amerique Latine (Paris: Editions du Seuil, 1982); or previous writings on the subject by the author, especially "Military Motivations in the Seizure of Power," Latin American Research Review (Fall 1975).

214   Martin C. Needler

15. Alden M. Cunninghim, "Mexico's National Security in the 1980's–1990's," in Ronfeldt, *The Modern Mexican Military*, 173, fn. 25.

16. Arturo Ramos Dalmau, "Estado, militarismo y sociedad en América Latina," *Anales: Revista de Ciencias Sociales e Historia*, nueva serie, vol. 1, no. 1 (1984): 81.

17. David P. Conradt, *The German Polity*, 3rd ed. (New York, NY: Longman, 1986), 121.

18. Delal Baer and John Bailey, "Mexico's 1985 Mid-Term Elections: A Preliminary Assessment," *LASA Forum*, vol. 16, no. 3 (Fall 1985): 6.

19. See also the full reports by Delal Baer, "CSIS Latin American Election Studies Series: The Mexican Mid-Term Elections," (Washington, D.C.: Center for Strategic and International Studies of Georgetown University, various dates during 1985).

20. Roderic Camp, *Mexico's Leaders* (Tucson, AZ: University of Arizona Press, 1983).

21. Note the attendance by Bernardo Garza Sada and Eugenio Garza Laguera, of the Alfa and Visa conglomerates respectively, at the inauguration of the PRI governor of Nuevo León in 1985. Delal Baer and John Bailey, "Mexico's 1985 Mid-Term Elections: A Preliminary Assessment," 9.

22. This is especially noticeable in the government's abandonment of its promised efforts at reform and "moral renovation" in the petroleum sector. See George Grayson, "Mexico's Oil Industry Under de la Madrid: a New Pemex?" (Paper presented at the Pacific Coast Council on Latin American Studies Meeting, October 19, 1985), 16.

23. In the Federal District, the PRI is able to recruit students and intellectuals for government positions without difficulty. In the north, there is some "leakage" of people from the PRI to the PAN. Carlos Martínez Assad and Alvaro Arreola Ayala, "La decisión de vencer o las elecciones de 1983," in Pablo González Casanova, *Las elecciones en México*, 383.

PART FOUR

Perspectives on the Political Opposition

9

"The Opposition" in Mexico: Always a Bridesmaid, Never Yet the Bride

Evelyn P. Stevens

After fifty years of almost glacial change in Mexico's political system, the process has shown indications of accelerating, and no one seems sure of what the outcome will be. At the center of the problem is the fact that one political party has dominated the process of decision-making for the whole nation, allowing only token participation in the process by other groups.

This does not mean that most Mexican citizens approve of all the official policies that restrict their opportunities to influence economic and political choices. Those who disapprove, either individuals or organizations, are numerous, but they are disunited, some because of divergent definitions of the problems, others over the formulation of new goals, and in general because of uncertainty about where their true individual and class interests lie.

It is impossible to calculate the strength of "the opposition" with accuracy because the term used in its broadest sense could easily apply to every member of the polity; surely no one, not even the highest-ranking office holders, approves of all government policies. Further, the use of the singular form of the word "opposition" overlooks the proliferation of groups of opponents, each in conflict with the other groups, and many plagued by internal conflicts about ends and means.

Booth and Seligson revive an old discussion about the nature of the Mexican polity.[1] Referring to Almond and Verba's 1963 study, *The Civic Culture*, they take issue with what they see as the authors' main conclusion: that Mexico's authoritarian political structure is the product of authoritarian attitudes of the citizens. Analyzing new survey results, they reach the conclusion that Mexicans support democratic values in preference to authoritarian ones, and they find "the paradox of a persistently authoritarian, yet popular, system sustained by a pro-democratic citizenry."

This paradox was once described to the present author by a Mexican attorney who observed, "We have the best constitution in the world, and one day it will become a reality." The gap between ideal and reality has narrowed, but full achievement may require much more time and effort.

Mexico's "civic culture" has been cleared of the charge of authoritarianism. The public record is full of accounts of opposition movements, rebellions, peasant uprisings, labor strikes, and electoral challenges. The fact that attempts to affect the operation of the system have failed to achieve the desired ends can be attributed to the state's monopoly of coercive power which has been employed whenever the outcome of a contest is in doubt.

In the present context, "opposition" refers to any organized group that manifests a critical attitude toward national political and economic goals as they are defined and implemented by the state, formulates an alternative agenda emphasizing economic and social goals that differ significantly from those pursued by the incumbent regime, and recruits new adherents and actively strives to increase its share of political power for the purpose of implementing its own agenda.

Because Mexican political life today is characterized by a greater number of such groups than at any time since the 1920s, it is appropriate that this period should be recognized as one of transition. Although the result of the process cannot be predicted with any certainty at this time, some of the participants can be described and the significance of their activities evaluated.

There is a sense of urgency today about every discussion of Mexico's present situation and future prospects. The word most used to convey the prevailing opinion is "crisis," although there is no general agreement about the nature of the problem or the elements that have gone into the making of it. Economic disaster, the worst in fifty years, figures importantly in assessments of the situation, but there is more than merely a sense of deprivation in the reactions of the populace. Although Mexicans have long been accustomed to revelations of fiscal fraud by government office holders, there is now a mounting outrage at the magnitude of the fraud in the face of falling petroleum prices, a huge external debt, and disastrous domestic inflation. The government has taken more than the customary token measures against the worst offenders, but public anger has not been assuaged.

Writing in 1972 the late Daniel Cosío Villegas, dean of Mexican politologists, concluded that the political system that had been successful for many years in containing the divisive elements of the nation, guaranteeing stability and achieving economic growth, was no longer adequate for modern needs and seemed unable to accept the necessity of basic changes to provide greater responsiveness and participation. The system, he implied, had exhausted its potential for growth and change; therefore, the change would have to come from without, i.e., imposed by events.[2] Those events have overtaken his predictions; the Mexican polity now stands on the brink of irreversible political and economic disaster, but no individual or group has stepped forward to lead the nation out of the wilderness.

Reflected in the analyses of the problem is a conviction that the regime as presently constituted is incapable of devising and implementing effective remedies. Some sectors of society have for many years insisted that deeply rooted problems can be solved only by a realignment of political forces that will reorder national goals and implement new policies. These groups are "the opposition" from among which observers hope to discover evidences of effective action.

Therein lies a dilemma involving questions about which opposition groups have formulated comprehensive analyses of the nation's problems, have prepared detailed programs of actions to remedy them, and can count on politically competent individuals to implement the program. Even the most thoughtful of analysts often focus on internal political economy, to the exclusion of consideration of world conditions.

While in the past observers often commented on the extraordinary stability of Mexico's political system, that stability has been largely an illusion maintained by the state apparatus that controls the rate and direction of change through a variety of measures. Although the repertory is rather limited, comprising such elements as temporization, coercion, cooptation, deceit, and tactical retreat from untenable positions, it is the flexible Mexican "mix" of these practices that has preserved an equilibrium of sorts for nearly six decades. The same resources are available to any government but may be combined in various ways, producing different and sometimes disastrous results for the polity.

Social groups have a limited array of resources for expressing their grievances and pressing for redress. Resort to violence is an option, but it is usually unsuccessful in an encounter with the overwhelmingly superior forces of the government. In the past half-century in Mexico there has been a progressive diminution of attempts to resist or change government policies by armed force.[3]

Toward the end of the 1930s, suppression of the *sinarquista* rebellion virtually closed off threats to political stability and made possible the reorganization of the ruling party. The new sectoral organization effectively defined the limits of participation in the system and drastically reduced structural conditions for the expression of dissent. This closing off of the escape valves for discontent seems to have fostered the building up of pressures that eventually led to outbreaks of protest, especially—but not exclusively—in the decade from 1958 to 1968.[4]

"The opposition" of that era cannot be described as a homogeneous mass of citizens who were acting in concert to oppose state power. Some groups mobilized on an ad hoc basis because their immediate interests were jeopardized by new threats to their economic or social rights and privileges. Others, inspired by awareness of new ideological currents, recognized their shared discontent, joined forces, and took action against what they perceived as oppression.

There were at least three types of groups with different viewpoints about the proper ends of political activity and the appropriate means for achieving them. The following description of some protest movements that occurred during the period in question, although by no means an exhaustive catalog, suggests the limitations experienced by the protestors and the resources used by the regime to suppress them.

Protest Movements

Peasant Uprisings

Compared to the number of organized peasant groups that exist throughout the countryside, only a few engage in protests against government policies such as the violent marches of the henequén farmers of Yucatán in the 1960s. Most organizations concentrate on collective purchasing of seed, fertilizer, tools, and other necessities directly related to their agricultural work. It is not peasant apathy but a concern for survival that makes them wary of direct hostile engagement with the power of the state. All their perceptions of the chances of economic, political, and even of biological survival indicate that they can fare better by lending token electoral support to the PRI (Partido Revolucionario Institucional), the dominant political party. In a study of participation in electoral politics, Reyna[5] showed that the least advantaged groups, among them the peasants, gave the strongest support to PRI candidates.

In the countryside, peace was broken when the Independent Peasants Union (CCI) in 1962 carried out a sustained campaign under the leadership of Rubén Jaramillo. The CCI demanded an end to exploitation and terrorization by local *caciques* (political strong men) and effective implementation of the agrarian provisions of the national constitution. The uprising collapsed when Jaramillo and his family were assassinated in 1962 by "unknown assailants" who were later identified as members of a police squad.[6]

After the demise of the CCI there were a number of smaller, short-lived peasant protests throughout the countryside that were suppressed by the local police or by special death squads. Until the advent of a viable alternative press, these events were rarely reported in the major Mexico City news media; the consequences of such publicity would have been dangerous to the journalists who reported the news.

An exception to the more usual pattern of agrarian political involvement is described by Hellman[7] in a history of the Central Union, established in the 1930s in the Laguna region. At the height of its success the Union had 30,000 members. Organizers were members of the Communist party but instead of recruiting party members they concentrated their efforts on building a large union membership that could improve its economic position by cooperative effort. The leaders never renounced their party membership, but neither did they challenge the central government directly; instead, they represented the Union members in contacts with government agencies to obtain benefits or concessions. Eventually the Union was destroyed by a "highly sophisticated co-optive technique"[8] whereby the government created parallel agencies bearing the same acronyms as the Central Union agencies. Many peasants were weaned away from the Union by the substitute agencies that offered them greater benefits. Similar techniques were employed in the 1964–1965 doctors' strikes.[9]

Student Movements

Since the advent of free public education at the university level, Latin American students generally have been more politically active than their angloamerican counterparts, with the possible exceptions of the Free Speech movement of U.S. students in 1964–1965 and the student agitation against continued U.S. involvement in Vietnam in the early 1970s. The old university buildings were located in a central area of Mexico City until a new campus was built at its present location during the presidency of Miguel Alemán (1946–1952). Although it was obvious that the old quarters could not have accommodated the expanding student and faculty population, students were convinced that the president wanted to isolate them from contact with the citizenry (and tourists). Whatever his motives, the students showed their disapproval of his policies by repeatedly defacing the statue of Alemán, in academic garb, that had been erected in the center of the new campus. University officials erected a box-like enclosure to protect the statue but in the face of continued student unrest it was finally removed and placed in storage.

One of the two most notable manifestations of student dissent was the strike of 1956 by students of the Polytechnic Institute, the scientific and technical school in Mexico City. The apparent aim of the strike was to support an accumulation of grievances related to the physical conditions of the school and the staffing of the faculty. After nearly a year of occupation of the campus by the strikers, government troops forcibly evicted them and closed down the school. Several students were killed and many others were jailed.

Twelve years after the "Poly" strike, students at the National University of Mexico (UNAM), south of Mexico City, in an apparently spontaneous case of political combustion, organized a mass protest on their campus in response to police assaults on high school (preparatoria) students in the historic center of Mexico City. After two months the strike was ended on 2 October 1968 with the massacre of hundreds of students who were peaceably assembled in the Plaza of Three Cultures. Police and army units were blamed for the indiscriminate gunfire, but no individuals were brought to justice.[10]

Catholic students from middle class or wealthy families were educated in private schools in Mexico or abroad and were expected to share their parents' conservative views. However, during the 1968 protest movements many students from the Catholic University broke out of their conformity and occasionally joined the UNAM students in marches, meetings, and leafletting brigades.

While peasant uprisings and student strikes clearly reflect group opposition to state policies, they fall into the special category of protest movements distinguished by two characteristics. The first of these is the difficulty they encounter in formulating a single agenda that lists specific grievances and proposes a set of attainable remedies. The second characteristic is a deficiency of political negotiation skills, of control of mobilized masses, of a delicate sense of timing, and of a Machiavellian flexibility.

At the same time, the state must be able to count on appointed officials who possess these skills as well as a commitment to use force only as a last resort. If there is no acceptance by the opposing groups of the minimal conditions under which agreement can be sought, the conflict is destined to end in stalemate or violence.

Government Employees

In another protest movement, the 1964–1965 strikes of the Mexican Association of Residents and Interns (AMMRI) at government hospitals, the government brought into play a new tactic. Taking advantage of the fact that the physicians had not registered their association in the appropriate government department (Gobernación), the labor sector of the PRI hastily and clandestinely assembled a small group of progovernment physicians who dutifully applied for official recognition as repesentatives of a union of all the physicians employed by the government. When AMMRI representatives tried again to press their case, officials refused to negotiate with them on the grounds that they were imposters.[11]

Other methods used by the Mexican government to break that strike were used later by the United States government to break a strike of the air traffic controllers' union. While some physicians were allowed to return to work, the most politically active ones were dismissed, although many were later rehired. This was a more lenient attitude than the one displayed by the U.S. government in the 1983 strike of air traffic controllers.

This review of a number of protest movements, each of which mobilized thousands of militants, was undertaken to emphasize the difficulties of challenging the enormous power of the state. The movements were for the most part short-lived, their leadership inexperienced, their objectives perhaps too ambitious to succeed. Although most of the militants eventually abandoned the cause in favor of matters of immediate and urgent concern, some of the leaders retained the knowledge and skills they had acquired, in the hope that they might be able to use them in some future cause.

The state suffered not at all from discontinuity of experience. Over a fifty-year period the skills developed by successive generations of bureaucrats grew by accretion to a body of expertise that covered a wide variety of techniques for containing dissent. The official family may have grown too complacent about its ability to prevail against any threat to its hegemony. Industrial development, demographic growth, economic boom and bust, structural change, and finally seismic disaster have significantly weakened the state's ability to satisfy demands on its resources and perhaps also its capacity for responding to challenges to power.

Although protest movements have been recurrent features of twentieth-century political life, there seems to have been little or no continuity between the sporadic outbreaks of those manifestations. They have flared up, burned brightly, and been brutally repressed without retaining organizational cores that could bank the embers of historic grievances and fan them back into a flame that would fire bigger and more disciplined movements. In brief, they lack a political genealogy.

Labor

In marked contrast to the spontaneous and short-lived protests, the labor movement in twentieth-century Mexico can trace its roots through the decades back to the anarchosyndicalist movement originating before the Revolution of 1910, and contributing significant support to the successful effort to overthrow the Díaz regime.[12] Because of the coexistence of old but still active unions and new unions whose activities have taken other forms, labor must be included in any discussion of sources of possible change. The question that must be asked is: Do the unions in any sense constitute an "opposition" and if so, to what—to the PRI, to "peak" union leadership, to the regime?

Since the triumph of the Revolution the labor movement has participated with great vitality and often volatility in the processes of change that have been a constant feature of twentieth-century Mexican life. Workers and their leaders served as the main source of support for and influence on the newly constituted regime. At the same time, labor leaders were informing themselves about the evolution of unions in Europe, the Soviet Union, and the United States, with the intention of adopting features that might prove useful in creating a model suitable for Mexican conditions.

Throughout its postrevolutionary existence labor has been united in agreement on its place as the most important constituent of society. Apart from that, however, almost every other issue has been a source of disagreement, ranging from rivalry for leadership to ideological controversy. Political attitudes range from the frank avowal of communist convictions[13] to professed aversion for any issues except bread-and-butter concerns. The latter attitude is the more prevalent one.

The CTM (Mexican Confederation of Workers) is one of the three sectors, or supporting pillars, of the nation's hegemonic political party, the PRI, and it is also a member of the umbrella labor organization, the Labor Congress, but some of its constituent unions display a critical attitude toward positions adopted by the CTM leadership.

For the past forty years the CTM has been headed and ruled by Fidel Velázquez, who developed a dual strategy, one aspect of which was the manipulation of the labor sector in defense of the PRI's hegemonic influence over Mexico's political system. The other aspect defended the economic interests of members of the unions that belonged to the CTM. Reconciling these two often conflicting interests was the accomplishment that gained general recognition of Velázquez as a master manipulator.

In 1986 as his eighty-sixth birthday approached, there were indications that Velázquez's retirement from the leadership post was imminent and that his successor would be Emilio González, governor of the state of Nayarit.[14] Although his retirement had been expected and his successor seems likely to continue his policies, many supporters of the regime have expressed concern about possible future changes in the CTM's role in the political changes that are already taking place.

Since the end of World War II Mexico's industrial structure has undergone continued growth and diversification, accompanied by new trends in the field of labor relations. Although recognition of the nature of these changes calls forth questions about their impact on the future of Mexican industrial development, our focus is limited to the possible emergence of organized labor's opposition to the government's political economic agenda.

Even more important, the evolution of labor organizations during the past fifteen years has brought about the breakup of some old established unions, the emergence of many new ones—partly in response to new trends in industrial activity—and a militantly critical attitude toward the government's labor policies. Bizberg comments that "in spite of the combination of forces that lean toward the official labor movement, the quantitative and qualitative presence of tendencies that reject the traditional alliance between the State and the labor movement is definite and significant."[15]

The peak progovernment organization, the Labor Congress, gathers under its "umbrella" the largest unions, whose total membership numbers nearly five million workers in diverse types of industry. Of that total, the CTM has a membership of two million. Five unions not affiliated with the CTM, with a membership of nearly 400,000, have taken strong stands against the government's and the party's positions on labor problems.[16]

In addition to these dissident unions of the Left, there is a "company" union (sindicato blanco), the FNSINL (National Federation of Industrial Unions of [the state of] Nuevo León), created and sustained by the directorship of private industries located principally in Monterrey. This union has a membership of about 50,000 workers who are committed to support the conservative views of business interests in the state, which in turn are an important source of support for the Partido de Acción Nacional (PAN), the conservative pro-Catholic, pro-business political party.

Roxborough's study of labor activities in the automobile industry pays particular attention to the behavioral characteristics of nine unions in plants engaged in the production of passenger cars. Six of the nine unions were "official," i.e., affiliated with the Labor Congress, while three were "independent," not affiliated with the Congress. However, when the behavior of both groups was analyzed in terms of "militancy," it appeared that two of the "official" unions engaged in strikes as often as did the three "independent" unions.[17]

Roxborough further argues that in spite of the grouping of most labor unions into "peak" organizations that have an official relationship with the regime, "rank and file insurgency has been a constant feature of Mexican industrial relations and . . . control by the state over the organized labour movement is far more fragile and subject to contest than appears at first sight."[18]

In a historical account of the growth of the automobile workers' unions, the 1984 Roxborough study concluded that the parent CTM was unable in an important number of cases to control insurgent movements of union members. The impression given by a detailed account of the in-plant activities of unionized auto workers, including elections of officials, is one of little or no control from above over the workers' choices of policies or representatives. This viewpoint is in sharp contrast with the orthodox view that entrenched union leaders manipulate the membership in such a way as to repress labor militancy.

The study recognizes the existence of "two styles of unionism, one militant and the other conservative," and indicates that the militant unions are characterized by a high degree of internal democracy. The nine unions, including both militant and conservative tendencies, actually account for a relatively small number of members; the largest of them has no more than ten thousand members.[19] Nevertheless the author seems to indicate that there will be a continued tendency toward an increase in the number of independent unions and that they will further undermine the ability of organized labor to "prop up the system."[20] This is an optimistic assessment that may in the long run prove to be justified, but in the near distance there loom enormous problems that could postpone the achievement until well into the next century.

Bizberg calls attention to the difficulties of converting a small grass-roots movement of union democracy into a powerful force for democratization of the whole polity.[21] He asks what will be the effect on labor militancy of increased unemployment, a slowdown in or even elimination of some fringe benefits, and inability of the government to satisfy demands for wage increases to compensate for the effects of severe inflationary trends.

Labor militancy in defense of its own interests is a normal reaction of workers affected by reduction of their incomes or loss of employment. This militancy is usually confined to a small area of the national territory. There is a question as to whether the regime's response to economic disaster of the magnitude experienced by Mexicans in the 1980s will push a significant number of workers toward revolutionary activity or, on the contrary, tend to reduce their militancy. Put another way, will disaster force people to concentrate their efforts to survive?

What seems to be happening at this time is that the labor sector is falling into a decline of ideological engagement. Neither workers in the traditional labor sector nor those associated with modern industries seem to be inclined toward participation in the vanguard of political reform. Referring to workers in the auto industry, for example, Roxborough suggests that "if an analyst believes that [they] ought, in some sense, to be imbued with a revolutionary class consciousness, and ought to use their unions as instruments of struggle against a capitalist state, then these workers—like most workers in Mexico—must be regarded as profoundly conservative."[22]

Asking "How did the bourgeoisie reduce the Mexican workers to such a state of impotence?" the radical critic José Revueltas responds that they were seduced with paternalistic policies couched in "revolutionary" language and they received certain benefits in exchange for their loyalty to the political system.[23]

As of early 1986 not even economic concerns had spurred labor groups to take aggressive action to defend their interests. In December 1985 the official increase for the minimum salary for 1986 was 32 percent. This rate applied to Mexico City and other high-cost regions of the country. The daily wage (when and where it was actually paid) rose from 1,250 pesos to 1,650 pesos at a time when the inflation rate for 1985 was expected to have rounded off at 60 percent. The fact that the CTM had publicly declared that it would "fight tooth and nail" for a 60-percent raise and then accepted a 32-percent raise without protest caused indignation among members of CTM unions.[24]

Parties and Elections

When the Mexican government announced in the late 1970s that the time had come to introduce reforms in the electoral system, the news was received by Mexican political activists with almost as much excitement as the 1963 announcement by Generalissimo Francisco Franco that Spain would begin the process of becoming a constitutional monarchy. The analogy is appropriate, as both governments had for many years been recognized as outstanding examples of authoritarian political systems.

After the 1975 accession of King Juan Carlos to the Spanish throne, the transition to democratic representative government proceeded very rapidly. In Mexico, however, the 1977 electoral reform law has been criticized by opposition parties as coming too late and allowing too little change.

The provisions of the law for changes in procedures for election of opposition candidates to the national Chamber of Deputies has been described in detail by Middlebrook.[25] The abstract offered here is a distillation only of those points that are necessary for the present discussion. Referred to as LOPPE (Law of Political Organizations and Electoral Processes), the reform enlarged the number of seats in the Chamber from 250 to 400, of which 100 are reserved for minority parties whose candidates are elected by proportional representation from party lists in the five districts into which the whole of the national territory has been divided for this purpose. The other seats are filled by simple majority elections in the 300 electoral districts, but if any party wins as many as 60 of the 300-seat bloc, it may not compete in the proportional representation contest for an additional share of those 100 seats.

Other provisions (described by Middlebrook)[26] place special restrictions on opposition parties competing for seats in the Chamber, but the law also provides new benefits such as guaranteed allotment of time on radio and television programs, financial support for certain types of monthly publications, free access to postal and telegraph facilities, and tax exemptions. The established press, careful to preserve its benefits from the ruling party,[27] usually provides perfunctory, often misleading, reports of the activities of the opposition parties, but new opposition newspapers and weekly magazines are now being published that present more complete and accurate information.

Another important provision is the guarantee that permanently registered parties are granted voting membership on the Federal Electoral Commission (CFE) and state and district commissions; provisionally registered parties may send observers. The Federal Commission is the ultimate arbiter of charges of fraudulent practices in the tabulation of electoral returns. The PRI as the majority party has a majority of seats on all electoral commissions and can overrule appeals from minority parties as to certification of "winning candidates."

Before the law was adopted, it was thoroughly discussed by all sectors of the political system and changes were made in many provisions in response to criticisms by legal scholars as well as representatives of groups anxious to preserve or enlarge their influence on the system. The effects of the reform were visible for the first time in the 1979 election of members of the national Chamber of Deputies. The pre-reform period of 1961–1976 included only four parties: the PAN, PRI, PPS (Partido Popular Socialista), and PARM (Partido Auténtico de la Revolución Mexicana). During that period the PRI slipped from 90.2 percent of the total votes cast to 80.1 percent. In the same period PAN rose from 7.6 percent to a high point of 14.7 percent and then fell to 8.5 percent in 1976 (principally as a result of internal dissension in the party). The other two contending parties picked up the remaining crumbs.

The next three elections (1979, 1982, 1985) revealed further slippage in the percentage of votes for the PRI slates from 69.7 percent in 1979 to 65 percent in 1985. In the same period PAN increased its percentage from 10.8 (1979) to 17.5 (1982) and dropped again to 15.5 in 1985—still a significant increase over the pre-1979 tallies.

By 1985, in addition to PRI and PAN seven other parties were participating in the national elections for deputies, garnering amongst themselves the remaining 14.5 percent of the vote. The biggest share of this residual category was obtained by the PSUM (Partido Socialista Unificado de México) with 3.2 percent but that party, representing the hopes of the Left, had lost ground since its initial achievement of 4.9 percent of the vote in 1979.

Baer and Bailey, referring to the 1979 results, conclude that "in response to [the erosion of the PRI's electoral strength] the . . . government, acting in hegemonic fashion, rewarded its allies and weakened its real opposition . . . of both Right and Left, PAN and PSUM." This was accomplished by "encouraging the proliferation and survival of micro-parties."[28]

Many observers agree that fraud is the chief method employed by the government to distribute electoral rewards and punishment.[29] Even with simon-pure tallies that would result in the gain of a greater number of seats for the opposition parties, the PRI would remain the hegemonic party. Riding comments that "in theory, so long as its formal legitimacy and political control were unaffected, the government could simply recognize opposition victories and live with a higher degree of political pluralism. Yet the political managers, while accepting the principle of power-sharing within the system, resent surrendering any control to an opposition party."[30]

The problem is somewhat more complex than this appraisal might suggest. Fear of a possible "band-wagon" effect on voters' behavior may threaten the sense of security the PRI leadership has enjoyed for such a long time by using increasingly blatant manipulation of vote counting. They may be convinced that some symbolic figure would signify a fatal slippage leading to a rush of voters toward one of the opposition parties, either the PAN or the PSUM.

The Right and the Left

The Right

At present, PRI analysts appear to believe that the biggest danger comes from increased strength on the right of the political spectrum. Baer and Bailey concur with a suggestion that "the system punishes parties that entertain expectations for real electoral strength" and the PAN is the primary victim at this time.[31] The PAN has never had the kind of organization, financing, or membership to support a successful nationwide *mano a mano* contest with the PRI for control of the national government. It has concentrated its resources on winning the votes of its natural constituency: the educated, conservative, Catholic businessmen and industrialists and their wives and employees in the large urban centers in the North. Without using the whole gamut of electoral tactics that were perfected by Tammany Hall and Chicago's erstwhile Daley vote-getting machines, which in Mexico are paralleled by PRI campaigners, the PAN has persuaded a large segment of Northern citizens that their economic and political welfare depends on the party's increased influence on local and national affairs.

The PRI never rests; there is only a slight lull between the successful conclusion of one campaign and the initial long-term planning sessions for the next one. The huge central headquarters of the party in Mexico City employs hundreds of people on a year-round basis and the workforce is doubled or tripled for presidential and congressional elections.

PRI hoplites fan out across the nation distributing posters and banners, painting campaign slogans on buildings and hillsides, while print and electronic media saturate the public with information and local officials organize rallies, requiring government employees to attend them and rewarding the employees with time off during the rest of the working day. No reliable accounting of the cost of these activities has ever been made public.

There are party offices in all large cities, as well as in many smaller towns where problems of voter loyalty to the PRI may have arisen. PRI strategists also direct special contingents from the national headquarters to those areas during state and local election campaigns.

While no other party or combination of parties has these resources, the PAN is not bereft of means with which to carry on its work; industrialists and businessmen support its campaigns in the expectation that each PAN victory at any level of the political system will further their aims. The party has a substantial following especially in the states of Nuevo León, Sonora, and Chihuahua in the North and Jalisco, Puebla, and Tlaxcala in the center of the country.

In the 1983 elections PAN candidates won an increased number of posts in local elections in Northern cities but none of its seven candidates for governorships was successful. Experienced observers expressed concern that large-scale "mistakes" in voting tallies compiled by the respective electoral commissions dominated by PRI officials may have accounted for some of the PAN defeats. Then in 1985 there were violent protests against the results of local elections in San Luis Potosí, Guanajuato, Chiapas, Chihuahua, Jalisco, Tlaxcala, Baja California, and Tamaulipas. The most inflamed incidents occurred in San Luis Potosí, where the municipal palace was set on fire, and to a somewhat lesser extent in Chihuahua. After these incidents the PRI-controlled Chihuahua state legislature approved a new electoral law that was expected to reduce further the possibility that an opposition candidate might win the governorship in 1986.[32]

PAN's survival owes much to the early successes of the Grupo Monterrey in establishing an independent stronghold of conservative capitalism in the state of Nuevo León. Although the group's roots can be traced to the late nineteenth century, it achieved political maturity in 1936 by entering a conservative challenger to Lázaro Cárdenas's chosen successor for the presidency of Mexico. While the regiomontano candidate did not win the election, the Grupo, led by the Garza-Sada family, established an independent role for itself by challenging the dominant party's position on capital-labor and capital-state relations.

Among the important factors contributing to this success were the cohesiveness of the members of the group, the coordination of their resources, and the national government's ambiguity concerning participation by the private sector. Saragoza suggests that "the historical importance of the Monterrey Group, and the Garza-Sadas particularly, hinges on the development of the Grupo Monterrey within the larger framework of the evolution of capital-state relations."[33]

In spite of the Group's strength in Nuevo León and the effects of its example on conservatives in some other states, it is hard to believe that the PAN can benefit in the near future from these successes to the extent of displacing the PRI from its preeminence, even in an honest election.

The Left

If the PAN, representing the Right, has little chance of becoming the hegemonic power in Mexican politics in the immediate future, the PSUM must have even smaller hopes. Although the acronym appears in the official records of the 1979 elections, the votes reported in its name actually represented the sum of ballots cast for five parties of which the Partido Comunista Mexicana (PCM) was the best known. The other parties that formally joined with the PCM to become the PSUM in 1981 were PSR (Partido Socialista Revolucionario), MAP (Movimiento de Acción Popular), MAUS (Movimiento de Acción y Unidad Socialista) and PPM (Partido del Pueblo Mexicano). Whether the chronicles of the party's origin figure in history as 1979 or 1981 is unimportant in comparison with the fact that the forces of the Left had subordinated their individual ideological agendas to the larger aim of exerting real influence on Mexican political life.

That this aim has not yet been fully realized is less a reflection of the new party's performance at the polls than of the fact that its principal figures, intellectuals of the Left, have thus far failed to agree on basic principles and objectives. That kind of agreement is a necessary precondition to forging a linkage of their philosophical views with the pragmatic methods required for popular success. As a result, some of its most dedicated militants find themselves working at cross-purposes with each other and accomplishing far less than they had hoped for.

Part of the problem arises from the fact that the unification movement did not have enough time to mature before the party was thrust into the struggle of a national electoral contest. Although many party strategists appear to recognize that PSUM's "natural" constituency is in the ranks of organized labor, there is little agreement as to how that sector can be won over to the party's cause.

In an analysis of the problem Arnaldo Córdova argues vigorously that just as the PRI has become powerful by mobilizing *organized masses*, so must the PSUM make its prime task the reorganizing and winning over of the working masses.[34] "Without mass organization," he insists, "other parties confronting the official party are not genuine contenders [for power], whether they are on the left or the right or in the center; which is to say that they are not real parties at all." He reminds his colleagues of the Left that the insurgency of organized labor groups during the 1970s was a more important achievement than the Left's theorizing "which in many ways," he comments scathingly, "continues to be elementary and primitive."[35]

Carr recalls that "the 1968 [student] movement and its bloody repression brought into the PCM a whole new generation of young people, students, intellectuals and others with varying styles of anti-capitalist critique."[36] Interviews conducted by the present author in 1983 with veterans of the 1968 movement revealed a wide range of opinions about immediate and long-term goals of political action. While the "generation of '68" is an important sector of PSUM, yet another generation of students is already beginning to enter the stream of influences on the party's position.

In 1981, without waiting for full achievement of consensus, the COCEI (Coalition of Workers, Peasants, and Students of the Isthmus [of Tehuantepec] affiliated with the PCM) seized the municipal government of Juchitán in the state of Oaxaca and administered the affairs of the town for two years. Issues that had mobilized the local populace in support of the COCEI included long-term problems of land tenure reform, corruption in the local government, and lack of basic services such as schools and hospitals. The term "seized" is appropriate because the PRI candidates, claiming to have won the election which was largely viewed by the populace as having been flagrantly fraudulent, barricaded themselves in the city hall. The national government through its fiscal and police powers put great pressure on the COCEI by isolating the town, cutting off operating funds, and finally in August 1983 dissolving the local government. A special election was held, as a result of which the PRI candidates were declared the winners, in spite of repeated widespread accusations of fraud.[37]

Bizberg suggests that the authors of the 1977 political reform law may have intended to give the Left a part in the electoral process in order to reveal its weakness.[38] The PSUM has indeed expended much of its energy in parliamentary activity and intraparty dissension over ends and means and perhaps has diverted resources away from efforts to enlarge its membership base. In a comment on this kind of criticism, Roxborough states that "the aim [of the reform] is not to create a viable democracy but rather to give legitimacy to a broad range of oppositional political tendencies."[39]

As this is being written, an atmosphere of tension and expectation permeates most sectors of the politically active population in Mexico. Opinions about prospects for change, expressed in writing and in oral communication, manifest a wide range of attitudes, from buoyant optimism about the possibility of a real breakthrough toward a more democratic political system to a sense of foreboding that the recent concatenation of catastrophes experienced during the past decade will cause a relapse into a new era of porfirianism. Insofar as "public opinion" can be gauged, it appears that many Mexicans are confused, frightened, and angry, but these emotions are unfocused. There is no general agreement as to who is responsible for the disasters, nor is there a consensus about who or what can lead the Mexican people out of the wilderness.

Any discussion of Mexico's political future must begin with a discussion of the PRI's prospects for continuing as the hegemonic party. A realistic appraisal might convince an observer that no party will ever be able to break the PRI's hold on the nation; that the PRI with all its resources, including electoral fraud, violent suppression of opposition *groups* (we are not referring here to opposition *parties*), and control of most information sources, will continue to rule at least until the end of the century and perhaps until it celebrates its own centennial of power.

On the other hand, a few optimists—without any concrete justification—cling to the hope that relief will come from inside the party itself; that is, that from somewhere within the ranks of career politicians will grow the resolve to defy the rules of the game and mobilize an internal reform movement that will rescue Mexico from its long political stagnation. If they were to take such an action, it would not be motivated so much by altruism as by a sense of self-preservation based on some premonition that the ship of the PRI is about to sink under their feet.

In the past a political "hopeful" could be almost certain that appointment to a PRI post in national, state, or municipal government would afford a measure of influence and an opportunity for enrichment. Party militants— the people who organized and conducted the election campaigns—and career bureaucrats, the vast army of employees in the national headquarters and state enterprises—could look forward to almost certain lifetime employment. During the past ten years, however, the fabric of party prepotency has begun to fray slightly at the edges, sending a premonitory shiver through the ranks. By the mid-1980s it appeared that the modest electoral reforms of 1977 had allowed many voters to express their preferences for candidates of other parties. The 1982 and 1985 elections did not produce a stampede away from the PRI, but the trend showed that the pluripartidist system might in the future oblige the PRI to cede larger shares of its power to the opposition.

Like the effect of a slow leak in a sinking ship, the PRI may lose its position little by little, in spite of efforts to stop the loss by more widespread electoral fraud. Opportunist PRI politicians may begin to think of "jumping ship" and at such a time each politician may have to make very crucial decisions as to which of the other parties—PAN or PSUM—to take shelter in. One can imagine the spectacle as the politicians wrestle with the problem of assessing the chances of either party for replacing the PRI.

Can the PRI arrest its decline? Can it adapt to changing conditions, welcome victorious opposition candidates into the ranks of decision-makers after they have shed their roles as petitioners? Reyna perceives the party's dilemma. "[A]s strong as it is, the Mexican political system has difficulty combatting independent or relatively independent political movements. The . . . political structure is designed for political manipulation of demands, but it has no structure to absorb autonomous political mobilization. The Achilles' heel of the system may therefore be that sort of political protest."[40]

If the PRI does not succeed in resolving this dilemma, the vacuum will be filled by some other political force. That force may not be inclined to observe parliamentary etiquette.

Notes

1. John A. Booth and Mitchell A. Seligson, "The Political Culture of Author-itarianism in Mexico: A Reexamination," *Latin American Research Review*, 19, no. 1 (1984): 106–24.

2. Daniel Cosío Villegas, *El sistema político mexicano: las posibilidades de cambio* (Austin, TX: University of Texas Press, 1972), 59–71.

3. Howard F. Cline, *Mexico: Revolution to Evolution, 1940–1960* (New York, NY: Oxford University Press, 1963), 162; Lesley Byrd Simpson, *Many Mexicos* (Berkeley, CA: University of California Press, 1971), 339.

4. Enrique Semo, Ilán Semo and Américo Saldivar, México: un pueblo en la historia, vol. 4 (Puebla, México: Editorial Nueva Imagen, Universidad Autonoma de Puebla, 1982), 11–17.

5. José Luis Reyna, "An Empirical Analysis of Political Mobilization: The Case of Mexico" (Ph.D. diss., Cornell University, 1971).

6. Francisco Gómez Jara, El movimiento campesino en México (Mexico City, México: Campesina, 1970); Semo, Semo and Saldivar, México: un pueblo en la historia; Evelyn P. Stevens, Protest and Response in Mexico (Cambridge, MA: MIT Press, 1974).

7. Judith Adler Hellman, Mexico in Crisis, 2nd ed. (New York, NY: Holmes and Meier, 1983), 146–165.

8. Hellman, Mexico in Crisis, 158.

9. Stevens, Protest and Response in Mexico.

10. See Stevens, Protest and Response in Mexico, for a brief account and extensive bibliography of both the "Poly" and the UNAM strikes.

11. Stevens, Protest and Response in Mexico, 127–173.

12. Frank R. Brandenburg, The Making of Modern Mexico (Englewood Cliffs, NJ: Prentice-Hall, 1964), 120–121; Ian Roxborough, Unions and Politics in Mexico: The Case of the Automobile Industry (Cambridge: Cambridge University Press, 1984), 9–12; Joe C. Ashby, Organized Labor and the Mexican Revolution under Lázaro Cárdenas (Chapel Hill, NC: University of North Carolina Press, 1967).

13. Valentín Campa, Mi testimonio; memorias de un comunista mexicano (México: Ediciones de Cultura Popular, 1978).

14. New York Times, 27 March 1986.

15. Ilán Bizberg, "Las perspectivas de la oposición sindical en México," Foro International, 23, no. 4 (April-June): 33.

16. Bizberg, "Las perspectivas de la oposición sindical," 137–41; Manuel Camacho, La clase obrera en la historia de México: El futuro in mediato, vol. 15, 3d ed. (México: Siglo Veintiuno Editores, 1984), 336–37. (The largest and most important unions affiliated with the CTM are: Confederación Revolucionario de Obreros y Campesinos (CROC, Revolutionary Federation of Workers and Peasants), Federación de Sindicatos de Trabajadores al Servicio del Estado (FSTSE, Federation of Unions of Civil Service Workers), Sindicato de Trabajadores Ferrocarrileros de la República Mexicana (STFRM, Union of Railway Workers of the Mexican Republic), Confederación Regional Obrera Mexicana (CROM, Mexican Regional Labor Federation), Sindicato Nacional de Trabajadores Mineros, Metalúrgicos y Similares de la República Mexicana (SNTMMSRM, National Union of Mining, Metallurgic and Similar [occupations] of the Mexican Republic); Sindicato Único de Trabajadores Electricistas de la República Mexicana (SUTERM, Sole Union of Electrical Workers of the Mexican Republic), and Sindicato Mexicano de Electricistas (SME, Mexican Electricians' Union).

17. Ian Roxborough and Ilañ Bizberg, "Union Locals in Mexico: The 'New Unionism' in Steel and Automobiles," Journal of Latin American Studies 15, no. 1 (May 1983): 120–121.

18. Roxborough, Unions and Politics, 1.

19. Roxborough, Unions and Politics, 38–39.

20. Roxborough, Unions and Politics, 175.

21. Bizberg, "Las perspectivas de la oposición sindical," 339–358.

22. Roxborough, Unions and Politics, 167.

23. José Revueltas, México: Una democracia barbara. (México: Ediciones Era, 1983), 14.

24. Latin America Weekly Report, (3 January 1986): 4.

234   Evelyn P. Stevens

25. Kevin J. Middlebrook, "Political Change and Political Reform in an Authoritarian Regime: The Case of Mexico" (typescript, 94 pp).
26. Middlebrook, "Political Change and Political Reform."
27. Stevens, Protest and Response in Mexico, 34–43.
28. Delal Baer and John Bailey, "Mexico's Midterm Elections: A Preliminary Assessment," LASA Forum, vol. 16, no. 3 (Fall 1985), 6–7.
29. Baer and Bailey; Daniel C. Levy and Gabriel Szekely, "Mexico: Challenges and Responses," Current History 85, no. 87 (January 1986): 16–20, 37; Elais Chávez, "Cuando actúa la aplanadora, el Colegio Electoral deja de serlo," Proceso, no. 460, August 2, 1985, 6–9; Donald Mabry, Mexico's Acción Nacional: A Catholic Alternative to Revolution (Syracuse, NY: Syracuse University Press, 1973), 171; Alan Riding, Distant Neighbors: A Portrait of the Mexicans (New York, NY: Alfred A. Knopf, 1985), 68, 99–100; Cosío Villegas, El sistema político mexicano, 52; Silvia Gómez Tagle, "Democracy and Power in Mexico: The Meaning of Electoral Fraud in 1979 and 1982" (paper presented at the Twelfth Annual Meeting of the Latin American Studies Association, 1985); Middlebrook, "Political Change and Political Reform," 27.
30. Riding, Distant Neighbors, 111.
31. Baer and Bailey, "Mexico's Midterm Elections," 7.
32. Latin America Weekly Report, (31 January 1986): 8.
33. Alex M. Saragoza, The State and Capitalism in Mexico: the Formation of the Grupo Monterrey, 1880–1940 (Austin, TX: University of Texas Press, forthcoming).
34. Arnaldo Córdova, "La política de masas y el futuro de la izquierda," in Pablo González Casanova and Enrique Florescano, eds., Mexico Hoy (Mexico City: Siglo Veintiuno Editores, 1979), 385–403.
35. Córdova, "La política de masas," 390.
36. Barry Carr, "Mexican Communism 1968–1981: Eurocommunism in the Americas?" Journal of Latin American Studies 17 (May 1985): 210, fn 26.
37. Leigh Binford, "Political Conflict and Land Tenure in the Mexican Isthmus of Tehuantepec," Journal of Latin American Studies 17 (May 1985): 291–292; Riding, Distant Neighbors, 291–292; Los Angeles Times, 5 February 1982.
38. Bizberg, "Las perspectivas de la oposición sindical," 338.
39. Roxborough, Unions and Politics, 174.
40. Reyna, An Empirical Analysis of Political Mobilization, 164.

10

Opposition in Mexico:
A Comparison of Leadership

Roderic A. Camp

Since the mid-1970s the formula for Mexican politics has taken on some new ingredients. Among the most important of these has been the expansion of opposition political parties. Surprisingly, although several short analyses exist of voter support for various parties, and several works in the early 1970s were written about the major opposition party, no analysis has ever been published comparing opposition leaders from the right and the left with each other and the official party, nor one which suggests the consequences of their leadership since the introduction of electoral reforms a decade ago.[1]

This essay analyzes significant background characteristics found among Mexico's legal opposition leadership, examines national electoral trends among opposition parties since 1982, and suggests differences between mass support for and leadership of opposition groups. Specifically, this analysis suggests important trends taking place within the three groups of leaders in their background characteristics, their education and their career experiences. Moreover, I suggest the significance of these changing trends in the larger context of the structural changes taking place in the electoral process and the political system as a whole. Finally, I speculate about the possible impact differing leadership characteristics may have on Mexico's future political stability.

The analysis is based on three primary sources, a biographical data bank, the official 1982 election statistics,[2] and a national opinion survey. The biographical data bank contains information on 1,850 individuals who from 1935 to 1984 have held the most influential posts or exerted the greatest political influence within the established system and among legal opposition groups. Although the absolute numbers of opposition leaders may seem small, they represent a nearly complete population (over 80%) of these leaders. This elite has been subdivided into three groups: the Right, a population of 108 party leaders and office-holders from the National Action Party, the Mexican Democratic Party and the National Sinarquist Movement;

the Left, a population of 44 individuals from the Mexican Communist Party, the Party of the Unified Socialist Movement, the Revolutionary Workers Movement, the Socialist Workers Party and the Popular Socialist Party; and the Establishment, a population of 1,698 government office-holders and leaders from the official party, the Institutionalized Revolutionary Party or its subsidized factions, such as the Authentic Party of the Mexican Revolution.[3] The data are taken from the author's Mexican Political Biography Project, the most comprehensive biographical data bank available on a complete population of Mexican political leaders.[4]

Mexican opposition leadership takes on added importance because of the changing nature of the political system since 1977. Since 1968, Mexico's political system has undergone a severe crisis of legitimacy.[5] As economic problems have become increasingly serious, political pressures have become difficult to contain. During the last two decades Mexico's leadership, whose direct antecedents dominated the political scene since the 1920s, tinkered with the electoral process as a way of encouraging political opposition and legitimizing their own rule. Their adjustments to the electoral process came about because some establishment leaders believe the time has arrived for a more pluralistic system and others cynically used the reforms to perpetuate their own vested interests. Regardless of the reasons for the electoral reforms, they have altered the rules of the political game.

The establishment has opened up electoral competition in order to channel opposition into the least offensive and uninfluential arenas. At present, opposition representatives at the national level have only achieved positions in the lower house of the legislative branch, the Chamber of Deputies. In the Mexican polity, the legislative branch exerts very little influence since constitutionally, and in practice, the country is dominated by a centralized, presidential system. Thus, access of political opposition to significant decision making posts at the federal level is non-existent. Nevertheless, organized political opposition plays an important role.

Mexican opposition party leadership needs to be examined and understood for several reasons. In the first place, the government introduced electoral reforms in 1977 which automatically expanded opposition representation in the Chamber of Deputies. Beginning with the 1979–82 legislature, the first elected after the introduction of the reforms, the Chamber of Deputies contained 400 seats. Three hundred of these seats are based on districts, similar to the United States system, while one hundred are confined to minority parties only, distributed on the basis of a complex proportional voting system. Therefore, 25 percent of the seats are automatically given to opposition parties, plus whatever other seats they can win in the 300 majority districts. Although establishment leaders expanded opposition representation to legitimate their own political control, they have legitimated an opposition role too. Opposition parties controlled only 26%, 25% and 29% of the seats in the last three legislatures respectively, so their influence within the Chamber of Deputies is limited.[6] But, by expanding and legitimating their role, the government provided them with an official forum from which they can express their opinions.

A second reason why the role of opposition leaders takes on added significance since 1977 is that the government increased the heterogeneity of groups having a legitimate political voice. In particular, the Left has been given a more significant opportunity to express itself. It is ironic that the government has taken the initiative to legitimate dissent in Mexico, especially since a tendency exists among some working class populations to not allow critics to seek public office. A selective study of industrial employees from the North and West demonstrated that 52% disapproved of critics seeking public office, in contrast to only 26% who approved.[7] The diversity of political party opposition comes at time when other interest groups are exerting increased and unpredictable influence. For example, business interest groups are recognizing the need to become politicized, and are using public channels to express their views.[8] Thus, the diversity and vociferousness of public criticism confronts a political system already facing pressures from other sources.

A third reason why opposition leadership must be examined is that the role of the Chamber of Deputies itself has undergone subtle, but significant alterations. President de la Madrid has encouraged a precedent begun by his predecessor of requiring cabinet officers to defend their policies before this legislative body. The press gives these sessions considerable coverage. Because opposition party deputies participate in questioning cabinet members, their views have received far more attention than in the past in the national media. Moreover, the Chamber of Deputies real role is one of contact and mediation with the masses.[9] With political technocrats, who have few mass brokerage skills, dominating establishment leadership, deputies who have grass-roots contacts and experiences, whether they are from the opposition or the official party, will be in greater demand.

Finally, each of the changes described above have legitimated, institutionalized, and expanded the role of opposition parties. Surveys demonstrate that many Mexicans from all occupational backgrounds identify with the ideological positions of these parties. Even among appointive public officials, only 77% sympathized with the PRI. Within the general population, 59% say they identify with the PRI, 21% expressed no feelings towards any political party, and 20% sympathize with opposition parties.[10] Once political organizations have legitimacy, and their role becomes regularized, it is difficult to wipe out the systemic alterations responsible for the changes. Furthermore, because one-fifth of the population has come to identify with these parties, and another fifth to provide a pool for potential sympathizers in the immediate future, the government would find it politically difficult, if not impossible, to retract the role organized opposition presently plays.

Two of the most important political trends occurring in Mexico since the 1910 Revolution are the rapidity of urbanization and the increasing centralization of power in the capital city. Mexican political leadership reflects these two trends, as have presidents themselves.[11] But as Mexico's leadership moves away from rural backgrounds (two-thirds from 1935–1984 are from urban birthplaces), they have done so in numbers disproportionate to the total population. Interestingly, opposition leaders share a similar urban bias. Leaders from leftist parties come in numbers slightly more urban (70%) than their establishment counterparts (66%). Actually, they are less urban proportionately since as a group they are much younger than establishment political leaders. Among those leaders born since 1930, 75% of the Left, 89% of the Right and 84% of the establishment politicians came from urban backgrounds. In the case of the Right's leaders, however, their urban backgrounds for the entire period can be described as extreme, since 85% of them were born in urban locales.

Most Mexican politicians, establishment and opposition leaders alike, are from urban backgrounds because they come from families with higher levels of income, they have access to the education necessary to a successful political career, they experience social contacts crucial to political recruitment, and they are politicized at an early age. Yet, on a mass level, an interesting paradox exists in the Mexican political system. Whereas established political leadership increasingly comes from urban backgrounds, its electoral support is strongest in rural areas.[12] On the other hand, those areas benefiting most from governmental policies, urban centers, especially Mexico City, are the source of greatest opposition to government candidates.

Discrepancies between leadership backgrounds and sources of support are likely to have important future consequences for Mexico. For the most part, opposition strength at present is concentrated in major urban areas, especially Mexico City and its suburbs in the state of México, as well as in Guadalajara, Leon, Tijuana, Ensenada, and Ciudad Juárez. They focus their efforts in the cities because scarce resources go much further among concentrated populations, especially when expended on advertising.

It can be argued, therefore, that both the Left and the Right's leadership more closely approximates than does PRI's their national constituencies. Furthermore, all three groups are competing most strongly in the same districts. Although long-range demographic trends in Mexico point towards an even larger urban population, opposition parties are battling each other and PRI head on for the same votes. In other words, those districts potentially providing the greatest opportunities to opposition groups are neglected. In particular, the Right is limiting itself, in its own leadership, to those individuals who share urban backgrounds and experiences. The traditional occupational group giving the lowest support to the Right, especially the National Action Party, its oldest and largest organization, is small farmers.[13]

Establishment leadership in Mexico has reason to be complacent about competition in rural areas. Peasants and small farmers have benefited least from government policies, and yet passively give the strongest support to PRI candidates. For example, PRI deputies in 1985 received 91% of the votes in Quintana Roo, 90% in Chiapas, 94% in Campeche and 83% in Colima, all rural states.[14] But as tensions increase within the political system, these neglected constituencies will become increasingly vociferous in voicing their complaints. Few Mexican government officials today have any personal experience or contact with rural populations. Personal sensitivity to and contact with rural people may become a valuable asset to future leaders. At the moment, the government is safe from opposition parties stealing peasant leadership, but it is not safe from itself since PRI may not be able to control traditionally coopted rural groups.

Urban backgrounds are not the only significant variable in the birthplaces of Mexico's leadership. Like many countries, Mexico has had a long history of regional conflicts, a pre- and post-revolutionary pattern where certain regions dominated in the backgrounds of her political leadership. As I suggested above, the most notable trend among Mexico's establishment politicians is the dominance of Mexico City in their backgrounds. (See Table 10.1.) The rapidity of Mexico City's growth does not account for the disproportionate number of leaders born in the capital. Again, the sharpness of the trends in Table 10.1 are partially hidden by lumping all politicians together with distinguishing their age. If age is controlled for, 29% of the establishment politicians born since 1920 came from Mexico City, among the Right the figure was 18%, and the Left counted 19% of its leaders from the capital.

Even without making age distinctions, trends in regional birthplaces are revealing. Except for the overrepresentation of the Federal District, establishment politicians have been well distributed among all regions. In this sense, as I have shown elsewhere, regional dominance is a dead issue, and a politician's birthplace is unlikely to have any significant impact on his receipt of any top governmental post, especially the presidency.[15] The increasing presence of Federal District birthplaces among all political leaders, opposition included, reflects the importance of centralization. Moreover, the fact that leaders share similar urban birthplaces, especially Mexico City, in their backgrounds, is another homogenizing element in Mexico's leadership, regardless of party affiliation.

A further explanation for the presence of the Federal District in the birthplaces of establishment and right-wing leadership is that many are from political families who came to Mexico City to hold governmental posts in an earlier era. As will be demonstrated below, political connections are critical to building a successful career, and second and third generation politicians have a distinct advantage in their level of contacts.[16]

In the case of the Left, however, a different explanation is necessary. Nearly two-thirds of their leaders were born after 1930, and since their opportunities to participate are recent, similar generational antecedents do not apply. Instead, the Left traditionally began its activities in Mexico City, where it has operated more freely than in other regions. Natives of Mexico City, through their union contacts and through major institutions of higher learning have been more likely to associate with peers affiliated with leftist parties than have natives of the provinces. Also, a small number of leaders are the children of Spanish immigrants, many of whom had to flee Spain in the 1930s because of leftist sympathies.[17]

Data in Table 10.1 also reveal the strength of the West and the North in the backgrounds of both the Left and the Right. National voting trends reveal the strength of the Right in both regions. For example, PAN, which obtained 18% and 16% of the votes cast for federal deputies in 1982 and 1985 respectively, 90% of the total votes going to the Right, did much better in the following states: Jalisco (27% and 24%), the major state from the West, and Baja California (34% and 29%), Coahuila (29% and 23%), Chihuahua (30% and 39%), Sonora (32% and 26%) and Nuevo León (26% and 24%), all from the North. On the local level, PAN has done well in these states and regions, having obtained victories in mayoralty elections of several major cities.

There is a relationship between the vote-getting ability of PAN and the regional background of its leadership because the party is strong locally, serving as a recruiting agent among natives from those regions. Deputyships are the only national government positions opposition leaders presently hold. The Right's strength in the West can be explained by the fact that they are well represented in the second largest city in Mexico, Guadalajara, located in Jalisco. Traditionally conservative, Guadalajara is a Catholic stronghold, having provided many of the guerrillas who bitterly opposed the government in the Cristero rebellion in the late 1920s.[18] However, the fact that the co-founder of PAN, Efraín González Luna, was from Jalisco, established right-wing leadership roots in Guadalajara from the beginning. Furthermore, the Mexican Association of Catholic Youth had a strong cell there, one producing many future leaders of the political Right.[19] Finally, one of the major private universities serving to recruit conservative political leaders is the Autonomous University of Guadalajara.

The Left has done well in the West for different reasons. In the West, in 1982 and 1985, it obtained its highest national vote in the state of Nayarit, historically a stronghold of the Popular Socialist Party (PPS) founded in 1947 by Vicente Lombardo Toledano, leading establishment labor leader and intellectual.[20] Two brothers, Julian and Alejandro Gascón Mercado, children of peasants, dominated political life in the state during the 1970s. Both were members of the PPS, and in 1964 Julian was elected governor of the state on a joint ticket with PRI. Alejandro, the more radical of the two, founded his own splinter movement and ran for governor against the PRI candidate in 1976. In what was according to critics a fraudulent election, the PRI candidate was declared the winner.[21] Thus, a strong core of support remains for former PPS leaders who have since become members of the newer leftist parties.

Other than historical accident or local circumstance, the most important reason why the northern and western regions are well represented in the backgrounds of opposition leaders is their location at the Mexican periphery and/or their close proximity to the United States. The Booth-Seligson study, based on six industrial cities in the North and Guadalajara in the West, concluded that these Mexicans came down on the side of pro-democratic values.[22] Studies by the U.S. International Communication Agency clearly indicate sizeable differences in values among middle-class groups residing in the northern cities, Guadalajara, and Mexico City.[23] In the North, proximity to the United States influences the political values of border residents, who tend to encourage greater political participation in emulation of their Northern neighbor.

The data in Table 10.1 also reveal a notable deficiency in the background of opposition leaders from the Right. Whereas their leadership overrepresents three of seven regions, they are sorely underrepresented in the South and Gulf regions, containing many of Mexico's least industrialized, but highly populated states. Again, the Right, and particularly PAN is deficient in leaders from rural backgrounds, but especially from these two regions, which traditionally, with the exception of Yucatán, give overwhelming support to the PRI. The Right will continue to be limited as a national party in its appeal until it can establish its credentials in the rural areas, especially in these important regions.

In the introduction, I argued that one of the consequences of the 1977 electoral reforms has been to increase the heterogeneity of politically legitimate groups. Birthplace data alone provide no evidence of this statement, if anything, they suggest several broad characteristics homogeneous to all three groups. However, one of the most important differences between the Left on the one hand, and the Right and the establishment on the other, is family background. In the first place, Mexico's political Right has much closer family ties to establishment political elites than does the Left. During the last half century, 27% of the establishment leadership has been closely related to others who have held important political office, suggesting the importance of political families in Mexico. In the case of opposition leaders from the Right, 15% of their numbers have also had close relatives in political office. For example, Abel Vicencio Tovar, who served as President of PAN in the late 1970s, and his brother, Astolfo, who was Secretary General, are the sons of Gustavo Vicencio, a Supreme Court Justice in the 1920s. Pablo Emilio Madero Belden, the presidential candidate of PAN against Miguel de la Madrid in 1982 is the nephew of Francisco Madero, apostle of the 1910 Revolution and the first elected revolutionary president.[24]

The Left cannot claim family credentials similar to the Right or the establishment. Only 5% of the leftist leadership is known to have strong family ties to the government or other political leaders. This fact not only distinguishes them from the other two groups, but suggests the newness of its leadership to the political scene.

An important explanation for this separation is the extreme difference in the socio-economic backgrounds of their parents. Among establishment leaders, 62% come from middle and upper-class families. The figures for the Right, not surprisingly, are higher, with 89% coming from parents with similar class backgrounds. (Class distinctions were made on the basis of parents' occupational activity, with manual occupations used to distinguish working from middle and upper-class backgrounds.) Among leftist leaders, only a paltry 17% could claim such an upbringing. Younger leaders among all three groups exaggerate these differences, with 81% of the establishment, 100% of the Right and only 25% of the left sharing this class background.

Therefore, the social contacts leading to kinship and career ties are missing between the Left and government leaders.

These data on family backgrounds of opposition leaders are evidence that for the first time in years, the government has implemented a structural change through the 1977 Electoral Reform Law that has a significant impact on the Mexican recruitment process. In the last several decades, studies show a narrowing in the funnel through which individuals must pass to arrive at the top of the political heap.[25] The impact of recognizing the Left has been to widen slightly that recruitment funnel, enough so that some individuals who do not share all of the characteristics of the established leadership can participate politically. Because the Left does not have family vested interests stemming from previous kinship ties to the regime, it is likely to be the freer and more unpredictable of the opposition factions.

If kinship ties are confined to a much more restrictive relationship, we find a decided lack of connection between the government and the Left. Nine percent of establishment leaders were the children of fathers known to have held high-level governmental or military posts. In the case of the Right, 6% were known to have such fathers. As for the Left, none were known to have a father who followed a notable government career. Again, these data suggest the distance which the Left has from traditional Mexican political families.

If long-term generational ties extending back to the Revolution and the Porfiriato or pre-revolutionary period are examined, several interesting comparisons are revealed. Interestingly, 7% of the leaders from the Right and from the establishment could trace their family ties back to the late 19th and early 20th century. For government politicians with these family ties, half were related to prominent Porfirian families, and half to Revolutionary families. What is striking here is that despite the vociferous rhetoric of the post-Revolutionary political elites, revolutionary family ties have been no more conducive to successful political careers than have ties to those families the Revolution sought to displace. Some politicians after the mid-1930s had Porfirian ancestors, but more important is that such ancestry was not an obstacle to political success. Mexico's two most recent presidents exemplify this tie to the past.[26]

For the conservative opposition, the nature of the ancestry is different. Only one individual, Emilio Madero Belden, is known to have Revolutionary credentials in his family background, but 7% of the Right's leaders, or twice as many as establishment politicians, had ties to the Porfirian families. Although not a large percentage, this figure suggests the degree to which many prominent families in the nineteenth century survived and enhanced their position in the twentieth century, even after a violent upheaval.

The Left, however, cannot lay claim to a notable ancestry among Mexico's indigenous Right, supporters of the Porfiriato, or its Revolutionary Left. None of its leaders are known to come from either type of family. Thus again the Left's newness is well established, having no tie to Mexico's recent past.

Family backgrounds are not only important indicators of past influence and ties to establishment politicians, but they also suggest connections opposition and establishment leaders have with other politically active groups. In Mexico, two such important groups are intellectuals and businessmen. Intellectuals historically have followed government careers in significant numbers, serving as close collaborators of the Mexican state. Since 1968, Mexican intellectuals began to move away from government service into academia and other, independent occupations.[27] Nevertheless, because so many prominent intellectuals have held public positions, one would expect family ties between Mexican intellectuals and prominent politicians to be rather strong. Actually, however, fewer than three percent of Mexico's establishment politicians are known to be related to members of the intellectual elite. Interestingly, the Right's kinship ties to intellectuals are strong, twice as frequent as those of establishment politicians. This is a surprising finding because Mexico's intellectual community is weakest, ideologically speaking, from the Right. One suspects that an important explanation for the relatedness between politicians of the Right and notable intellectuals is their comparable urban and high socio-economic backgrounds.[28]

Intellectuals with leftist sympathies have been prominent in the establishment of left-of-center opposition parties. For example, Narciso Bassols, Vicente Lombardo Toledano and Víctor Manuel Villaseñor, all of whom followed distinguished public careers, founded the Popular Party, later the Popular Socialist Party. More recently, several intellectuals participated in the establishment of workers parties in the late 1970s.[29] Therefore, it is logical to expect many family ties between the intellectual left and the political left. No such relationship exists. The Left has no family ties to Mexico's intellectual elite. This finding suggests, similar to their lack of ties to establishment political families, that leftist opposition leaders are a fresh group, newly recruited from various sectors of the population.[30]

To many observers of the Mexican political scene, the group exerting the greatest influence on policy-making, if only indirectly, has been business.[31] Rhetorically and structurally, business elites have been forced to maintain their distance from the political system. Their exclusion, in both respects, is best illustrated by the fact that the business sector is not represented within the PRI. However, because top businessmen individually and collectively have exerted considerable influence over economic decision-making, analysts suspect that ties between Mexican entrepreneurs and government leaders are strong. Family relationships between the two groups do not support this suspicion since only 3% have known relationships to Mexico's economic elite.

The Right's social relationship to the private sector should be quite strong. They both share similar ideological attitudes, and evidence exists, especially recently, of direct financial support from top business leaders to rightist parties' political campaigns.[32] Furthermore, some entrepreneurial families, especially from Monterrey, have not hidden their affiliations with PAN from public view.[33] The evidence bears this relationship out. Thus, of all the family ties between a political organization and occupational group, that between the Right and business is strongest. Seven percent of the Right's leadership has known kinship ties to Mexico's most powerful economic families.

Leftist opposition leaders predictably have no relationship through family ties with the private sector. None of their leaders were known to be related to prominent entrepreneurial families.

Several general conclusions can be drawn about the interrelationship of Mexican political leaders to intellectual and business leaders. A small number of establishment politicians come from families producing elites in the intellectual and business community. It would be difficult to conclude, however, that a power elite, in C. Wright Mills' terms, dominated by a small group of families, controls cultural, economic and political leadership. On the other hand, the most well-connected political leadership, measured in terms of family ties among cultural and business elites, is the political Right, 11% of whom have ties with one or both elite groups. This fact is striking in that it is double the political establishment's own ties. The higher proportion of family ties to intellectuals among the Right is most surprising. Such a relationship may foretell a stronger alliance between intellectuals and political opposition from this ideological perspective, an alliance beneficial to the political Right.

The fact that the Left is completely divorced from the establishment and right-wing leadership in having elite family antecedents suggests that it is the most unique among political leaders today. The Left should be given closer attention, not because of its electoral strength, but because it represents an opening in the overall composition of the legitimate political leadership. A generation or more must pass to see if the Left will establish the same ties with traditional leadership groups, whether governmental, economic or intellectual, that have existed with the Right or contemporary establishment politicians.

Social contacts through kinship ties are only one means of elite integration. Career experiences also determine access to other groups. Such experiences can be significant in facilitating special skills, especially brokerage skills useful in dealing with mass-based or special interest groups. Politically speaking, the most important occupational interest groups in Mexico have been: business, labor and the military. The data in Table 10.2 are revealing about the career experiences of political leadership among the three.

Each of the three political leadership groups have had some experience in the private sector, but the important finding is that in no case have successful Mexican business types been attracted to political careers. Most politicians in Mexico, regardless of ideological conviction or party membership, are professional people. Despite the small numbers of prominent businessmen within each group, it is quite obvious that the degree of ideological sympathy each political faction shares with the private sector correlates with the proportion of businessmen found among their leaders. Again, the Left has very few leaders with business experience, whereas the

Right, among all Mexican politicians, has the greatest ties to private sector interests, having worked in the business community before entering politics. The experiences of governmental leaders fall half way in between the two opposition groups.

In the case of organized labor, establishment politicians still can claim to be the most well connected since nearly one out of six government leaders pursued labor careers. However, the Left too has strong credentials among organized labor. This fact is important for several reasons. A group critical to the legitimacy of the present political system and its leadership is organized labor. Any opposition party claiming support from this group is battling PRI where it needs most to maintain its supremacy. Since most of the urban population as yet is unorganized, they provide fertile ground for political organizing. Furthermore, many middle-class professions, especially education, are organized into unions, and the Left has already demonstrated some success among these employees, particularly at the universities.

Mexico's Right has absolutely no contact with organized labor. Ideologically, this posture is consistent with its criticism of organized labor as corrupt and its sympathies towards business interests. Although 5% and 1% respectively of the working class say they are members of PAN and the PDM, the Right has done very little to increase its support among the working class.[34] The Right, by confining its contacts to middle class professional sectors and business, limits its potential support.

The Left has the greatest potential for exploiting a political weakness in Mexico's current leadership. If we limit establishment politicians only to those holding cabinet-level posts, in Mexico those figures exerting the greatest influence on decision-making, contact with labor is quite small. In earlier administrations in the 1950s and 1960s, one out of four cabinet secretaries were union leaders. By the 1970 generation, only 9% of Mexico's most important political figures had union careers, and for the group who will dominate these posts in the 1980s, a mere 2% have labor experience.[35] As I have argued elsewhere, the lack of experience with organized labor is a primary weakness of establishment politicians, one which the Right cannot use to its advantage. The Left, however, will be unable to exploit this advantage in the future if their youngest leaders continue to follow in the footsteps of establishment politicians. None of the Left's leaders born after 1940 have union posts in their backgrounds.

The data in Table 10.2 suggest some very clear patterns about the direct influence of, and experience which opposition politicians have had with, the officer corps. The fact that the Left has had no experience with the military is no surprise. What is notable, however, is that the Right too has had little contact. Unlike Latin American countries where retired officers pursue political activities among conservative parties, the Mexican Right offers little opportunity to the military. This fact illustrates, to some degree, the uniqueness of Mexico's military and the degree to which it has subordinated itself to civilian authority. But more importantly, the military has yet to involve itself closely with any opposition party, thus limiting its political role to bureaucratic, institutional channels, or to an extra-legal coup. The military as a political actor, however, is so isolated from politically active groups that its potential allies presently are limited to dissidents *within* governmental leadership.

Establishment politicians do have the closest ties with the military, and the most frequent experience in the officer ranks. The overall numbers (3%) in Table 10.2, however, are deceiving as to the extent of their strength. Again, if we control for age or examine only those politicians responsible for policy making, we find that with the exception of the two ministries responsible for defense and navy, no cabinet-level officer in recent years is from the military, and only one individual since 1982 at assistant cabinet rank served as a career officer. In fact, among top-ranking politicians in general, only 1% born since 1930 were career officers. The Mexican military partly by design, is isolated from all other political groups both in their family ties and as an occupational source of future politicians.

Among establishment politicians, the most important agent of recruitment, and a significant determinant of their values and political skills, has been the specialization, level and location of leaders' education.[36] Recent analyses also suggest similar influences for Mexican army officers and intellectuals.[37] One of the major changes in Mexican education during the last ten years is the rapid expansion of private secular and parochial schools at the primary and secondary level. Mexican studies suggest that even at these levels the impact on political values are substantial.[38] Daniel C. Levy's recent studies of private education in Latin America clearly demonstrate the distinct orientation between private and public institutions at all levels in Mexico.[39]

It is valuable to track the early educational experiences of the three leadership groups to identify which institutions produced them. Among government leaders, three our of four attended public primary or secondary school. Among leftist politicians, 62% attended similar institutions. But among leaders from the Right, only 40% graduated from public grammar schools. The differences in these figures are important.

Most Mexican private primary schools are affiliated with the Catholic Church or its religious orders. Politicians educated in these schools are beginning to receive, contradictory to the educational provisions of the 1917 Constitution, ideological orientations different from products of public schools. Moreover, much larger numbers of intellectuals and business leaders have attended these same schools than have establishment politicians. Right-of-center and younger establishment political leaders are associating with each other and are being influenced by values contradicting the official political rhetoric. Thus, a division in the backgrounds of establishment political leaders is producing one set of individuals who have more in common with the background of many rightist politicians than with their immediate peers. Traditionally, however, the educational backgrounds between the Left and the establishment are much more compatible.

As political leaders continue their education, they join an elite 3% of the Mexican population completing a college education. The data in Table

10.3 show first that Mexican politicians have graduated from college in large numbers. Nearly three-quarters of leaders from the government and the Right are college graduates.

In comparison, the Left, which is younger, and therefore generationally has had greater educational opportunities, should be better educated. Instead, only slightly over half of its members have achieved similar education attainments. Among Mexican politicians, as among all other sectors of the population, parents' socio-economic background is the most significant determinant of a child's educational achievements. More than half of the Right's leadership without college degrees, who come from middle and upper class backgrounds, have preparatory school educations, the academic program for college-bound students. Among the leftist leaders who did not complete a college degree, 60% had only primary, secondary or normal schooling, those levels most accessible to children of working class parents.

Because institutions of higher education are the key to Mexican political recruitment, the greater the proportion of all politicians with college degrees, the more important universities become. For the Left, other institutions provide alternative recruitment channels because a sizable majority do not achieve university educations. Even for the Left, however, the trend is strongly towards a college-educated leadership.

Institutional location is significant in determining what type of university is most responsible for socializing and recruiting political leaders. Among establishment politicians, I have shown that the National University of Mexico (UNAM) has been an overwhelming agent of socialization and recruitment. Forty-five percent of all Mexican government leaders attended that institution, and among those politicians graduating from any college, the National University accounts for 63% of their degrees. The National University has been equally important to the college educated politicians from the Left and the Right, for although fewer of their leaders altogether attended it, among college educated leaders only, 61% and 55% of the Left and the Right were UNAM alumni. The most obvious conclusion presented by the data in Table 10.4 is that Mexico's National University dominates college educations among all types of political leaders, Right and Left included.

The data in Table 10.4 further indicate that a tiny number of Mexican institutions are responsible for educating political leaders and that several institutions predominantly produce one type of leader versus another. For the Left, two institutions have been notable: the University of Michoacán and the National Polytechnic Institute. Both institutions for historic reasons are important sources of leftist leaders. The National Polytechnic Institute (IPN) was President Lázaro Cárdenas' answer to what he considered to be the elitist teaching staff and conservative ideological orientation of the National University in the 1930s. Although he hoped to create a competitor to UNAM in producing future political leadership, his goal failed, but the IPN did produce many left-of-center figures within the political establishment, some of whom formed the first leftist political factions establishing the Popular party, later the most important single source of PSUM leaders.

Interestingly, the impact of Cárdenas also explains the unusual role of a provincial institution, the University of Michoacán, in the college educations of Mexico's leftist opposition. Cárdenas governed the state of Michoacán in the 1920s, surrounding himself with a group of radical intellectuals from Morelia, the site of the Colegio de San Nicolas de Hidalgo (later the University of Michoacán). Many of these individuals became prominent in national political life, while others remained at the University, producing successive generations of disciples who retained some of the radical ideologies of their mentors.[40]

For the Left, 90% of its leaders who attended college went to a public institution. From the Right, 84% of its leaders graduated from public institutions. A greater percentage of opposition leaders from the Right than from the Left or the government attended private universities, which account for a small proportion of all college graduates in Mexico (only 10% in 1970).[41] Two institutions are important as sources of right-wing politicians: the Monterrey Technological Institute of Higher Studies (ITESM) and the Free Law School. The first institution is unabashedly connected with the private sector, founded by leading entrepreneurs in Monterrey to produce a rigorously trained and technological competent managerial elite.[42]

The most important institution for the Right has been the Free Law School, the oldest private university in Mexico. The Free Law School has produced prominent establishment politicians, and was created at the instigation of students attending the National University during the revolutionary decade.[43] It has been more important to future leaders from the Right because law, as a professional discipline, has been much more prevalent among all types of political leaders. As the leading independent law school, the Free Law School produced several generations of PAN militants. As economics replaces law in importance, it is likely that greater numbers of politicians with right-of-center sympathies will come from the ITESM, the Autonomous Technological Institute of Mexico, and Ibero-American University. Of lesser importance to the Right is the University of Guadalajara and the University of Puebla, both located in communities traditionally strongholds of the Mexican Right.

On the undergraduate or professional school level, future politicians from the Right have attended United States universities in far greater numbers than establishment or leftist politicians. The influence of United States educational methodologies is playing a more significant role on Mexican government leaders today than in the past. This influence can also be found among opposition leaders from the Right. Although the establishment politician's initial college degree is taken in Mexico, one-fifth of all government leaders pursued graduate work, 68% of those in the United States and Europe. Opposition leaders from the Right emulate this trend closely, although only one-sixth continue on with graduate studies, and only 47% of those travel abroad for their training.

The Left, however, experiences graduate work in smaller proportions, with 7% continuing their formal education beyond a professional degree.

More importantly, not one of their numbers has studied abroad. This finding is significant in that it indicates the indigenous quality of the intellectual training of party leaders from the Left. Furthermore, whatever views most leftist leaders share of the United States, they are not based on any long-term residence there.

In addition to political leaders' place and location of education, their choice of disciplines reveal the importance of individual faculties in Mexico, the formal skills they bring to their leadership, and often their ideological orientation. If all non-college educated leaders are excluded, the data identify important differences among the three groups of leaders.

It is not surprising that right- and left-wing opposition leaders most often are trained in the field of law, similar to their establishment peers. The reasons why 51% of the college-educated political establishment, and 53% and 43% respectively of the Right and the Left come from this discipline are well-known. Law traditionally is one of the most important disciplines in Mexico; it provides formal skills most closely related to the practice of politics, and on-campus recruitment and political activity have always centered in law schools within the Mexican public university system.

In recent years economics, an offshoot of the law faculty at the National University, has attracted increasingly large numbers of future establishment politicians.[44] Along with such traditional disciplines as medicine and engineering, economics has taken second place to law, with 9% of Mexico's political leadership trained in this field. The figure is even larger among younger politicians. Surprisingly, however, only one politician (that is, fewer than 1% of the Right's leaders) graduated in economics. On the other hand, substantially more politicians from the Left (14%) have economics degrees.

This discrepancy in the economics training among the three groups can be explained by the ideological orientation of the major economics programs at the public universities. The National School of Economics, which produces the largest number of graduates, has had for many years a decided Marxist philosophy. Therefore, many of its graduates have been affiliated with the populist left within the establishment leadership, or have joined the newer leftist parties. Much of the economic literature in Mexico stresses the discrepancies between the goals of the state and the economy's actual achievements, especially its failure to achieve a more equitable distribution of wealth. Economics graduates of public universities during the last few years are perceived unfavorably for the first time, compared to their private university counterparts, by establishment politicians.

When those individuals in charge of political recruitment change their perception concerning the credentials appropriate for public leadership, they alter the recruiting structure. Therefore, the youngest generation of establishment political leaders, especially those with economics degrees, will come increasingly from private universities. The Left is a beneficiary of this change to the extent that economic programs at public institutions, as reduced sources of establishment leaders, become more important pools for future leftist politicians.

The Right counts almost no economics graduates among its leaders because a student with ideological preferences leaning toward right-wing political activism would not be welcomed by or attracted to a public university's economics program. It seems odd, however, that economics graduates from the older private schools, notably the Monterrey Institute of Higher Studies and the Autonomous University of Guadalajara, have not entered politics. This pattern is explained by the fact that in addition to being anti-Marxist, these programs encouraged an apolitical attitude. In contrast, public service, and by implication, political concerns, are built into the public universities' economics programs. As businessmen become more politically involved, it is likely that economics graduates, even from private schools, will play a more important role among the Right.

An additional explanation for the poor representation of economics among the Right's leadership can also be seen in the figures for accounting graduates. Among rightist politicians, 7% were graduates of certified public accounting programs, twice that of leaders from the other two groups. Accounting is traditionally a non-political degree field, attracting a generally more conservative clientele whose views are reinforced through educational socialization.

The Right is strongest and the Left weakest in engineering. As a discipline it preselects students with a more conservative mentality, hence 16% of the Right but only 4% of the Left received engineering degrees. Studies of college graduates in the United States clearly show that certain disciplines, including engineering and the hard sciences, attract and produce a dispro-portionate number of students with views on the right of our political spectrum.[45] It would seem that this phenomenon applies to Mexico too.

The importance of individual educational institutions, and the significance of higher education as the focus of political recruitment in Mexico, is determined in large part by the presence of politicians among college teaching staffs. Establishment politicians, both numerically and proportionately, have an edge in teaching over their political competitors, as is to be expected, because the tie between the university and the state is a well-established tradition. Clearly, however, many Mexican politicians are professors, since 44% of the establishment and 39% and 36% of the Right and the Left have part or full-time careers in academia.

There is a definite correlation between where politicians attend school and where they choose to teach. The National University captures the lion's share of politicians who are college teachers, with 60% of the establishment politicians working there. In contrast, 33% of the Right and 40% of the Left teach at UNAM. Again, whereas a small percentage of establishment politicians take posts at private colleges, nearly one out of four among PAN and PDM leaders can be found teaching at these institutions. On the other hand, whereas neither establishment nor right-wing students in large numbers graduated from or taught at the National Polytechnic Institute (see Table 10.4), the Left has strong ties to that university, and 13% of its teaching leadership taught there.

The importance of these figures is that educational backgrounds among political leaders will continue to be separated on the basis of private-public institutions, or in the case of the Left and the establishment, between the UNAM and the IPN. Leadership trends, as determined by education, will only be altered by future politicians' changing choices in their schooling and in their teaching.

Conclusions

Opposition politicians share many characteristics with their establishment peers. Among the most important is the fact that the majority of them tends to come from urban backgrounds, that Mexico City is overrepresented in their backgrounds, that each group is a well-educated elite, that many of them are graduates of and teachers at the National University, and that none of them has strong ties, measured according to occupational experience, with the military.

The significance of these homogeneous characteristics is that the political leadership shares little in common with the average Mexican of comparable age, who comes from a rural background, who does not live in Mexico City in such large numbers, and who has not attended, taught at or graduated from college. A sharing of similar backgrounds with the masses is not as significant in a society in which participation is limited. But as the structural reforms which produced the growth of opposition leadership itself take effect, more emphasis on the relationship between constituencies and their leaders will occur. Mexico's politicians from all ideological perspectives have little in their background on which to build and strengthen their ties to the masses.

Opposition leaders demonstrate more important differences between each other, and with establishment figures, than they do similarities. For the Mexican Right, several characteristics are important to understand. As an opposition group, they come closest to being a "loyal opposition" to the extent that they are more closely tied to the establishment political elite. Moreover, the data further demonstrate that the Right has many kinship ties to leading economic and intellectual elites, even more so than the establishment politician.

Such ties are significant because they imply that the Right can draw on allies from two traditionally influential groups. Not only does the Right have a potential source of financial support, but it shares certain vested interests with other, established groups. The Right and the establishment have much more in common with each other than each would want to publicly admit. Thus, in future times of political crisis, if an unexpected change in leadership were to come from within the establishment, especially if it were conservatively oriented, it could easily find support from the Right.

The Right's orientation stems in part from its strong ties to private education. This eduction affects only a minority of Mexicans. But as establishment leaders themselves move away from public education, an important group of government leaders are being formed who share more strongly the experiences and backgrounds of the Right.

The Left, however, offers a generally different set of characteristics from both the Right and the establishment. On the whole, it has little relationship to the establishment, either through its family ties, its class background, or to a lesser extent, its career and educational experiences. The strength of the Left is that it comes from a lower socio-economic background. This background is translated into a natural affiliation with organized labor. Yet, their youngest leadership has not developed close ties with organized labor, rather they tend to appeal to unorganized masses, to students, and to intellectual professions. It is also the reason why leftist leadership continues to attend public, rather than private schools, a choice most working class Mexicans must follow.

The distinguishing characteristics of the Left separate it both from the Right and the establishment. It is truly an independent set of leaders in the sense that it has few ties to establishment groups, whether they are political, economic or intellectual. This independent quality makes them politically more unpredictable. They do not have vested interests to protect, at least not to the same extent as both the Right and the establishment. On the other hand, they are the most isolated of political leadership groups in their potential ability to find ready allies. Thus, their independence is both a strength and a weakness.

Politically speaking, on the basis of leadership characteristics and ideological appeal, political opposition groups in Mexico compete strongly against one another in urban centers, where the government is at its weakest. As Joe Klesner argues, in 1982 the opposition mobilized many new voters, but PRI did this much more successfully.[46] Whereas the Right has done the best against PRI in these districts, the Left has the greatest potential for exploiting the weaknesses of the government's leadership, its urban, middle-class bias. But the Left has been unable to exploit its strong ties to organized labor or indeed translate them into votes for its candidates, because its grass roots support and the source of its leadership is unevenly distributed throughout the republic. The Right is equally ill distributed, for example, producing strong leadership and support from the Federal District, but not as yet having a national leader from Veracruz, one of Mexico's most populous states and a traditional PRI stronghold.

The only group with the power to successfully implement an extra-legal change in Mexico's political leadership is the army. The army does not have the expertise, numbers, organizational ability, or mass support to accomplish this alone. But among potential allies, the Right structurally has no advantage over the Left since both have little direct ties to the military. Although the political establishment cannot make a much better claim for similar ties to the military, its day-to-day working relationship over many decades gives it an advantage. But in a crisis situation involving a change in the present political system, during which new alliances might be formed, none of the three existing groups has any substantial advantage in initiating such an alliance.

In the past, PRI has maintained its support by converting support from a large group of voters who are non-aligned. During this same period, PAN was able to gain new supporters by converting non-aligned voters and former supporters of PRI to its banner.[47] The expansion of parties on both the Right and the Left increases the electorate's choices, and the electorate has become more partisan. But as indicated in opinion polls, the present Right and Left may be reaching the upper limits of their ideological appeals nationally, if not regionally. If so, other leaders, with a different political philosophy, and with support in rural and urban areas, will provide the only effective opposition to the political establishment.

Notes

1. The best general work is that by Robert R. Bezdek, "Electoral Oppositions in Mexico: Emergence, Suppression, and Impact on Political Processes" (unpublished Ph.D. dissertation, Ohio State University, 1973). The National Action Party has been the subject of two studies. The most comprehensive is that by Donald Mabry, *Mexico's Acción Nacional: A Catholic Alternative to Revolution* (Syracuse, NY: Syracuse University Press, 1973). A different perspective is offered by Franz A. Von Sauer, *The Alienated "Loyal" Opposition, Mexico's Partido Acción Nacional* (Albuquerque, NM: University of New Mexico Press, 1974). An insightful case study of PAN on the local level, completed since 1977, is Haskel Simonowitz, "The Partido Acción Nacional in Baja California, the Electoral Struggle for Power in an Authoritarian System" (paper presented at the Pacific Coast Council of Latin Americanists, Tijuana, 1982). The only analyses of the Left since 1977, but without an analysis of electoral strength or leadership, are Cecilia Imáz, "La izquierda y la reforma política en México," *Revista Mexicana de Sociología*, vol. 43 (July-September, 1981): 1103–1120 and Barry Carr, *The Mexican Left and the Politics of Austerity, 1982–84* (La Jolla, CA: Center for U.S.-Mexican Studies, University of California, San Diego, 1985). The only study of national electoral support until 1985, but confined to the PRI, is that by Barry Ames, entitled "Basis of Support for Mexico's Dominant Party," *American Political Science Review*, vol. 64 (March 1970): 153–167. In 1986, the studies by Juan Molinar Horcasitas, "La costumbre electoral mexicana," *Nexos*, January 1985, 17–25 and Delal Baer and John Bailey, "Mexico's Midterm Elections: A Preliminary Assessment," *LASA Forum* (Fall 1985): 4–10. For the best description of organizational history and platforms of those parties qualifying in the 1982 elections, see Centro Antonio de Montesinos, "Los partidos políticos ante las elecciones de julio," *Serie Análisis Políticos* (1982).

2. Election statistics are available in Volker G. Lehr, ed., *Manual Trienal del Congreso de la Union*, 2 vols. (México: UNAM, 1983).

3. For evidence of PARM's financial dependence, see party leader Mario Guerra Leal's inside account, *La grilla* (México: Editorial Diana, 1978), 232.

4. For a detailed explanation of the composition of this data bank see the author's, *Mexico's Leaders, Their Education and Recruitment* (Tucson, AZ: University of Arizona Press, 1980).

5. A crisis of legitimacy has been most thoroughly argued in Roberto Newell G. and Luis Rubio F., *Mexico's Dilemma: The Political Origins of Economic Crisis* (Boulder, CO: Westview Press, 1984).

6. In the 1979 elections, the National Action Party won 4 of the 300 legislative districts, with the remaining 296 going to PRI. In 1982, PAN captured only one seat and PRI claimed victory in 299 districts. The Left won no districts in either election.

7. John A. Booth and Mitchell A. Seligson, "The Political Culture of Authoritarianism in Mexico, A Reexamination," *Latin American Research Review*, vol. 19, no. 1 (1984): 111.

8. As expressed in numerous interviews with leading entrepreneurs and business chamber leaders by the author, Mexico City and Toluca, Mexico, 1982, 1983, 1984. For additional evidence of this changing attitude, see Roberto Newell G. and Luis Rubio F., *Mexico's Dilemma* and Miguel Basañez, *La lucha por la hegemonía en México, 1968-1980* (México: Siglo XXI, 1981), 192ff.

9. Alejandro Portes, "Legislatures Under Authoritarian Regimes: the Case of Mexico," *Journal of Political and Military Sociology*, vol. 5, no. 2 (Fall 1977): 196-197.

10. Partido Revolucionario Institucional, Instituto de Estudios Políticos, Económicos y Sociales, *Encuesta Nacional de Partidos Políticos* (Mexico City, 1983).

11. Roderic A. Camp, "Mexican Presidential Candidates: Changes and Portents for the Future," *Polity*, vol. 16, no. 4 (Summer 1984): 588-605.

12. See Barry Ames, "Basis of Support for Mexico's Dominant Party," for elections up to 1970. See Volker Lehr, *Manual Trienal* for the 1982 election results.

13. Partido Revolucionario Institucional, *Encuesta Nacional*.

14. Miguel Basañez, "Pronósticos y resultados electorales: México 1985" (unpublished paper, appendix).

15. Roderic A. Camp, "A Reexamination of Political Leadership and Allocation of Federal Revenues in Mexico, 1934-1973," *Journal of Developing Areas*, vol. 10 (January 1976): 198.

16. Roderic A. Camp, "Family Relationships in Mexican Politics, A Preliminary View," *Journal of Politics*, vol. 44 (August 1982): 848-862.

17. Evidence of this influence can be found in Patricia Fagen, *Exiles and Citizens: Spanish Republicans in Mexico* (Austin, TX: University of Texas Press, 1973).

18. For the best single study of this period, see Jean A. Meyer's classic *The Cristero Rebellion: The Mexican People Between Church and State (1926-1929)* (Cambridge: Cambridge University Press, 1976). For its connection to the Sinarquistas, later the source of most PDM party members, see Jean Meyer's *El sinarquismo, un fascismo mexicano?* (México: Joaquín Mortiz, 1979).

19. It also produced several notable establishment politicians including Agustin Yáñez and J. Jesús González Gallo, both governors of Jalisco.

20. For background details on the establishment of the party, see Víctor Manuel Villaseñor, *Memorias de un hombre de izquierda*, vol. 1 (México: Editorial Grijalbo, 1976).

21. *Proceso*, April 24, 1978, 23; and *Latin American Report*, November 11, 1977, 349-50.

22. Booth and Seligson, "The Political Culture of Authoritarianism in Mexico," 118.

23. William J. Millard, "Media Use by the Better-Educated in Major Mexican Cities" (Office of Research, United States International Communication Agency, December 18, 1981).

24. For background on Abel Vicencio Tovar, see Roderic A. Camp, *Mexican Political Biographies, 1935-1980* (Tucson, AZ: University of Arizona Press, 1982), 314; for Pablo Emilio Madero Belden, see *Excelsior*, April 16, 1979, 16, *La Nación*,

September 16, 1981, 10; *Almanaque de México* (México, 1980), 15, and *Hispano Americano,* October 5, 1981, 9.

25. Peter H. Smith, *Labyrinths of Power, Political Recruitment in Twentieth Century Mexico* (Princeton, NJ: Princeton University Press, 1979); and Roderic A. Camp, *Mexico's Leaders.*

26. José López Portillo (1976–1982) was the grandson of a prominent Jalisco politician who served as Secretary of Foreign Relations in the cabinet of Victoriano Huerta. Miguel de la Madrid comes from a distinguished Coliman political family, and his grandfather was governor of his home state during the Porfiriato.

27. Roderic A. Camp, *Mexican Intellectuals and the State in 20th Century Mexico* (Austin, TX: University of Texas Press, 1985).

28. Camp, *Mexican Intellectuals,* 76, 81. Eighty-six percent of Mexico's leading intellectuals come from urban birthplaces, and 94% were from middle- and upper-class parents.

29. Personal interview with Luis Villoro, Mexico City, August 20, 1978.

30. Historically the Mexican Communist Party has been devoid of intellectuals. See Karl Schmitt, "Communism in Mexico Today," *Western Political Quarterly,* vol. 15 (March 1962): 114.

31. For this view see Roger D. Hansen, *The Politics of Mexican Development* (Baltimore, MD: John Hopkins University Press, 1971) and Susan K. Purcell, *The Mexican Profit-Sharing Decision, Politics in an Authoritarian Regime* (Berkeley, CA: University of California Press, 1975).

32. For example, the powerful Vallina family, prominent industrialists from Chihuahua, supported PAN candidates in the 1982 elections. In the past only 6% of all industrialists even claimed party membership. See Flavia Derossi, *The Mexican Entrepreneur* (Paris: Development Centre of the Organization for Economic Cooperation and Development, 1971), 187. For a more recent view of their changing attitudes see Dale Story, "Industrial Elites in Mexico, Political Ideology and Influence," *Journal of Inter-American Studies and World Affairs,* vol. 25, no. 3 (August 1983): 367.

33. *Quién es Cada Quién en Monterrey* (Monterrey: Graphos, 1952).

34. Partido Revolucionario Institucional, *Encuesta Nacional.*

35. Camp, "Mexican Presidential Candidates," 22.

36. Camp, *Mexico's Leaders,* 197–198.

37. David Ronfeldt, ed., *The Modern Mexican Military: A Reassessment* (La Jolla, CA: Center for U.S.-Mexican Studies, University of California, San Diego, 1984) and Roderic A. Camp, "Intellectuals and the State in Mexico, 1920–1980, the Influence of Family and Education," in Charles A. Hale, Roderic A. Camp and Josefina Vazquez, eds., *Intellectuals and the State in Mexico, Proceedings of the VI Conference of Mexican and United States Historians* (Los Angeles, CA: Latin American Center, UCLA, forthcoming, 1986).

38. Rafael Segovia, *La politización del niño mexicano* (México: El Colegio de México, 1975).

39. Daniel C. Levy, *Higher Education and the State in Latin America: Private Challenges to Public Dominance* (Chicago, IL: University of Chicago Press, 1986).

40. For background on this interesting university see Alberto Bremautz, *Setenta años de mi vida* (México: Ediciones Juridicas Sociales, 1968), 45–46; Luis Garrido, *El tiempo de mi vida: memorias* (México: Editorial Porrua, 1974), 149, 172; and Eduardo Villaseñor, *Memorias-Testimonio* (México: Fondo de Cultura Económica, 1974), 26.

41. Villaseñor, Chapter 4. Levy estimates that 13% of the Mexican university enrollment as of 1984 is private.

42. Richard A. LaBarge and T. Noel Osborn, "The Status of Professional Economics Programs in Mexican Universities," *Inter-American Economic Affairs*, vol. 31 (Summer 1977): 12–13.

43. Personal letter to the author from Emilio Portes Gil, former president of Mexico and student founder of the Free Law School, October 20, 1972.

44. Roderic A. Camp, "The Technocrat and the Survival of the Political System," *Latin American Research Review*, vol. 20, no. 3 (1984).

45. For evidence of this, see Everett C. Ladd, Jr., and Seymour Martin Lipset, *The Divided Academy* (New York, NY: Norton, 1976).

46. Joseph Klesner, "Party System Expansion and Electoral Mobilization in Mexico" (Paper presented at the National Latin American Studies Association, Albuquerque, April 18–20, 1985).

47. Charles L. Davis and Kenneth M. Coleman, "Electoral Change in the One-Party Dominant Mexican Polity, 1958–73: Evidence from Mexico City," *Journal of Developing Areas*, vol. 17 (September 1983): 537.

TABLE 10.1
Regional Birthplaces of Mexican Politicians (percentage)

Region	Type of Leader			General Population
	Establishment	Right	Left	
Federal District	17	22	19	6
East Central	15	17	9	20
West	15	18	21	16
North	15	20	23	12
South	10	4	7	1
Gulf	13	5	12	13
West Central	14	14	10	19
Foreign	1	0	0	--
Totals	100	100	101	101

(a) Census data for the general population is their place of residence in 1920, the date closest to the birth date of most of our three populations.

258

TABLE 10.2
Career Experiences of Political Leaders in Mexico (percentage)

Career Experience	Type of Politician		
	Establishment	Right	Left
Business	5	10	2
Labor	15	0	11
Military	3	1	0

(a) A business career is one defined as holding a management level position. A career in labor signifies that the person has served in an important state or national leadership capacity in organized labor. A military career describes someone who has reached the rank of Colonel or higher in the Mexican armed forces.

TABLE 10.3
Educational Levels of Mexican Politicians (percentage)

Level of Education Completed	Type of Politician		
	Establishment	Right	Left
Primary	7	3	17
Secondary	6	9	2
Normal	7	2	7
Preparatory	6	15	17
University	51	55	43
Post-Professional, Ph.D., M.D., D.D.S.	23	17	14
Totals	100	101	100

(a) Percentages do not add up to 100 due to rounding.

TABLE 10.4
Location of College Educations Among Mexican Politicians (percentage)

Institution	Type of Leader		
	Establishment	Right	Left
UNAM	45	37	31
University of Michoacán	1	1	7
Military Academies	5	0	0
Free Law School	2	5	0
National Polytechnic Institute	2	1	5
University of Guadalajara	2	4	0
Monterrey Institute (ITESM)	0.2	3	0
University of Puebla	1	3	0
United States Universities	1	3	0
Other Public Universities	12	7	3
Other Private Universities	1	3	5
No College Degree	28	33	49
Totals	100.2	100	100

11

The PAN, the Private Sector, and the Future of the Mexican Opposition

Dale Story

The candidacy of Fernando Canales Clariond for the governor's seat of Nuevo León in 1985 once again raised the issue of the ties between the Mexican private sector and the major opposition party, the Partido Acción Nacional (National Action Party, or PAN). Canales Clariond, of course, was the nominee of the PAN, and as a relatively young, dynamic, wealthy entrepreneur from the industrial center of Monterrey was seen by many as a serious threat to the successive string of gubernatorial victories for the ruling party, the PRI (Partido Revolucionario Institucional). Recognizing this challenge, the PRI nominated Jorge Treviño Martínez, who was also relatively young, dynamic, and wealthy. Predictably, Treviño won by over a 2-to-1 margin and the PAN cried fraud and staged numerous protests. But one of the most important repercussions of this race was to renew the charge that the PAN was the party of big business, since Canales Clariond was considered the epitome of the large entrepreneurial class of northern Mexico.

Entrepreneurial support for Canales Clariond, both before and after the election, was quite evident. If anything, his defeat seemed to increase business disaffection with the PRI in Monterrey. The PAN attempted to upstage Treviño's inauguration by holding a "Democratic Electoral Congress" in late July of 1985 in order to publicize the alleged illegitimacy of the Treviño victory. In attendance were top officials of the state's business associations (COPARMEX, CANACO, and CAINTRA), executives from major Monterrey industrial groups (Alfa, Visa, Vitro, and Cydsa), and several influential *Priistas* who became disenchanted with the governing party.[1]

This election and other indicators of business support for the PAN have created great speculation both within and outside the party that the PAN has become the chief voice of private sector political opposition to the PRI. The purpose of this chapter is to examine critically the thesis that the PAN is the party of the large capitalists in Mexico and to assess the future of the major opposition party.

The PRI and the Business Sector

Substantial evidence exists to document the distance between the dominant party and the private sector in Mexico. Of the groups and institutions outside the PRI, the most powerful and the most independent is the private sector.[2] Only small businesses and some individual entrepreneurs officially belong to the PRI, while the bulk of the Mexican private sector and its political associations remain outside the confines of the Party. The business organizations are in an advantageous position outside the PRI, since they can achieve their objectives through other channels (particularly their trade associations) while escaping the rigors of party discipline.

Though entrepreneurs are not subject to the political controls placed upon the three functional sectors of the Party, the chambers and confederations of industry and commerce are governed by the so-called Chambers Law, which at least provides the potential for strong state control over the private sector. However, the actual degree of government control over entrepreneurial groups has not been great. Despite the extensive regulatory powers of the state over the business associations, the chambers and confederations have always maintained their autonomy from either government or Party control.

Particularly as the private sector developed in the postwar period in Mexico, its relations with the state assumed an adversary nature and the willingness of business groups to criticize PRI-dominated policies increased.[3] The critical stance of industrialists is evident in survey data, especially in the attitudes prior to the López Portillo administration. In surveys in 1969 and in 1980, Mexican entrepreneurs are quite critical of many economic policies and staunchly oppose the state's increasing role in the economy.[4] Also, Peter Smith, in comparing the backgrounds of economic and political elites, finds that they belong to different social strata, frequently disagree over policies, and are really competing elites.[5]

The distance between the private sector and the state was particularly great during the Echeverría administration and the last year of López Portillo's term. In the 1980 survey, industrial leaders viewed Echeverría as the most unfavorable president to the private sector since the creation of the ruling party in the late 1920s. Specific Echeverría policies opposed by business groups included the proposed fiscal reform, price controls, the extension of public ownership and of the state role in distributing basic goods, and the agrarian reform.[6] In addition to public criticism, efforts of business groups like the Entrepreneurial Coordinating Council (CCE), and a business strike in 1976, an even more important form of business opposition to Echeverría was the withdrawal of business confidence, followed by refusals to invest and a growing problem of capital flight from Mexico.

Though cooperation between the private and public sectors was partially restored when López Portillo came into office, the entrepreneurs did not yield from pressuring the government when business interests were being threatened, as exemplified in a business strike in Puebla, in concerns being voiced by the National Confederation of Chambers of Commerce (CON-CANACO) and others over the fiscal reforms proposed in 1979, in opposition by the Chamber of Transformation Industries (CANACINTRA) to Mexico's entry to the GATT in 1980, and of course in the outcry against the bank nationalizations. The decision regarding the banks, which was announced September 1, 1982, in López Portillo's last *Informe*, began a period of discord between the state and the private sector that spilled over into De la Madrid's first few months.[7] Soon after the state takeover of the remaining private national banks, entrepreneurial leaders began to decry what they felt was encroaching "socialism" and "statism." They also manifested their opinion that the current political system, as dominated by the PRI, was bent on depriving individuals of their political and economic rights. One De la Madrid was inaugurated, the private sector focused its attacks on the previous government and the official party and was careful not to criticize the new President or his economic team.

The split between the private sector and the PRI escalated in January of 1983 when CONCANACO organized a conference in Toluca (with representatives from the Mexican Employers' Confederation—COPAR-MEX—and the CCE also attending) to criticize the "arbitrary acts" (referring to the bank nationalizations and the exchange controls) of the previous administration. On January 28 the PRI took the unusual step of publishing an advertisement in the major newspapers that was a direct response to the private sector criticisms. The official party stated that private sector chambers "are not political institutions nor adequate channels for the expression of ideological positions" and reminded them, in an indirect threat, that they were subject to the control of the Secretary of Commerce and Industrial Promotion. However, indicative of their relative autonomy, the entrepreneurial groups were not intimidated and continued their criticisms of the PRI and the previous government.

Business support for the PAN in local elections in the state of Chihuahua in 1983 seemed to have provoked further hostile rhetoric from the PRI toward the "anti-nationalist and anti-revolutionary programs" of the *neopanistas* (those linked to private sector interests).[8] Most recently, in November 1985, COPARMEX charged that a number of entrepreneurs had been pressured by government officials to refrain from politics. The seriousness of the allegations prompted the Minister of *Gobernación*, Manuel Bartlett Díaz, to issue an unusual denial, which was printed on the front pages of the major Mexico City newspapers. One example cited of these pressures was the removal of Rogelio Sada Zambrano as chief executive of Vitro (a major Monterrey industrial conglomerate) by the company's board of directors, allegedly because he had attended a public meeting in support of José Luis Coindreau, the PAN candidate for mayor in Monterrey.[9]

Manifesting the opposition of many entrepreneurs to the PRI, the possibility of establishing a political party to represent business has often been raised. In the aftermath of the July 1979 elections, when an unusually large number of entrepreneurs were elected to the 51st Legislature, some commentators forecasted that the trend would lead to the formation of a political party solely representing the private sector.[10] In 1981 COPARMEX supported the idea of creating a new party for entrepreneurs and the "middle class";[11] and again in 1983, after a series of verbal battles with the PRI, some entrepreneurial leaders said that the private sector was ready to form its own political party.[12] This step is unlikely, however, so many have suggested that the private sector is turning to the PAN as its principal means of political representation. Table 11.1 shows the nine parties that participated in the 1985 elections for the federal Chamber of Deputies. Of the eight opposition parties, only two have garnered any significant level of support: the PAN on the right and the PSUM (the Mexican Unified Socialist Party) on the left. With the PRI dominating the labor sector and relying upon its traditional barrage of revolutionary rhetoric, the accomplishments of the PSUM have been minimal. Thus, the only threat to PRI dominance—and the only political alternative for the private sector—is the PAN.

The National Action Party

The National Action Party was organized in September 1939 predominantly by Catholic university students, but its founders also included many entrepreneurs and other professionals. Its roots can be traced to a number of earlier political and social movements, although its initial leaders were primarily motivated by reactions against the anticlericalism of the 1920s and the perceived radicalism of the Cárdenas regime in the 1930s. The earliest remnants of the PAN are actually claimed by some to be found in the movement of Francisco Madero.[13] The traditional liberalism of the PAN and its belief in a pluralistic democracy and in "effective" reforms are said to have been inspired and influenced by the *maderista* philosophy. Several founders of the PAN were even supporters of Madero or actual members of his government.[14] Another early political phenomenon that has been associated with the PAN is the presidential candidacy of José Vasconcelos in 1929. Many Catholics and other opponents of the emerging PNR dynasty rallied to the side of Vasconcelos. One of these dissidents was Manuel Gómez Morín, a former government official under both Obregón and Calles, a principal adviser to the Vasconcelos campaign, rector of the national university (UNAM) in 1933 and 1934, and finally one of the chief founders of the PAN in 1939.[15]

Even more important to the PAN than these political ties was its foundation in the more conservative and politicized lay associations of the Catholic Church. Three groups in particular had links with the PAN and its early followers: the *Cristeros* who rebelled against Calles in the 1920s, the semi-secret corporatist organization created in 1949 called simply the Base, and the pseudo-fascist group that spun off from the Base in 1937 labeled the

Union Nacional Sinarquista (UNS). All three were composed of relatively militant Christian rightists who at times would resort to violence or physical intimidation to promote their ideology of anti-secularism. The *Cristeros* and the UNS were the most radical, with their support coming primarily from the peasantry. Their members have been described as "disciplined soldiers of a militant theocratic faith" who were extremely alienated from the Mexican state.[16] The Base was a somewhat more moderate and multi-class group committed to combating anticlericalism and communism. Actually, both the PAN and the UNS emerged from the Base, with the PAN being the organizational structure of the Christian right, which tended to attract the upperclass elements, and the UNS being the unstructured but action-oriented group, which basically included peasants passionately devoted to establishing a Christian state.

Especially in its formative years the PAN was ideologically conservative and staunchly proclerical. The Party was born out of the 1930s struggle between the Christian right (led by Gómez Morín who organized the PAN) and the socialist left (epitomized in Lombardo Toledano with whom Cárdenas sympathized). The early *panistas* wanted to restore to the Church many of its prerevolutionary powers, especially in the areas of religious education and political participation. And they vehemently disagreed with the statist policies of President Cárdenas. Strong believers in the inalienable rights of private property, the PAN followers opposed the nationalizations and the agrarian reform achieved in the 1930s. The Party actually supported the redistribution of land which would grant peasants title to small, private holdings. However, its criticisms of land reform in Mexico focused on the collectivization of agriculture. The massive *ejidos* were seen to be philosophically indefensible and economically counter-productive and were cited as another example of the ineffective and communist-inspired reforms of the period. In the early 1940s, the PAN shifted even further to the right, particularly in its foreign policy. Through the first three and one-half years of its history, the party advocated neutrality in World War II, and several leaders openly supported Franco in Spain and professed pro-fascist sympathies.[17]

Motivated by a desire to protect their financial interests from the encroaching "socialism" of Cárdenas, many businessmen were among the early founders of the PAN.[18] An analysis of the original (1939) National Executive Committee of the PAN shows the important role of entrepreneurs in the establishment of the party. As in most political parties, the leading occupational group was lawyers with 31.0 percent of the 29 members of the Committee. Bankers were the second best represented group (with 24.2 percent of the membership) followed by businessmen and journalists (with 13.8 percent each). Monterrey industrialists and leaders of the conservative COPARMEX (often most closely associated with the so-called Monterrey Group) were especially committed to the establishment of the PAN.

The two founders of the PAN, the previously mentioned Gómez Morín and Efraín González Luna, had strong links to the private sector. Trained as a lawyer, Gómez Morín specialized in financial affairs during his stints in governmental service in the 1920s. In his periods as a private lawyer, he focused on corporate law and the banking industry. He helped organize such joint enterprises as the Euzkadi (Goodrich) rubber company, was on the board of directors of many private enterprises, and was an officer of the private Banco de Londres y México. González Luna also had a law degree and became a prominent lawyer in Guadalajara, where he established some very influential capitalist connections. He founded the employers' center in Guadalajara and was one of the stockholders of that city's Banco Capitalizador. González Luna also represented the links between the party's entrepreneurial and clerical roots, since he was a militant Catholic. Though he rejected violence as an alternative, he did sympathize with the demands of the *Cristero* rebellion.

The election of the conservative Miguel Alemán as president of Mexico in 1946 brought much of the business sector back into the fold of the PRI, and PAN-business links deteriorated in the 1950s and 1960s. In these years the PAN flirted more with Catholic social thought and the international Christian Democratic movement (which it officially abandoned in 1962). In particular, the PAN began to focus more on issues of political democratization in Mexico. The PAN has always been quite serious about following democratic principles within its own decision-making processes and promoting these principles in the national political system. Contrary to the PRI, candidates and leaders for the PAN are selected in an open, pluralistic manner, and dissent and competition within the party are usually accepted. At the national level the PAN consistently argues for a more democratic Mexico and views itself as the best hope for creating a genuinely free system. It has criticized the history of political repression, presidential dominance, and fraudulent elections in Mexico, and on many occasions it has sided with the leftist opposition in a common struggle against PRI control.

The question of its own participation in the system poses the greatest dilemma for the PAN. Its presence adds legitimacy to the authoritarian one-party state, and so far the PAN has proven powerless in significantly altering the rules of the game. But if it chooses abstention as a means of protest, then it is vacating its role as the "loyal opposition" and is allowing the PRI to monopolize the political debate. Since it has almost always chosen to participate, the PAN has played a very crucial legitimizing role for the PRI. When it did not run a candidate in the 1976 presidential election, the reason was primarily the inability to agree on a single candidate and not the desire to prevent the PRI from achieving its aura of legitimacy.

On economic and social issues the PAN in recent years has also not perfectly fit the model of a conservative party favoring free enterprise over economic justice and growth over equity. Certainly the Party's philosophy has been pro-business and oriented toward private ownership. But at least since the 1960s the PAN has also stressed social consciousness. In an important document issued at the close of the Party's twentieth national convention in 1969, the PAN advocated a third path of development between capitalism and socialism: "*solidarismo*" or, as described by one author, "political humanism."[19] Private property is viewed as positive so long as it also contributes to the society at large. The individual should not be alienated from his environment but has a responsibility to improve the general human condition. The Party's Declaration of Principles contains constant references to the common good, national harmony, the community, and the collective well-being of all Mexicans.[20] The Party even sees itself working in "solidarity" with the state to promote "order, progress, and peace."[21]

If the PAN can be seen as partially abandoning its close association with the business sector after 1950, a split has developed in the party in the late-1970s and 1980s over its ideological and political proximity to conservative economic policies. As PAN president, José Angel Conchello attempted to lead the PAN into a more critical stance vis-à-vis the reformism of Echeverría and closer to the economic liberalism of the Monterrey Group. Conchello's followers wanted to nominate Pablo Emilio Madero as their presidential candidate in 1976, but the social reformist elements within the PAN blocked this attempt and the party did not run any candidate against the PRI's José López Portillo. But in 1982 Madero did gain the PAN's presidential nomination and the party presidency in 1984. A number of the more moderate *panistas* left the party, including Efraín González Morfín Luna, son of González Luna and PAN presidential candidate in 1970; and thus the so-called *neo-panistas*, with close business links, became an influential force within the PAN.

The *neo-panista* wing was particularly strengthened after the bank nationalizations in 1982. Entrepreneurs in general reacted by urging greater political input by the private sector, with many suggesting that input be channeled toward the PRI.[22] But a larger number apparently joined the PAN, especially in the northern border states like Nuevo León and Chihuahua. The presidential candidacy and party presidency of Madero, a Monterrey businessman, in part marked the ascendancy of the *neo-panistas*. As a result, the PAN has generally moved toward the right as it has profited from popular discontent arising from the Mexican economic crisis. It has identified itself more closely with an ideology of favoring private enterprise and combating the increasing state role in the economy.[23] While the middle-class has been a fertile ground for recruiting voters, many entrepreneurs have played key roles in the leadership of the PAN in the 1980s.

Electoral Successes

Since its inception in 1939, the PAN has nominated a presidential candidate in every election except 1940 and 1976. In 1940 the fledgling party decided to support the candidacy of General Almazán; and in 1976, after a very divisive national convention, the party was unable to decide on a candidate. The PAN ran its own candidates for the first time in the 1943 elections for federal deputies. Its 21 candidates garnered 25,000 votes nationwide. In 1946 it nominated its first presidential candidate, the former Carranza adviser Luis Cabrera. However, Cabrera refused the nomination, saying he was "too old and had too many enemies."[24] Its first genuine presidential contender then was Efraín González Luna who won 7.82 percent of the vote in 1952. Since that time each PAN presidential candidate has received a successively higher percentage of the vote (see Table 11.2). In 1982 Pablo Emilio Madero, a nephew of Francisco Madero, was nominated and collected 15.68 percent of the vote—the highest total ever for the PAN.

The Party has also been steadily increasing its representation in the Chamber of Deputies. Its first deputies were elected in 1946, and throughout the 1950s it retained at least five seats in the Chamber (see Table 11.3). With the advent of the "party deputies" in 1963, the number of PAN deputies increased to 20. And after the political reform of 1977 the PAN elected 45 and 51 deputies in the elections of 1979 and 1982, respectively. The PAN's delegation of federal deputies fell to 40 in 1985 (8 "majority" and only 32 "party"), but the opposition parties claimed widespread fraud. Its delegation in the Chamber has always been the largest of all the opposition parties, and the PAN deputies have been the most significant counterweight to the PRI in the legislative branch.

In recent years the PAN has also been quite successful in a number of municipal electoral contests and actually poses the greatest threat to the PRI at the local level in those states where the PAN is the strongest. Altogether, of the 2300 municipalities in Mexico, the PAN controls 33 and 22 are held by other opposition parties. The most significant PAN victories have been concentrated in northern Mexico, where the PAN controls the mayor's office in Chihuahua, Durango, and Hermosillo (all are state capitals), Ciudad Juárez (the fourth largest city in Mexico), and eight other important cities.

After the 1983 elections that brought the opposition its greatest local electoral successes ever, the PRI reasserted its control in 1984 with sweeping victories in Baja California and Coahuila. However, the charges of fraud were louder than ever, and *panistas* in Piedras Negras, Monclova, and Escobedo (cities in the state of Coahuila in which the opposition claimed the PRI had committed widespread fraud) staged the most violent protests against the PRI in many years. The international bridge at Piedras Negras was closed down and municipal offices were set afire; and in Monclova the defeated PAN mayor refused to relinquish city hall until the state legislature finally appointed a neutral mayor acceptable to both sides. These incidents showed the growing strength of the PAN in the north and the determination of its followers to oppose what they perceived as fraudulent tactics by the PRI. The PAN was more confident than ever going into the 1985 elections for the Chamber of Deputies and seven governorships and even hoped for its first gubernatorial victories in the states of Sonora and Nuevo León. When the PRI swept all the gubernatorial races and the PAN received some 2 percent less of the total vote in 1985 than in 1982 (and 11 fewer federal deputies), the frustrations of the *panistas* in northern Mexico once again produced violent protests against the alleged electoral fraud.

Analyses of recent elections show the bulk of the PAN's strength coming from two areas: the northern border states and the more urbanized states.[25]

Statistical analysis of the 1982 electoral results provides further confirmation for these conclusions. Though these results do not prove the depth of business support for the PAN, certainly electoral strength in the north and in urban areas would be a necessary factor in showing private sector support. Though the PAN has made some surprising inroads with the labor sector (especially since the onset of the economic crisis), its northern and urban support is predominantly middle- and upper-class.

Table 11.4 shows the average percentage of the 1982 presidential vote won by the PAN, the PRI, and the PSUM, broken down into seven geographic regions. The strongest region by far for the PAN was the north, with the center and the center-north its second and third best areas. A variety of factors undoubtedly explain this relationship. Though the north provided most of the early Revolutionary leaders, in the postwar period it has become more autonomous and isolated from the core area surrounding Mexico City. This separation has contributed to the feeling of alienation from the federal government held by many Mexicans in the north. In addition, the north has been traditionally more conservative, especially the industrial center of Monterrey, and more heavily influenced by the U.S. For example, Monterrey is closer to San Antonio than it is to Mexico City. Northerners visit the U.S. more frequently and have easier access to U.S. radio, television and other cultural factors. The sense of alienation, the economic conservatism, and the influence of the U.S. have all contributed to the increased vote for the PAN.

The identification of the PAN with the U.S. (especially the present conservative administration) and with northern Mexico was exemplified in the controversy involving the U.S. Ambassador to Mexico, John Gavin, and PAN leaders. Suspicions that the U.S. Embassy during the Reagan administration favored the PAN were fueled in 1984 when several *panistas* attended the Republican Party National Convention in Dallas and when Ambassador Gavin met with PAN leaders and Church officials in Hermosillo in August. Many commentators in Mexico charged Gavin with interfering in the internal affairs of Mexico, and PRI President Adolfo Lugo Verduzco issued a stinging attack on Gavin. In the minds of many leftists, the PAN, the Catholic Church, and the U.S. Embassy form a united front threatening the progress of the ongoing Revolution. Though the ties are considerably exaggerated by most Mexican leftists, the Reagan administration was undoubtedly sympathetic to the more conservative domestic and foreign policy stands of the PAN. And it was no surprise that Gavin met with the PAN in Hermosillo, one of the northern centers of power for the Party.

Independent of its northern base, the PAN attracts considerable support from urban areas all across Mexico. Again, the 1982 data confirm the conclusions of earlier studies associating a stronger PAN vote with measures of urbanization. In this analysis at the state level, the PAN's percent of the 1982 vote has been correlated with three measures of urbanization: the percent of the population in metropolitan areas of more than 80,000 people; the percent of the population in municipalities with more than 5,000 people;

and the percent of the economically active population engaged in the manufacturing sector. For each measure of urbanization the correlation coefficient with votes for the PAN is positive and statistically significant (see Table 11.5), and the strongest relationship is with the most urbanized areas (>80,000). If we divide the states into those above the mean value in terms of urbanization ("urban") and those below the mean value ("non-urban"), the association of the PAN with urban regions is even more obvious (see Table 11.6). The PAN receives from 18 to 21 percent of the vote (depending upon the variable) in urban states and only eight to nine percent of the vote in non-urban states.

The reasons for the relative strength of the PAN in urban areas are varied. For one, urban voters tend to be better educated, more sophisticated, and less vulnerable to socialization by the ruling party. The PRI has been most successful in controlling rural politics, while the PAN has made its best inroads with the urban electorate. Urban areas also tend to be more developed economically with higher average income levels—demographic characteristics that suggest a natural attraction to the PAN's pro-business and pluralistic ideology. Finally, the urban centers are evolving rapidly and contain segments of the population (particularly in the middle-class) that are emerging politically and economically, have fewer ties to the traditional political organizations, and enjoy more independence from the PRI.

Summary and Conclusion

PAN-Business Links

A number of facts substantiate the proposed close association between the PAN and the business community in Mexico. In the first place, the disenchantment of the private sector with the PRI is evident at various points in Mexican history, particularly during the administrations of Cárdenas and Echeverría and the last year of the López Portillo *sexenio*, which brought exchange controls and bank nationalization. This alienation caused many business leaders to participate in the founding of the PAN. Though entrepreneurs drifted away from the PAN in the 1950s and 1960s, the reformism of the Echeverría presidency motivated many in the private sector to return to the major conservative opposition party. Today the *neo-panistas* (the most economically liberal wing of the party) are in ascendance.

The electoral success of the PAN in the north and urban areas further suggests an industrial base for the party, and many of its current leaders are powerful entrepreneurs. The key city of Monterrey in the northern state of Nuevo León provides a number of examples of *panistas* who are also important business leaders.[26] As previously mentioned the PAN gubernatorial candidate in 1985, Fernando Canales Clariond, is an important businessman in Monterrey (associated with Grupo IMSA). Other leading *panistas* from Monterrey include Adán Elizondo (President of COPARMEX in Nuevo León), José Luis Coindreau (former president of COPARMEX and PAN candidate for mayor of Monterrey in 1986), Jorge Eugenio Ortíz and Mauricio Fernández (of the powerful Garza Sada family), Rogelio Sada (head of Vidriera Monterrey), and Andrés Marcelo Sada (director of Grupo Monterrey).

Weaknesses in Business Loyalty to the PAN

Considerable evidence also exists that the private sector in Mexico does not profess united and unquestioning loyalty to the PAN and that the major opposition party has more important support outside the upper-classes. Several commentators have recognized that the PAN has encountered surprising obstacles in its appeals to the upper-class, whose voters appear to recognize that the PRI still dominates the reins of power.[27] Most of the business support for the PAN is limited to the northern states and to the state of Puebla. And even in the *panista* stronghold of Monterrey, a number of industrialists are leading *priistas*. Alberto Santos, of the Grupo Gamesa, is a PRI federal deputy, and Javier Garza Calderón (leading stockholder in the Grupo VISA and the Grupo Gentor) is a PRI official.[28] Other PRI militants include Javier Lobo (another deputy and leader in the Grupo Protexa), Eugenio Clariond (cousin of the PAN's Fernando Canales Clariond and founder of the League of Nationalist Entrepreneurs within the PRI), and Genaro Leal (former PRI mayor and owner of Industrias Químicas). Even the PRI gubernatorial candidate in Nuevo León in 1985 was a "wealthy Monterrey tax lawyer who has made a career of finding tax breaks for big business."[29] And the PAN's current president, Pablo Emilio Madero, has been quoted as saying that "big business is still in bed with the PRI," because they find it too risky to oppose the ruling party.[30] Other business leaders emphasize their distance from the PAN without directly affiliating with the ruling party. Jorge Chapa, president of the CCE, "scrupulously avoids any connection with the PAN."[31]

The private sector has often been opposed within the PAN by many of the long-standing leaders of the party, who in part resent the influence of the business "new-comers" to the party. The previously mentioned doctrine of social consciousness (favored by many traditional *panistas*) was not supported by the Mexican business community, which even opposed the 1970 presidential candidacy of Efraín González Morfín (who as son of González Luna was the acknowledged heir of original *panismo*). At the 1985 National Convention, the traditional *panistas* won a substantial victory with the approval of ideological statements stressing the pre-eminence of labor and recognizing the problems of injustice and marginalization.[32] Thus, even in a period in which the *neo-panistas* are claimed to be assuming a dominant role in the party, the old-line base of the PAN and the social consciousness ideology retain a significant influence in party decisions.

The argument that the entrepreneurial sector provides the PAN with substantial financial resources would appear to be vacuous. In the first place, the PAN's budget is quite austere compared with that of the PRI (estimates of the PRI outspending the PAN range from ratios of 10 to 1 up to 100 to 1). In addition, the meager revenues for the PAN come principally from two sources; lotteries and quotas of the salaries of elected *panista* officials. Thus the PAN has received its most important support, both financial and electoral, from outside business circles.[33] The predominant PAN support comes from the urban, middle-class voter, who perceives the manipulative nature of the PRI and sees no rewards in being coopted by the dominant party. These voters typically feel they have not gained their fair share of the benefits from the system and cast their lot with the PAN as a protest vote against the PRI.

The fact that PAN electoral support is predominantly a protest vote against the ruling party is indeed one of the greatest challenges facing the opposition party. As mentioned, the PAN does not have significant financial resources. Also its political organization (from its headquarters in Mexico City to its poll-watchers across the country) is notoriously weak. Without a base of electoral support or strong party roots among important segments of Mexican society, the PAN is reduced to being a negative voice for those disenchanted with the PRI. Its support is more anti-PRI than pro-PAN. With the PRI continuing to maintain the image that it is a sure winner, the voice of the Mexican Revolution, and the guarantor of social stability in Mexico, the future of the PAN would appear to be its relegation to the status of a permanent minority party.

Notes

1. John G. Conklin, "Prospects for Mexican Democracy: Summer Elections of 1985" (Paper presented at the 1985 meeting of the Pacific Coast Conference on Latin American Studies, Las Vegas, October 18, 1985), 14.

2. Dale Story, *Industry, the State, and Public Policy in Mexico* (Austin, TX: University of Texas Press, 1986), chapter 4.

3. Peter H. Smith, *Labyrinths of Power: Political Recruitment in Twentieth-Century Mexico* (Princeton, NJ: Princeton University Press, 1979), 211–216.

4. Flavia Derossi, *The Mexican Entrepreneur* (Paris: Development Centre of the Organization for Economic Co-operation and Development, 1971); and Story, *Industry,* chapter 5.

5. Peter Smith, "Does Mexico Have a Power Elite?" in José Luis Reyna and Richard S. Weinert, eds., *Authoritarianism in Mexico* (Philadelphia, PA: Institute for the Study of Human Issues, 1977).

6. John F.H. Purcell and Susan Kaufman Purcell, "El estado y la empresa privada," *Nueva Política,* 1, no. 1 (1976): 229–250; and *Análisis Político,* March 29, 1976 and August 22, 1977.

7. *Decisión,* December, 1982; *Excelsior,* January 27, 28, 1983; *Proceso,* January 3, 1983; *Razones,* February 7–20, 1983; and *Expansión,* March 2, 1983.

8. John J. Bailey, "What Impact Will Major Groups Have on Policy-Making?: Trends in Government/Business Relations in Mexico" (Issue Paper #5 prepared for working group on "Mexico: The Next Five Years," October 23, 1985), 22–23.

9. *Latin America Regional Report—Mexico and Central America,* November 29, 1985.

10. *Excelsior,* July 16, 1979.

11. *Nexos,* April, 1983.

12. *Excelsior,* January 29, 1983.

13. Franz A. Von Sauer, *The Alienated "Loyal" Opposition: Mexico's Partido Acción Nacional* (Albuquerque, NM: University of New Mexico Press, 1974), 15, 45–60.

14. Octavio Rodríguez Araujo, *La reforma política y los partidos en México* (México: Siglo Veintiuno Editores, 1983), 126.

15. Donald J. Mabry, *Mexico's Acción Nacional: A Catholic Alternative to Revolution* (Syracuse, NY: Syracuse University Press, 1973), 32–33.

16. VonSauer, *Opposition,* 38.

17. Mabry, *Acción Nacional,* 39.

18. Mabry, *Acción Nacional,* 34–36.

19. Partido Acción Nacional, *Cambio democrático de estructura* (México: Editores de Acción Nacional, 1969); and Kenneth F. Johnson, *Mexican Democracy: A Critical View* (New York, NY: Praeger, 1978), 144.

20. Partido Acción Nacional, *Nuestros Ideales: Principios de Doctrina* (México: Ediciones PAN, 1984).

21. José Angel Conchello et al., *Los partidos políticos de México* (México: Fondo de Cultura Económica, 1975), 11–144.

22. *Análisis Político,* August 15, 1985 and January 15, 1985.

23. *Análisis Político,* March 15, 1984.

24. Mabry, *Acción Nacional,* 43.

25. John Walton and Joyce A. Sween, "Urbanization, Industrialization and Voting in Mexico: A Longitudinal Analysis of Official and Opposition Party Support," *Social Science Quarterly* 52, no. 3 (December 1971): 721–745; Rafael Segovia, "Las elecciones federales de 1979," *Foro Internacional* 20, no. 3 (1980): 397–410; and Joseph L. Klesner, "Party System Expansion and Electoral Mobilization in Mexico" (paper presented at the XII International Congress of the Latin American Studies Association, Albuquerque, New Mexico, April 18–20, 1985).

26. *Proceso,* July 15, 1985.

27. Roger Bartra, "Viaje al centro de la derecha," *Nexos,* April, 1983, 15–23; and *Wall Street Journal,* December 13, 1984, January 16, 1985, February 13, 1985, and April 26, 1985.

28. *Proceso,* July 15, 1985.

29. *Wall Street Journal,* February 13, 1985.

30. *Wall Street Journal,* February 13, 1985.

31. *Wall Street Journal,* December 13, 1984.

32. *Análisis Político,* March 15, 1985.

33. Mabry, *Acción Nacional,* 164.

TABLE 11.1
Political Parties Participating in the 1985 Elections

Party	Pronounced ideology[a]	Date of establishment	Date of registration	% of votes for deputies, 1985
PAN	traditional liberalism; Catholic democratic	1939	1948	15.45
PARM	revolutionary; nationalist; populist	1954	1957[b]	1.65
PDM	democratic; populist	1972	1978	2.73
PMT	democratic; anti-imperialist	1974	1985[c]	1.53
PPS	marxist-leninist; anti-imperialist	1948 (PP)	1960	1.97
PRI	social democratic; populist	1929 (PNR)	1946	64.99
PRT	trotskyite	1976	1981	1.25
PST	social democratic; anti-imperialist	1975	1979	2.45
PSUM	marxist-leninist	1919 (PCM)	1981	3.24

[a]Ideology here is designed to reflect only the stated philosophy of the party, not its actual policy, preferences, goals, or candidates. Most of these descriptions come from Pablo González Casanova, El estado y los partidos políticos en México (México: Ediciones Era, 1983), 78–79.

[b]Lost full registration in 1982 but received conditional registration for 1985.

[c]Conditional registration.

TABLE 11.2
Presidential Vote by Party, 1929-1982

Year	PRI	PAN	PPS	PARM	PCM/PSUM	PST	PRT	PSD	PDM	OTHERS
1929	93.55	---	---	---	---	---	---	---	---	6.45[a]
1934	98.19	---	---	---	---	---	---	---	---	1.81
1940	93.89	---	---	---	---	---	---	---	---	6.11[b]
1946	77.90	---	---	---	---	---	---	---	---	22.10[c]
1952	74.31	7.82	1.98	---	---	---	---	---	---	15.89[d]
1958	90.43	9.42	---	---	---	---	---	---	---	0.15
1964	87.82	11.05	0.68[e]	0.45[e]	---	---	---	---	---	0.00
1970	83.32	13.85	0.86[e]	0.54[e]	---	---	---	---	---	1.43
1976	86.89	---	3.65[e]	3.05[e]	---	---	---	---	---	6.42
1982	68.43	15.68	1.53[e]	1.03[e]	3.48	1.45	1.76	0.20	1.84	4.60

[a]5.32 percent for José Vasconcelos (National Anti-Re-electionist Party).
[b]5.72 percent for General Almazán (Revolutionary Party of National Unity).
[c]19.33 percent for Ezequiel Padilla (Democratic Party).
[d]15.87 for General Henríquez (Federation of Mexican People's Parties).
[e]From 1964 through 1982 the PPS and the PARM endorsed the PRI candidate, so their votes were actually votes for the PRI nominees.

Sources: Comisión Federal Electoral, Reforma Política: Memoria del Proceso Federal Electoral 1981-1982, vol. IX (Mexico: Secretaría Técnica, 1982), 128-129; Pablo González Casanova, Democracy in Mexico (New York: Oxford University Press, 1970), 199-200; Daniel Levy and Gabriel Székely, Mexico: Paradoxes of Stability and Change (Boulder, Colorado: Westview Press, 1983), 69; and Octavio Rodríguez Araujo, La reforma política y los partidos en México (México: Siglo Veintiuno Editores, 1983), 144-48, 157-59.

TABLE 11.3
Representation in Chamber of Deputies by Party, 1943–1982

Year	PRI	PAN	PPS	PARM	PCM/ PSUM	PDM	PST	OTHER
1943	147	---	---	---	---	---	---	---
1946	143	4	---	---	---	---	---	---
1949	142	4	1	---	---	---	---	---
1952	154	5	2	---	---	---	---	---
1955	154	6	1	---	---	---	---	---
1958	152	6	1	1	---	---	---	1
1961	172	5	1	---	---	---	---	---
1964[a]	175	2+18	1+9	0+5	---	---	---	---
1967[a]	176	1+19	0+10	1+5	---	---	---	---
1970[a]	178	0+20	0+10	0+5	---	---	---	---
1973[a]	189	4+21	3+10	0+7	---	---	---	---
1976[a]	196	0+20	0+12	0+10	---	---	---	---
1979[a]	296	4+39	0+11	0+12	0+18	0+10	0+10	---
1982[a]	299	1+50	0+10	0	0+17	0+12	0+11	---
1985[a]	290	8+32	0+11	2+9	0+12	0+12	0+12	0+12

[a]The first number shows the number of representatives elected in single-number districts. The second number is the number of representatives elected through a proportional representation system.

Sources: Comisión Federal Electoral, Reforma Política, vol. IX and X; Robert K. Furtak, El Partido de la Revolución y la estabilidad política en México (México: Universidad Nacional Autónoma de México, 1978), 105; González Casanova, El estado, 68–69; Levy and Székely, Mexico, 70; Martin C. Needler, Mexican Politics: The Containment of Conflict (New York: Praeger, 1982), 87; Rodríguez Araujo, La reforma política, 148–149, 158–60; and Robert E. Scott, Mexican Government in Transition (Urbana: University of Illinois Press, 1964), 243.

TABLE 11.4
Party Mean Vote, 1982 Presidential Election, by Region

| | | PERCENTAGES | |
Region[a]	PAN	PRI	PSUM
North	19.6	69.1	2.2
Center-north	13.8	75.1	1.2
Center	14.0	69.7	3.4
West	11.1	74.2	5.1
East	3.4	86.2	1.4
Southeast	9.3	84.9	0.6
South	4.3	85.1	2.6

[a]The regions are broken down to include the following states: (1) North = Baja California, Baja California Sur, Coahuila, Chihuahua, Durango, Nuevo León, Sinaloa, Sonora, and Tamaulipas; (2) Center-north = Aguascalientes, Guanajuato, Querétaro, San Luis Potosí, and Zacatecas; (3) Center = Federal District, Hidalgo, México, Morelos, Puebla, and Tlaxcala; (4) West = Colima, Jalisco, Michoacán, and Nayarit; (5) East = Tabasco and Veracruz; (6) Southeast = Campeche, Quintana Roo, and Yucatán; and (7) South = Chiapas, Guerrero, and Oaxaca.
Source: Comisión Federal Electoral, Reforma Política, vol. IX, 96-127.

TABLE 11.5
Pearson Correlation Coefficients, 1982 Party Vote with Urbanization

(levels of significance in parentheses)

Variable	PAN	PRI	PSUM
percent urban (>80,000)	.7609	-.8230	.2300
	(0.000)	(0.000)	(0.103)
Percent urban (>5,000)	.7157	-.7287	.1617
	(0.000)	(0.000)	(0.000)
Percent labor force	.4977	-.4947	.0890
in manufacturing	(0.002)	(0.002)	(0.314)

Source: Comisión Federal Electoral, Reforma Política, vol. IX, 96-127.

TABLE 11.6
Party Mean Vote, 1982 Presidential Election By Urbanization (in percentages)

Party	Per cent urban[a] (>80,000)		Per cent urban[a] (>5,000)		Per cent labor force in manufacturing	
	Non-urban	Urban	Non-urban	Urban	Non-urban	Urban
PAN	8.9	21.3	8.0	18.3	9.8	18.9
PRI	80.8	63.6	81.5	68.2	79.8	66.6
PSUM	2.2	2.9	2.5	2.3	2.3	2.6

[a] Non-urban are those states below the mean value and urban are those above the mean value.
Source: Comisión Federal Electoral, Reforma Política, vol. IX, 96-127.

12

The PSUM:
The Unification Process on
the Mexican Left, 1981-1985

Barry Carr

Introduction

The last ten years have witnessed a dramatic process of reorganization and regrouping within the Mexican left, culminating in the formal dissolution of the Mexican Communist Party (PCM) and the creation of a new broad left party, the United Socialist Party of Mexico (PSUM) in 1981. There have also been mergers further to the left of the PCM. In February 1982, the Organización de Izquierda Revolucionaria Línea de Masas (OIRLM) was established out of a number of influential regional organizations of urban *colonos* (of maoist origin).

During the same period the last vestiges of the short-lived experiment with armed struggle in the early 1970s disappeared. Some of the former *guerilleros* of the 1970-1974 period returned to the "above-ground" political arena, particularly to the Communist Party and to the newly formed Corriente Socialista.[1]

The reorganization of the left took place against the background of the political reform (*Reforma Política* or LOPPE) initiated by the Echeverría administration but implemented during the first year of the López Portillo government. The *Reforma* was just one of the ways in which the Mexican state attempted to overcome the economic and political difficulties of the late 1960s and 1970s by attempting to radicalize the image of the ruling

---

Editor's Note: In the spring of 1987, several political parties on the left agreed to form a new Socialist Party of Mexico, PSM. The process of merger is set to conclude in the fall of 1987 and involves the following parties: PSUM, PMT, PPR (Partido Patriótico Revolucionario), MRP (Movimiento Revolucionario de Pueblo), and the UIC (Unidad de Izquierda Comunista). Notable among parties still remaining outside the unified left is the Trotskyite PRT. Barry Carr's analysis was completed prior to this latest merger.

Institutional Revolutionary Party (PRI) and to weaken radical opposition by channelling it in a parliamentary direction.

The left responded cautiously to the new opportunities opened up by the LOPPE with the most substantial reservations about the place of "electoralism" being expressed by the Trotskyists and the most interest being shown by sectors of the Communist Party. Overall, however, the decade which followed the introduction of the *Reforma Política* was characterized by a grand march into the electoral arena during which nearly all the large parties of the left obtained their formal registration as legal groupings, as well as parliamentary representation. By 1985, there were three independent socialist/marxist parties represented in the Chamber of Deputies (PSUM; the Revolutionary Workers Party, PRT; the Mexican Workers Party, PMT) in addition to the "left-wing" parties of the so-called loyal opposition, the Socialist Popular Party (PPS) and the Socialist Workers Party (PST).

The reunification and reorganization theme has not only affected political parties. The ever more important complex of urban social movements and independent peasant organizations has also undergone major changes.[2] A number of important broad fronts and organizations have emerged to coordinate the activities and struggles of hundreds of these local and regional centers of resistance to declining living standards and conditions. The major coordinating bodies (*coordinadoras*) established since 1979 are the National Coordinating Committee of the Urban Popular Movement (CONAMUP) and the National "Plan de Ayala" Coordinating Committee (CNPA), while the National Worker and Peasant Assembly (ANOCP), founded at the end of 1982, has organized two nationwide civic strikes (*paros cívicos*) in October 1983 and June 1984.[3]

While parties of the left and the union movement have traditionally focused their attention on the work place and on the sphere of production, the newer organizations active within the "urban popular movement" are concerned more with the sphere of consumption and are territorially organized. Their concerns tend, therefore, to be centered not so much on the factory, mill, mine or workshop but on the *barrio*, street and school, and ground struggles over access to land, housing and urban services such as potable water, roads and power.

Many of these groups are suspicious of, and sometimes hostile to, involvement in their activities by the traditional parties of the left. These suspicions are generated by bitter memories of the way in which certain sectors of the left have subordinated the concerns and needs of specific movements to the interests and goals of national political parties. The symptoms of this malaise were painfully and vividly evident, for example, in the tension between CNPA peasants and militants of the PSUM, PRT and PMT during a march held in Mexico City in April 1984 to commemorate the assassination of Emiliano Zapata.[4] One CNPA leader denounced the actions of the representatives of political parties present, declaring to the press:

We are not interested in whether any of our leaders are members of political organizations. What we reject are attempts by parties to manipulate the CNPA. They see us as "booty" and want to take advantage of our strength, something we will never allow . . . the vanguard of the left is among the masses not in the parties or in the Chamber of Deputies.[5]

The *coordinadoras* and the ANOCP have been responsible for organizing one of the most dramatic and innovative of the responses to the programs of austerity and economic stabilization launched in the early and mid eighties. In October 1983, and again, in June 1984, two civic strikes (*paros cívicos*) were held throughout Mexico. The *paros* were designed as a form of protest most appropriate to a period of acute economic crisis. It was recognized that the possibilities of prolonged industrial action by workers were very limited, while there existed a great variety of alternative forms of registering popular opposition which could be combined under one banner within the space of a single day.

The *paro cívico* was a new tactic involving the simultaneous realization in hundreds of locations throughout Mexico of an extraordinarily wide variety of protest movements and actions—work stoppages, slowdowns, late entry to work, meetings, marches, *plantones* in front of public buildings, land seizures, road blocks, hunger strikes, boycotts of stores, power blackouts and cultural and political festivals.[6] Between 1.5 and 2 million people took part in the first *paro*. However, the second strike, in June 1984, was far less widely observed with barely half a million people involved.[7]

While the organizers of the *paros* did not expect a large participation by industrial workers, the involvement of the organized labor movement was disappointingly small. The only significant worker contingents present came from the powerful dissident grouping within the National Union of Educational Workers (SNTE) and from small groups of workers in government ministeries like Health, Hydraulic Resources and Fisheries. The commitment of such an important nuclei of independent left unionism as the university workers union (STUNAM) at the National Autonomous University (UNAM), and the Nuclear Industry Workers Union (SUTIN) was at best lukewarm, reflecting divisions within the left over the usefulness of actions like the *paros cívicos*.

The sector in which the theme of unification and reorganization has been least visible has been the organized labor movement itself. A number of new democratic trade union groupings have appeared, the most important being the Trade Union Unity and Solidarity Pact (Pacto de Unidad y Solidaridad Sindical or PAUSS) and the National Union Coordinating Body (Coordinadora Sindical Nacional or COSINA), but the labor movement still lacks an organizing focus which is as effective as the Democratic Tendency of the Electricians Union (SUTERM) had been in the early and mid-1970s.[8]

One union which, in spite of its smallness, had been playing a crucial role as a rallying point and source of inspiration and advice to independent labor groups was the nuclear industry workers' union SUTIN. The SUTIN, through its national leaders Arturo Whaley and Antonio Gerschenson, also had strong links with the PSUM. During 1983 and 1984, however, the De la Madrid government launched a series of attacks on the union, the most serious of which involved the closing of a para-state company, URAMEX, which employed 2,300 men and women, about half of SUTIN's total membership.[9] SUTIN's membership in the Congress of Labor (Congreso de Trabajo), which distinguished it from most of the unions in the independent sector, proved in the end of little use in halting what appeared to be a deliberate government ploy to destroy the union and at the same time abort one of the most effective rallying points for the non-government unions.[10]

The PSUM

The United Socialist Party of Mexico (PSUM) was founded in November 1981 after a merger between five political parties and tendencies, of which the most important, and by far the biggest, was the Mexican Communist Party (PCM). The decision to dissolve the PCM was a very significant act of itself. Few communist parties in the western hemisphere have voluntarily dissolved themselves; the only well-known case involved the party liquidations of the Browderist phase in the development of U.S. and Latin American communism during the period 1944–1945.

Moreover, the PCM was the oldest political party in Mexico (founded in 1919). It had survived periods of intense government repression and, until the mid-1960s at least, it was the most substantial and conspicuous focus of independent socialist activity and ideas.[11] The decision to dissolve the party, therefore, was a particularly painful one, especially for some of its older members. Although there was little overt opposition to the decision to dissolve the Communist Party, many of its members demonstrated their unhappiness over the change by failing to join the PSUM.

At the time of its dissolution, the PCM could be described as a partially "eurocommunized" party with its social base firmly established within the state intelligentsia and certain segments of the skilled working class, particularly among metal workers, railroadmen, and miners.

Beginning in the early 1970s, the PCM had begun to modify aspects of its traditional program, tactics and style. The areas of convergence between the PCM and Eurocommunists included the issue of the sovereignty of socialist states and the principle of non-intervention by the Soviet Union in the affairs of national communist parties. Regarding these matters, the PCM had by the end of the 1970s become fully eurocommunized. In 1968, the party condemned the Soviet Union's intervention in Czechoslovakia and it later reopened its relations with the Chinese Communist Party. The party also began firmly to criticize the *socialismo realmente existente* practiced in the socialist bloc, and by 1978 the PCM had reached a conscious decision to use the non-party media to publicize its concerns about the continuing heritage of Stalinism in Eastern Europe.[12]

Secondly, the PCM's debates over the concept of the dictatorship of the proletariat paralleled similar discussions within certain European communist parties.[13] In fact, at its XIX congress (held in March 1981) the Mexican party ultimately decided to abandon the term replacing it with the notion of "democratic workers power."

A third area of similarity between the PCM and Eurocommunism concerned the erosion of the narrow conception of the party as a "vanguard organization" in relation to other left formations. In the 1970s, the PCM demonstrated a new openness to the broad left and played a leading role in the creation of the Left Coalition (Coalición de Izquierda) in 1977. Actions like these signalled the party's abandonment of its earlier claim to be the sole interpreter of revolutionary Marxism in Mexico and paved the way, as we shall see, for the path-breaking decision to create a single party of the left in 1981.

However, in a large number of areas, the politics of the PCM diverged from Eurocommunist currents. With the exception of a small number of figures within the PCM leadership (the best known being anthropologist Roger Bartra and historian Enrique Semo), no formally designated Eurocommunist current developed within the party.[14] Moreover, the process of unification of the left which began in 1979 and which was consummated in 1981 with the formation of the PSUM, intensified debate within the party and its allies over the correctness of the seemingly Eurocommunist modifications in the party's style and tactics.[15]

Although the PCM was by far the biggest of the parties which merged to create the PSUM, two of its new partners, the Party of the Mexican People (PPM) and the Movement for Political Action (MAP) were to play important roles in the new party. The PPM was a split from Vicente Lombardo Toledano's old Popular Socialist Party (PPS) which had been the traditional focus of the "loyal opposition" of the left to the official party, the Institutional Revolutionary Party, PRI. The PPM was created in 1977 after the PPS engaged in a maneuver of more than normal cynicism and unprincipledness by selling its clear victory in the 1975 elections for governor of the state of Nayarit for a place in the national Senate for Jorge Cruickshank Garcia, Lombardo's successor in the leadership of the party.[16]

The PPM developed a major political base in the northwestern state of Nayarit where its leader, Alejandro Gascón Mercado (a former Mayor of Tepic, the state capital and brother of a former PRI *gobernador*) has enjoyed a strong personal following.[17] The party also has considerable influence among students in Guadalajara, Jalisco, where its cadres control the powerful Guadalajara Student Federation (FEG). Despite the bitterness of the split with the PPS, however, it is important to note that the PPM and its leading figures retained a firm commitment to the ideological positions of Lombardo Toledano on the issue of revolutionary nationalism although their attitudes towards the De la Madrid government were taking on a steadily more belligerent tone after 1982.[18]

The last of the five groups to abandon its separate identity in the merger was a relatively new formation, the MAP. Established only a year before the creation of the PSUM, the MAP's leading figures already constituted a clearly defined current attached to the ideas and memory of the late Rafael Galván of the Democratic Tendency within the Electrical Workers Union (SUTERM). It is made up of a number of leading university-based intellectuals (Arnaldo Córdova, Rolando Cordera, José Woldenburg, Carlos Pereyra) and has links with some important new trade unions within the democratic camp, particularly among highly skilled workers; these include the nuclear workers union, SUTIN and the university workers of STUNAM.[19]

The MAP developed a very well-elaborated and coherent vision of Mexican society and of the appropriate socialist strategy to deal with its problems. The MAP's orientation was characterized by a strongly statist and populist approach to socialist issues, and it defined its radical nationalism as the recovery by the nation (implemented on its behalf by the state) of its resources.[20] Rafael Galván, from whom the MAP drew a great deal of its philosophy, put it very succinctly, "In our history we grow and advance by nationalizing."[21]

Not surprisingly, in view of its intimate links with the union movement, the MAP's positions were also fiercely workerist and its ideologues showed little interest in the activities or potential of groups on the margin of organized production. Next to the PCM, it was the MAP whose influence was most clearly visible in the new party in terms of both the high public profile enjoyed by some of its leading personalities and the size of its representation on the Central Committee of the PSUM.

Two much smaller groups also merged to form the PSUM. Both the Movement for Socialist Action and Unity (MAUS) and the Revolutionary Socialist Party (PSR) were the products of ancient splits and expulsions from the old Communist Party.[22]

The Background to the Merger

The PSUM emerged remarkably quickly; only four months elapsed between the first announcement of the holding of discussions on a merger (August 1981) and the formal emergence of the PSUM in November.[23] The whole process took the rank and file of the merging parties by surprise, and there is some evidence that Heberto Castillo made absolute secrecy one of the conditions for the preliminary negotiations between himself and the leaders of the Coalition of the Left.[24] The suddenness of the move and disquiet over the elitist character of the negotiations (denounced as the politics of the cupula) led to many party members failing to transfer their affiliation to the new party.[25]

If the timing and details of the negotiations to form the PSUM came as a surprise to most observers, the idea of a united left party built around the old PCM goes back to the mid-1970s, even before the formation of the Coalition of the Left in 1976. In 1979, the Coalición de Izquierda (made up of the same parties which eventually made up the PSUM—minus the MAP) made a reasonable showing in the mid-term congressional elections. The Coalition, led by the now legally registered PCM, received three-quarters of a million votes and won eighteen seats in the Chamber of Deputies under the complicated proportional representation provisions of the LOPPE electoral reform law.[26]

The demand for left unity also went as far as calling for the formation of a single party of the socialist left, although the heterogeneous character of the Coalition placed difficulties in the way of discussion with some groups, in particular the Trotskyist PRT. In spite of the opposition of the PCM's still Stalinist-tinged allies like the PPM and MAUS, short term electoral alliances were arranged with the PRT in the late 1970s and early 1980s. Less controversial were the local and regional electoral alliances which the Coalition partners established from time to time with the Corriente Socialista and the PRI-leaning PPS and PST.

Interestingly, the first push for the merger came from a party which was outside of the Coalition of the Left and which did not in the end take part in the unification process. This was the Mexican Workers Party (PMT) led by a distinguished engineer and former activist in the 1968 student-popular movement, Heberto Castillo.[27] The initial proposal for the merger was launched by Castillo shortly after the PMT's application for registration as an electoral party had been turned down by the López Portillo government in the summer of 1981.[28]

The immediate background of the PSUM's birth, therefore, was a mood of anxiety about the future of the PMT in a political arena which was increasingly dominated by the logic of electoralism. The PMT was not alone, however, in its preoccupation with the future of the left. The Mexican Communist Party had only just emerged from a particularly intense year-long internal struggle in which its leadership had been challenged by an influential current of opinion which received the title of "the renewers" (*renovadores*).[29]

The *renovadores* attacked the PCM for paying only lip service to internal democracy and criticized the party for what they saw as its excessive devotion to parliamentary activity at the expense of "mass work." They also denounced the party's uncritical and often incoherent incorporation of new issues, questions and members as "ideological dispersion." Although the *renovadores* were defeated in a formal sense, their challenge had met with considerable support within the party, and the public and often messy brawling (particularly at the PCM's XIX congress) had brought on a mood of demoralisation among many members. The discussions about a possible merger between the Coalition of the Left and the PMT in July and August 1981 provided a brilliant opportunity, therefore, to transcend the left's internal difficulties through the sketching out of a splendid vision of a united left political force.

In the end, the PMT did not reach agreement with the other left groups and it refused to join in the establishment of the PSUM. At the heart of the dispute was a serious clash over whether the new force would espouse the ideas of scientific socialism and employ the traditional emblems of the international socialist and communist movement. The PMT rejected both notions as it does not formally label itself a socialist party and is fiercely nationalist.[30] But behind these disagreements over matters of principle there lay a personality clash between the headstrong Castillo and the leaderships of the constituent groups of the Coalition of the Left, a reminder that the scourge of *caudillismo* afflicted the left as severely as it did other parts of the Mexican political spectrum.

The central preoccupation of the parties and groups involved in the merger was the need to create a "party of a new type."[31] The resonances of this term, borrowed from Lenin, clearly recall events in the classical age of Russian revolutionary Marxism. But forging a party of a new kind in Mexico in the early 1980s was no easy task, and it is far from having been achieved at the time of writing.

There were many obstacles in the way of the development of a united left party. The founders of the PSUM, for example, were highly conscious of the need to roll back the fragmentation of the left which the *Reforma Política* was encouraging. But old party and group loyalties (or "party patriotism" as it is termed in Italy) were difficult to erode, and the organic evolution of the PSUM suffered as a consequence.

In any case, the parties and groups which merged with the old PCM were not a completely representative cross section of socialist currents in Mexico. They all sprang from one of two traditions. They were either the product of earlier splits from the PCM (this is the case of the MAUS and the Revolutionary Socialist Party [PSR]) or were linked with the current of revolutionary nationalism or *lombardismo* with its faith in the anti-imperialist and socialist potential of the Mexican Revolution (the case with the MAP and the PPM). Moreover, all the merging parties, with the partial exception of the MAP, tended to have more "backward" and "stalinist" notions than the partially transformed and eurocommunized PCM. Attempts to incorporate parties to the "left" and "right" have not prospered. The PCM and later the PSUM failed to make headway in negotiations with the Trotskyist PRT, due in part to the opposition of groups still steeped in the anti-Trotskyist mythology of the 1930s and 1940s.[32]

On the "right" of the PSUM, the PMT of Heberto Castillo has not been able to reach an agreement on a merger with the new party, although talks have been held periodically ever since the disagreements of the summer and fall of 1981. Cooperation between the two parties has not been helped by the defection to the PSUM of a large number of key PMT figures (the best known being the railroad workers' leader and major activist in the 1958–1959 rail strikes, Demetrio Vallejo).[33] Moreover, the PMT's success in obtaining its electoral registration in 1984 and its modest success in the 1985 congressional elections (winning six seats) have reinforced its status as a "competitor" of the PSUM.

Attempts to extend the unification process further by incorporating other parties and tendencies have been similarly unsuccessful although the PSUM has developed very close relations with the Corriente Socialista and the Unidad de Izquierda Comunista (UIC). There was, though, some success in building a common Electoral Front (Plataforma Común Electoral) in the electoral campaign of 1985. The Front was endorsed by the PSUM, PPS and PST, although opposition from conservative elements prevented the alliance from incorporating the Trotskyist PRT.[34]

Finally, as we shall see later, the first years of the PSUM more or less coincided with the spectacular economic debacle of 1982–1985. If the PSUM was created amid the last moments of the oil-boom euphoria it was confronted almost immediately with the task of responding to the crisis of austerity and economic stabilization imposed after 1982. As though this were not challenge enough, there were also indications of a radical recomposition of Mexican politics away from the corporatist traditions of the Mexican Revolution. One could not imagine a more difficult conjuncture for the birth of any new political force.

A "Party of a New Type"?

A new party that is something more than a mere aggregation of the forces that it replaced has not yet fully emerged. A basic problem present from the very first days of the PSUM has been the uneven distribution of influence within the party. Since the Communist Party was clearly the biggest of the merging forces, the PSUM started its life with a generalized suspicion held by many members that the entire unification process was simply a device which would enable the former PCM to expand its authority under cover of a new party. This suspicion was later reinforced by the increased presence of ex-PCM figures in the PSUM's Central Committee elected at the party's second congress in 1983.

While these and other inter-group suspicions were partly the product of differences in policies, they were also caused by personalist rivalries and the tendency to see political parties as an extension of the personality of particular individuals. The case of the former PPM and its national leader Alejandro Gascón Mercado best illustrates this tendency. Gascón had built up over the years an impressive electoral and political base in the state of Nayarit where he had held several important positions including Mayor of the state capital; there were in fact very few examples within the PSUM of such strong regional nuclei of support.[35]

Gascón was also the major rival of Pablo Gómez, the PSUM Secretary-General, and it was painfully clear that he saw himself as a more suitable candidate for the office than the former PCM figure.[36] Various methods were used by representatives of the former PPM (the *ola verde* or green wave as they were popularly known) to get their way and they included such traditional sectarian tactics as trying to pack the Second Congress of the PSUM with its own delegates. After this tactic had failed Gascón issued several warnings that he might withdraw his forces from the PSUM, a threat which he finally carried out in February 1985.[37]

One of the key demands made by the ex-PPM elements was that the PSUM should return to a system which would allocate positions on its

Central Committee and Political Commission following a formula which would reward each of the merging parties on the basis of its pre-merger size. This was a highly retrograde step since in effect it would have institutionalized the tendency towards the survival of party patriotism in the new PSUM.[38] Meanwhile, slowly, and without much publicity, another of the founding parties, the PSR, also left the PSUM. Although the defectors did not by any means take with them all of the ex-PPM and PSR members the PSUM was a much weakened force on the eve of the congressional elections of July 1985.

The organic construction of the PSUM also exhibits a number of deficiencies. This is especially clear in the area of party finances. In line with the experience of most Mexican parties of the left, dues payment by members is very poor. In 1983, for example, 61 percent of the PSUM's total expenditure came from one source, the salaries (dietas) received by the party's deputies in Congress. Not surprisingly, therefore, the decision in 1984 by a number of deputies not to hand over their dietas to the party caused a good deal of alarm, as well as a major internal political scandal.[39]

Global membership figures for the PSUM show a doubling of militants between 1982 and the middle of 1984 with the party claiming a figure of 63,000 for the latter date.[40] Of these, nearly 37% percent, it was claimed, were wage workers in industry and agriculture and 29.4% were peasants. 10% of members were students while teachers and university workers made up another 8.7%. Approximately 27.5% of members were women with more than half being either wage workers or peasants.

Overall, these figures were rather disappointing for a new party which had aroused such great enthusiasm when it was launched at the end of 1981. Particularly striking was the relative newness of the PSUM's membership. Although there are no published figures on the previous political affiliations of current PSUM members, the evidence of senior party cadres points overwhelmingly to the conclusion that a large number of the members of the merging parties, particularly of the PCM, failed to join the PSUM. One must also assume that the departure of a large number of ex-PPM figures in early 1985 represented a signficant erosion of the party's base, especially in areas like Nayarit and Jalisco.

By the summer of 1984, however, the PSUM had at least laid down a basic organizational network throughout Mexico. Thirty-one state committees were in existence; the only state without one was Campeche in the southeast of the country. The quality and depth of organization, however, varies immensely from state to state. Something remotely resembling a "party of a new kind" is emerging in about eight states, Zacatecas, Durango, part of Chihuahua, Northern Sinaloa and Tamaulipas, Guerrero, Oaxaca and Chiapas. It is interesting to note that, with the exception of Sinaloa and Tamaulipas, these are not states in which the old PCM, the largest of the PSUM's founding members, was strong in the post-1950s period.[41]

These are also states which are predominantly peasant and several of them (Guerrero, Oaxaca and Chiapas) possess large Indian populations.

Quite what the significance of this latter factor is remains unclear but it is worth remembering that one of the most vigorous sources of union opposition to the state in recent years, the CNTE, or dissident section of the teachers union (SNTE), has received its strongest push precisely from these same regions (Oaxaca and Chiapas, in particular). Similarly, a large percentage of the municipal victories of the PCM/PSUM have been in strongly Indian oriented areas like Juchitán and Magdalena Ocotlán[42] (Oaxaca), Alcozauca (Guerrero); Papalotla (Tlaxcala) and several *municipios* in the state of Puebla like San José Miahuatlán which are Nahuatl speaking communities.[43]

Thus it would appear that where the structures of the merging parties, especially the old Communist Party, were weakest before the merger, the PSUM has been developing most smoothly. This seems eminently logical, given the difficulty the party has had in dissolving the identities of its founding groups. The great exception to this general conclusion is the Federal District and State of Mexico which have always been major centers of communist strength and which today also account for a very high percentage of the PSUM's electoral support (approximately eight to ten percent of the total votes cast in both the 1982 and 1985 elections).[44]

In some other states where the old Communist Party was strong, such as Yucatán, Puebla and Veracruz, many elements within the old leaderships of the PCM and PPM have been shunted aside and new cadres have emerged who are more committed to building the PSUM as a new political project. This has not been without its problems—the old guard has rarely yielded without a struggle.

There have been serious problems in important states like Jalisco where the leadership of the PSUM was initially in the hands of university figures associated with both the former PPM and the powerful Federation of Guadalajara Students (FEG).[45] The tension between Gascón Mercado and the PSUM leadership, and the withdrawal of many former PPM people from the party in early 1985, were responsible for the poor electoral performance of the PSUM in Jalisco in the July 1985 congressional elections. More seriously, in view of the PSUM's desire to become a *"partido de masas,"* there are also states with major concentrations of industrial workers where the PSUM is pathetically weak. The northeastern state of Nuevo León is the best example: only 650 members were affiliated by the middle of 1984.

The Electoral and Parliamentary Question

It is fair to say that the merger process and a large part of the energies of the PSUM have been driven by electoral considerations. The *Reforma Política* in this sense has, from the PRI's perspective, been successful in channelling much of the left's enthusiasm towards parliamentary and electoral activities. An examination of the electoral performance of the PSUM since 1981 does not, however, suggest that the early expectations of the PSUM have been fully realized.

In the 1979 congressional elections, the old Coalition of the Left won 703,000 votes (giving it 19 deputies) while in the presidential elections of 1982 the new PSUM won 905,000 votes (according to the officially recognized figures—although over two hundred thousand votes seem to have disappeared from the PSUM's total between the initial post-election announcements and publication of the final figures).[46] Taking into account the increase in the total number of votes cast, the PSUM appears to have obtained a smaller percentage of total votes in 1982 than it had done in 1979.[47]

This was a disappointing result since the PSUM was numerically a much larger party than the Coalition of the Left had been in 1979 and its creation had aroused enthusiasm among a large constituency of Mexicans who were heartened by the unusual sight of the left uniting rather than fragmenting its forces. On the other hand, the PSUM was being challenged for the first time by a second independent Marxist party, the Trotskyist PRT, which fielded as its presidential candidate the indomitable human rights campaigner Rosario Ibarra de Piedra.[48] Some of the PSUM's loss of votes can be explained by a leakage to the PRT which mounted a vigorous campaign of denunciation of economic and social injustice and human rights abuses which was considerably more radical and questioning of the regime than the PSUM's equally intense but more restrained efforts.

The 1985 congressional elections also had mixed results for the PSUM and demonstrated that three years of drastic austerity programs have not increased the influence of the Mexican left within the parliamentary arena. Although the number of independent left parties represented in the Chamber of Deputies was increased by two, the weight of the PSUM was substantially reduced. The party won 578,000 votes (3.24% of the total votes cast) giving it twelve deputies, a drop from the 17 it won in the 1982 presidential elections. As in previous contests, the PSUM polled most strongly in the Federal District where it won approximately 8% of the vote.[49]

The erosion of the PSUM's position undoubtedly had something to do with the party's internal squabbles and with the defection of much of the former PPM's contingent. It was also, however, connected with the emergence for the first time of two new electorally viable (they were both newly registered) parties of the left, the Trotskyite PRT and the PMT, each of which received six seats.[50] There are now more self-styled socialist parties represented in Congress in Mexico than in any other Latin American legislature. In addition to the three independents (PSUM, PRT and PMT) there are two members of the "loyal opposition," the PPS and PST, which identify with the revolutionary nationalism of the official party.

Thus the elections have also confirmed that the ruling PRI has lost none of its political skills in handling the opposition. By registering two additional parties it succeeded in substantially expanding the range of left options open to the electorate while at the same time increasing competition among the forces of the left and weakening the dominance of the PSUM.

At the regional level, the PSUM has obtained deputies under proportional representation in twelve states—with a total of 28 local deputies by the end of 1984.[51] It also won six town councils (*ayuntamientos*) (Zaragoza in Chihuahua, Alcozauca in Guerrero, Juchitán in Oaxaca which was stolen from the PSUM-COCEI alliance in 1983 in a brutal show of government force, and a number of small *municipios* in Puebla state). In 1984 the PSUM could also boast 162 councillors (*regidores*).

Although the PSUM is the third party in Mexico in electoral terms, it has not been able to duplicate the PAN's success in posing a serious threat to the hegemony of the PRI in particular areas of the country. In numerical terms its performance represents little more than a drop in the ocean. The PSUM's overall percentage share of the votes cast in the states in which there were elections in 1983 was a tiny 2.86%. The highest figures it achieved in state elections in 1983 under the proportional representation system was 6.94% of total votes (Sinaloa) while its normal performance fluctuated between 1.4 and 3.7%. Its electoral success in the federal sphere was very much of the same order.

It would be unwise, however, to conclude that the PSUM's electoral efforts have been universally unsatisfactory. As the party discovered in its electoral campaign in 1982, the LOPPE and formal registration gave it a unique opportunity to reach millions of Mexicans who had previously been beyond the reach of socialist propaganda. The campaign was also used to improve the PSUM's still very shaky organizational structure. All in all, the 1982 national *gira* of PSUM presidential candidate, Arnoldo Martínez Verdugo, which concluded in a magnificent rally in the Zócalo of Mexico City (the first time since 1968 that this nerve-center of the capital had been used by the left) was an extraordinary logistical achievement for the young party.[52]

Economic Crisis and Austerity

The economic crisis has paralyzed the PSUM as it has done broad sectors of the left and popular movements. Since the beginning of the acute phase of the crisis in 1982 there have been surprisingly few major challenges to Mexico's political and economic system either from parties of the left or from the organized working class and urban popular movements. In contrast, the opportunities opened up by the economic debacle appear to have been mostly seized by the right or, less clearly, by sectors of the ruling party and state apparatus.[53]

The state bureaucracy and certain sectors of the PRI have tried to take advantage of the crisis in order to implement a new politico-economic project, radically opposed to the populist and statist tradition bequeathed by the *cardenista* social pact of the mid-1930s. The new project embraces many of the postulates of economic liberalism—an end to the so-called "fictional economy," price liberalization and cuts in subsidies. It also involves a commitment to a liberal recomposition of Mexico's political system centering on greater openness to the opposition and an erosion of the crucial mediating role of mass organizations. In neither of these cases are the trends entirely free of contradictions. This is especially true of the latter where the ferocious repression unleashed against the PSUM/COCEI alliance's control over Juchitán in 1983, and the continuation of electoral fraud throughout the country, gave the lie to much of the pluralist and "moral renewal" rhetoric of the De la Madrid government.

It is unfortunate, therefore, that the bold steps in the direction of greater unity on the left should have coincided with the country's worst ever economic crisis and with the signs of a radical shift in the direction of the Mexican polity. These two developments exacerbated the difficulties that are inherent in any unification exercise. They pushed the left onto the defensive, and tended to exacerbate age-old disputes over definitions of the character of the regime and of the Mexican state, and over how the left, and particularly the PSUM, should respond to the government's violent economic stabilization policies.

As a result, the left has been submerged in endless debate over the relative merits of different projects. These include limited cooperation with austerity measures in order to force a fair division of the burden; a willingness to exploit fissures appearing within the political bureaucracy and leadership of the mass organizations in order to establish "convergencias" between the left and displaced elements; and a policy of frontal opposition to the regime and its socio-economic program. In addition, the left has only had limited success in reaching agreement on the issue of how far it should link its struggle against austerity measures and for the defense of popular living standards to a program of demands for an *alternative* economic strategy. Only on the issue of foreign debt has the crisis produced near unanimity among the PSUM and the other sectors of the "independent" and "loyal" left.[54]

In the immediate aftermath of the bank nationalization of September 1982, much of the left, in particular sections of the PSUM, were caught up in a mood of euphoria over what some claimed to be the demise of finance capital in Mexico and a "break with the ruling class."[55] The bold move of the López Portillo government in its last months appeared to strengthen the arguments and positions of the powerful "revolutionary nationalism" current within the left, represented within the PSUM by the former MAP, and by sections of the old PCM. This tendency with its strongly statist and populist orientation to socialist issues had been increasingly marginalized within the old Communist Party, but was greatly strengthened by the formation of the PSUM.

Shortly after the nationalization, Arnaldo Córdova, a PSUM deputy and one of the founders of the MAP, provoked strong reactions from within and outside the party when he praised the López Portillo administration for pursuing domestic policies which were congruent with the progressive line it was maintaining in foreign affairs, especially around Central America.[56] Córdova was saluting what he and other MAP theoreticians considered a victory of the "national-popular" current over the "neo-liberals" within the eternal Struggle for the Nation (*Disputa por la nación*) waged during the Mexican Revolution.[57]

The dramatic demonstration of the Mexican state's strength and "relative autonomy" during the bank nationalization episode was interpreted as proof that a national and popular resolution of the economic crisis was possible. It also seemed to confirm the view that the left's goal was to intervene actively to promote further and deeper political and economic reforms in the tradition of the radical nationalism and populism of the Mexican Revolution. Such reforms could be facilitated, it was argued, by the inevitable appearance of more and more points of "convergence" between the left and reformist elements within the mass organizations (eg. CTM, CNC) which gave sustenance to the *cardenista* social pact, but which were being crudely displaced by the neo-liberal and technocratic project of the De la Madrid government.[58]

The position espoused by MAP figures like Rolando Cordera and Arnaldo Córdova, both within and outside of the PSUM, was challenged by other forces on the left, which denied the possibility of a democratic resolution of the crisis within the framework of Mexico's peculiar model of capitalist accumulation and "mass politics." Particular concern was expressed at the way in which the nationalization euphoria had led some PSUM figures like Rolando Cordera to propose policies of "austerity with compensation" (*austeridad con compensación*), an idea that owes something to the Italian Communist Party's policies in the early 1970s.[59]

The tension between these two different positions was demonstrated with particular clarity by the establishment of two broad anti-austerity organizations at the end of 1981, FNDSCAC and CNDEP.[60] FNDSCAC was the broadest of the two, but was criticized by the PSUM for its narrowly economistic and *gremialista* outlook, and for giving excessive weight to calls for mass mobilization. Its activism, so the PSUM argued, was at the cost of a more balanced campaign which would involve agitation for an alternative left political economy. Although the PSUM and affiliated unions like SUTIN participated in FNDSCAC's activities, most of their efforts were directed towards the CNDEP.[61]

In turn, the organizations and forces represented in FNDSCAC accused their opponents of harboring illusions about the possibility of democratizing and modernizing capitalism, and of ignoring the necessity for rallying mass opposition to government assaults on popular living standards. Implicit in this critique of the PSUM's early responses was a condemnation of the way in which the *Reforma Política* had caused the PSUM to emphasize parliamentary activities at the expense of mass work. This critique of "parliamentarism" was also shared by an important current within the PSUM itself. Fortunately, the tension between the two anti-austerity fronts was quickly resolved by their merger in June 1983. The subsequent creation of the ANOCP signalled the inauguration of a new tactic of popular protest, the *paros cívicos*.

While the dispute between FNSDCAC and CNDEP was quickly resolved, the tension between the tendencies each represented—political negotiation for a popular solution to the crisis—and frontal assaults on the state through constant mass mobilization—continued to wrack the left. In the summer of 1983, the PSUM issued its alternative economic strategy for dealing with the crisis. Its National Development Plan was concerned to show that there was an alternative strategy for coping with the crisis which was not destructive of the human and physical resources of the nation and which established as its principal goal the satisfaction of the basic social needs of the majority of the population.

The Plan called for a reorientation of Mexico's fiscal and productive apparatus towards the broadening of the domestic market, redistribution of wealth, and a reordering of priorities in the field of public investment. As in previous economic programs the PSUM called for radical tax reform, the imposition of exchange controls, the indexing of wages in line with inflation (the *escala móvil*), the introduction of unemployment insurance and greater support for small and medium-sized businesses.

The language of the Plan echoed the concerns of both competing projects outlined above. On the one hand, it expressed hopes that the Plan would act to promote convergence between sectors interested in radical democratic change, and it repeated the familiar anti-monopoly and left-Keynesian recipes of the Mexican left. On the other hand, it called for direct worker control over public enterprises and for a break with the development models followed since the 1940s.[62] The Plan and other economic pronouncements of the PSUM were clearly designed to win the support of as broad a segment of the "popular and anti-monopoly" constituency as possible. But if previous experience is any indication such moderation runs the risk of the left "having its clothes" stolen by the government and organizations like the Congress of Labor.[63]

If the PSUM's National Development Plan tried to have it both ways, the party's Second National Congress in August 1983 inaugurated a marked radicalization of the PSUM's political stance, at least at the level of rhetoric. Gone were the references to *convergencia* and the possibility of implementing a different state economic policy even within the framework of austerity programs. In its place was an emphasis on the necessity of promoting and deepening everyday struggles of the people by incorporating the energies not only of traditional socialist forces but of new mass organizations forged in the heat of the anti-austerity battles.[64]

The radicalization of the party's attitude towards the state's economic and political policies was the product of a political alliance between certain sections of the old PCM and the forces of Gascón Mercado. Nevertheless, while these two tendencies were united in their determination to intensify the "oppositionist" stance of the PSUM, the alliance did not embrace a common platform on ideological questions. On issues such as feminism and the civil rights of the Church, the *gasconistas* parted company with former PCM figures like Enrique Semo. The sharp radicalization of the PSUM's language, combined with the Congress' reversal of previous policies on women, the civil rights of clergy and youth questions, evoked worried responses by proponents of gradualist and parliamentary paths to socialism like Roger Bartra, the leading figure in one of the two eurocommunist currents within the party.[65] Subsequent events would show, however, that the PSUM's radicalization was more form than substance.

An examination of the Mexican state's response to the issues debated by the left provides little evidence to support the more optimistic scenarios outlined by the proponents of revolutionary nationalism. In spite of the drastic assault on its legitimacy and perquisites, the leadership of the *oficialista* mass organizations showed little interest in *convergencia* with their left-wing critics. At the same time the PRI continued to practice its traditional policies of cooptation and divide and rule in its dealings with the left. In 1982 it gave the PRT its *registro* and two years later, in the summer of 1984, it granted the PMT its electoral registration.

The PSUM and Mass Organizations

The PSUM aspires, as we have seen, to become a mass party and not a mere "party of cadres." It has also firmly committed itself to a path which eschews dogma and sectarianism and aims for a radical democratization of Mexican society. These aspirations necessarily confront the PSUM with the age-old project of the left to secure the autonomy and internal democratization of the mass organizations of workers and peasants which play such a crucial role in the corporativist structure of Mexico.

The party's resources in the labor and peasant area are not insignificant. It has inherited much of the experience and influence of its predecessors in the PCM, MAP and to a lesser extent the PPM. The PSUM now has a somewhat stronger team of union organizers than the PCM had in 1981, and it has benefited not only from the skills of ex-MAP people like Antonio Gerschenson and Arturo Whaley but also from the talents of older and more experienced men like Demetrio Vallejo, Angel Reyna Menchaca and a number of skilled organizers in the Teachers Union SNTE.[66] The situation is less clear in the area of peasant organization. The PCM brought to the new party its long standing relationship with the rural work force, most clearly seen today in the activities of the Independent Confederation of Agricultural Workers and Peasants (Central Independiente de Obreros Agricolas y Campesinos, CIOAC). On the other hand, the conflicts around the demands of the PPM forces in the party weakened the PSUM's links with the PPM-affiliated General Union of Mexican Workers and Peasants-Red Wing, (Unión General de Obreros y Campesinos-Roja, UGOCM-Roja).

Labor and peasant organizations remain, however, tricky and dangerous terrain for parties of the independent left. The *Reforma Política* was aimed at changing the country's electoral system and in no way attempted to modify the sensitive linkages between the mass organizations and the state. Thus official tolerance for the left's parliamentary and electoral actions does not extend to its activities within worker and peasant organizations, especially those which are tied to the *oficialista* federations.

Secondly, during the economic crisis, oppositional currents within the union movement have suffered a number of defeats. Several of these currents were closely tied to the PSUM. In addition to the nuclear workers of the SUTIN, whose fate has already been detailed, the PSUM has taken a beating in another important center of democratic unionism, the STUNAM, an organization of university workers at the National Autonomous University (UNAM). Here, though, it has been divisions within the left (particularly between conflicting currents within the PSUM and between the PSUM and rival left factions), rather than government actions, which have been responsible for the union's impotence.[67]

Conclusion

"El que con el Estado se acuesta, con lombardo se levanta."[68]

Four years is not a long time in the life of a new political party and it is probably too early to reach definitive judgments on the success or failure of the PSUM project during such a short period. In any case the task of building a democratic and autonomous political force in Mexico (let alone one that is also revolutionary and socialist!) is an extraordinarily brave and bold one.

As has often been pointed out, conditions in Mexico do not favor the development of parties which rely heavily on counter-hegemonic strategies and parliamentary tactics. Civil society has been greatly impoverished by the growth of an over-mighty state, itself the most visible achievement of the Mexican Revolution. Furthermore, congress has been traditionally weak and ineffective in the face of a powerful and even despotic presidency; since the 1910 Revolution, the federal legislature has been largely impotent, with the exception of a brief period from 1911 to 1913 and during the 1920s. In the Chamber of Deputies itself, the odds are clearly and crudely stacked against opposition parties. These factors and frequent state repression have combined with the Mexican left's lingering anti-state consciousness (derived from its powerfully anarchist and syndicalist heritage) to limit rank and file enthusiasm for parliamentary activity.

The unfortunate conjuncture of a severe economic crisis which put the left as a whole on the defensive, and the emergence of the PSUM unification project has also created obstacles in the way of the new party. What opposition there has been to the politics of austerity has tended to be channelled not towards national *political* parties but into more spontaneous *social* movements of a local variety. The PSUM has so far been unable to connect in a permanent fashion with these newer forms of popular action.

More seriously, the PSUM has sent out ambiguous signals about its attitude towards the changed conditions of lives of many Mexicans and towards the new social movements which have arisen in the wake of these changes. Some of the forces represented within the PSUM, for example, abhor any discussion of specifically feminist politics. Since representatives of the old PPM, MAUS and PSR considered feminism outside the traditional labor-capital struggle, it was not surprising to see the PSUM reject a resolution at its 1983 Congress which described the party as feminist and echoed the PCM's earlier support for an independent women's movement.[69] Moreover, the PSUM's seventy-five members Central Committee elected at the Congress included only four women, three of whom were former members of the PCM.[70]

Overall, the PSUM's political discourse still centers around the question of the relationship between party and state, the age-old problematic of the Mexican left. It is here that the depth of the economic crisis may be having its most negative impact. The obsession with the topic of *convergencias*, intermittent and heavily contested though it might be, suggests that the party still harbors illusions about the viability of the revolutionary nationalist project which has such a long pedigree in Mexican politics. One of the costs of unity may have been the strengthening of these illusions.

The PSUM appears now to be wavering between the option of promoting a "popular and democratic solution to the crisis of capitalism" and the posing of solutions which challenge the very structure of Mexican capitalism itself. Thus far the weight of the party's rhetoric and actions is clearly inclined towards the first option. But by urging the former path the PSUM runs the risk of being handmaiden to the strengthening of a populist and authoritarian state which may promote "progressive" measures but which cannot eradicate the anti-democratic features so central to its corporativist heart.

Notes

1. A prime case of this return to legal political activity is the involvement of Gustavo Hirales in the PCM and then the PSUM. Hirales, a former member of the urban-based armed front, the 23rd of September Communist League, has written an account of several movements involved in the armed struggles in Gustavo Hirales, "La Guerra secreta, 1970–1978," *Nexos*, No. 54 (June 1982): 34–42.

2. On the rise of urban popular movements, see the special issue of *Nueva Antropológia* devoted to the topic. *Nueva Antropológia*, vol. VI, no. 24 (June 1984).

3. ANOCP arose out of two organizations, the National Front in Defense of Wages Against Austerity and Measures in the Cost of Living (Frente Nacional de Defensa del Salario Contra la Austeridad y lo Carestia, FNDSCAC) and the National Committee for Defense of the Popular Economy (Comité Nacional de Defensa de la Economia Popular, CNDEP) that were established in 1982 to confront the austerity crisis. The fusion of these two rival organizations was itself a sign of disunity overcome. ANOCP is made up of more than 100 left organizations.

4. On CNPA see "V Encuentro Nacional de Organizaciones Campesinas Independientes," *Pueblo*, ano V, no. 96 (July 1982).

5. Guillermo Corea, "La marcha rechazó oportunismos," *Proceso*, no. 389, April 16, 1984, 28–33.

6. "El pueblo se organiza" and "Balance de la Jornada y el PCN de la ANOCP," *Pueblo*, ano VI, nos. 110–111 (November-December 1983): 3–8.

7. "Documentos Básicos de la ANOCP" and "Síntesis Informativa del Primer Paro Cívico Nacional," *Espacios,* no. 3, May-July 1984, 38–47; 56–57; Manuel Aguilar Mora, "Balance del II Paro Cívico," *Uno Más Uno,* June 13, 1984, 3.

8. Barry Carr, "The Mexican Economic Debacle and the Labor Movement: A New Era or More of the Same?" in Donald L. Wyman, ed., *Mexico's Economic Crisis: Challenges and Opportunities* (La Jolla, CA: Center for U.S. Mexican Studies, University of California, San Diego, 1983), 91–116.

9. Salvador Corro, "Por castigar al SUTIN, Escofet reniega de su proyecto nuclear," *Proceso,* no. 348, July 4, 1983, 20–25.

10. See the interview with Arturo Whaley in *Solidaridad,* December 1980, 6.

11. On the history of the PCM see, Karl M. Schmitt, *Communism in Mexico: A Study in Political Frustration* (Austin, TX: University of Texas Press, 1965); Manuel Márquez Fuentes and Octavio Rodríguez Araujo, *El Partido Comunista Mexicano* (México: Ediciones "El Caballito," 1973); Arnoldo Martínez Verdugo, *Historia del comunismo en México* (México: Grijalbo, 1985).

12. Barry Carr, "Mexican Communism 1968–1983; Eurocommunism in the Americas," *Journal of Latin American Studies,* vol. 17, part 1 (May 1985): 201–228.

13. Antonio Franco, Gilberto Rincón Gallardo and Pablo Gómez, "Acerca de la dictadura del proletariado," *Socialismo* 2:6 (1976).

14. Christopher Domínguez, "Conversación con Roger Bartra: Leña del arbol de la utopia," *Buscón,* no. 10, 1984: 26–45. Bartra's political essays have been published in two volumes, *El reto de la izquierda* (México: Ed. Grijalbo, 1982) and *Las redes imaginarias del poder político* (México: Ed. Era, 1981).

15. Roger Bartra has been the bitterest critic of the revival of stalinist currents (disguised as *lombardismo*) within the PSUM and has attacked the party for its failure to engage critically with the errors of the Cuban and Nicarguan revolutions. Domínguez, "Conversación con Roger Bartra," 36–41.

16. Octavio Rodríguez Araujo, *La reforma política y los partidos en México* (México: Siglo Vientiuno, 1979), 231–234.

17. Miguel Angel Granados Chapa, *La reforma política* (México: Universidad Autonoma Metropolitana-Azcapotzalco, 1982), 25–45.

18. *Mexico en el capitalismo y ante el socialismo: informe de Alejandro Gascón Mercado, Secretario-general del Comité Central del Partido del Pueblo Mexicano al Primer Congreso Extraordinario* (Oaxtepec, 1980). "Lombardismo" is explored in Lourdes Quintanilla Obregón, *Lombardismo y sindicatos en América Latina* (México Ediciones Nueva Sociología, 1982) and Roger Bartra, *El reto,* 177–193.

19. For a detailed and moving account of what the Galván tradition signifies see the special issue of *Solidaridad* published on his death. *Soldiaridad,* Número Extraordinario, September 27, 1980.

20. Movimiento de Acción Política, *Tésis y programa* (México, 1980).

21. Arnaldo Córdova, "Nación y nacionalismo en México," *Nexos,* no. 83, (November 1984): 27–33.

22. The best-known spokesman for the MAUS was the veteran communist Miguel Angel Velasco, one of the PCM's earliest militants and a prominent figure in the party's leadership until his expulsion in 1943.

23. Partido Comunista Mexicano, Movimiento de Acción y Unidad Socialista, Partido Mexicano de Trabajadores, Partido Socialista Revolucionario, Partido del Pueblo Mexicano, *Un solo partido por la democracia y el socialismo* (Mexico, no date or place of publication).

24. Octavio Rodríguez Araujo, "Preguntas a Heberto Castillo," *Uno Más Uno,* August 20, 1981, 20. Heberto Castillo himself notes the surprise of delegates to the

PMT's Second Extraordinary National Convention when the news of the merger was announced. Heberto Castillo, "Sorpresa, entusiasmo, socialismo," *Proceso*, no. 251, August 24, 1981, 34.

25. For a criticism of the merger process by a leading PCM figure, see Rodolfo Echeverría Martínez, "Carta de renuncia: el PSUM no es un partido nuevo" (México: Circulo José Revueltas, no date). The author's impression that a large number of communists failed to join the new party was confirmed by speakers such as Arnaldo Córdova, Valentín Campa and Rodolfo Echeverría (el Chicali) at a public meeting of the PSUM in the Casa de la Cultura del Periodista on January 21, 1983.

26. *Coalición de Izquierda: su presencia en la cámara* (México: Ediciones del Comité Central, 1981).

27. The Mexican Workers Party was founded in 1974 by Heberto Castillo and Demetrio Vallejo. Heberto Castillo and Francisco J. Paoli, *El Poder robado* (México: Edamex, 1980). On Heberto Castillo, see Jorge Sotomayor, "Seguire lunchando," *Razones*, no. 43, August 24–September 6, 1981, 12–14.

28. The Federal Electoral Commission denied the PMT's application for conditional registration on May 15. Heberto Castillo, "Fé y confianza, pero en la nación," *Proceso*, no. 246, July 20, 1981, 31–32; "La mancuerna PCM-H Castillo," *Razones*, No. 43, August 24–September 1981, 7–8.

29. The name of the current was a reference to an open letter titled "For the renewal of Mexican Communist Party" which the *renovadores* published in the Mexican press in December 1980. *Por la renovación del Partido Comunista Mexicana: prolegómenos de un debate* (México, 1981).

30. Heberto Castillo, "Aclarando posiciones sobre la fusión," published in five parts in *Proceso* during November and December 1981.

31. Author's interview with Gilberto Rincón Gallardo, Mexico City, January 1983. See also, *La creación del PSUM* (México: Ediciones del Comité Central, 1982), 32–38.

32. The fiercest opposition to any form of cooperation with the Trotskyists came from the forces of the PPM and MAUS.

33. *Proceso*, no. 331, March 7, 1983, 6–11.

34. This has not prevented the PSUM from entering into alliances with Trotskyites and others at the state level as, for example, in the November 1984 state elections in the State of Mexico.

35. Gascón claimed in 1984 that the PSUM had 15,000 militants in Nayarit of whom 12,000 were members of party units. *Así Es*, no. 96, March 5, 1984, 20.

36. Gómez was typical of the newcomers who joined the PCM after the student-popular movement of 1968. Having joined the Communist Youth in 1963, Pablo Gómez became one of the leaders of the student movement (1966-1969) and a member of the National Strike Council at the National University (UNAM) in 1968. After spending three years as a political prisoner, he resumed his activities in the PCM, attaining membership of the party's Central Committee in 1972 and the Political Commission in 1977. He was elected a member of the Chamber of Deputies in 1979.

37. Gascón and the nucleus of former members of the PPM who followed him out of the PSUM later established the Party of the Socialist Revolution (PRS).

38. For a brief period (November 1981 to February 1982) positions on the Central Committee were allocated in this fashion. At the new party's first congress (February 1982) leadership positions were filled on a one-delegate-one-vote basis.

39. The *dietas* represented a significant financial gain for the party especially after the salary of a *diputado* went up to 300,000 pesos in 1983, representing an increase of over 300 percent.

40. In September 1984 there were also an additional 7,000 membership applications awaiting processing. *Hacer del PSUM un gran partido de masas: Documentos de la Conferencia Nacional de Organización (16 al 18 de agosto de 1984) y del VII Pleno del CC (8 y 9 de septiembre de 1984)* (México: Ediciones de Comité Central, 1984), 13–14.

41. Before the World War II, the PCM had enjoyed some influence in areas of Chiapas and the party continued to enjoy significant support among peasant *ejidatarios* in the Laguna areas of Durango well into the fifties.

42. The PSUM-COCEI (Coalition of Isthmus Workers, Peasants and Students) control of the Juchitán town council was overturned in August 1983 and army and police forces brutally expelled *coceistas* from the town hall in November of the same year.

43. San José Miahuatlán is a small community of 15,000 people in which the worst traditions of rural caciquismo are the rule. Numerous militants of the PSUM have been assassinated in the region including four in September 1984. The key issue for many of the region's poor inhabitants is access to water and this was a cause which the PSUM embraced with enthusiasm in 1982–1983 prior to winning the *ayuntamiento* in November 1983. The four victims made a total of 36 PSUM members who have been killed during the governorship of Jiménez Morales, *Así Es*, no. 95, February 27, 1984, 11.

44. In 1982, for example, the PSUM obtained 9.2% of the total vote cast in the D.F. compared with 27% for the conservative Party of National Action (PAN). In the same elections the PSUM obtained 150,000 votes (16.5% of the total votes obtained by the PSUM) in the State of Mexico. The latest figures on membership show that there are 4,326 members of the PSUM living in the D.F and 6,000 in the State of Mexico, *Así Es*, no. 125, November 2, 1984, 24.

45. The FEG holds anti-imperialist and radical nationalist positions, but its leading figures are closely involved in the PRI-dominated political establishment of Jalisco. The FEG members of the PSUM in Guadalajara introduced many of the dubious practices of this world into the new party. "Jalisco: en defensa del proyecto PSUM," *Así Es*, no. 128, December 21, 1984, 17–19.

46. The PRT also appears to have "lost" votes during the counting process. This development was linked to the government's concern to deny its seats in the Congress to which it was probably entitled.

47. On the PSUM's loss of votes see *Di*, no. 87, August 1982, 33 and Miguel Angel Granados Chapa, Elke Knöppen and Pablo González Casanova, "Las elecciones de 1982" in Pablo González Casanova, *Las elecciones en México: evolución y perspectivas* (México: Siglo XXI, 1985), 201. See also, Nuria Fernández, "La izquierda mexicana en las elecciones," *Cuadernos Políticos*, no. 33, (July–September 1982): 45–58.

48. Rosario Ibarra de Piedra is the leading figure in the campaign against political repression, torture and the "disappearances" of political activists in Mexico. She was the founder of the National Committee for the Defense of Prisoners, the Persecuted, the Disappeared and Political Exiles which undertook campaigns around the fate of the participants (including her own son) in the armed struggle movements of the early 1970s. Later she helped found the National Front Against Repression (FNCR).

49. The elections were preceded by the dramatic kidnapping on July 1 of the former Secretary-General of the Communist Party, Arnoldo Martínez Verdugo, now a PSUM deputy in the new congress. The kidnappers allegedly were members of the Poor People's Party (*Partido de los Pobres*), one of the best-known guerrilla groups active in the state of Guerrero in the early 1970s. After being held for

seventeen days, Martínez Verdugo was released on payment of a ransom of 100 million pesos representing, so it was claimed, the money (plus interest!) given to the former PCM for safe-keeping by the guerrillas over twelve years earlier after they had kidnapped the wealthy Guerrero state governor, Ruben Figueroa. The affair was given considerable publicity by the Mexican press and clearly embarrassed the PSUM. Since the Party of the Poor no longer exists, observers were left wondering whether the incident was a maneuver by the security forces aimed at damaging the left's electoral chances.

50. The PRT had already received its *registro* following the 1982 presidential elections. It was denied any deputies, however, during these same elections.

51. Local deputies elected under the proportional representation schemes in 1983 were as follows: Sinaloa (3), Zacatecas (1), Durango (2), Baja California Norte (1), Baja California Sur (1), Veracruz (1), Michoacán (1), Guerrero (1), Oaxaca (1), Puebla (1).

52. For a lively account of the *gira* see Rogelio Hernández and Roberto Rock, *Zócalo rojo* (México: Ediciones Oceano, 1982). Martínez Verdugo's speeches during the campaign have been published as *El proyecto socialista: selección de discursos de la marcha por la democracia, junio de 1982* (México: Ediciones del Comite Central, 1983).

53. Nora Hamilton, "State-Class Alliances and Conflicts; Issues and Actors in the Mexican Economic Crisis," *Latin American Perspectives*, issue 43, vol. 11, no. 4, (Fall 1984): 6–32.

54. In mid-November 1985, representatives from twelve left-wing parties and groups met to elaborate a plan of joint action and to discuss a possible long-term unity pact. *Uno Más Uno*, November 13, 1985, 6.

55. For a discussion of the left's responses to the bank nationalization from an ultra-left perspective see Carlos Morera Camacho, "La izquierda y la nacionalización de la banca," *Teoría y política*, año IV, no. 9, (April–June 1982): 143–168.

56. "Debate en el CC," *Así Es*, no. 36, October 8–14, 1982, 12–15. For Córdova's views on the nationalization and other topics, see the interview with him in *Crítica Política*, November 15, 1982, 17–23. A small minority on the party's Central Committee reserved judgment on the long-term significance of the bank nationalization issue. See the arguments of Enrique Semo, "Donde quedó la nación?" *El Buscón*, no. I, November-December 1982, 22–23.

57. This was a reference to a key text of the revolutionary nationalist position written by a leading PSUM economist, Rolando Cordera, and former government minister, Carlos Tello, which appeared in 1981. Rolando Cordera and Carlos Tello, *México: la disputa por la nación. Perspectivas y opciones del desarrollo* (México: Siglo XXI, 1981). A good critique of the Tello-Cordera approach can be found in Wayne Olsen, "Crisis and Change in Mexico's Political Economy," *Latin American Perspectivas*, issue 46, vol. 12, no. 3, (Summer 1985): 7–28.

58. In its conclusions, the January 1984 plenum of the PSUM noted increasing evidence of "the struggle between the bureaucracy and the public officials, especially the so-called populists, who have been displaced." *Uno Más Uno*, January 27, 1984.

59. This controversial position was modified soon after during second congress of the PSUM in 1983.

60. For the manifestos of FNDSCAC and CNDEP, see *Pueblo*, ano VI, no. 103, March 1983, 9–15.

61. René Bejarano, "En el camino de la ANOCP: PSUM y movimiento de masas," *Espacios*, no. 3, May–July 1984, 97–100; José Luis Hernández, "La ANOCP, va," *Espacios*, no. 3, May–July 1984, 82–89.

62. Oscar Hinojosa, "Plan alterno del PSUM: producir lo básico y gravar a los ricos," *Proceso*, no. 345, June 13, 1983, 26–27.

63. On this point, see Carr, *Mexican Communism*, 23.

64. Gustavo Hirales, "La radicalización del PSUM," *Así Es*, no. 73, July 29–August 4, 1983; "Restauración y modernización," *Así Es*, no. 81, September 23–29, 1983.

65. Roger Bartra, "Un no a la política, un sí al activismo," *Así Es*, no. 78, September 2–8, 1983. At the level of ideology and politics there has been some backsliding by the PSUM, especially on those issues where the old PCM had made the greatest strides in ridding itself of dogmatism, sectarianism and jacobinism. The key issues here were Poland (in the first year), women and youth matters (the issue of autonomy) and the civil rights of the clergy (discussed at the second congress of the party). On the party's internal conflict over the Polish state of emergency and the role of Solidarity, see the comments of Manuel Stephens García and José Woldenberg, *Así Es*, no. 1, January 28–February 4, 1982, 16.

66. Angel Reyna Menchaca left the PCM in 1954 and became a leading figure in the Revolutionary Labor Confederation (Confederación Obrera Revolucionaria, COR.)

67. María Esther Ibarra, "La presencia del PSUM divide al STUNAM ante las proximas elecciones," *Proceso*, February 27, 1984, 24–25; *Uno Más Uno*, March 25, 1984, 1.

68. "Those who go to bed with the State—in the morning alongside Lombardo awake." This aphorism was collected by Hector Aguilar Camín in the aftermath of the bank nationalization of September 1982. Hector Aguilar Camín, "Memorias de una expropriación," *Nexos*, no. 58 (October 1982), 27.

69. The party's resolution on women was published in *Así Es*, no. 70, July 8–14, 1983, 8. The resolution was modified to remove references to the PSUM as a feminist party. See Alba Martínez Olive, "Feminismo en el PSUM? Doble opresión, doble militancia," *Así Es*, no. 78, September 2–8, 1983.

70. The 1983 Congress also rejected the document on youth matters, which championed the autonomy of youth organizations and openly discussed such issues as sexual politics. For a rank-and-file response to the debates on youth questions, see the letter by Lohengrín Martínez Flores, *Así Es*, no. 86, October 28–November 3, 1983.

About the Contributors

John Bailey (Ph.D., University of Wisconsin) is associate professor of government at Georgetown University and adjunct chairman of the Advanced Area Seminar on Mexico of the State Department's Foreign Service Institute. He has written on interest groups and policymaking in the fields of agriculture, public finance, and education. A recent publication is "Politics and Agricultural Trade Policy in the Western Hemisphere: Trends and Issues in the 1980's," in F. LaMond Tullis and D. Ladd Hollist, eds., *Food, the State and International Political Economy*. His recent work on Mexico includes essays on government-business relations and on the PRI, published in Roderic A. Camp, ed., *Mexican Political Stability: The Next Five Years* (Boulder, Colo.: Westview Press, 1986). Professor Bailey is currently completing *Governing Mexico, 1976–88: The Statecraft of Crisis Management*.

Miguel Basáñez is a graduate of the UNAM Law School, the University of Warwick, England (public administration), and the London School of Economics (political science). He has taught law and Mexican politics at UNAM and currently teaches at the University of the State of Mexico. He is the author of *La lucha por la hegemonía en México, 1968–80* (Mexico City: Siglo XXI, 1980) and of several articles on Mexican politics. Basáñez was also recently attorney general of the State of Mexico.

Roderic A. Camp, director of Latin American Studies at Central College, Pella, Iowa, has engaged in field research on Mexico since 1966. A former Fulbright scholar to Mexico, Camp has been a visiting researcher at the Colegio de México and fellow at the Woodrow Wilson Center for International Scholars, Smithsonian Institution. He is the author of numerous articles and books on Mexico, and his most recent work is *Intellectuals and the State in Twentieth Century Mexico*. Current research interests include Mexican entrepreneurs as well as the military.

Barry Carr is senior lecturer in history and chairman of the Institute of Latin American Studies at La Trobe University, Melbourne, Australia. His research has dealt with the history of the Mexican workers' movement, labor-state relations, the regional history of the Mexican Revolution, the impact of austerity and economic stabilization on the Mexican labor movement

1982–1986, and most recently, the development of Marxism and communism in Mexico. His publications on these subjects include *El movimiento obrero y la politica en Mexico, 1910–1929* (México: Ediciones Era, 1981) and numerous articles on the history of the Mexican Communist Party. He is the editor of a collection of original essays by Mexican scholars and political organizers, *The Mexican Left, the Popular Movement and the Politics of Austerity, 1982–1984.*

Wayne A. Cornelius is the Gildred Professor of Political Science and director of the Center for U.S.-Mexican Studies at the University of California-San Diego. He is also president of the Latin American Studies Association. He has lived and done field research in Mexico for a total of more than four years and has specialized in studies of Mexican politics, urbanization in Mexico, and Mexican labor migration to the United States. His publications include *Politics and the Migrant Poor in Mexico City* and *Politics in Mexico.*

Judith Gentleman is an assistant professor of political science at the State University of New York at Geneseo. She has been the recipient of Fulbright awards for research in Mexico and Colombia. Her study, *Mexican Oil and Dependent Development,* examined the impact of the Mexican oil boom upon the nation's development. Her current research focuses on the political implications of chronic economic crisis in Mexico.

Silvia Gómez Tagle has been a research fellow in the Centro de Estudios Sociológicos at El Colegio de México since 1973. She studied at the National School of Anthropology in Mexico City and at the Anthropology Department at Cambridge University. Her research has previously focused on the Mexican labor movement, and she has published *Democracia e insurgencia en los sindicatos electricistas,* as well as other articles on this subject. Since 1981, Gómez Tagle has been engaged in research on political reform in Mexico and has published several articles exploring various aspects of the reform. Gómez Tagle has served as the editor of the journal *Nueva Antropologia* since 1976, a journal that she founded in 1975, along with other colleagues.

Joseph L. Klesner teaches political science at Kenyon College. He is a doctoral candidate at the Massachusetts Institute of Technology where he is writing his dissertation on the 1977 Mexican electoral reforms in the context of post-revolutionary Mexican regime evolution based on research conducted in Mexico from 1983 to 1984 under a Fulbright grant.

Martin C. Needler is professor of political science and sociology at the University of New Mexico, having previously taught at Harvard, Dartmouth, and the University of Michigan. His A.B. and Ph.D. are both from Harvard, and he has held research appointments at Harvard and Oxford Universities. Dr. Needler's publications have been concerned primarily with politics in

Mexico and Ecuador, the theory of political development, the military seizure of power, and U.S. foreign policy. He has published two books on Mexico, *Politics and Society in Mexico* and *Mexican Politics: The Containment of Conflict*. *The Problem of Democracy in Latin America* is in press.

Evelyn P. Stevens is a research associate at the Center for Latin American Studies at the University of California in Berkeley. She has lived and worked for more than twenty years in the Caribbean, Central America, and Mexico and has written numerous books and articles about the politics of those areas.

Dale Story is an associate professor of political science at the University of Texas at Arlington. He is the author of two books on Mexico: *Industry, the State, and Public Policy in Mexico* and the forthcoming *The Mexican Ruling Party*. He has numerous articles on Mexican politics appearing in such journals as *Latin American Research Review, Journal of Interamerican Studies and World Affairs, International Organization,* and *Social Science Quarterly*. His research has principally focused on the role of the private sector in Mexican politics.

Index